Spire Publishing
www.spirepublishing.com

SAFFIA FARR

REVOLUTION BABY

Motherhood and Anarchy in Kyrgyzstan

Spire Publishing
www.spirepublishing.com

Spire Publishing Books, September 2007

First published in Canada 2007 by Spire Publishing.
Spire Publishing is a trademark of Adlibbed Ltd.

Note to librarians: A cataloguing record for this book is available from the Library and Archives Canada. Visit www.collectionscanada.ca/amicus/index-e.html

Printed and bound in the US or the UK
by Lightningsource Ltd

ISBN: 1-897312-50-4

www.saffiafarr.com
www.revolution-baby.com

To Tom – in recognition of the hours I spent writing when I should have been playing with you.

Forward

I read Saffia Farr's Revolution Baby while securely in Somerset on leave from foreign adventures. As a trailing spouse myself (with a couple of decades more postings under my belt than young Saffia) I recognised every word she writes and I found myself smiling all the way through, and often laughing out loud: Ms Farr has an irreverent sense of humour. But it also made me want to cry, so vividly does she recreate the grim arrival, the bewilderment and homesickness, and the bizarre daily life of the ex-pat wife desperately trying to fill her empty days while her husband does his job in whatever strange place he has dragged her to. In Ms Farr's case, her husband, a water engineer, was sent to remote and unknown Kyrgyzstan when she (by training a lawyer) was pregnant with their first baby, and at a time when the country was going through huge political upheavals.

I recommend Revolution Baby to anyone who has ever had to travel abroad with a spouse – we may not share her exact experience but we will all identify with her and delight in the way she tells 'our' story.

Brigid Keenan, August 2007
Author of Diplomatic Baggage: The Adventures of a Trailing Spouse

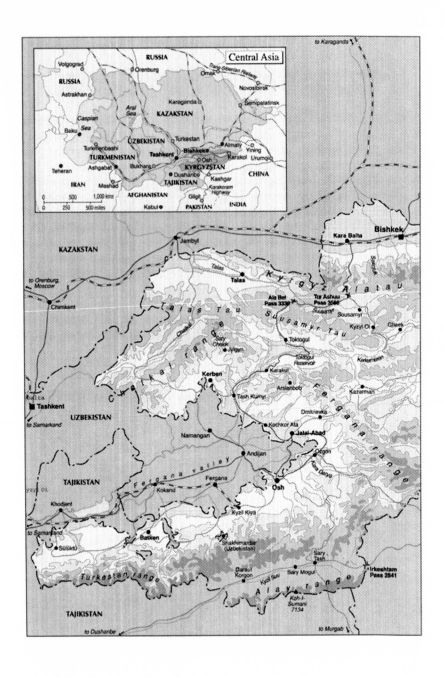

Central Asia

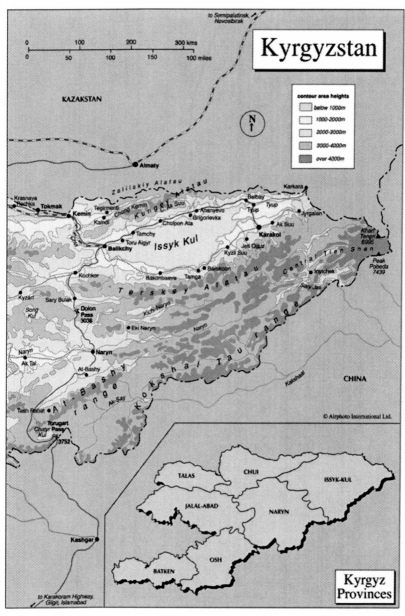

Kyrgyzstan

Map supplied courtesy of Odyssey Books & Guides
(www.odysseypublications.com)

Prologue

Angry protesters set up a tent camp between Lenin's statue and parliament. "Kulov's a murderer," they claimed in impassioned speeches. Teams of intimidating men with firearms concealed under black leather jackets cooked huge vats of rice and boiled gallons of tea to fuel the protest. Blue portaloos tilted against oak trees and a large beer tent impeded Lenin's view of proceedings.

The catalyst for the unrest was the violent murder of Tynychbek Akmatbayev, a member of parliament attacked while visiting Prison 31. His brother, Ryspek, was accusing Prime Minister Kulov of organising the killing with a Chechen crime lord called Batukayev. Batukayev allegedly controlled the Kyrgyz underworld from his cells in Prison 31; cells well-stocked with machine guns, knives, mobile phones, computers with Internet connections, three mares and fifteen goats.

The complication was that Ryspek himself was an alleged crime lord, the murderous leader of a rival gang in this primitive land of clan loyalties. He was due in court to face charges of killing Batukayev's brother-in-law: Kyrgyzstan was said to be descending into the chaos of organised crime.

A gathering of angry young men and dissatisfied mafia bosses was unlikely to end peacefully. Already that year the people had risen up and overthrown their president. Revolution was the new national sport.

Before we go any further, let me introduce myself. My name's Saffia, rhymes with mafia. I've brown hair, green eyes and boobs the same size as Jordan's, difference is mine are real. I grew up north of Bristol where cider starts with Z and Asda ends in L. At the age of 13 I decided to become a lawyer so worked hard for the grades I needed, went to law school and ended up in London, paginating in a room without windows.

Then I met Matthew Bullock, a water engineer with blond hair, blue eyes and a nice bum. He worked in Laos, Tunisia and Waltham Cross while we struggled to live together-apart. It's his fault my programmed life took an unexpected turn when at twenty-six I abandoned my legal career and moved to Egypt to retrain as a housewife. We weren't even married.

For two years Matthew tried to stop Aswan's drinking water running down the road while I learnt how to haggle in Arabic, fight off Egyptians admiring my breasts and make bread which wouldn't crack our teeth. We left in December, spent Christmas in France with Matthew's family, married in England in January and honeymooned in The Seychelles, where I realised I was expecting a baby.

Next stop was Matthew's headquarters in Denmark. It was freezing. I tried to find a midwife who'd be nice to foreigners until Matthew's boss decided we were going to Kyrgyzstan – the following week.

This is my story about how our baby grew in the shadow of the Tien Shan mountains, we survived a revolution and I learnt to love Bishkek, even though it's made of concrete and people spit on your feet.

Part One – Bump in Bishkek

Chapter One – Dawn Arrival

I hadn't heard of Kyrgyzstan until I watched the traveller Ian Wright eating sheep's eyes up a mountain on the Travel Channel. He didn't encourage me to go. We were living in Egypt at the time and I laughed at his discomfort, unaware that I'd end up there one day.

I forgot the episode until, based in Denmark, Matthew phoned from his Copenhagen office.

"You don't like Danish midwives do you?"

"They don't like me." I was bitter because no-one would see me before I paid a £1000 deposit – so much for EU reciprocity.

"So you'd welcome an excuse to go elsewhere?"

"Anything would be an improvement on unfriendly Danes."

"So if I say we're moving to Kyrgyzstan next week you won't yell at me?"

"Kyrgyzstan?"

"The place with the eyeballs."

"I remember. Do they have nice midwives?"

I wasn't completely flippant about leaving the safety of European medicine, however expensive. If the Kyrgyz still ate sheep's eyes in felt tents, would pain relief have advanced beyond vodka? Matthew's answer to everything is to look on the Internet but any sites mentioning Kyrgyzstan were dominated by advertisements for brides. We resorted to the telephone, calling Kumashai, office manager in Bishkek.

"I understand if you want a middle wife when you arrive," Kumashai answered after listening to our problem. Matthew tried to explain but Kumashai seemed distracted by what sounded like a hen clucking in the background. "Many visitors do this, our young girls are liking foreign men."

"No! A midwife is a type of doctor who looks after pregnant women. Do you have those?"

"Of course, we have many. Kyrgyz doctors are best in world." This sounded frighteningly like Soviet propaganda.

"Do they speak English? It would be helpful if Saffia could talk to them directly."

"Of course."

"Is there a clinic where she can have an ultrasound?"

"Of course. The Canadian clinic has many modern equipments." A Canadian clinic sounded reassuring and I started to feel more comfortable about going. I didn't want to stay behind, split from Matthew at this pivotal time of our life. I tried to look outside the paranoia of the West and remember that women all over the world survived pregnancy without the tests and paraphernalia of British ante-natal care. Unfortunately I'd discover that Kumashai was optimistic about the state of Kyrgyz medicine, her 'of course' meaning 'I've no idea but I'm not admitting that to you'.

I agreed to incubate our first baby in a Central Asian wilderness and we returned to Bristol to play hokey-cokey with our boxes. Matthew had negotiated an extra week in England so we could explain to family and friends exactly where we were going – difficult because I still couldn't spell K-whatsit or find it on a map.

Once I realised it wasn't Kurdistan and the chances of being shot were reduced, I started searching by the Black Sea, thinking our 'stan' bordered it, comforted by the proximity of Europe.

"It's not here," I wailed to Matthew. "Where are you taking me?"

"Try beyond the Caspian Sea." Matthew's geography education had included more than precipitation and where to site supermarkets. Moving further east my finger swept across steppes and 'stans' but I still couldn't find the Kyrgyz, however you spell them.

Our bickering only stopped when we realised I wasn't being stupid but using an atlas printed before 1991, when the country now known as Kyrgyzstan was lost within the Soviet Union. To cartographers Central Asia is one of those friends who keep moving and messing up your address book; boundaries constantly changing so that you have to keep crossing names out and starting again.

Before Stalin the only borders were mountains and rivers and the Kyrgyz, who'd wandered down from Siberia, were just one of many tribes moving over the steppes with horses, herds and tents. Over centuries the region was conquered by Alexander the Great, Huns, Arabs, Persians, Genghis Khan, Tamerlane and the Uzbek khanates of Khiva, Bukhara and Khokand. Trade, religion and technology flowed east and west along the Silk Routes.

In the nineteenth century, while the Khans brawled for territory and supremacy, Tsarist Russia crept steadily across mountain and desert like a red wine stain on a white table cloth. Every step was a planned move in The Great Game of espionage and subterfuge against the British Empire, advancing tentatively into Afghanistan from India. Russia tried to control the territory by resettling it with ethnic Russians but indigenous nomads resisted, resulting in brutal repression and mass slaughter of animals and people. When the Bolshevik revolution of 1917 rocked Russia's centre, tremors were felt in Central Asia but it took years of massacring wild bandits yelling 'get off my land' to formally establish Soviet power in the snappily named Turkestan Autonomous Soviet Socialist Republic.

This was only the beginning of territorial Twister – it was no surprise I was having trouble finding the Kyrgyz. In 1924, fearing united Islamic and Turkic uprisings, the Soviets carved Central Asia into nations: Kazak, Kyrgyz, Tajik, Turkmen and Uzbek; forced and unnatural categorisations which still cause problems today.

Stalin is credited with drawing arbitrary borders, deliberately slicing valleys and splitting tribes to ensure everyone was too busy arguing whose sheep could graze in which field to unite against the communists. Each country was kindly given an ethnic profile, language, history, and purpose – Kyrgyzstan allegedly produced sufficient buttermilk, yoghurt and cheese for the whole Union. But nomads were trapped in countries they weren't sure they belonged to, wondering which category to tick on identity cards they couldn't read, having happily been hybrids all their lives.

To add to the confusion, titles were changed more often than underwear: Kara-Kyrgyz Autonomous Oblast became Kyrgyz Autonomous Oblast then Kyrgyz Autonomous Soviet Socialist Republic while Pishpek, the capital, was renamed Frunze after the captain of their Red Army 'liberators'. No-one really knew who or where they were and concentrated on being good Soviets and staying out of the gulags – which is exactly what Stalin intended.

His geographical suppression worked until the late eighties when revolutionary ideas about owning land and eating McDonald's snuck in under the Iron Curtain. The Soviet Union started to crumble, cracks appearing at the edges as republics declared sovereignty, Kyrgyzstan in December 1990. After a failed hard-line communist coup attempt in Moscow, reaction to a renegotiated Union Treaty, the Kyrgyz Supreme Soviet voted for independence on 31st August 1991, the central Soviet parliament formally acknowledging the dissolution of the Union on 26th December.

To the shock of the world the powerful Soviet Union had disintegrated and anyone who'd been given an atlas for Christmas was fuming. Red pens were brought out as names changed again – the Kyrgyz Soviet Socialist Republic branded the Kyrgyz Republic, colloquially Kyrgyzstan. Its capital was renamed Bishkek, the Kyrgyz form of its old Kazak name meaning a large wooden spoon for stirring fermented mare's milk, suitably domestic after years of oppression.

Finally, everyone stayed still long enough to be caught on a map and in a modern atlas I found our destination, a tiny country encircled by mountains and nestling against China, the baby in a set of Russian dolls with Kazakhstan and Russia fanning out above with increasing immensity. I was amazed, and slightly ashamed, that I knew so little about such an enormous region, one which was considered a centre of civilization in ancient times, criss-crossed by trading routes which shaped the modern world. But I wasn't the only ignorant one: most of our friends had never heard of Kyrgyzstan and still can't spell it. The surprising increase in sales of atlases in South Gloucestershire can be attributed to them valiantly trying to find us.

When you land at Manas airport there are no comforting city lights: it's four in the morning and everyone's asleep. The only activity is from American marines unloading the week's supply of Oreos from the bellies of Hercules. They live next door at a coalition airbase, opened to help fight the War on Terror and the pilots need home-comforts to soothe them on return from missions in Afghanistan. 'Dark' is your first thought; 'concrete' the second as you walk into a grey terminal building which someone forgot to paint.

We first touched down on a cold Friday in April, Matthew, me and my 'Secret Treasure'. In the glare of fluorescent lighting a hopeful youth held a sign eagerly above his head: 'MR with SaNdra BulloCK'. I was sorry to disappoint. No Hollywood celebrity in lip gloss and shades, just me feeling crumpled and grubby after ten hours of pressurised air.

Matthew's company had paid for us to arrive through the VIP lounge, which meant we sat on a plastic couch while someone else stood at the carousel wondering which continent our underwear had been sent to. The lounge had turquoise walls, porn magazines wrapped in cellophane and four clocks marking time in London, New York, Tokyo and Bishkek. Britney Spears was entertaining from a television screwed to the ceiling, gyrating in red PVC for an audience of men in creaking leather. They smoked and salivated under fur hats, changing the channel when a boy band came on.

"Shy?" asked a flimsy girl. She wasn't, wearing minge-line mini, chiffon blouse and scarlet bra. "Café? Shy?"

"Ah *chai* – tea, same as Arabic. She's offering us a drink." Matthew ordered sweet tea. I'd had enough burnt caffeine on the plane. "I wonder where Luigi is?"

Luigi was the Sicilian boss, employed by the same Danish consultancy as Matthew who were paid by British taxpayers to implement the aims of a World Bank loan taken out by the Kyrgyz government – truly international aid. The project was to design and construct drinking water supply systems for hundreds of remote villages where water, and nasty diseases, were collected from muddy puddles and dirty rivers.

"Sorry I late!" Luigi burst through the door, cold air cutting the smoky fug. "We were stop randomically by police."

"Is there a problem?"

"No, no. They think we speeding so we pay small fine. Is Friday, police just want money for weekend vodka. Kyrgyzstan is high on BMI."

"BMI?"

"Black Mercedes Index. The more black Mercedes you see driving round poor country the more corruption you know it is. But, enough bad talk, welcome to Bishkek!" He opened his arms and for a moment I thought I was expected to place a kiss of respect on each cheek as if he were the Godfather. "You still wait for visa and luggage? Okay, we talk."

While Luigi trapped Matthew with an animated soliloquy about the trials of finding good pasta, a tall blond man in neatly pressed jeans and cream cable-knit jumper conversed politely with me.

"The lake is now too cold to swim in," he advised. This was Dema, the office driver. It seemed a non-sequitur but I'd been primed by guidebooks. Lake Issyk-Kul, second highest alpine lake in the world, was the Kyrgyz pride. Dubbed 'Riviera of Central Asia' it wasn't unusual to discuss its merits at 5am, even in winter.

Unable to think of a sensible reply, I asked whether he was from Bishkek.

"I am Kyrgyz with Russian parents."

"That sounds confusing."

"It's because of Stalin."

"Ah yes, the dichotomy of ethnicity and nationality so that people are foreigners in their own birth place, identifying themselves first by extended family or tribe." I'd been reading Colin Thubron's scholarly 'The Lost Heart of Asia' on the plane.

"I'm sorry, I don't understand, my English is not good."

"It's better than my Russian." So far I knew that *nyet* meant 'no' and *wodka* meant 'vodka'. I'd no idea what Kyrgyz sounded like.

"What are you?"

"I'm English with English parents."

"You have a simple history. In former Soviet Union people are complicated."

Luigi sent Dema to chivvy the immigration officers with a bribe. At least I didn't have to worry about my visa. In Egypt I'd been a stowaway wife, sneaking through paperwork with illegitimate status. We'd married three months ago so I now had a matching surname and genuine wedding band and engagement ring, symbols of being grown up. As this was our fifth country since marrying I regretted not rewriting our vows: *"I give you this boarding card as a sign of our departure. With my passport I trust you and all my duty free I share with you. All that I have is in that suitcase, within the care of British Airways baggage handlers so help me God."*

Here I was in Kyrgyzstan: another country, another culture, another currency, another language, another new set of taxi drivers to argue prices with. It felt tedious to be starting again, having to find a home, safe butcher, decent hairdresser and somewhere to have my legs waxed. I felt displaced and depressed, which I tried to blame on lack of sleep, but all my old worries were coming back – would I make friends, should I get a job – who would employ a pregnant woman – where would we live, would we be able to find Kellogg's cornflakes? It's the small things that become important to displaced people.

I watched the half-dressed waitress empty ashtrays, wondering whether she and I were the only women in Kyrgyzstan. The flight had been a masculine reunion of oil workers and gold miners who drank whisky and discussed which bars they'd visited on home leave. I'd felt self-conscious with my book and pregnancy. And *everybody* was smoking. Matthew seemed to be taking me on a tour of the world's nicotine capitals, disquieting when posters in English clinics showed gruesome images of damaged babies in the womb and warnings that the chances of cot death were increased by passive smoking.

In Copenhagen I'd been on the equivalent of twenty-a-day because Danish hobbies are smoking, eating dodgy hot dogs, smoking, buying designer kitchenware, smoking, wearing dead animals with feet and tails still attached, smoking, dyeing hair red, smoking, cycling whilst smoking and smoking: similar to Kyrgyz I'd learn, without the designer kitchenware. Danes smoke *everywhere*, even the hairdressers. Paying fifty quid to emerge with Friday night pub hair and increased risk of lung cancer wasn't my idea of a good deal.

The pale light of dawn was illuminating the edges of the sky when we entered Bishkek. First impressions: had I gone back in time? It was every cliché from Russian history; grey, drab and cold with faceless tenements and huge institutions stamped with hammers, sickles and stars. I thought of boiled cabbage and freezing fingers, peasants herded into state farms and women queuing for food.

I assumed we'd got off at the wrong stop – this wasn't what I'd expected from Central Asia. In the in-flight magazine I'd read about Bukhara and dreamed of ancient mausoleums and camel caravans laden with rugs. With turquoise domes and huge tiled arches, Bukhara is a stunning product of the Silk Routes and Central Asian Islam. With concrete high-rises and grubby municipal parks, Bishkek is not. It has a Soviet face, more Soviet than Russia because it was new-built for convenience not aesthetics.

As we passed an empty square where taxi drivers huddled against another chilly night without business I wondered where we'd live. I was a spoilt westerner from the country, used to sunbathing in her own garden. Bishkekers lived in shoe-box-blocks with three variations: grey or brown; standing horizontal or vertical; balcony open or enclosed. If you wanted anything else, best move to Paris. I tried not to dismiss my new home in the first hour, knowing my sense of adventure was anaesthetised by tiredness but I felt the fear of unfamiliarity and wondered if I was crazy to move to a country still struggling to stand after its release from the Soviet Union.

Luigi, unaware that Matthew and I were trying not to cry on the back seat, commentated on landmarks as we drove along *Chui Prospect*, the main road through town.

"This is a market for fruit and other things."

"Osh bazaar?" I'd read about it and hoped to practise my bartering skills there, accustomed to Egyptian *souqs*.

"Yes, is very big and too much busy. You can buy everything from fabric to walnuts and have your wallet stolen at same time." I'd heard such hype before and wasn't discouraged – I was a market veteran. "They slash your bag randomically with knives, is very dangerous." Maybe I wasn't so keen. "Products is cheap because they, how you say, tip over front of truck from China?"

"Fall off the back of a lorry?"

"Yes, many people do this because drivers is too much bad. Here is Beta Stores, great Turkish supermarket. It has three storey of clothes, food and toys, a restaurant for kebabs and you can even take photo outside with golden lions."

"There are supermarkets?"

"Oh yes, at least three." The idea of stacked shelves and trolleys was exciting. If there was an English cinema and bookshop, Kyrgyzstan would achieve my definition of 'developed'. "But please don't be happy about food. These shops just sell too much cabbage and too much sheep head. Nowhere can you find good pasta or mozzarella."

While Luigi ranted about the quality of cheese we passed the White House, a square, white building chequered with small windows; office of the President. Next door was Ala Too Square, a plaza so huge troops could line up for inspection before their leader, proletariat workers cheer and wave banners and crowds rally to the marching band – and still leave space for the popcorn man. A bronze statue of Lenin stood on a high plinth. His right arm was raised, in welcome or warning I wasn't yet sure, orating to an unseen audience. Behind him was the State Museum, another square, white building. I'd read that the second floor ceiling was a violent mural glorifying Lenin and communism. The recommendation was to see it quickly before it was replaced with 'What the Americans have done for us'.

We turned left off the square and the road narrowed and darkened under cover of trees. Dema pulled in beside a squat building floating in mud. If this was a shoebox someone had stamped on it. The stairwell stank of piss and rotting vegetables and the concrete was damp and cold.

Luigi unlocked a metal door on the third floor and flicked a switch. A bare bulb hanging from the ceiling gave off pale light. It's usual to spend at least the first night of a posting in a hotel so that free toiletries, tea and coffee making facilities and satellite television distract you from homesickness. Luigi appeared to have confused 'hotel' with 'hovel'.

"Is temporary," he mumbled. Italian euphemism for 'it's a shit-hole but cheap'. I'd always imagined my ex-pat years would be spent in elegant bungalows with verandas overlooking gardens of palms and bougainvillea. In Egypt we'd had an amazing view of the Nile from our flat roof but the house was in the middle of a building site. Even then I never imagined I'd downgrade to a Soviet tenement. I started to feel very depressed.

Dema gave us survival rations – bread, cheese, tea bags and fizzy water – promised to return at midday and advised us to lock ourselves in. Then he and Luigi ran away before we started clinging to their coats crying 'don't leave us here!' As Matthew banged the door and clicked the locks I felt like a Lifer on her first night in prison.

Tentatively we explored. The flat smelt of mould and other people's lives. The wallpaper was smothered in pink roses. A study and sitting room were crowded by oversized dark furniture, their surfaces cluttered with white crochet doilies. In the kitchen a brick propped up a gas stove and a photograph of Khrushchev was stuck to the wall with tape yellow with age. A quick search of cupboards revealed an extensive inventory – bread board, serrated knife, two cups without handles, a stove-top kettle and a box of three matches. Orange smears scarred the sink and bath where water dripped in Chinese torture; cracked linoleum peeled at the edges. Worse was the toilet. Hidden in a room diminished by roses, its seat was padded, stained foam escaping from gashes in the plastic. This could not be hygienic.

Too scared to use the tap I rinsed my teeth with fizzy water, bubbles failing to relieve dehydration. The beds were low wooden cots so we pushed them together and curled under thin, stiff sheets searching for warmth. The most difficult part of a posting is arriving. You've waved goodbye to family and home, flown into another time zone, been dumped in an alien environment and told to sleep. I tried not to think that in Bristol I'd be happily snuggled under my duvet: I was in Bishkek now and had to learn to survive, for better, for worse.

The narration of ex-pat life is always more glamorous than reality. 'I live in Kyrgyzstan' does sound thrilling and mysterious, especially as no-one knows where it is. Inspired by guidebooks I'd fantasized about vast green valleys, snowy mountains and tea with cheery locals in alpine pastures; so that's what everyone believed we'd be doing. Flying through the night, stinking of dirty aeroplanes, homesick for familiarity and squatting in a flat with a padded loo seat weren't such appealing images. But they were the reality. Holding hands across the gap we drifted into uneasy sleep.

Chapter Two – The Mountains of Heaven

"We'd better get up, Dema'll be here soon," Matthew whispered, reluctantly rolling out of bed to find the pile of clothes he'd discarded four hours earlier. "What's wrong with the heating, it's freezing in here." I twitched back grey net curtains: dismal Bishkek was still there. While we'd slept the city had started another day. Fat women squatted behind roadside stalls, youths leant on cars and a scraggy dog cocked its leg against a broken slide.

"Are we mad to move to a place like this?"

"Don't think about it now, we're still tired and disorientated. You know the first weeks always feel horrible."

"It's only four months, it's only four months," I mumbled to myself in desperate mantra. Although Matthew's contract was for a year, I was leaving at the end of August to give birth in England. British Airways let you fly until thirty-six weeks with a letter of reassurance from a doctor. I just needed to find a doctor.

A hot powerful shower would have been wonderful but after shivering under a drizzle of water at least I smelt of shampoo rather than stale sweat. I tiptoed over the sticky linoleum, pulled on the first clothes to fall out of the bag and found Matthew in the kitchen boiling water, two of the precious matches charred on the stove.

"*Chai*? No saucers I'm afraid," he apologised handing me a chipped cup.

"What's for breakfast?"

"Dry bread with rubbery cheese."

"That's not a breakfast suggested in The Books."

'The Books' were my collection of pregnancy manuals. They had charts, diagrams, tips and photographs and I referred to them obsessively for every detail of my development. At fifteen weeks Baby was supposed to have a large head, proper legs, arms and all its vital organs. They didn't offer advice on what to do if you were stranded in an ex-Soviet republic without muesli.

"Do you want to come with me this afternoon?" Matthew asked as I chewed the cheese, trying to work out where my next vitamin was coming from. Dema was taking Matthew to the office to meet his colleagues. Although I could think of wilder adventures I decided it would be more stimulating than staring at the floral wallpaper wondering if it always rained in Bishkek.

It was the right decision because en-route I experienced an epiphany. As Dema drove south towards Ala Too Square, grey clouds parted revealing glistening white mountains rising majestically above damp pavements. I had no idea they were lurking there. Dwarfing the Soviet tenements they formed a jagged line across the horizon, closing off the city like a huge fence at the bottom of the garden. They looked close enough to touch but were actually 25 kilometres away, something I discovered the morning I set off to walk to the mountains.

It was a biblical vision, but then these were the Tien Shan – Mountains of Heaven. God was telling me to look beyond padded loo seats and dry bread because Kyrgyzstan did have something worth flying ten hours for. Matthew and I smiled across at each other, furtively squeezing hands. For the first time I thought I might be able to stay longer than the weekend.

The office was in an impressive building with a colonnade of arches. Disappointingly this was just a façade to hide a now defunct knitwear factory. Inside it smelt of boiled cabbage and sinister guards in olive uniforms glared from behind a reception desk. They wore large caps which curved stiffly to peaks above their foreheads like ski-jumps.

An ancient lift cranked us up to the fourth floor and we stepped into a gloomy corridor. In Egypt I'd envied Matthew going to work because it gave him a daily purpose and someone to chat to. This time I was relieved I'd stay at home. The office was bare and unfriendly and locals wearing anoraks nodded curtly from behind computer screens before resuming Russian conversations.

"No English," Kumashai explained.

In Luigi's room we met Ken, chief engineer and OAP. He would have retired under a tartan blanket long ago had he not collected a second wife in Manila who was helping his first wife spend his savings.

"*Dobra ootra*!" Luigi greeted us. "Is Russian for good morning."

"It's afternoon," Ken added helpfully.

"Yes, yes good afternoon. You sleep well? Lovely, now we talk again. This time, work!"

For what felt like hours I tried to be a dutiful wife and listen attentively while Matthew threw me sympathetic looks and Ken dozed in the corner. I hoped Luigi might take pity on an expectant mother with jet lag but he seemed to have forgotten why Matthew had negotiated paternal leave into his contract.

Telling – or reminding – people you're pregnant is not as easy as assumed. Slipping it into conversation just doesn't seem auspicious enough but it's difficult to make an announcement without appearing overdramatic. I'd been saved any awkwardness informing my family by my brother: when I declined a glass of wine he'd said, 'what, are you up the duff or something?'

Eventually I asked for a drink, hoping Luigi might take the hint. He dispatched Kumashai without missing a syllable. She returned with a bottle of fizzy water and a cabbage.

"More cabbages?" Luigi asked. Kumashai nodded. "I tell you, this is joke of work in Kyrgyzstan. You know our project is village people steering..." He meant 'community driven' Matthew explained later. "...so people must contribute with time and money. It supposed to make them feel responsible for success of project but is really a bullshit because they so poor and no money because live by bartering. So randomly they deliver sack of cabbage and chicken and they think this is 5% of many dollars. What I do with chicken who run around and say 'brawk brawk'? I no time to sell in Osh bazaar."

"Last week we got a sheep," Ken added from the corner.

"Mama mia the sheep!" Luigi drew breath, ready to narrate the story.

"I think I've gone into labour," I said quietly.

"Labour!" Matthew, Luigi and Ken yelled in unison.

"Only joking. But can I go and rest now?"

Before we left the office we phoned England.

"We're fine," I reassured my mother unconvincingly. What I wanted to say was, "I'm lost. It's raining. I can't understand anyone, everything is grey and stinks of cabbage and I want to come home," but I thought that an unfair burden when there was nothing she could do to help.

Standing by the window I listened to her news. Our ancient cat Kizzy was purring on her lap; there'd been a crisis at the church council meeting and the sun was so warm she'd been sitting in the garden. I looked out across Chui where Ladas splashed through puddles and Lenin saluted the rain, wondering if I could feel more isolated from the home I loved. I couldn't believe we were actually in Kyrgyzstan, a country hidden behind the Iron Curtain for most of my life. Taking deep breaths I composed a smile to hide my unhappiness from Matthew who, judging by the way his bottom lip trembled every time Luigi said 'long time in Kyrgyzstan', had huge doubts of his own.

"Every Friday a group of us meet in a restaurant," Ken explained as we walked to the lift, "you should join us tonight". It would be our first experience of city ex-pat society: in Aswan there'd been nowhere to go out and in Copenhagen we'd had no friends. I imagined myself leaning casually on a polished bar, laughing with women wearing glossy piles of hair, glittering earrings, floating chiffon tops and bangles which clattered as they lifted stemmed cocktail glasses with manicured hands. It would be the type of evening depicted in advertisements, the nauseatingly good time people with tans and perfect white teeth always have.

"I hope I can find something decent to wear."

"I wouldn't bother, we don't make a fuss. I just go like this." As Ken was wearing faded jeans and a saggy blue cardigan I realised I needed to manage my expectations better.

The Navigator was allegedly the smartest restaurant in Bishkek: a smoky conservatory with marble-effect plastic tables and dusty fabric plants. Ken waved to us from a long table where assorted ex-pats yelled at each other above the noise of rain pounding on the roof. We sat at one end and I concentrated on smiling to stop myself swinging a table-mat at the smoke Ken was blithely exhaling in my direction.

Etiquette demands that you swap banal pleasantries when meeting strangers. Pregnant and hungry, I had no time for small talk.

"Hello, I'm Saffia, we arrived this morning. Can you pass the menu please and does anyone know a good doctor?" While everyone reeled from shock I ordered. Eating was no longer a simple pleasure interrupted only by concerns that my bum was widening. Aware that everything I consumed was channelled through the placenta to my baby I was attempting to achieve 'five portions a day' from something other than Cadbury's 'Fruit and Nut'.

Mindful that Secret Treasure and I had only eaten a plastic airline meal and dry bread and cheese in the last twenty-four hours, I chose the most healthy sounding dish on the menu: *Vitaminka* salad. To follow I ordered a kebab, which came with rings of raw onion as a side dish.

"I've been to the German clinic," said Mary-Lou, an astonishingly large American lady dressed in an emerald-green velour tracksuit. Her accent was a southern drawl and she exaggerated vowels as if thinking I'd have trouble understanding. "It wasn't very nice and there weren't any Germans so I don't know why they call it that."

"I heard a Jap died there on the operating table," Ken added cheerfully.

"He was Korean," corrected Brian, an Australian.

"But he still died."

"Oh yeah. You'd be better off goin' to VIP clinic."

"VIP!" Mary-Lou yelled. "All you get there are vi-tamin injections. Your leg's broken, stomach's aching, head's cut but they just give you vi-tamins."

"Or an onion and vodka remedy."

"There's always an onion and vodka remedy."

The whole table was involved in the conversation now, all ready to share their hospital horror stories. This was a favourite ex-pat pastime, second only to 'who can phone the most important person in government' whenever there was a problem.

"What about the Canadian clinic?" I threw tentatively into the discussion.

"Canadian? That'll be Kumtor's," Mary-Lou explained. "You can't go there honey, it's only for people who work for the company, they're the ones who mine gold up east." This wasn't a good start. I'd only felt comfortable about moving to Kyrgyzstan because Kumashai had mentioned a Canadian clinic.

"Why d'ya need a doctor, you've only just arrived?" Brian asked.

"I'm pregnant."

"That's great honey, congratulations. But bad timing. You'll have trouble in summer; it gets real hot, ninety degrees!" I didn't like to tell Mary-Lou I'd walked to market in a hundred degrees in Egypt.

"D'you know what it is yet?" asked Tina. Tina was also Australian, married to Brian who kept telling Matthew he'd be 'vodka-ising' him later. She was short with dark dyed hair. I knew this because I'd listened politely for ten minutes while, undeterred by my natural brunette, she'd explained how difficult it was to get the right colour and you had to be careful who you trusted or you'd end up with the Orang-utan orange hair favoured by locals.

"No, we don't know the sex and we don't want to. We'd like a surprise."

12

"You're not giving birth here are ya honey? I know a girl who gave birth in Bishkek last year. She was from Moscow and spoke Russian so she thought she'd be alright but she had a terrible time. Her labour went on-an-on and then the baby got stuck so they said she needed a C-section but the clinic couldn't do it so her husband had to drive her across town to the hospital. She thought she was gonna die."

"I'm going home to England," I said resolutely.

"That's if Brit Air will let ya. My friend, at Quilt Camp…"

"Is there a Women's Club?" I interrupted, tired of Mary-Lou's pessimism. "Where do you go to meet people in Bishkek?"

In Denmark I'd had trouble meeting anyone. In one lonely week the only people I'd chatted to, apart from Matthew, were Brian the fishmonger and Jamie Oliver, in Copenhagen for a cooking demonstration. With few distractions I'd wandered expensive department stores fighting hormonal urges to sweep my arms across shelves of designer crystal and hurl stone lamps at mirrors. Desperate to divert me Matthew had sought friends on the Internet. He'd found the 'Ladies International Network' who offered bridge, tennis and shopping outings. I'd been in negotiations to join until told we were leaving. But I'd learnt the first lesson in ex-pat survival – find the Women's Club, they'll supply comfort, a social life and important local information like where to get your legs waxed.

"Sure there's a Women's Club," said Mary-Lou. "They meet first Tuesday of the month at the Hyatt. I can't make it in May but Tina'll take ya, won't ya Tina."

"Aw yeah, no worries."

"You can go bazaa ba bee caarfool cothey try stea yoo monay."

"Er, hi." A petite oriental lady was nudging a chair up to the table next to my elbow.

"Hey, this is Leyla," Tina introduced. "She's married to Derek. She likes buying shoes."

"And she's the same age as his daughter back home," Mary-Lou added in a whisper.

"Der say I spen awl monay ba I always see bargeen."

"That's very interesting." Embarrassingly, I couldn't understand a word.

"You lie shaw wi mee?"

Energised by food I started to enjoy myself. I worked out that Leyla was inviting me on a shopping tour of Bishkek – potentially exhausting but useful. Mary-Lou talked endlessly but I learnt, between Quilt Camp anecdotes, about the International Women's Club Ball at the Hyatt. This sounded the ultimate in ex-pat chic and I started worrying about what I'd wear, relieved that I'd thrown in a pair of black kitten-heels at the last minute.

In friendly company Bishkek didn't seem so dreary. It was a different start to our posting in Aswan where we hadn't met anyone who spoke English for a month. Bishkek had the advantage of being a capital city with an ex-pat community propping up the economy. The disadvantage was segregation –

most foreigners used the same shops, restaurants, bars and beauty salons and most locals ignored you unless hunting for work, husbands, visas or all three.

I slipped effortlessly into ex-pat banter, a growing sense of comradeship making me think that maybe I could cope in Bishkek for four months, until Frank, a fat bald-headed Englishman started arguing loudly with a woman in a crocheted smock. He was ranting about George Bush being a gormless ape – quite possibly true but not an accusation you throw at Americans on a Friday night. Especially not in politically-charged Central Asia where not everyone is who they say they are: I learnt this the hard way by criticising George Bush to someone I later found out played ping-pong with his dad. This woman looked like a hippy but she might have been an undercover CIA agent reporting on us all. The CIA was bound to be out there somewhere running covert operations in the name of US values.

As their voices escalated the restaurant went silent, other diners staring while languidly exhaling smoke rings. I felt embarrassed to be sitting at the table, associated with the expatriate arrogance. The argument had exposed the shallowness of these forced relationships and I realised this was not my choice of company. Matthew and I paid our bill and left quietly as an uneasy truce mingled above the table with the cigarette smoke and shrill conversations about who'd worked in the most dangerous country resumed.

Outside it was cold and very dark – there weren't many street lamps in Bishkek. The only agreement of the evening had been that it wasn't safe to walk at night. Brian had been mugged outside a hotel, Frank was beaten up in his stairwell and Mary-Lou knew three foreigners who'd had their wallets snatched. While Matthew hailed a taxi I looked nervously around expecting someone to creep from the shadows.

Dema had written our address in Russian. We handed the note to the driver and were disconcerted by his hacking laugh. Disorientated by the one-way system it was embarrassing to learn that our luxury lodgings were one handbrake turn around the corner. It was a short but dangerous ride, only marginally safer than being mugged. The radio volume was connected to the accelerator, windscreen blotted by spiders' webs of cracks and seat springs treacherous as we bounced over potholes. The driver laughed at my attempts to find a seatbelt.

"You no need with me." As his headlights were smashed and bumper dented into a vee I disagreed and prayed we'd avoid ending our posting prematurely, mashed in a ditch.

The final challenge was paying.

"Don't take any shit from taxi drivers," Mary-Lou had counselled. "They take you round the block and want a hundred *som*. You say *n-yet* and pay 'em forty, you got it, four-tee." Matthew had reassured her that after two years bartering with Egyptian taxi drivers there wasn't much I didn't know – apart from Russian. Fortunately our driver let us go without an argument, blasting a triumphal fanfare with his horn as he wheel-spun out of the mud.

"I'm not sure I can face going back into that building," I said, hesitating on the steps.

"Flat hunting tomorrow and we'll move, I promise," Matthew said as he took my hand. But I was worried where we could be comfortable in grey, Soviet Bishkek.

Chapter Three – Nomads

Saturday's breakfast was the same as Friday's – just a day staler. At ten Dema arrived with Cholpon, Luigi's secretary who would help with translation as we searched for a flat with hygienic loo seats and a kitchen with crockery. Cholpon was a typical Bishkek girl: petite and immaculately dressed in trousers so tight I marvelled she could walk. Although Kyrgyzstan is officially Muslim, after seventy years of Soviet atheism Islam isn't practised seriously by the urban masses and the dress-code for women is anything but modest. I'd already realised that as in Egypt it would be my clothes which would make me different – but this time because they were *too* loose and shapeless. According to Mary-Lou, summer clothes were short, transparent and low cut as well as tight. 'Slavic Slut' was her summary of the fashion.

Cholpon wore dark blue jeans, a burgundy leather jacket and pointed boots with heels so high her ankles wobbled when she walked. A Louis Vuitton handbag was tucked under her arm. I wondered how she looked so immaculate when Bishkek was so filthy. I'd learn that Kyrgyz women, especially young ones, spend hours on appearance and wouldn't dream of popping to the corner shop without three tones of eye-shadow. In my jet-lagged lethargy I'd recycled yesterday's clothes and scraped greasy hair into the same scrunchie. Cholpon looked me up and down with ill-concealed contempt: 'this piece of shit is the new engineer's wife?'

Luigi had spent weeks researching suitable accommodation – and failed. There was a very short list of two flats: modern Kyrgyz – chiffon drapes, velour sofas and huge chandeliers, or Soviet – small, dark rooms with brown linoleum. We chose the first because without a padded loo seat it had potential.

I bit my lip to stop myself crying. Finding a place where you can feel comfortable is crucial to the success of a posting. Our new home was in a vertical, brown shoebox with enclosed balcony and graffiti decorating the metal front door. A stuffed pheasant lived in the concrete stairwell. Outside the gates two women in coats tied up with string rummaged through skips, congratulating each other on finding a plastic bottle and loaf of bread. Opposite, surly youths smoked and spat from the steps of a horizontal, grey shoebox modelled on an NCP car park.

"Is this a good area?" I asked Cholpon, worrying that we'd agreed to move into Bishkek's ghetto. Her look was withering but how was I to know this was a prime location for ex-pats, somewhere locals could only dream of affording?

"This is nice, you have garden," Cholpon said. She was referring to a muddy flowerbed at the edge of a chipped parking area.

As the flat wasn't available for a week Matthew insisted we move somewhere else. In Bishkek, flats can be rented nightly like hotel rooms, the only difference being the number of zeros in the price. We considered blowing our life savings to stay in the Hyatt but instead Luigi took us to another temporary place on a grimy shoebox estate. It was a slight improvement as the toilet seat wasn't padded but there were only Chinese tea bowls in the kitchen so I still couldn't cook for us. It smelt of well-worn trainers and made me want to vomit.

The estate looked like the perfect location for gang warfare: three ten-storey blocks of monstrous concrete with lightening-bolt cracks running down the walls, cardboard replacing window panes, paint peeling from sills and rubbish festering under the stairwells. Loitering kids with fags pinched in lips watched us drag suitcases through the mud. My homesickness was raw.

On Monday, when Matthew left for work, I turned over in bed. What was the point of getting up to watch more rain? I let the lethargy of depression dig its claws in, feeling sorry for myself because I was living in Bishkek, dreary capital of Kyrgyzstan which no-one had ever heard of.

First Mondays are always difficult, the moment Husband leaves you alone and you have to work out how to fill empty weeks. Some postings offer exciting choices for spouses; university degrees, cordon-bleu cookery courses or diverse sporting facilities. As Matthew wasn't likely to be posted anywhere blessed with such conveniences, because they'd already have drinking water and sewers, I'd learnt to rely on my own resourcefulness for entertainment. So far in my ex-pat life I'd never been bored but I had been lonely and it's loneliness that makes you depressed. I wasn't sure I had the stamina to start all over again.

I adjourned to the brown sofa in the sitting room and switched on the television. I missed BBC. In England I could lose myself in pointless hours of hunting for antique bargains in attics or ruminations about moving to the country. In Bishkek the choice was President Akayev making a very long speech, 'Back to the Future' dubbed into Russian by a bored man reading all the parts or the Sky News cycle.

I knew I should be exploring the city, making tentative starts at the new language and understanding Central Asia. But I felt lost; scared and alone with my mysterious bodily functions, fearful of the alien city. It was easier to skulk around the flat cussing Matthew for dragging me to a place with the architecture of a public toilet. Maybe Denmark hadn't been so bad after all.

I didn't aspire to be one of those ex-pat wives who moan about wanting to be happy but not knowing how. I intended to be a supportive wife, greeting Matthew with delicious dinners rather than floods of tears, modelled on the resilient ex-pat women of history I'd read about in Katie Hickman's 'Daughters of Britannia'. They travelled overland to Kashgar in corsets, lived in cramped spaces with limited washing facilities, picked cockroaches from their beds and didn't even have email to connect them with home. In comparison Bishkek was luxurious.

It's easier for Husbands to settle, they have work as a distraction. Left at home the domestic problems of nomadic life always affect the wife more. Dumped in a new place you have to learn how to cater for your family and adapt to your environment, which isn't always easy in a different culture and language. You can be in the most exciting city in the world, somewhere you've always wanted to go, but if the oven breaks and you don't know who to call you still feel isolated and homesick.

A friend once asked whether I resented Matthew because I'd given up my career for him.

"Only when I want to," I'd answered. This was one of those times. I could have been dictating letters about breaches of contract; instead I was trying to open a tin of jam with a corkscrew. Being an ex-pat wife is a strange existence; 'Trailing Spouses' Brigid Keenan calls us. Despite being educated and independent you agree to sacrifice a career and separate identity to follow Husband around the world, your only purpose being Cook and Companion in places where cooks are cheaply hired – as are companions in Bishkek.

When I told friends that I was giving up work to move to Egypt, they'd responded with a mix of awe and horror. Awe because I was living the dream we'd all talked of but never dared realise – swapping a safe office job for Adventure in the pages of a Lonely Planet guidebook. Horror because I'd studied for ten years and written sixty application letters to become a lawyer and what was I going to do when I was fifty and wasn't a partner and didn't have a pension? I didn't mourn my lost career – after four years in the City I was already disillusioned. I'd naively hoped for John-Grisham justice and found paperwork and presenteeism. It wasn't law I missed but the companionship of a busy office.

When the brown sofa got too uncomfortable I moved to the balcony, cautiously at first as I worried it might collapse. I leant on the concrete balustrade and stared out across the towering shoeboxes of Bishkek. In Denmark I'd watched snowflakes swirl over a wasteland, pondering the joy of pregnancy: I'd been nine weeks and felt sick if I did eat and sick if I didn't. Now I admired a grander view, the Tien Shan skirting Bishkek's southern districts on their journey from the Pamirs into China, pondering whether I could spend four crucial months of my life in this ex-Soviet republic.

I'd agreed to meet Matthew for lunch. Our flat was on *Sovietskaya* and I walked north until it met *Chui*, turning left towards the office. Bishkek was designed by Russian military planners in the late 1800s and built on a grid system. This makes it easy to orientate, despite street names being changed regularly to suit political fashions. The lid of cloud had lifted from the city and the sun was pleasantly warm. I thought I'd dressed appropriately for the weather in a t-shirt and three-quarter trousers but felt very conspicuous as everyone else was wearing leather coats.

The people were an interesting mix: big-nosed Russians, oriental gypsies, Mongoloids with flat eyelids. Round faces, broad faces, brown faces; black hair, orange hair, blond hair; gold teeth, brown teeth, no teeth; high ruddy cheekbones, slanting eyes, all calling themselves Kyrgyz. How did you know who was Kazak, Uzbek, Tajik or Uighur, for Kyrgyzstan is home to eighty ethnic groups?

Central Asia's history is reflected in these faces, nomadic tribes who roamed the steppes fighting and intermarrying, unconcerned with nations and nationalities until Stalin 'identified' them. Ask about ancestry and you're told, 'my mother was Turkmen and father Tajik but my grandparents were born in Bukhara so I'm Kyrgyz but Uzbek but until I was twelve I was a Soviet'. Confused? So are they. It's no wonder the new Republics have problems with ethnic identity and rivalries. Can you imagine being English but French? Who would you support at rugby? It was something I'd have to investigate.

My destination was a restaurant unappetisingly called 'Fatboys'. With purple walls, green plastic chairs, beer posters, tea served in chipped mugs and a seedy answering service offering: 'When the wife calls we'll tell her we haven't see you all day for 50 *som'*, it couldn't decide if it wanted to be a student union, transport café or brothel.

Embarrassingly, it was home of the Honorary British Consul. The Americans had a high-security bunker outside town, staff of seventy and suave Ambassador smiling from front pages of newspapers; the Germans had a neat compound and white Range Rovers flying black, red and gold pennants. We had Bill at Fatboys, head chef when he wasn't calling the Foreign Office or drinking vodka with his Kyrgyz in-laws. The contact address on the Foreign and Commonwealth website was *'Osoo* Fatboys' which sounded so ridiculous we'd heard of people booking Silk Road Tours just to see if it were true. Its only redeeming features were fat sour-dough pancakes and shelves of books left by understanding ex-pats. As there were no English bookshops in Bishkek this was a precious resource – as long as you liked reading nothing but Tom Clancy.

Matthew had spent the morning discovering he wasn't wanted. Understandably, he was a little upset. It's not nice to commute 7000 kilometres to be told by a man called Mr Turd that you're not welcome. Mr Turd – full name Turdibayev – was head of the Rural Water Department. He wanted Matthew fired so that a local design institute could do the work. Matthew would have agreed with him if the design institute were competent and 95% of the fees weren't destined for Mr Turdibayev's black Mercedes fund.

"If they reject everyone who comes to help they're never going to achieve their Millennium targets," Matthew muttered, flicking through the menu.

In 2000 the Kyrgyz government had pledged unilateral access to clean drinking water by 2010, an enthusiastic response to the UN's Millennium Development goals, designed to free those suffering from 'dehumanising conditions of extreme poverty'. Goal Seven, Target 10 was to halve the number of people without clean drinking water by 2015, of which there are two billion. Fortunately for the 1.8 million Kyrgyz without safe water, the World Bank, DFID[1] and ADB[2] had agreed to help.

The Kyrgyz government is good at getting others to do, or at least pay for, development work. From the outset politicians understood that the only way for their small country to survive Independence was to talk loudly about democracy and a market economy, encouraging foreign investment. But ultimately Kyrgyzstan's success at attracting Aid is due to favourable comparisons with authoritarian neighbours and its geographical position.

Snuggled near Russia, Afghanistan and China, Kyrgyzstan sits in the middle of major drugs routes and borders countries bursting with oil and Islamic extremists. As a result it's the only country in the world to accommodate both Russian and American airbases, symbols of a rivalry for influence in Central Asia. America opened its base in December 2001 to support the war in Afghanistan; deploying troops on former communist territory an amazing reversal of cold war policies. Any ideological reservations Kyrgyzstan had were soon forgotten: co-operation with the US meant dollars and military assistance to counteract the growth of Islamic militancy in the south.

Moscow's base was operational a year later, ostensibly to control terrorists and Afghan drug flow but really to halt US encroachment on what traditionally was Russia's sphere of influence. Not wanting to be left out the Chinese organised joint military exercises with Kyrgyzstan, the first time soldiers from the People's Liberation Army had conducted manoeuvres abroad. They formed the Shanghai Cooperation Organisation with Russia and Central Asian states, to combat terrorism and 'support multi-polarity in the world', but this again was really just to counter America's moves. Little Kyrgyzstan was the board on which huge international political games were being played. It had never been so popular.

Conveniently, some say, the War on Terror is being fought across the continent which is thought to contain the world's largest untapped fossil fuel resources. Although Kyrgyzstan doesn't sit on any oil itself, President Akayev was clever in prostituting his country as a strategic outpost so that keeping Kyrgyzstan friendly and free from Islamic militants is an important facet of the New Great Game of 'power and pipelines'.[3] Aid plays a critical part in this, being a tool of foreign policy.

The more I've learnt about Aid the more cynical I've become. I'd naively assumed the idea was to help the world's poor who desperately need clean water, hospitals, schools and other necessities we take for granted. But I've learnt that Aid is actually about buying allies and ensuring support for donors' international politics. This means that politically important countries are

---

[1] Department for International Development – British Government aid
[2] Asian Development Bank
[3] The New Great Game: Blood and Oil in Central Asia – Lutz Kleveman

assisted in priority to the most needy and dollars usually buy more bribes than useful equipment. If a few wells get dug, diseases cured and classrooms built, that's a bonus.

"At least I've solved Luigi's cabbage problem," Matthew said.

"How?"

"I suggested he ask the villagers to sell them and just bring the proceeds. He thought this was the most amazing idea he'd ever heard and ordered Kumashai to send his memo to every *Oblast*. She's grumbling that this is a waste of time because most of them can't read Russian."

While Matthew talked, I poked at what was allegedly hummus with rubbery carrots. I was still searching for elusive vitamins, desperate to crunch something fresh. In the corner three ladies were noisily discussing whose drive was the straightest that morning on the golf course. Mary-Lou was with them and waved us over for introductions.

"Hey everybody, this is Saf-fee-ya and Matthew, they're having a baby. Guys, meet Gina and Penny. Gina's with the American embassy and Penny's husband works for Kumtor."

"You're birthing here?" Gina asked, burger halted midway to her mouth, red lipstick smeared by the bun.

"No." The best thing about moving to Bishkek was the excuse to go home and give birth in English. If we'd stayed in Denmark I couldn't have justified the travelling and I hadn't been looking forward to going through such an intimate experience with fierce Danish midwives.

"Oh, thank God because I knew this woman who was induced by having wires fixed to her nipples and electric shocks…"

"Saf-fee-ya's looking for a doctor," Mary Lou interrupted, "d'you know one Gina?"

"Well, we use the clinic at the base but my friend Chloe, she went to see someone who spoke English, might even have been English, a woman called Helen or Hilary or something so I'll ask her. But I gotta tell you about my housekeeper…"

I tuned out while Gina moaned about how Svetlana kept losing the children's homework, politely nodding and hmming in appropriate places while watching two taxi drivers argue about who'd skidded into who outside the window. When Matthew excused himself to return to the more pressing issue of drinking water in Kyrgyzstan, I felt obliged to accept Mary-Lou's invitation to shop with her – after all, I'd already spent two hours staring at mountains that morning.

Everyone needs a Mary-Lou when they arrive in a new place. Someone to show you which butcher sells something other than sheep heads and explain how to find butter in a dairy counter full of mysterious packets. For Mary-Lou it was a treat to have a captive audience.

"Let me tell you about shopping in Bishkek. At home if you want a new dress you just go to your favourite store in the mall and buy your size. Well here you gotta hunt. Maybe they sell a dress in your size in Bishkek but you gotta know which stall in which corner of which bazaar to go to and that's where I can help ya. Every ex-pat in Bishkek knows the frustration of not being able to easily find what you need. As I told my friend at Quilt Camp…"

I was already exhausted and we hadn't got to Beta Stores yet.

"…shopping is a full time job 'cos there's no Wal-Mart where you can go buy everything. Bey-da's ow-kay but you still have to go to three markets just to get what's on your list for dinner. Penny says you can get everything you *need* here but not everything you *want* which I think is real brave of her 'cos really there's just so many necessities you have'ta live without. Like anchovies. They come in real rare so when you see 'em buy the lot 'cos you never know when that lorry's gonna get over the pass from China again."

We toured Beta Stores, visited Mary-Lou's tailor who was making a huge turquoise creation for the ball, and hiked across Bishkek searching for the correct shade of hair dye: not my idea of fun but at least it helped acquaint me with the city – and practise crossing the road. In Bishkek red lights mean 'stop if you want to' so stepping off pavements is virtual suicide. In fact, walking on pavements is virtual suicide because all the slabs are loose and every man-hole cover has been sold to China as scrap[4]. Rubbish from skips is scattered across the street by beggars looking for food and the locals hawk and spit at your feet. Mary-Lou told me she called it 'dodge-the-gob' and gave a lengthy explanation about a vendor in a market who kept a spittoon under her stall, a bowl full of foamy saliva which put her right off buying the peaches.

Despite aching legs I was feeling more positive about living in Kyrgyzstan. The sun was shining and Mary-Lou's soliloquy on the merits of every hairdresser in Bishkek – and there are *a lot* of hairdressers in Bishkek, nearly as many as pharmacies – was at least distracting. All was well until Matthew telephoned to say we couldn't take the new flat because the landlady's second-cousin's-neighbour's-dad had died and she was rushing to Moscow to commiserate. Unable to find anything else, Luigi was advising we stayed where we were. I spiralled back down into tearful depression, returning to the sofa weighed down by misery.

There was a flight to Heathrow that night and I desperately wanted to be on it, racing back through time to comfort and familiarity. I tried to remember what had first attracted me to expatriate life from behind my boring lawyer files: dreams of 'doing something very different, and a bit adventurous',[5] the idea of being a pioneer who'd left behind the cosseted West so that Matthew could get clean water to people. Or simply that I wasn't very good at living together-apart when Matthew was weekly commuting.

Unable to recreate the buzz, I kept asking myself why I was fifteen weeks pregnant in a country where 'health' meant only smoking at the weekend.

---

[4] They use it to make steel to sell to countries who give Kyrgyzstan aid to buy more man-hole covers.
[5] Catherine Young quoted in 'Daughters of Britannia'

"You must be mad going to Bezerkistan," friends had said, "especially with a baby coming."

"I'll be fine," I'd reassured, full of bravado, marketing myself as an intrepid adventurer when really I was just a scared girl who felt most comfortable in her home village. I was lonely, worried for my child's health – I'd resorted to sniffing beetroot for vitamins – and felt helpless, disabled by language.

"We're never living abroad again," I informed Matthew when he returned from work. "Why do we choose to live in remote places? So we have something exciting to tell our grandchildren? A test to find the limits of our emotional endurance? I'm a lawyer you know. Why am I shopping for hair dye with the chairman of the Alabama Quilting Society when I spent six years training to write contracts?"

Rants like this are normal in the first weeks when rationality is swamped by desolation.

"I can't eat because every kitchen makes me gag, Kumashai was wrong about the Canadian clinic and I can't believe I'm going to find a decent doctor. Is this the sort of place I should be growing our first child?" Matthew calmed me down with reassurances that we'd return to England and find a home. But we'd had the same conversation on arrival in Egypt and I'd still agreed to move to Bishkek. If only I'd remember that the days of misery pass I'd feel so much better when we started our postings, but the depression is so consuming I assume I'll hate the place for ever. The reality is that when we come to leave I cry again, this time because I don't want to go. Nomadic life is a rollercoaster of confusing emotions.

By the end of the week we'd found another flat. It was in the same block as the flat we'd just lost, the vertical, brown shoebox with the stuffed pheasant on the stairwell and muddy flowerbed as a garden. This flat was on the third floor. I counted fifty-eight steps; it would be like jumping on a Stairmaster every time I wanted a loaf of bread.

This place was unusually modern, open-plan with a real wooden floor and white walls. There were two lavatories, both with hard seats, a twelve piece dinner service and even a view of the mountains from a bay window in the sitting room. The kitchen was tiny with grey tiles, brown shelves and a sink which wobbled away from the wall. But as it had saucepans and didn't whiff of rancid yoghurt I was happy. At least the oven wasn't on the balcony, like Tina told me hers was.

The landlady was called Aigul and always dressed neatly in dark jeans and cream jumpers, her glossy, black hair cut into a smart bob. The caretaker, Larissa, was the antithesis of Aigul's Central Asian chic. She wore dumpy brown dresses, smelt of stale vodka and had brittle Orang-utan orange hair. As she only spoke one word of English, 'problem?' explaining that the boiler had burst and water was flooding across the bathroom was going to be fun.

It was cold. I asked Cholpon, there to help with translation, why the heating wasn't working.

"There is no heating," Cholpon explained as if telling children the earth wasn't flat.

"No heating in a country under snow for half the year?"

"No, no heating *now*. It's turned off."

"Can't we turn it on," I whined, "it's five degrees." Cholpon patiently described district heating, the impressive Soviet system which warmed the whole city through a network of pipes conveying hot water from a power station at the edge of town. It was regulated by the government who turned it off promptly on 31st March, whatever the temperature, and on again on 1st November, if they had money for fuel.

It was raining when Dema helped carry our suitcases and boxes upstairs, again. Every time we'd moved in the last few months, and we'd moved a lot, it had been raining: I thought I'd read somewhere about Bishkek enjoying 270 days of sun a year. It was bliss to unpack our boxes, hang up clothes, put away suitcases and cook a meal – I managed beans on toast. As we snuggled under our duvet I calculated that since leaving Aswan the previous November we'd slept in eighteen beds in six countries. I was glad that our nomadic days were over, for the summer at least.

Chapter Four – Dr Bucket

The joy of living in transit is that you don't have to bother homemaking; you make-do, complain and move on. As we were going to be in Aigul's flat for more than a week I wanted to make it as cosy as possible. Unfortunately Aigul loved brown and we didn't so we spent Saturday rolling up brown rugs, removing brown cushions and taking down brown paintings.

We might not like packing and unpacking but we're good at it. Matthew can guess the weight of a suitcase within one kilo and I'm an expert in maximising box space and writing inventories. It's difficult not to become obsessive about stock-taking in modern nomadic life. Before leaving England we always calculate how much Marmite, Bisto, PG Tips and safe, identifiable medicine we'll need for the trip; Matthew, being 'Techno Matt', has spreadsheets for this purpose. I agree that living abroad is about experiencing a different culture, but it's much easier to do that when you can have a decent cup of tea.

To carry all these necessities the company had given us a baggage allowance. Our boxes had come with us as cargo on the plane as we weren't going to entrust our books and Marmite to the overland journey through Pakistan, Afghanistan and Tajikistan. Dema had taken Matthew to collect the boxes from Customs and given him a demonstration in Kyrgyz bribery:

Dema: 'I'd be very grateful if you'd release these boxes today.'

Customs Officer: 'How grateful?'

Dema, reaching for wallet: 'How grateful do I have to be?'

We brought a hundred kilos of junk in six boxes, an eclectic mix of scarves and sun cream because it's difficult to know what to pack for a country advertised as freezing one day and 30 degrees the next. We'd forgotten things that would have been most useful – wellies, an umbrella and some decent ornaments. Aigul's collection of china cats and decorative vases, all brown, had been relegated to the cupboard with the pictures.

"At least the flat has furniture," Matthew reasoned. In Denmark we'd chosen an unfurnished loft and filled it with modern Scandinavian pieces – IKEA – just in time to be told we were moving continents. It was now stacked up in boxes in my parents' attic with all our wedding presents and souvenirs collected in Egypt. My father was worried about the ceiling collapsing, as was my sister who slept in the room underneath.

On Sunday we treated ourselves to lunch at the Hyatt. Despite being built in post-Independence Kyrgyzstan, the architect had been tainted with a Soviet lack of imagination and the hotel was a horizontal beige shoebox without balconies. It was like walking into another world: from grey Bishkek with spit splattered across cracked pavements into the hushed marble of a five-star cosmopolitan foyer. There were red Bukhara carpets, brocade sofas, lilies curling from tall vases and waitresses in starched aprons gliding silently between bar and tables. I felt glamorous by association.

We sat outside on the terrace under square canvas umbrellas, declining brunch then enviously watching others return with salmon slivers and chocolate mousses in tiny glasses. There appeared to be hordes of jolly ex-pats greeting each other with pecks on cheeks and vigorous handshakes. We observed but felt too shy to introduce ourselves, unwilling to intrude on family lunches. 'Hi, I'm Saffia, I'm new and lonely' was too burdensome for Sunday relaxation. I was waiting for the Women's Club meeting where I hoped to meet friends who weren't my mother's age and obsessed with hair dye.

That day I was absorbed with finding a doctor who'd monitor my pregnancy and write my 'you're healthy to fly at thirty-six weeks' letter for BA so I could get home. I'd not yet found anyone able to cope with the complications of my nomadic pregnancy. In Denmark the doctor had been more concerned about how I'd pay for my healthcare than discussing my debilitating headaches. In England a midwife, who I'll call Fiona, had panicked me about all the checks and tests I wouldn't be able to have and was blatantly disapproving of me going to a country she'd never heard of. I'd felt completely abandoned and was planning to give birth in a field without ever bothering the medical profession again, until learning I needed an official letter.

I was surprised how disinterested everyone was; I'd expected someone to at least check I wasn't making it up for attention. But these are the contradictions of the first trimester: it's full of crucial development but no medical support or practical advice. It's when you feel the worst and want to sleep a lot, eat everything or be sick and yet, made superstitious by The Books who caution against early announcements while there's a higher risk of miscarriage, can't explain to anyone why you're behaving so strangely.

In Bishkek I just wanted a doctor who I could talk to in English – I didn't want to play Chinese whispers through a translator about intimate bodily functions. So far I'd learnt that the Canadian clinic was exclusive to gold miners and the 'German' Clinic was only so named because a German had donated some money to it a long time ago. The gynaecologist recommended by Bill at Fatboys only spoke Kyrgyz; a lady called Ulla had given birth in Maternity Hospital Number 5 and survived and there were rumours of a female English doctor but my only hope of finding her lay with a mad American woman called Gina.

I didn't really want to give birth in a field and I was worried Fiona would tell me off even more if I arrived home without a graph plotting my monthly blood pressure. That Sunday in the Hyatt I vowed to ask the next pregnant woman I saw about her doctor. Walking into the cloakroom I was confronted by a petite woman preening her bobbed blond hair and checking her immaculately made-up face in the mirror. My mouth went dry – she had a round, protruding belly.

I stepped to the sink and reached for soap, examining her out of the corner of my eye, searching for the courage to fulfil my resolution which moments before had seemed so simple. She wore a cream dress with matching jacket and her snub nose was raised even higher by the superior approving look she was giving herself. She didn't seem the type who'd sit cross-legged on the sofa eagerly discussing swelling ankles and maternity pants. She turned to leave and I let her pass without asking what I was so desperate to know.

"Was this my first failure for our child," I asked Matthew?

"Don't be ridiculous," he admonished. But Matthew, unaffected by pre-natal hormones, had the luxury of sensible thought.

On the way home we continued our research on where to shop. Although Mary-Lou had criticised Bishkek's three main supermarkets and declared the country 'backward' I was still excited by the mere existence of aisles and trolleys in my new home. The difference was our benchmark: she was used to Wal-Marts bigger than the Isle of Wight whereas I'd just spent two years haggling in Aswan's *souq*; a truly raw experience – when I'd wanted chicken I'd chosen a live one and watched it being slaughtered.

Unfortunately I'd already been put off Beta Stores by flaccid carrots, security guards who proof-read your receipt before letting you out and over-zealous assistants who insisted on packing each product separately so that you went home with twenty carriers wedged on each hand and the feeling the ozone layer was doomed.

When I'd mentioned that I didn't like 'Bey-da', as Mary-Lou called it, Leyla had dragged me around Bishkek City Market, a large warehouse with a supermarket at one end and stalls selling firm vegetables and plaited sheep intestines at the other. It was quieter than Beta Stores, shoppers probably deterred by the fish section where dead pike floated in paddling pools. In the supermarket the irritating assistants mopped the floor at your feet and rearranged packets into gaps the moment you picked up something. But it always amused me that they sold condoms called 'Favourite' at the checkout.

Europa, our destination that Sunday afternoon, sold condoms called 'Spicy' at their checkouts. Europa was favoured by ex-pats because it stocked barbecue sauce and cake mix. Unfortunately, such imported luxuries cost more than most Ladas so the shop was protected by obsessive security. Two guards stalked us and hovered so close I worried my skirt was tucked in my knickers and they didn't know how to tell me. They slunk around, ducking behind piles of tins, hovering between freezers and knocking over stacks of crackers in their haste to trail us to the cereal. I felt like a criminal just being there and considered an attempt at shoplifting simply to justify their existence, before remembering I'd have to rely on Bill at Fatboys to get me out of Kyrgyz prison.

Most women admit they spend their first week in Bishkek wandering around supermarkets trying to find tins and packets they recognise. It's the simple, everyday chores which present the greatest challenges to ex-pat wives and shopping in a foreign language is a game of chance. Unless there's a helpful picture you have to resort to telepathy or a dictionary and cruising aisles with a Rough Guide phrasebook is embarrassing. I'd already done it in Denmark and felt like a nerd – maybe that's why no-one wanted to be friends.

In Bishkek there was the added problem of the Cyrillic alphabet. Before you could start searching you had to work out which letter the strange squiggle was. On my last encounter with the dairy section the closest match to a word on a label was 'death' so I'd given up. I was going to have to reach new levels of resilience and resourcefulness if I couldn't even find milk.

That Sunday I was busy attempting to distinguish cream from *keffir*, a sour yoghurt drink – what *was* the woman on the carton churning – when I saw a lady with a baby who looked European. It's easy for foreigners to spot foreigners in Kyrgyzstan – they're the ones who don't dress like prostitutes or dye their hair orange. Determined to redeem my earlier failure I lingered by the chill cabinet, psyching myself to approach her.

"Hello. Do you speak English?"

"Yes, I am English." This was a miraculous find. I thought the only other Brits in Kyrgyzstan were Frank and Fatboys Bill, and he was Gibraltarian.

"This is a rather strange request but I've just moved to Bishkek and I'm pregnant and having trouble finding a doctor and I wondered if you lived here when you were pregnant and whether you could recommend someone to me?"

I should have taken it as a sign of her eccentricity that she didn't even flinch at my gabbled soliloquy. Instead she smiled serenely at her baby who was reaching for a packet of pasta.

"Yes, I was pregnant but went home for the birth. You're not planning on giving birth here are you?"

"No, no, I'm going home for that."

"Good, because hospitals are really terrible. They're dirty, ill-equipped, staffed by morons and rarely have electricity..." I didn't need more persuading. "...and I knew this woman whose ribs were broken by doctors pushing down on her to force the baby out. I left when I was four months pregnant but I did find a doctor with an ultrasound."

"A scan? Here?"

Despite Kumashai's reassurances, I had no expectations of having a scan in Kyrgyzstan. I wanted to have one before we left Europe, hoping for ultrasonic confirmation that there was a healthy baby in there and I wasn't just bloating with wind before we announced my pregnancy. I'd feel pretty foolish if after a big fart my periods resumed and I had to phone the Grannies and say 'stop knitting!' But due to my international timetable, neither the Danes nor Fiona were willing to scan me so I'd flown to Bishkek believing that I wouldn't meet my baby until the birth, hoping all was well in there.

Gabriella told me that the doctor's name was 'Bucket'.

"He doesn't speak much English but he's very nice. He's at the Rotdorm Hospital Number 2. Do you know it?" I shook my head.

"Rotdorm? Sounds unpleasant."

"It means 'maternity' in Russian. I'd draw you a map but I'm terrible with directions. Why don't I take you; I'd like Bucket to meet Omar. How about next week? Shall we meet for lunch first?"

Matthew returned from researching frozen fish to find Gabriella and I chatting like old friends. He was astonished by our bonding speed, it's not usual to discuss foetal heartbeats with a stranger in Tesco on a Sunday afternoon. But being pregnant in Mahé-Bristol-Copenhagen-Bristol-Bishkek isn't usual and you have to make the most of any help you can find.

We met at the Navigator on Wednesday. I tried to eat another *Vitaminka* salad and concentrate on Gabriella's tales of her affair with an Uzbek nomad but I felt sick with nerves that Bucket was going to tell me there was something wrong with Baby because I'd missed Fiona's tests and told friends I was pregnant without a reassuring scan.

"Saf-fee-ya! Woo-hoo!" Gina was striding across the restaurant waving a piece of paper. "I've got that number for Dr Hilary. My friend Chloe said she was real nice. Can't stop to chat, we're teeing off at two. Ciao!"

I explained to Gabriella about Dr Hilary.

"Do you mind if I try now? We don't have a phone in our flat yet."

"Of course, no problem. Why don't you use the one at the bar? Local calls are free so they won't mind."

I dialled the number while the barman bashed wet coffee grounds from the machine, refilled with fresh and screwed the handle into place.

"*Da?*"

"Can I speak to Dr Hilary please?"

"*Shto?*" The receiver was passed around while I attempted a variety of phrases in an amalgam of languages.

"Er, *pajalsta* – please – Dr Hilary?" I was so proud of my few Russian words – when they didn't come out as Arabic. My pronunciation was undoubtedly appalling. I tried a different approach, repeating "Hilary, Hilary, Dr Hilary," so many times they probably thought I was suffering from delusions that *I* was Dr Hilary. I could hear women ranting in shrill Russian, voices fading as I hoped someone went to fetch Hilary.

I waited five minutes listening to the echo of babies crying before feet approached the telephone.

"Hello, Hilary speaking."

"Dr Hilary? I was beginning to think you were a fantasy for desperate ex-pats." I could sense her thinking, 'how did this weirdo get my number?' so tried to be normal which wasn't easy because the coffee machine had started belching out thick liquid.

"How can I help?" I shoved a finger in my ear against the hiss of milk frothing and explained my predicament. Hilary was calm, English and professional and willing to see me despite my madness. Four cappuccinos later I'd made an appointment; I could now concentrate on meeting Baby Bullock for the first time.

My excitement about meeting Baby Bullock was brief because the Rotdorm was closed, nurses locked in a smoky office downing shots of vodka.

"Bugger!" Gabriella cussed. "I'd forgotten it's May Day tomorrow. It's a really important festival, proletarians around the world unite and all that, so they've bunked off early." Labour Day, 1st May, had been designated a holiday to celebrate workers by an international meeting of socialists in 1889. Celebrated throughout the Soviet Union with military parades, banners, fireworks and lots of vodka, it had become a symbol of solidarity and was too much fun for Kyrgyzstan to give up with Independence.

Disappointed, we wandered back through the crumbling buildings to *Moskovskaya*, the road on which I now lived. It was oppressively cold and grey. When the clouds came down, being in Bishkek was like walking around a multi-storey car park searching for the exit. When the sky was clear, mountains hovered at the southern end of every street, comforting reassurance that some things were more enduring than Soviet concrete.

"The Kyrgyz will blame grey skies on the war in Iraq," Gabriella explained.
"Why?"
"They believe that dropping bombs causes meteorological changes, same as when rockets are launched from Baikonur, the Russian space centre in Kazakhstan. Something to do with cosmic disturbance."

It was an interesting theory and an anti-war campaign I doubted George Bush had heard, yet. People shoved past us, heads bent against the wind. Shrivelled *babushkas* hunched behind rugs displaying items they hoped to sell. Their stalls were memory games from childhood parties: a teaspoon, comb with missing teeth, a plug and two clothes pegs; a depressing image of grandmas reduced to bartering random pieces of their lives for survival.

"They didn't expect retirement to be like this," Gabriella mused. "They worked hard in Factory Number 5 and wore the Order of Lenin for being good citizens. Then they woke up in the independent Kyrgyz Republic where there was no money for pensions and everything they'd been brought up to believe was condemned. They're the lost Soviet generation. They don't know who they are now because they've never been Kyrgyz or Kazak, just Soviet. Their grandchildren tell them this is the new age of freedom but they can't find it." We each bought a jam jar, offering support but preserving pride. The *babushka* nodded her head and wrapped the notes in a grubby hanky which she tucked in her bra.

On the next corner a woman sat on an upturned box, stout legs in brown woollen stockings splayed around a bucket of carrots. She wore a thick shawl over her head, folded forward at her ears and tucked under her chin. There was someone like this on every street, farmers converging on the city to sell surplus from their gardens. As well as carrots this woman had a pail of white eggs, three beetroots and first strawberries in a jam jar.

While Gabriella selected carrots I watched Omar kick the blanket from his legs. A boy cycled past with a sack of cabbages on the handle bars and opposite three men lifted bloody carcasses from the boot of a Nissan Sunny. On their heads were *ak-kalpaks*, tall white felt hats, shaped like Kyrgyzstan's mountains and revered as symbols of heritage, purity and brotherhood. They looked comical to the uninitiated but local men proudly wore them all year, claiming the air trapped inside kept heads warm during winter and cool during summer and that *ak-kalpaks* contained protective magic.

Bishkek still felt like a National Geographic documentary rather than somewhere I could call home. A friend who'd moved to New York had emailed me that morning. 'I always think new places look and feel strange for the first few months, then familiarity sets in and all seems normal', he'd written. By the summer, would men wearing conical hats and roads pitted with open sewers seem normal?

"Dyevooshka, what do you mean by taking a child out like this?"

"I'm sorry?" A woman in a black fur coat with what looked like a dead cat on her head was yelling at me in Russian and pointing at Omar who smiled back.

"You should be ashamed, that child should be wearing a hat and his ankles are showing."

"There's really no problem, he's not cold," Gabriella calmly replied, nodding passively while the woman chastised us abrasively before stomping to the trolleybus stop.

"You'll learn that locals are obsessed with wrapping children," Gabriella explained. "Every good Kyrgyz mother knows that children should be smothered in four blankets and wear at least three hats, even in summer. So expect interference when you bring your baby back." 'If', I thought silently. Although our tentative plan was for me and Baby to return to Bishkek in January and stay until Matthew's contract ended in April, I wasn't convinced I was brave enough – or willing to commit to four months of winter concrete. Becoming a mother for the first time is daunting enough without worrying about coping in a country so remote terry towelling nappies are an initiative. Having discovered the state of the hospitals we'd agreed to see if Baby was healthy before making a final decision but I was already rehearsing the arguments I'd use to persuade Matthew I should stay at home.

On Friday Gabriella, Omar and I returned to the rotting dorms of Maternity Hospital Number 2. Sunshine slightly improved its image but it still stank of urine – cat or human I couldn't tell. The clinic was in a building which looked as though it should be listed for demolition. Pieces of render were dropping off in clumps and the roof was patched with Beta Stores shopping bags.

The door was propped open to reveal eight miserable women sitting on benches around the edge of a small waiting room. Gabriella was in an uncharacteristic flap.

"Do you mind if I put you in the queue and leave? There's something wrong with Omar and a friend said they can take me to a doctor now but I must go today as there's another public holiday on Monday. Bucket's always late so you'll probably have to wait for an hour and I should be back by then. Will that be alright?" I nodded, suppressing the urge to cry 'don't abandon me in a Soviet institution with eight surly women'.

"You'll follow this lady in the orange top," Gabriella explained after a stilted conversation with one of the women. "And don't drink too much. The loo is in that shed over there and is the most disgusting in Bishkek. I resorted to going behind a tree. Good luck."

I took my place on a bench. Eight ladies stared and I smiled weakly back, trying not to look conspicuous or foreign. This wasn't easy as thanks to Gabriella's announcement everyone in the room knew I was foreign and I was the only person not wearing stiletto boots and a leather jacket. I wondered how they walked along Bishkek pavements in heels like knitting needles without breaking ankles or inducing miscarriage.

The waiting room was decorated with cracked mint-green ceramic tiles, smudged brown by sweaty hands and greasy hair. Craters were worn into the brown linoleum where thousands of women had visited Bucket. Looking at the dirt I wondered if I was being irresponsible seeking antenatal care here. If something was wrong would I end up being admitted to a Rotdorm ward and plugged into a vitamin drip before Gabriella could save me?

We waited for Bucket in silence. No-one spoke, even when people arrived and asked when Bucket was expected and who was last in the queue. This was Stalin's legacy. Unlike Egyptians who take friendliness to the point of harassment, Central Asians don't talk to strangers. They grew up learning that careless gossip could send someone to the gulag.

To pass time some women flicked through thin newspapers, some dozed and some stared at the walls. The lady opposite picked her nose. I studied a Russian poster about breastfeeding. According to my interpretation of the hand drawn pictures, if you fed your baby while lying in a wheelbarrow your nipples would grow to three inches.

The front door banged, jerking us all from our reveries. A man with thick, black, spiky hair wearing a short, turquoise lab coat and black-framed glasses strode across the room. Time seemed to slow as women quivered and leant towards his magnetic force. They shuffled handbags, twitched hairstyles and sighed with anticipation. This could only be Doctor Bucket.

Breaking the pheromone trance, a butch matron ordered the first patient through a side door and everyone else into a tiny dispensary to collect small bottles of white liquid. There was panic and confusion as women ran in and out of doors, shrieking and pushing to get to the front.

I had no idea what to do. Should I be queuing? Did I need white liquid? What was the lady in the orange sweatshirt trying to tell me? Why was everyone staring and pointing helpfully in different directions? Living amid a foreign language of which you understand three words is debilitating. It's like watching television with the sound off – you get the gist of the story but you don't really know what's going on. In Egypt I'd become an expert in mime but acting 'my friend has taken her baby to another doctor but will be back soon to help me' was testing even my skills.

Gabriella had warned that Dr Bucket didn't linger over examinations and women were popping out of his room faster than marbles from Bagatelle. The lady in the orange top was waving her arms in exaggerated gestures for me to follow her. I was too scared to go alone so phoned Gabriella who'd promised to protect me.

"I'm having a terrible time. The doctor's just put a metal band around Omar's head and hung him on a meat hook to give him an x-ray and he's really screaming. I should be there in twenty minutes, can you wait?"

"It's fine, my friend's coming once her son's off a meat hook," I explained to the ladies who'd stopped jostling to listen to my phone call. I returned to the bench and concentrated on pretending that I didn't need a wee.

"I'm so sorry," said Gabriella, crashing through the door.

"Don't worry. How's Omar?" Curious to see who was talking to me in English, matron came out of her dispensary. She yelled in surprise at Gabriella and pinched Omar's cheeks, which was probably just what he needed after being hung from a meat hook.

"Bucket!" she said laughing and pulled us towards the door he'd disappeared through. It opened onto a long empty corridor painted lime green. To the left was a small room with a grubby curtain hanging limply from the lintel. When a girl came out zipping up her trousers, matron pushed me through.

Chapter Five – Bishkek International Women's Club

Dr Bucket's consulting room was dark because all the curtains were drawn. An assistant scribbled notes at a desk in the corner and Bucket's spiky hair stuck out above a huge computer monitor. Matron guided me onto a wooden bench where I wriggled self-consciously, trying to find comfort on the hard surface.

Bucket and Gabriella reminisced in fast Russian. He clicked his fingers and dangled a pen in front of Omar who rolled his eyes and farted at more abuse from mad foreigners. Without warning Bucket yanked at my trousers and smeared a cold probe covered in green jelly across my lower belly. I flinched; this was intimate contact and the moment of revelation had finally come. While Bucket studied footage of unexplored cavities of my body I watched his face for clues.

"Can she see?" Gabriella asked. He turned the screen and I gazed at the greeny-black picture. This was my baby but I wouldn't believe it unless primed.

"Heart!" Bucket, zoomed in on a small, dark, pulsating shape. He moved the transducer and the spine flashed white down the screen, reassuringly bold. "Liver. Kidney. Head." I hoped he was checking off vital organs rather than practising English anatomy. "Foot! See, see!"

"He's very concerned that you see this foot."

"Why, has it only got one?"

"No, he's just excited by the toes."

I wished *I* could be; I could only see shadows. I squinted at the screen, hoping that like a magic hologram I could bring the picture into focus. Bucket looked at me, eyebrows raised expectantly.

"*Da, f*oot," I lied. I didn't want Bucket to think I was a useless mother who couldn't even distinguish her own baby's limbs but I was having problems comprehending that this shimmering splodge was someone growing inside me. It looked more like a nature video of underwater pond life. Did Bucket have the monitor tuned to the right channel? I was disappointed that after months of anticipation baby was a blur. I wasn't expecting it to smile and wave but being able to tell its head from its arse would have been nice.

"Is everything alright?" I asked?

"Okay, okay," the mad doctor said, grinning and putting both thumbs up like a kid who's scored a goal. Not the comprehensive diagnosis I'd been hoping for but a positive start at least.

"He says you should come back in a month…and that it doesn't look like you." Bucket thought this very funny. I hoped it meant that my child had escaped my big chin, rough feet and propensity for gaining weight.

"You don't want to know the sex do you? He's dying to tell."

"No thank you, we'd like a surprise."

The next girl walked in and lifted her dress – my cue to leave. I buttoned my jeans and spelt my name for the assistant, paying the dollar fee.

"Seventeen weeks," Bucket called as we walked out of the door. I was reassured he was correct.

"I presume baby's healthy," I asked Gabriella as we emerged into the sunlight. It had all happened so quickly I couldn't help feeling nervous he'd missed something. Pregnant friends in England told me they had half-hours of detailed measurement. How could Bucket have determined that organs as complicated as heart and brain were functioning normally in a three minute session?

"Oh yes, Bucket was very happy. He's the best in Bishkek you know." This wasn't necessarily comforting as he was probably the only person who knew how to turn the machine on. I decided to change the subject.

"Are you going to the Women's Club meeting on Tuesday?"

"No, I went once but was scared off by their manicures and intense do-gooding. And they're all old enough to be my mother. But give it a go, there may be some new people, ex-pats are always coming and going in this transient life. You never know who you might meet. I saw Ralph Fiennes in the Hyatt once."

"At the Women's Club?"

"No, he was visiting orphanages. But anything's possible in Bishkek."

Bishkek International Women's Club meet on the first Tuesday of every month at 10 am in the Hyatt. Anyone is welcome to join as long as they're a woman, international and willing to buy raffle tickets for crap no-one else wants. Australian Tina and I walked to the May meeting together. It was a warm spring day of chirruping Blue-tits and oak leaves desperate to burst from buds. In recognition of this Kyrgyz mothers had removed the outer layer of bonnets so that round cheeks and brown staring eyes were discernable among the blankets.

With blue sky and no rain, this was a good Bishkek day. In the first weeks of a posting you have good days and bad days: the challenge is to get through the bad ones without crying for home. No-one bothered us as we wandered along Chui, past Lenin and through Dubovy Park where stone sculptures tumbled into long weeds. This was a novelty for me because in Aswan I'd looked so different to everyone else I was hassled every time I left the house. In Bishkek, foreigners were only obvious to each other and I tried not to feel upset that no-one was proposing marriage or telling me I had nice breasts three times a day.

That morning I'd fussed uncharacteristically about what to wear. I wanted to make a good first impression, which was difficult because I was at the awkward stage where it wasn't clear whether I was pregnant or unable to resist the lure of the biscuit tin. I'd eventually settled on a baggy white shirt and red hipsters – the first pair I'd ever dared buy as I now had an excuse for a fat belly. It wasn't very subtle compared to the locals who rarely deviated from jeans and black leather jackets.

The Women's Club meeting was advertised by a car park full of huge four-wheel-drives with red diplomatic plates. We entered the foyer and followed the sound of chinking cups and female voices to a boardroom overlooking the swimming pool. The snippets of conversation I heard did not encourage me to stay.

"Honey, I can't make Bridge this week coz I have a pedicure."

"We took the orphans sweets and they lined up with their mouths open like baby birds. It was *sooo* cute!"

"They've got cake mix in Bey-da Stores today."

I was preparing to flee when Tina grabbed my arm saying we should meet her friend Ulla who I'd really like. Ulla was sitting on the far side of a huge square table which filled the room. She was wearing a magenta shirt which contrasted strikingly with her dark skin. A badge clipped to a breast pocket stated that she was from Papua New Guinea. Having lived in Bishkek on-and-off for seven years Ulla was a veteran of Women's Club meetings and let the nonsense wash over her while she sipped coffee. Her fame was widespread.

"You're the lady who gave birth here," I exclaimed after we'd been introduced.

"Wow, you know that already!"

"It's local folklore but I have a vested interest, I'm pregnant."

"Congratulations!" I sheepishly explained to Ulla that despite her surviving the ordeal I was running home to mummy to have my baby.

"Don't feel bad about that. Hospitals have got worse since I had Lily because no-one's spent money on health since the Soviets left."

"Did you have wires fixed to your nipples and male doctors breaking your ribs?" I appreciated that this was a little personal for a first conversation but I was dying to know just how bad hospitals were.

"No, but I did have a lot of vitamin injections."

As the room filled up chattering ladies took places around the table. Ulla pointed out various women, sharing important details like names, home countries and reason for moving to Bishkek. Most were Trailing Spouses, brain surgeons and scriptwriters reduced to the status of 'wife' so that their husbands could help Akayev run the country. And he needed their help.

While being celebrated, Independence brought immense financial and social difficulties. Kyrgyzstan was a fledgling dropped from Moscow's nest, suddenly expected to survive on its own without subsidies from mother, confused because communism was now wrong. With economic decline, ethnic bickering, severe poverty and businessmen who thought the Stock Exchange was a swap-shop for cattle, there were enough problems for everyone to get involved. This was fortunate because everyone wanted to get involved: Soviet subsidies had been replaced by Aid, loans and entrepreneurs.

Kyrgyzstan was a popular beneficiary because it offered a less contentious way to gain power in the region. Labelled an 'island of democracy' in a sea of dictators because its president didn't boil political prisoners, donors knew that in helping Kyrgyzstan they could interfere in Central Asia without being criticised for colluding with the bad guys.

Central Asia was hot political property: drugs and oil passed along the Silk Routes and Islamic militants thrived in the Ferghana Valley. With millions of new customers discovering consumerism, Central Asia was also hot commercial property. Through Aid, loans and entrepreneurs countries and institutions competed for trade and influence in socialism's wake. I could just imagine the annual co-ordination meeting of the Ministry of Finance.

"So, what have we got on this year Minister?"

"Well, the Americans are educating our children, updating the banking system, helping small businesses, working with Customs and donating medicines; the Japanese are replacing trams; the British are providing clean drinking water, sanitation and developing an HIV programme; the UN is sorting our refugees, the Swiss are promoting culture and tourism and supporting agriculture; the Russians are giving police cars and everyone's nagging about corruption, which is getting a bit tedious."

"What's left for us to do?"

"Adjourn to Issyk-Kul."

The development boom had swelled membership of the Women's Club. Years before there were barely enough ladies for a bridge four. Now there were sub-groups and clubs and almost enough cliques for international bitching. I sensed an unofficial hierarchy according to what your husband did; a top table of ambassadors', chief executives' and bankers' wives. As Matthew was only part of an Aid project offering clean drinking water I didn't expect to be fêted.

"Ladies, ladies, welcome to today's meeting."

"That's Marjorie, she's the president," Ulla whispered. "British, ex-pat for thirty years, husband works with Customs." Marjorie was comfortingly plump, dressed in fawn trousers with matching short-sleeved jacket and wearing a gold pendant of the African continent around her neck. She would have been running a WI if not posted to Bishkek.

"I understand there are some new members. Would they like to introduce themselves?" Suddenly the room went silent and everyone looked at me. I stood awkwardly, the chair scraping back with a fart.

"My name's Saffia, I'm English. My husband's an engineer working on a DFID project, trying to get clean water to half a million people in remote villages." I thought I might as well give him a plug. I was warming up now, encouraged by smiles and nods of approval. "*My* project for this year is that I'm four months pregnant. So that will keep me busy." Everyone laughed and I sat down to enthusiastic applause.

"You should win the quilt for the baby!"

"Pass the tickets along!"

"There's a raffle every meeting," Tina explained. "Usually we just have things people don't want any more, like candles or vases, but today the prize is a quilt we made at Craft Group." The quilt was hanging proudly on the wall at the far end of the room. It was square with a checked design of pink, white and green fabrics, punctuated with buttons in the shape of tiny pink roses. Although it wasn't my taste, I dutifully bought two tickets, tucking them into my pocket while Marjorie continued the meeting.

"Today we have a guest speaker, Dr Peter, Marcia's husband. He's an expert on virology. As some of you are concerned about SARS, Penny suggested Dr Peter come and tell us the facts." Murmurs of approval hummed around the table and expectant faces gazed at Dr Peter. Unnerved by the rapturous attention he described the SARS virus, its transfer and symptoms. When he paused a lady sitting next to Tina raised her hand.

"Can we ask questions? What's your advice on going to bazaars where Chinese products are sold? Is it possible that the virus might be passed on them?"

"I think it's unlikely to stay on a product, although it is possible..."

"But the Chinese come here all the time, to the bazaars."

"That's why they're closing the borders," Marjorie reassured.

"Yeah, and there are ten checkpoints through the Torugart pass, it took us days to get to China and that was before this SARS business."

"But I'm sure some will sneak through, they'll risk anything for money."

"Oh my gawd!"

"I'll tell you one way to avoid infection," drawled a voice from the back of the room. It was Gina. She waved a manicured hand to attract attention. "I'm real concerned about this SARS thing so last time I went to the bazaar with my housekeeper we wore surgical masks." There were concerned gasps from around the room, women worrying about their last shopping trip without a mask.

"Those masks don't actually offer full protection," Dr Peter added calmly.

"But they sure keep people away. I've never had so much space at Dordoi. Everyone was thinking, 'oh boy, are they infected', and moving back, but that suited me real fine."

"What about restaurants, can it pass on dirty crockery?"

"In theory, yes."

"Oh my gawd!"

"Can you clean it off?"

"If you use bleach the virus won't survive."

"So if restaurants don't wash plates in bleach we can catch SARS right?"

"Well, in theory yes, but..."

"Oh my gawd!"

"But we have to remember that SARS isn't actually *in* Kyrgyzstan so there's very little risk," Marjorie called above the swell of voices.

"Will the government announce if it is?"

"The newspapers say it isn't."

"But they just print what they're told, they don't investigate."

Questions and concerns started ricocheting off walls like squash balls, bashing against each other in the panic. Dr Peter looked embarrassed, wishing he could get back to his viruses – a lot easier to deal with than fussing women.

"D'y think we should take our kids outa school?"

"Should we be bleaching crockery?"

"Will an-tie bacterial handwash save us?"

"They've sold out at Bey-da."

"I gotta order me some from NetGrocer."

"If we think we've got it, what do we do?"

"Get out of here," called a late-comer who was pouring herself a coffee.

"But no country is gonna let you in with SARS are they?"

"So we're stuck here with it?"

"Oh my gawd!"

"Ladies please!" Marjorie was on her feet. "We must remember that SARS isn't in Kyrgyzstan."

"But the government won't say if it is."

"Yeah, and y'know a lot of the kids had a real bad flu at Christmas. What if that was SARS and no-one knew."

"Did you hear about the man who coughed on a Kyrgyz Air flight," Ulla whispered mischievously. "He told the other passengers, 'don't worry, it's not SARS, just TB!'" We sniggered conspiratorially. This was the rational reaction to SARS; a problem, but a minor one in comparison to other killers in Kyrgyzstan: tuberculosis, AIDS and even dysentery because not all rural Kyrgyz understood the concept of pooing in a designated place then washing hands. You were more likely to get run over in Bishkek than catch SARS and one inhabitant of the Chui region died of tuberculosis every three days. Spitting probably didn't help.

But rationality was lost that morning in the Hyatt; the Bishkek International Women were worried about SARS and preparing to trample each other in the dash for bleach and masks. Panic was infectious. Before the meeting SARS was just another news story and I'd been looking forward to eating in local restaurants and wandering around bazaars. Now I wondered if that was irresponsible. Or was this a plot by Hyatt to ensure the international community only dared dine there?

"What are you doing next Friday?" Ulla asked, bored of the hysteria. "You know there's another public holiday."

"What's it for this time?"

"Victory Day, celebrating the famous Kyrgyz successes of the Second World War, on behalf of the Soviet Union of course. Soldiers will parade around Ala Too Square in front of Akayev and everyone will drink too much vodka. It's the same every year. We thought we'd get out of town. Would you and Matthew like to come to Ala Archa National Park with us, for a picnic? There's a group of us going, Tina and her husband included."

I was surprised by the speed with which Ulla had befriended me, but then she'd lived in Bishkek a long time and knew how lonely first weeks could be and how cathartic it was to see the beauty of Kyrgyzstan outside city limits.

"We must thank our expert for coming to talk to us," Marjorie declared, forcefully concluding the hysterics of question time. Dr Peter smiled weakly and ran whimpering from the room as Marjorie told everyone she presumed they were feeling reassured. "Next item on the agenda are the cooking classes at the Hyatt..." After discussing ticket sales for the ball, selecting a committee of enthusiastic ladies to decorate the tables and announcing a concert at the Philharmonic Hall, Marjorie waved the basket of tickets to signal it was time for the raffle.

"Today we have a very special prize. A quilt made by the Craft Group. I think we can all agree they did very well."

"Good job!"

"It's real cute."

"Who sewed on those adorable buttons?"

"Would our new member like to choose the winning ticket?" I leaned across the table, looked away from the basket, pulled out a scrap of paper and passed it to Marjorie who unfolded it.

"Seventy-eight." The room buzzed with excitement as everyone checked their tickets, commiserating with each other on not winning. "Seventy-eight," Marjorie called louder, "who's the lucky winner?" Sitting down I casually glanced at my tickets.

"Oh-my-god it's mine!" My cheeks burned as red as my trousers and I looked up expecting to see narrow-eyed bitchiness. Instead everyone was smiling and laughing.

"It's for the baby!"

"What a fantastic welcome gift!"

"Hope it's a girl with all those pink buttons!" I just blushed bashfully like a grateful mother who couldn't believe her luck.

With the meeting adjourned people started moving away from the table, gathering in small groups to discuss where to go for lunch without catching SARS. Tina and Ulla were arranging where to lay Sunday's Hash run. The Hash House Harriers are an international network of enthusiastic ex-pats who meet at weekends to follow paper trails before competing over who can drink the most beer. My first encounter with Hashers had been in Kuala Lumpur where I'd been distressed to find a note pushed under my hotel door reading, 'Are you hashing tonight?' Convinced I'd been trapped in a drugs ring and would be thrown into a dingy Malaysian prison, I ran for the lift to find a jolly bunch of Australians wearing 'International Hash 1999' t-shirts and talking loudly about 'great hash' without fear of being overheard and arrested.

I declined Ulla and Tina's offer to join: chasing bits of paper and downing beers didn't appeal to me. Besides, with big boobs and short legs I wasn't designed to run.

"Ataturk Park is too dodgy, that guy asked if I was a prostitute last time we ran there," Tina was admitting to Ulla. I decided that although feeling shy, I should make an effort to meet more people so left the safety of my seat for the sideboard where tea and coffee were laid out. Clutching a cup and saucer I studied the truly international group. Rowdy Americans; petite Indians in bright saris; tall Dutch with tortoiseshell glasses and chic French in pearls: a diverse mix from all nations, united by being foreign and unable to pronounce 'hello' in the local language.

"So you won the quilt, how wonderful!" I swung round, tea-cup midway to my mouth. It was Marjorie, the President.

"I'm very embarrassed about drawing my own ticket. I hope no-one thinks I cheated."

"Don't be silly, we don't fuss about such things here. This is a small international community with a lovely friendly atmosphere, there's none of the bitchiness I've experienced in other places. Living abroad you should pull together and look after each other. There are far more important things to worry about than cheating at the raffle, not that I think you did of course. How are you getting on, homesick I should think? Nothing to be ashamed of, we've all been there. I've been travelling for the whole of my husband's career and can remember being so miserable on my first posting. I recall crying over a bowl of soup at a restaurant because I'd got lost in the market or something ridiculous and I said to my husband, 'I want to go home'.

'I'll get the driver', he replied and I said, 'No, stupid, I want to really go home'. Thirty years and four children later I love this life and all the homes I've had. And there's no need to be lonely in Bishkek. Everyone understands the difficulties of living in the former Soviet Union, so we all support each other. Do you sew? You must join the Craft Group, speak to Marcia, she'll give you the details. Excuse me while I talk to Penny, enjoy your morning."

Before I could replace my cup on its saucer a bouncy lady in a pink tracksuit pounced on me.

"I love your pants, where did you get them from?" I panicked, was I making the classic hipster mistake and showing some g-string? "What a great red colour." Of course, she meant trousers, being American. "I bet they're not from Tzumingdales."

"Where?"

"Tzumingdales! It's what I like to call Tzum, Bishkek's department store. It's more a collection of shabby stalls than a real store but I love it coz they sell everything from Dior to Prada, all fake of course." Now I knew how Cholpon afforded Louis Vuitton. "And my husband luuurvs the third floor which is fulla music and films. You can always get the latest thing – premiers in Hollywood Saturday, released in Tzum by Tuesday, awesome!"

"Really? That's impressive."

"They're pirate copies sweetie! All that fussin' Stateside about illegal Internet downloads. Here you just go shop at Tzumingdales and no-one cares. So, how ya doing? You can always spot the new girls, they look like rabbits

41

in the headlights. Don't be miserable about Bishkek, we all have lotsa fun. Oh hi there Birgit, come to meet our new little mom, isn't she cute?" Birgit looked as bewildered as I did about my being 'cute', but smiled and shook my hand.

"I've come to invite Saffia to Playgroup at my house tomorrow."

"Playgroup! Oh I remember those days. It sure was great to learn that it's not unusual to want to throttle your two-year-old but the scariest thing you'll ever do in Bishkek is host Playgroup. Fifteen kids tearin' up your home and the moms, who are all expert bakers, chewin' on your pumpkin pie. My gawd I hated it, I'm so glad my Tula grew outa that and goes to bal-let instead. Anyway, why'd she wanna go to Playgroup, her kid's not born yet?"

"I just thought she might like to meet some other young mums and hear how we all manage."

"She's not gonna..."

"I'd love to," I interrupted.

"Oh gee, well I'll leave you two discussing diapers. Great to meet you Safi and call me when you wanna see round Tzumingdales."

"Will do, bye."

"Phew, that's Clorise, she's extraordinary but a lovely, generous woman." Birgit was Swedish, her husband a paramedic training local doctors. She was petite with cropped grey hair and long, delicate fingers. She'd looked terrified of Clorise. "So how long are you in Bishkek?" I explained, again, about flying home for the birth and being unsure whether we'd bring baby back to this harsh city of concrete.

"I know how you feel. I came here with a three-month old."

"You did?"

"Oh yes, everyone thought I was mad and I wondered whether I was the only woman in the world to leave her country with a tiny baby. But when I arrived I met some other mums and we formed the playgroup and helped each other out and it's been wonderful."

"That makes me feel better already. I'm just not sure I can cope so far from home, especially where there's no medical back up."

"Yes, that's a worry for all of us, even me with my husband a paramedic. I fear we're all a little reckless and rely on prayer, crossed fingers and good insurance so we can get flown out. Thank God, there's not been an emergency yet. So how are you settling in? Not too miserable?" Why was everyone obsessed with my being miserable? Had my first-week rant been broadcast over the Internet? "Moving to a new country where everything's strange is always difficult. Wait 'til you do it with children, then you'll know what pressure is. If they're not happy you don't stand a chance. Would you like to join us tomorrow? It may reassure you to see how other mums cope. And we're all a bit younger so don't talk about hot flushes and support pants," she added in a whisper.

How lovely these women were, I concluded as I sipped cold tea. In England there'd be snide murmurs in corners and bitching about whether I'd cheated to win the coveted quilt. Here everyone was too busy congratulating me and inviting me for coffee. It seemed I'd be pretty busy in Bishkek – if I survived SARS.

Chapter Six – To the Mountains

Life changed with membership of the Bishkek International Women's Club. I had friends and a phone list and somewhere to go on Wednesday afternoons. In Aswan there hadn't been a Women's Club. There'd been me, a Colombian and an American who'd sunbathed together and shared books, but no monthly meetings, no minutes, no membership fees. In Bishkek I was dazzled by emailed agendas about orphans, craft fairs and who was sitting on which committee. I'd even been invited out for lunch after the meeting and listened to discussions about a new restaurant in the mountains and where to go hiking. At Playgroup I'd met Susi, Anthea, Penny, Chitra and children and learnt that *kaimak* was thick local cream suitable for making tiramisu and that if your gardener over-watered the roses you should fire him. It was all thrilling for someone whose life had revolved around episodes of Fame Academy in Denmark.

Ulla followed up her picnic invitation and the following Friday sixteen of us squeezed into a *mashrutka* with seating for ten. This was very Kyrgyz. *Mashrutkas* are battered mini buses which race around town attempting to run over pedestrians as they pull in and out of traffic. Passengers pay 5 *som* (about 7 pence) for any destination; arriving without whiplash is a bonus. Ulla had hired a man who was willing to drive slowly and hadn't yet ruined his suspension and Matthew and myself; Ulla and family; Tina and Brian; Noreko, a Japanese girl volunteering with the UN; Ajara, a Kyrgyz friend of Ulla's; a missionary called Madeline, her four children and a guinea pig – the children's pet, not lunch I was corrected – crammed into the seats.

I was very excited. I'd never been on a picnic with a guinea pig before. It was also wonderful to be escaping to green hills beyond the concrete. We drove south down a road called *Manas*, the mountains rising tantalisingly before us. *Manas* is the label given to everything in Bishkek no longer called 'Lenin', the name of a super-hero folk legend on horseback who fought endless foes to find a homeland for his people. His exploits are recorded in an epic twenty times as long as the Odyssey, recited through generations by lyrical *manaschi*. Supposedly it tells of great courage and battles, of single-handedly tossing enemies from their saddles, but the first excerpt I read involved *Manas* and a mate sucking an old lady's breasts.

The road *Manas* is one of the major arteries through town, a wide boulevard without potholes because it's the route to the President's house. It was usually a melee of traffic and kamikaze pedestrians crossing between the pharmacies, hairdressers and grandiose universities on either side. As it was a holiday its lanes were quiet, Bishkekers at home recovering from the previous night's consumption of booze and fags until it was time to converge on Ala Too Square for parades, speeches and music. Matthew had watched cadets practise from his office window, boys on national service who were too young to remember winning any war. They were to be inspected by Akayev from the back of an open-topped Zil, suitably Soviet and very ceremonial.

The guinea pig and I waved goodbye to the shoebox towers as we raced out of town. Above us trolleybus wires rattled and billboards advertised Kyrgyz vices: cigarettes, vodka, gambling and mountains. The Kyrgyz are proud of their celestial Tien Shan, said to symbolise 'the high spirit of our ancestors, their striving for freedom, wisdom and philosophy'.[6] In recognition of this worship the President declared 2003 'Year of the Mountains' and insisted that huge posters of him were used to promote the celebrations.

It was difficult to take Askar Akayev seriously when you saw him superimposed on a snowy vista, grinning like a cartoon character. He had shiny round cheeks, eyebrows like black slugs and an *ak-kalpak* on his bald head. You couldn't help thinking, 'this buffoon was Father of the Nation?' But Akayev led Kyrgyzstan from Communism's cocoon into Independence, and survived. Chosen for President by the Supreme Soviet in October 1990, the first non-communist Central Asian premier, he was re-elected, conveniently running unopposed, in Kyrgyzstan's first presidential elections in October 1991.

Commentators write that emerging states' politics were determined by the character and style of whoever was local boss at the time of Independence, four of whom are still in power. Therefore, Uzbekistan became a repressive secular autocracy under Karimov; Kazakhstan a presidential dictatorship under Nazabayev; Turkmenistan a theme park for the cult of Niyazov, better known as Turkmenbashi, Father of all Turkmens; and Tajikistan a mess because without a strong leader it fell into civil war.

In comparison, Akayev, although not exactly a liberal democrat, was the most moderate Central Asian president. According to his contemporaries his tolerance was his weakness and would be his downfall. From newspaper coverage it seemed the style of his leadership was to smile and philosophise and make so many fantastic speeches that 'Words of Akayev' was a favourite feature in the Bishkek Observer. The editor had yet to realise it would be better on the coffee break quiz page under 'what does Akayev actually mean?'

In a region of political and economic instability many worried what would happen if he abdicated before the next election, which he couldn't win without constitutional abuse. They looked at the good achieved by his administration – improved international relations, an American airbase generating lots of dollars and extensive road resurfacing, on *Manas* – saying 'better the Disney character you know than the dictator you don't'. Others concentrated on the bad aspects of his reign – lingering corruption, nepotism, abused elections and his books – and looked for alternatives to the ruling family. Either way he was more popular than Michael Jackson, according to the polls, and you couldn't get to Ala Archa without smiling back at him.

---

[6] Kyrgyzstan: The Word about Homeland – Imanaliev

Within ten minutes we'd passed the last billboard and were speeding down an elegant avenue of poplars. We flashed by the American Embassy bunker and a new housing estate of red, blue and green roofs. On a patch of tarmac cars bunny-hopped and reverse-parallel-parked into each other – the next generation learning to drive before bribing officials for a license. Nearby cows grazed, watched by motionless *babushkas*; this was where city and country merged, nudging each other at their edges.

At the end of the avenue soldiers paced in front of a gate.

"That's Akayev's house," Ulla explained.

"One of them," Mark, her husband, added.

"According to newspaper reports he's only got a car, an apartment, a gun and a horse," I said.

"And why d'you think they wrote that?" Mark asked rhetorically. "Kyrgyz papers are so dull my dog wouldn't poo on them."

"We don't have a dog," Ulla remarked.

"But you get my point." Mark pulled a paper out of his bag and read from the front page. "'*The President congratulated the new foreign minister on his appointment to the high post and noted that there was a good relation between their countries expressing thanks for visit.*' It's always the same bland drivel. No comment, no analysis, they're too scared of being sued until bankrupt or imprisoned for libel." Freedom of speech isn't sacrosanct in Kyrgyzstan – tabloids wouldn't last long. Adverts for strip clubs are allowed but too many lurid stories about which politician owned a million-dollar apartment in Moscow and they'd be closed down before you could say 'get your tits out'.

We turned right off the tarmac and bumped through deep ruts.

"No need to maintain the road now the President's got home," Australian Brian drawled. The guinea pig burrowed deeper into its basket and I tried, again, to fasten my seat belt.

"You no need with me," the driver assured with a grin before ramming us violently through a widening pot-hole.

Our journey to the mountains took us through villages of whitewashed cottages and donkey carts. Steep alpine meadows arched ever higher, grazing horses silhouetted against the blue sky. We bounced and swerved past fields of delicate poppies and herds of shaggy sheep, their bottoms round and protruding; lumps of fat which were traditionally presented to the most senior woman at a banquet, considered a delicacy sliced and served cold. Shepherds were barefoot children waving sticks or men slouched on horses, dozing under grubby *ak-kalpaks*.

Along the roadside on muddy river banks, people were already picnicking, choosing to eat in a crowded swamp despite the beauty spots of Kyrgyzstan. Families were lighting cooking fires and washing dishes in the river – just like being at home for most of them. Picnicking is a national pastime in Kyrgyzstan. At weekends and on national holidays the city empties as people dash for the nearest piece of grass. Weather isn't an issue; Kyrgyz are like Brits and barbecue even if it's snowing. But they don't just char burgers, there's more to a Kyrgyz picnic than shuffling Tupperware. The fire smoulders for hours while *shashlik*, kebabs of mutton, beef, pork, chicken and chunks of fat, sizzle in embers fanned with pieces of cardboard. Women sit cross-legged on blankets, screeching with laughter at foreigners' soggy sandwiches while they chop buckets of green pepper, onions and carrots for Kyrgyz specialities: noodles with fatty mutton – *lagman* – and rice with fatty mutton – *plov*, both cooked in huge basins over the fire. This is washed down with vodka, tea from the samovar and round loaves of flat *lepioshka* until it's time to load all the equipment and at least eight people into a tiny Lada and drive back to the city.

It was another beautiful spring morning – two days without rain in one week, I felt blessed. My only worry, apart from being flung through the windscreen, was altitude sickness. When I'd realised that Bishkek was 800 metres above sea level and someone had commented that you're not supposed to go to high altitudes when pregnant because it affects blood flow, I'd panicked and set Matthew researching on the Internet. The general consensus was that climbing Everest at thirty weeks wasn't a good idea but unhelpfully no-one answered the question of whether I'd be safe living in a third floor apartment on *Moskovskaya*. As we were planning to picnic at 3000 metres that day I wondered how Baby Bullock – and the guinea pig – were going to react.

We passed under an arch declaring something Soviet and on the fat curve of a hillside I saw an assortment of metal gazebos and bird cages clinging to the slopes.

"What are they?" I asked the guinea pig. One tower looked as if it would blast off to space if given suitable power.

"Graves," Ulla replied, the guinea pig too car-sick to comment. "It's a cemetery. The tower's a memorial to Baitik Khan who rebelled against the Khan of Khokand and asked Russian troops for help in storming Pishpek, as Bishkek used to be called."

"Unlike the rest of Central Asia the Kyrgyz aren't ashamed of displaying their history," Mark explained. "Lenin's still here but he's been torn down everywhere else."

"How long do you think he'll last?" I asked.

"Until the government realise he's worth more to them as scrap sold to China."

Leaving Bishkek is like travelling back a century. Although the capital is stuck in a Soviet time-warp, rural villages are living illustrations of history book rusticity. That morning families were preparing fields for planting, unaware of the holiday. A decrepit tractor, probably a remnant of Stalin's Five-Year Industrialisation Plans, was dragging a plough ineffectually across cloying mud. Women in woollen smocks and headscarves swung large hoes like blunt pick-axes into the ground, turning clods of earth. As we passed a *babushka* paused and wiped a soiled sleeve across her forehead, indifferent to the sight of fifteen foreigners and a guinea pig peering at her. Her flat, round face was browned by the sun and framed by a red headscarf. I wanted to stick her in my photo album.

From the comfort of the minibus the scene was so charming I wished we could live in a cottage with a shaggy hayrick in the garden. Fetching water from a brook and dining by candlelight seems quaint and appealing – when you can return to hot showers and electricity once the novelty's worn off. Life is hard for rural Kyrgyz. They'd grown up on *kolkhoz*, Soviet collective farms, and many pined for the support and guaranteed salaries which vanished when the Soviet Union collapsed. Farmers lamented in the Central Asian Times about lack of funds and knowledge to maximise land allotted to them, hoping for Aid to save them.

But Aid is a slow and cumbersome saviour. Matthew was working to bring clean drinking water to villages, but don't imagine flushing toilets and kitchen sinks. It was taking seven years and a lot of World Bank and DFID money to put *kalonka*, standpipes, in the streets, one per 350 people. People would still have to walk half a mile for a cup of tea, but it was an improvement on using dirty puddles.

Water is a basic need we take for granted in the West, a precious resource which many predict wars will be fought over. In Kyrgyzstan there's plenty of water but pumps and pipes haven't been operational since perestroika. Being an ex-pat was teaching me what an extraordinary standard of living we enjoy in England, giving me perspective on true hardship. Fortnightly rubbish collections, waiting months to see free doctors and other calamities hyped by the media were mere inconveniences compared to life in Kyrgyzstan.

The Kyrgyz were remarkably apathetic about their poverty. Having been taught conformity and obedience by the Soviets they never thought to question why their lives had stagnated. One reason for their lethargy was that they probably had little idea about the rest of the world. Cocooned by communism, illiteracy and no access to media, there was nothing for them to compare their lives against.

Civil society projects were slowly changing this by opening centres where Kyrgyz could watch international news, read papers or search on the Internet. Critics worried this might have a detrimental effect, warning that forced emancipation could be dangerous. The sheltered Kyrgyz being educated in these centres weren't being told that with modernisation came different problems, a new generation of social ills. They were being exposed to the vices of the West; excessive consumerism; obesity; dire reality television; pollution; the assumption being that families hand planting potatoes for next year's survival would happily trade their life for those corruptions.

The projects were also condemned for deliberately stirring discontent. The most extreme critics claimed that they were simply covers for the Western governments funding them who planned to use the angered Kyrgyz as pawns to undermine regimes which didn't fit into their world order. Across Kyrgyzstan was a gradual awakening, a growing awareness that a rich president whose family dominated parliament wasn't normal.

Out of the village we skirted the mountains I'd gazed at from Bishkek. They fanned out in layers of ridges, each higher and whiter as they ascended into the distance until undistinguishable from clouds gathered around them.

"Look, skiers," one of Madeline's children yelled. Black dots swerved down steep slopes, zooming towards each other then careening away as if repelled by a magnetic force. At the entrance to the gorge we stopped to pay fees for the national park. We didn't try to bribe the official, unlike a local reporter who'd happily described this corruption in his article: an interesting illustration of the things journalists were happy to admit and those they dared not report.

Behind the toll booth was an archetypal alpine scene, as if laid on for tourists' benefit. Wooden houses with steeply sloping, corrugated roofs nestled on the valley floor, scattered around the river. Plumes of smoke rose towards meadows where cattle grazed, insignificant specks against the vast landscape. Above them the snow line hung like a curtain, clinging to slopes as the sun nibbled its hem.

As we wound deeper into the park the mountains closed in on us like towering walls. They rose harshly and precipitously, in serrated crags both threatening and unreal to my eyes more used to desert sands. The landscape was so wild I wouldn't have been surprised to see two Hobbits looking for Mordor. Instead herds of fluffy brown yaks grazed on herbage which pushed through thinning snow.

The road ended by a cluster of dumpy buildings, one of which I could already read in Cyrillic was a bar. Above them a tall chalet was being constructed. It had a steep red roof, tinted windows and three large satellite dishes.

"Wow, who can afford that?" I asked Mark.

"Who d'you think?"

"The President?"

"Or a son. Anything in Bishkek which is new, shiny and profitable belongs to someone in the ruling family."

"How are you finding the altitude?" Matthew asked as he helped me out of the *mashrutka*.

"I haven't popped yet. What are we at?" Matthew consulted his pocket GPS.

"2150 metres. 74° 30.6' E, 42° 40.2' N." You can't get lost with Matthew around, he has a gadget for everything.

Grabbing rucksacks, baskets and the guinea pig we climbed over a stile onto the track. The air was cool and fresh, a rasp at the back of your throat if you breathed too quickly but a pleasant change to smoggy carbon monoxide in

49

Bishkek. The path was shaded by tall pine trees with clumps of snow clinging to branches, remnants of winter icing.

"Too much vodka!" Tina called as Brian puffed with the exertion of the slight incline. Ulla's girls, Madeline's children and the guinea pig had run on ahead, oblivious to the dragging effect of altitude. As I stopped to steady my breathing I was glad my excuse was pregnancy.

"Give us a break," Brian yelled, "I am carrying a huge eskie, three bottles of water and the wardrobe of clothes you brought with you."

"Ulla said to dress for all seasons, you know the weather can change real quick up here."

So far we were lucky and warmed by exercise and the sun we peeled off coats, jumpers and sweatshirts like layers of onion. The children had chosen a patch of grass still unbending from the weight of snow and laid a rug between two fir trees. The guinea pig was tentatively nibbling fallen cones. To the right was a vast dried-up riverbed. In summer it would be filled with roaring melt-water. So far only a small stream hurried over smooth grey boulders, the wooden footbridge a monument amidst dry stones.

Benches and tables hewn from tree-trunks were already taken by Kyrgyz drinking vodka toasts and peeling skins from phallic salamis while their fires burnt down. Kyrgyzstan is about the size of Great Britain but has an average population density of 25 people per square kilometre – Britain's is 377. You'd think residents would enjoy such spatial luxury but in our square kilometre all 25 were sitting under the same tree. The problem was logistical. While Brian and I weren't able to walk much higher, locals chose not to. Their devotion to picnicking didn't extend to trekking to a secluded site – as we'd seen, most barely made it out of Bishkek. The Kyrgyz favoured parking the car and lighting a fire under its bumper so those around us felt they'd done well to get this far, especially the girls who were still wearing stilettos.

We laid out rugs and an eclectic mix of food patched together by the different nationalities: pizza, Kyrgyz *samsi* (meat or cheese pies), sushi, chicken wings, bread rolls and salads. While the guinea pig was evicted from the lettuce I attempted conversation with Madeline.

"Are you going to the Valentine Ball?"

"No." It was a short and disapproving answer. How stupid of me to ask. Not everyone aspired to waltz with ambassadors. The missionaries were here to immerse themselves with locals so they could teach them that Jesus was better than vodka or Allah.

"I am," chirped Noreko, "and so is Ajara. We're having our dresses made by Dilbar." Dilbar was Kyrgyzstan's only fashion designer, a talented woman who combined traditional embroidery with exotic fabrics to create stunning clothes.

"I can't wait," Ajara said eagerly. "It's going to be *so* glamorous; champagne beside the pool, dancing to a live band, like something from a fairytale!"

There was a buzz of anticipation about the ball around town, the demand for gowns causing electricity surges as every seamstress in Bishkek worked overtime to dress over-excited women in rustling silk and taffeta. I was excited too, assuming I'd finally discovered the fabled high-society glamour. Although the uninitiated perceive ex-pat life to be nothing but cocktail parties and soirees with ambassadors, my Trailing Spouse experiences so far had revolved around finding food and trying to be understood.

"I hear you're seeing Dr Hilary on Monday," Ulla said, passing the sushi.
"How did you know?"
Ulla laughed. "Nothing is private in Bishkek, especially if you tell Gina."
"What's wrong with you?" Noreko asked from behind her camera where she was encouraging the guinea pig to smile for a photo.
"I'm pregnant, nineteen weeks today!"
"Congratulations."
"Praise Jesus!" Madeline said emphatically, raising her arms in thanks. "I will pray for you when it gets hot in August, pray that you don't get too uncomfortable."
"Thank you." People seemed obsessed with August's heat. Was I going to be trapped inside, beached in front of our one air conditioner?
"Have some more pizza as you're eating for two," Tina suggested.
"Being pregnant is a great excuse to eat what you want and not worry about a fat stomach."
"It's one of God's gifts," Madeline reminded.
"Yes, of course." I didn't know how to explain that behind my flippancy I was in awe of the miracle of gestation. That a tiny person was lodging in my body, turning pizza and Mars bars into finger nails and eyelashes was beyond comprehension.
Unlike Kyrgyz our picnic didn't take all day and we were soon fidgeting for new entertainment. Brian dozed in the sun with the guinea pig; the children ran back down the path with Ulla to try and find horses to ride and the rest of us strolled further up the valley. We crossed the dry river bed; grey, pink, blue and white stones dull without water's shine. On the bank was a large *yurt*, a round, felt tent used by nomads. This one had electricity wires running to it and a satellite dish perched incongruously on its roof.
"Don't even ask me who that belongs to," Mark pre-empted. "There's only one answer."
We headed into the heart of the valley, the dip where the two sides appeared to meet. Dark pines bristled on steep slopes and the river rumbled in the distance where, compressed between narrower shores, it tossed boulders in torrents of water. Matthew and I walked with Ajara. She was Kyrgyz with Kyrgyz parents, born in a village called Tokok which teetered at 3000 feet near the Chinese border.
"That's one of my projects," Matthew exclaimed. "What's your water supply like?"

"We have to walk fifteen minutes to fetch it from a river. When you're little you think it's fun because you chat to all your friends and don't go to school but when you're older you think the men should do it. My mother still lives there. You can't imagine the hardships. In winter it's so cold everything freezes. From October until May the ground is hidden by snow and my mother must hack through the ice to find water. She wears so many clothes she can hardly move because there's no electricity for heating and spends the whole winter living in the kitchen warmed by the bread oven and lit by candles. I much prefer to be in Bishkek in an apartment but my mother is happy in our house. She says she's busy sewing *shyrdaks*, our traditional felt rugs, for my wedding."

"You're getting married?"

"Nothing is fixed yet but I hope to soon."

As Ajara's boyfriend was an American from the airbase it was unsurprising she was keen to get hitched. She'd join hoards of other Kyrgyz fiancés airlifted from a life of lugging water to a white picket fence and SUV somewhere in the States, a statistic in what many joked was the base's most successful humanitarian aid effort. Although the population had been discouraged from rebelling against an American airbase with propaganda promising increased revenue, the only benefits for normal Kyrgyz, apart from marriage if you wanted it, were increased sales of pirate DVDs in Tzum and 'friendship' candies handed out by patrols in nearby villages. Farmers didn't profit because all food and water was insultingly flown in, for alleged health and hygiene reasons and the Akayev family controlled the companies with the lucrative fuel supply contracts.

Ajara considered herself lucky. "I want to have big wedding with white veil and long limousine. All my friends will ride with me around town blasting car horns and I'll be a princess in a tiara. How was your wedding?" I told her about my corseted dress, the church, bridesmaids and heated marquee because it had been in January. I could sense Madeline trying to count nineteen weeks backwards on ten fingers without tripping over a boulder.

"Ours is a wedding night baby," I added conspicuously.

"Praise Jesus," said Madeline.

Over the crest of a small hill I stopped to rest while the others walked on to explore a hidden waterfall. I lay back on a warm boulder, rough grass scratching my legs where I'd rolled up my trousers. I closed my eyes, comfortable in the sun's warmth. In the silence I could hear snow melting, a sensation of delicate dripping from tips of pine needles. When I opened my eyes it took me a while to orientate. Above me eagles spiralled leisurely against a blue sky, dark trees framed my view and a mountain soared from the end of the valley, its glacier a smooth ribbon of white, lower summits dusted with snow.

Kyrgyzstan is almost completely mountainous; 40% of the country is over 3000 metres high and 30% permanently under snow. My boulder was a mere speck in the Ala Archa gorge which swept up to *Semenov Tianshanskii*, the highest peak in the Kyrgyz Alatau range at 4895 metres. But the Kyrgyz Alatau is just a spur of the great Tien Shan which runs across Central Asia for 2414 kilometres, cutting through Kyrgyzstan, Kazakhstan and China, vast mountains which have evolved over millions of year. I would leave Kyrgyzstan, have my baby, grow old and die and the Tien Shan would remain, unchanged but for a few landslides. I felt dwarfed by statistics.

With unconquered summits and virgin passes, Kyrgyzstan is an explorer's dream, if you're willing to trust Kyrgyz mountain rescue – three *babushkas* with a pick axe. On Victory Day the mountains looked silent and deserted but I knew that deep within the folds were base camps, ski chalets and adventurers with thermal sleeping bags and crampons, impossible territory for me, unfit and pregnant.

This scene was as striking as the guidebook pictures which had made me fantasize about a picturesque life in Kyrgyzstan. At last I felt I was seeing some of the country's beauty and although wouldn't have believed it three weeks before, felt lucky to be there. The trip had inspired me to travel; I wanted to see what was behind the mountain façades, visit a *jailoo*[7], stay in a *yurt* and experience the vast emptiness of Kyrgyzstan. Unfortunately I would realise that most of Kyrgyzstan was inaccessible if you were pregnant and cautious.

We returned to our *mashrutka* just as Kyrgyz fires were ready for cooking. Men shook their heads in bemusement at hasty foreigners, unscrewing the top of another vodka bottle while laying long skewers of *shashlik* across glowing embers. We slipped back down the valley, the mountains behind us shadows as the sky turned thunderously purple over the plains and lightening danced across horizons. By the time we reached Bishkek huge rain drops were lashing against our windows and the Tien Shan were lost in grey clouds. Were the Kyrgyz picnickers still up there, stoically chewing on kebabs while their Ladas floated down swollen rivers?

"I hope the sun comes out again soon," I lamented to the guinea pig, my buoyant mood dampened by the monotonous streets of Bishkek. He seemed not to notice the rain, relieved by the return to a lesser altitude, the four walls of his cage comparatively inviting.

"Are you coming to Craft Group next week?" Ulla asked as we pulled up outside our shoebox.

"Yeah, and there's Mahjong on Friday," Tina reminded.

"See you at the ball!" Noreko yelled.

"May God be with you," Madeline said sedately.

"Good luck with Hilary on Monday," Ulla called as the mini bus door slammed shut. "And don't forget to take a book; they're not very good at keeping appointments!"

---

[7] Pastures high in the mountains where shepherds take animals for the summer, living in *yurts*

53

Chapter Seven – Blooming in Bishkek

It rained all day Saturday, trapping us inside with squalls lashing around the building. On Sunday the Tien Shan were back in focus, faces of white and shadow shifting with the sun's trajectory. I gazed at them from the kitchen, chin cupped in my hands, elbows resting on the windowsill. Since my biblical vision on our first day I'd become Kyrgyz in my obsession with mountains, never tiring of watching their shifting shapes and colours. Their beauty kept me from becoming depressed about the most disgusting parts of Bishkek – currently the huge, open dustbins outside our flat.

The rubbish of Kyrgyzstan has replaced oppressive Soviet care as the social security system. Our three bins overflowed with rotting vegetables, rancid *keffir* cartons and congealed food, rummaged through by shuffling pensioners, bare-foot street kids and drunks with faces swollen by exposure and vodka. The resident *babushka* watched from her low wooden stool, legs crossed and hands clutching grubby *som*. She always wore a blue headscarf, thick brown overcoat, brown skirt, woollen tights and black snow boots. Her face was soft and wrinkled, her chin bristling with short hairs like a raspberry. She looked impassive as she waited for passers by to contribute to her welfare. Once cared for by the Soviet state she'd been abandoned to the waste and small change of others.

On Monday morning when I set out for my appointment with Dr Hilary the sun was warming the city and the skips stank of old cheese. If they were this bad now, how would they smell in August's heat? I held my breath and slung a bag onto the pile. It split open, gushing its contents across the ground. An old man dashed excitedly towards it. When I returned I'd find the bits he didn't want scattered across the path.

Dr Hilary worked at the Family Clinic on *Bokonbayeva*, one of many medical institutions in Bishkek; another Soviet legacy. She was part of a project to try and improve general practitioner skills, a challenge because most staff were Soviet trained to diagnose and treat patients by following instructions on a *precass* rather than listening, thinking and adapting. According to Gina, Grigor, her first driver, had been to hospital with a swollen foot. Mentioning that he was diabetic the doctor had consulted his *precass* on diabetes and injected the foot with insulin. The following week Grigor returned to hospital for an amputation. Such rumours were another reason I was so keen to see a Western trained doctor.

According to my map the quickest route to the clinic was through a small park squashed between *Moskovskaya* and *Bokonbayeva*. Paths were laid out like white lines on a Union Jack and in the wedges between were oak trees, scrubby grass, squirrels, condoms and beer bottles. It wasn't somewhere you'd want to sprawl on a rug and read the Sunday papers. At its centre a pink, granite bust of the poet *Togolok Moldo* watched from his bed of marigolds. Lovers intertwined on benches, snogging and sharing cigarettes. Mothers chased waddling toddlers who were so wedged into padded coats and trousers they struggled to bend limbs. On the dilapidated swings teenagers competed to see who could arc the highest and a burly Rottweiler, its coat groomed to a smooth black sheen, tugged at its lead, desperate to bite a man in a red tracksuit who was pulling himself up on high exercise bars in slow repetitions.

I turned left out of the park and walked through a gate beside a ditch blocked with litter. The stagnant water was thick and green, an unfortunate border for a hospital compound. I knew a clinic must be close because men in white coats strode past with stethoscopes swinging from their necks and women in dressing gowns and slippers shuffled towards stalls selling loo roll.

While I waited to cross an ambulance limped over the road, siren bleating pathetically. It was an old VW van driven by an ancient Uighur man with skull cap and grey goatee. Imagining the emergency call didn't help my nerves.

"Please help, I have terrible pains. I think I'm about to give birth prematurely."

"Don't panic. The ambulance will be there once we've changed a tyre and welded the door back on."

Ulla had told me to look for a grey building with '144' painted on it but all the buildings were grey and too decrepit to be hospitals, I hoped. I wandered up and down paths, through gates and up a stairwell which had '144' scraped promisingly from the stone. It was dark, quiet and all the doors were locked. Presuming this wasn't the clinic doing a sponsored silence I returned despondently to the road. What good was Doctor Hilary if I couldn't find her?

I was too scared to phone the receptionists for directions; it seems that doctor's receptionists are rude and unapproachable throughout the world. Instead I decided to ask someone in the street. Looking around I noticed there were lots of chefs in tall white hats and I wondered where all the restaurants were. Nearest to me a large group were chatting and laughing but I felt too intimidated to interrupt.

Eventually I settled on a newsagent, a lady sitting in a wooden booth with twenty thin newspapers pegged by their corners across the front. Also on sale were cigarettes, toy cars, sweets, glue and greetings cards with fluffy kittens in ribbons.

"Do you know the Family Clinic?" I asked through a small opening above the newspapers. The woman just sniffed and pointed up to where porn magazines were spread across the window, peroxide women with faded boobs pressed up to the glass.

"No thanks. Er, baby, doctor, me, where?" Registering the English she pulled a magazine down from a rack and pushed it across the ledge. It was called 'Shaven Asian'. "*Nyet*, a doc-tor." She shoved a card towards me with a smirk. A cartoon lady with boobs bursting from a short nurse's uniform was bending suggestively, exposing her bum. There was a condom inside. I hurried away before embarrassing myself further.

I was in despair. I now knew where to buy smutty birthday cards but I was no closer to Hilary. I wondered what would happen if I stood in the road and cried. I'd probably be pitied and handed dirty *som* notes by the chefs. I considered yelling "Hil-ar-ree" until she found me, or I was arrested. I hated being lost and foreign.

Trudging back towards the park I spotted '144a' and an arrow painted on a wall. There was an official sign and six people waiting outside looking bored. A chef was smoking on the doorstep. Ulla had said the clinic was on the first floor so I groped up the dark stairs and tentatively pushed a door. It opened onto a corridor which smelt of bleach; comforting even though the flooring was the same brown curling linoleum as Dr Bucket's hospital.

The receptionists were as unhelpful as their telephone manner suggested, refusing to acknowledge me until I started chanting, "Hil-ar-ree! Hil-ar-ree!" It's in coping with everyday things made complicated that ex-pat wives show the greatest resourcefulness. Recognised as the mad foreigner on the telephone I was led away to a small room at the end of a long corridor with 'Kabinet 3' on the door. I wasn't sure I'd be let out. Inside paint peeled from walls and the window panes were cracked. My interrogator wore a white lab-coat over a beige roll neck and brown tweed skirt. She appeared to have dyed her stiff hair with a red spray can. I was expecting to be put in a straitjacket until she pointed at the scales.

"Ah!" I thought, "booking in."

Having already been through the process in Danish and English I was familiar with the format. In English it involved admitting how unhealthy our families were, peeing all over a pot and lying on the sitting room floor while Fiona hunted for a foetal heartbeat. In Danish it had been more intrusive with Dr Henrik, latex gloves and endless questions about financial stability.

'Booking in' in Russian was simple at first as I was able to understand the purpose of each piece of equipment pointed at. I stood on the scales, pressed against the measuring chart, held out my arm for the blood pressure wrap and allowed a disposable thermometer to be thrust under my tongue. The next stage was trickier as it involved incomprehensibly long Russian sentences ending in questions. I shrugged and smiled apologetically.

"Mother, father, *babushka*?"

"*Da.*" Yes, I had family.

"*DA!*" Oh dear, wrong answer. I shrugged again and she resorted to miming, shaking violently, clutching her right breast and slumping forward. I understood. This was the 'what diseases are in your family stage' and that was a heart attack. How embarrassing to have to explain to another medic that between them our relations had almost every illness on the list. I'd not realised how sickly we were: cancer, heart problems, diabetes, indictments of modern living. What hope did this child have?

We went through the list with interesting mimes, most of which I didn't understand so answered "*nyet*" as the safest option. When she started coughing, hawking and banging her chest I looked desperately for the panic button, until realising this was the tuberculosis demonstration.

"*Nyet*," I replied, I didn't have that either, despite all the spitting.

Once all the boxes had been filled in I was led away to a narrow corridor and pushed onto a bench. Opposite me a mother held what I assumed was a baby cocooned in blankets. An ancient *babushka* shuffled over to sit next to me. Her skin was white and doughy, her face so patterned by webs of wrinkles it looked as though it was retracting into her puckered mouth and eyes. She sniffed and flicked a grubby handkerchief at her nose. I looked forward to catching whatever she had – in Kyrgyz hospitals you leave with more germs than you came with, but at least only colds rather than MRSA.

I read my book and tried to pretend I wasn't there. Doors slammed, matrons in white coats barged past, the old lady coughed, but I read on. The soundtrack of Russian buzzed around me, interrupted by tantalising snatches of female English which gave me hope of meeting Dr Hilary. I was therefore disappointed when I was led away along another corridor to another small room where a young Kyrgyz girl was sitting behind a desk, another leaning against the wall. They both wore shabby white coats and had mobile telephones hanging around their necks, as was the fashion in Kyrgyzstan. I sat down and the seated girl looked at me expectantly.

"What is your problem?" She tilted her head and wore a concerned doctor's frown.

"I'm pregnant. I was expecting to see Doctor Hilary."

"Ah, Doctor Hilary. How many pregnant?"

"Nineteen weeks." It seemed like the logical answer.

"Do you have wormit?"

"What? Worms?"

"Wormit, you know," she projectile vomited spit across the table.

"Ah! No, I don't have morning sickness."

"Smokey?" She lifted a packet of cigarettes from the pocket of her white coat.

"*Nyet!*" I'd heard Kyrgyz doctors were poorly trained but offering cigarettes to a pregnant woman seemed extreme. Hadn't she been taught about nicotine stunting a baby's growth?

"No, not for now," she said hastily. "I just ask question for form." She marked something in her notes. "Bishkek good? You like climate?"

Kyrgyz were obsessed with whether you liked their country, derived from a tradition of hospitality and the huge inferiority complex of a new nation. The girl was just interrogating me as to whether it was raining in London when a young blond woman in glasses, a white lab coat flapping over a floral dress, strode through the door.

"Sorry about that. I was accosted by an ex-KGB officer threatening unspeakable violence if I didn't give him pills. I'm Dr Hilary." At last, a friendly doctor, someone to save me from my ignorance of pregnancy. I was so excited I stood to hug her but sat down abruptly; hugging might be considered forward for a first meeting.

It was wonderful to discuss vaginal discharge in flowing English without pausing to calculate how much I should pay at the end of every sentence. Hilary answered my long list of questions and even explained what pre-eclampsia actually was.

"Don't worry about medical care during pregnancy. All you really need is someone to check your blood pressure and test your urine once a month, and we can do that here, just. Have you felt any movement yet?" As we talked two men in tall white hats burst dramatically through the door.

"Sorry, more trainees," Hilary apologised. "But this is a training school."

"Trainee chefs?" I asked.

"Chefs?" Hilary frowned. "Oh, the hats! They're not chefs, just unlucky. Soviet doctors had to wear those and no-one's thought to change the rules yet."

In Bishkek antenatal care was bizarre, but at least I was being examined. I lay on a rickety trolley and tried not to giggle as five doctors clustered around: two men in silly hats prodding my ankles, two women trying to measure my uterus with string and Hilary teaching that in England, girth wasn't considered an indicator of whether vaginal birth was possible.

"Medicine here is at the level we hit in the Fifties, mixed with local superstitions," she explained, unravelling a tape measure.

"That's comforting."

"Doctors are still convinced sitting on cold concrete will make you infertile and a favourite 'flu remedy is to prescribe rubbing vodka on your neck and putting mustard and onions in socks. Nargiza, can you find the heartbeat?" Nargiza moved a grey box across my belly until it screeched so loudly the two male doctors jumped back from their close inspection of my tummy.

"Don't panic! That's the battery running out not your baby. Sorry, no heartbeat today, equipment failures are common." I wasn't too disappointed. Fiona had found the beat and I'd listened to the syncopated pop-popping with awe, the first evidence that my Secret Treasure was in there.

Hilary explained that I had to come back in the morning for the urine test.

"Bring this form and a urine sample, preferably *not* in a huge vodka bottle you've emptied the night before like everyone else does, and go to Room Six opposite reception. Look for the technician, Gulzat; she's the one in blue gloves up to her elbows and a perpetual scowl. She'll test immediately but the results take time. Do you have your notes?"

Pregnant friends in England had fat booklets with graphs, boxes and charts to fill in. I had a pink piece of paper given reluctantly by Dr Henrik. Not able to read Danish, Hilary guessed where to record what she'd learnt and I left the clinic happy. Baby and I had just been examined by a friendly doctor. We were healthy, growing properly and I had Hilary's home number to call if I thought I was going into labour. Bishkek didn't seem like such a dump after all. I felt so relieved I skipped home through the park and wanted to dance with our 'Bin *Babushka*'. Instead I pressed some notes into her grimy hand.

"Bless you dear, and your unborn child." Well that's what I hoped she said, it could have been "is that all you stingy bitch?"

Early next morning I dutifully returned to the clinic, pausing only to gag indelicately at a man blowing his nose into his hand and wiping it on a tree. Asians believe that snorting bogies into a hankie and putting it in your pocket is disgusting, which possibly it is, but not as disgusting as smearing snot on a tree-trunk.

Two other women were waiting outside Room Six, both clutching vodka bottles. I joined them, placing my hand hopefully on my bump. Last night I'd felt bubbles popping inside me, a sensation of movement, a presence but nothing tangible for Matthew to share. I looked forward to Baby saying hello with its first kick.

In England the monthly urine test takes two seconds: a paper tester is dipped into a little pot and fades into a rainbow of purple, green or blue. In Bishkek it takes two hours – on the fast-track scheme. By eight-thirty the laboratory resembled a bottle stall at a fete with dozens of vodka bottles and jam jars full of golden urine. My little pot seemed timid in comparison.

Gulzat the technician, safe behind her huge gloves, jabbed pipettes into test tubes which spun in a mini Ferris-wheel for five minutes while she emptied the bottles into a sink. She then sat at her microscope, painstakingly examining each drop of blended pee between two slides.

I read, Gulzat noted results on forms, the man next to me snored under his *ak-kalpak*. Two hours later she gestured me in and carefully explained, in Russian, the significance of all the empty boxes on the form. I had no idea what she was talking about. Had her pen run out? Had I provided insufficient urine? Should I come back with two litres? Being pregnant in a foreign country was very confusing.

Depressed by my lack of test results and needing to stretch my leg muscles, I decided to walk to Mo-Soviet bazaar. I'd learnt at Playgroup that this was *the* place for fruit and vegetables because it stocked broccoli. What they didn't tell me was that it was *the* place to get ripped off, the broccoli a lure to snag stupid ex-pats. The bazaar was on *Moskovskaya,* near the junction with *Sovietskaya,* hence the name. I'd tentatively asked whether any of the women were wearing masks when shopping but the SARS hysteria seemed to have abated, the reality of lunching at home too tedious.

Mo-Soviet was a dark warehouse crammed with rows of stalls selling pyramids of tomatoes, carrots and aubergines, piles of strange green stalks, which apparently were for Kyrgyz soup, and of course broccoli. The selection was limited but everything was temptingly fresh, smelling tantalisingly of soil where it had been recently pulled from the ground. Fruit and vegetables are truly seasonal in Kyrgyzstan, which means you have to like cabbage during winter but summer tomatoes are a succulent deep red and don't taste of soggy cardboard.

I walked slowly up and down aisles, followed by dark-skinned gypsies cradling comatose babies and begging with outstretched palms. Vendors lurched across tables trying to snare me with crooked fingers and exhortations to buy. I was easy prey: clearly foreign and oozing ignorance and fear. They could smell their profit.

Knowing I couldn't circumnavigate the place all day I stopped at a corner where a man was smiling sycophantically rather than yelling. I should have known it was a trap.

"How much are those carrots?"

"100 *som* a kilo, special price for you." They looked so clean and fresh I didn't think it unreasonable. I knew I'd made a mistake the moment I turned; sellers were leaping at me like tidal waves, desperate to entice the stupid foreigner to buy from them. The atmosphere was grasping and malicious and I now understood why lots of ex-pats sent their drivers or housekeepers shopping for vegetables.

I fled from the building, weighed down with failure. I'd thought I had Bishkek sorted because I knew the way to the supermarket and had new friends who phoned me. But my confidence was superficial and it only took one kilo of carrots to destroy it. I wanted to cry, longing for home, familiarity and the ability to converse with a greengrocer. Language is a fortress not a barrier. I felt alone as I pushed through crowds, always on the edge of Bishkek life. I couldn't read notices, listen to the radio, eavesdrop on conversations or understand announcements in supermarkets. Individually these were small and seemingly insignificant details but collectively they denied me a depth of culture, lost nuances of Kyrgyzstan.

Clorise and Penny were waving to me from the Navigator's garden. Behind them two local girls in micro minis were sucking on long thin cigarettes, crossing and uncrossing legs in the hope male customers would pay their bill.

"Hey Saf-fee-ya, we were just talking, about you, how you won the quilt and your cute red pants and how you've taken Bishkek by storm." I wasn't sure whether to be flattered or insulted, but it seemed that once these woman had finished criticising their housekeepers they didn't have anything more exciting to discuss.

"Why don't you join us for lunch?" Penny suggested.

"It's kind of you to offer but I won't thanks." I just wanted to get home and call Ulla to discover the real price of carrots and how much of a fool I'd been.

"We've had such an exciting morning," Clorise said animatedly. "We've been to a craft fair at the Fine Arts Museum. The Blind Artisans of Kochkor are exhibiting cute table runners made with traditional embroidery. But you look sad today, Saf-*fee*-ya, what's up?" I wasn't going to confide in Clorise.

I didn't think she'd understand if I said my life lacked dimension because I couldn't communicate with local people. Her life lacked dimension if the manicurist ran out of peach nail varnish.

"How do you manage with language?" I asked. Penny started to explain about having lessons through Kumtor but Clorise interrupted.

"Oh boy, don't try learning Russian, it's got too many syllables. Anyway, it's just English in a stupid accent, you can add 'ski' to most words and be understood. Why waste time studyin' when you can say your husband's a *biznizman* and order *shampanski* with just a dictionary?" Clorise's husband was fighting the Central Asian drugs war for the American Embassy and so bizarre were her thought processes I was starting to wonder whether Clorise took some of the opium he confiscated.

I made my excuses and rushed home to call Ulla who confirmed that the appropriate rate for carrots was currently 40 *som*. I sobbed for baby who would suffer from iron deficiency through lack of broccoli because I was never going back to Mo-Soviet. I also phoned the clinic, eventually speaking to Hilary who reassured me that it was good to have empty boxes on my form; it meant I didn't have any protein in my urine. She told me to stop worrying and come back in a few weeks for a blood test. Unfortunately that blood test turned out to be more sinister than the urine experience.

I knew that the answer to my communication problems was to stop sulking and make more effort to learn more words than 'yes, no, please, thank you and vodka'. Arabic, my first ex-pat language, had been a novelty but not being a natural linguist – Matthew says I speak French with a Chinese accent – I didn't relish having to remember more grammar, verbs and stock phrases. A friend from home wrote enthusiastically about how she'd love the opportunity to throw herself into linguistics while living in a country. What she failed to realise was that this was a necessity not a hobby. Studying is less fun when you have to be fluent before the carrots run out. By the time I remembered enough Russian to be useful we'd be moving on to our next destination: one member of the Bishkek International Women's Club told me she was on her eleventh language and fifth alphabet.

In Bishkek the real dilemma was: Russian or Kyrgyz? I wasn't the only one with the problem; this had been a contentious issue since Independence. Although only approximately 60% of the population were Kyrgyz, language was seen as the key to redeveloping a sense of national identity, lost when the Soviets removed Kyrgyz, amongst other things, from school curricula. When Kyrgyz was declared state language in 1989 the Russians got upset and started leaving, which panicked the government because Slavs were the only ones who knew what doctors, teachers, engineers and other useful professionals should be doing. When it was announced that by 1994 Kyrgyz would be spoken in all administrative and educational institutions, everyone in Bishkek panicked because only those living in the mountains spoke Kyrgyz and they didn't want to come down.

Meanwhile President Akayev kept orating about civic harmony and ethnic peace – in Russian – conflicting with his speeches about nation building and the importance of wearing an *ak-kalpak*. Eventually a political genius realised that if they only spoke Kyrgyz, officials wouldn't be able to chat with generous foreign donors so Russian was declared 'language of inter-ethnic communication' in the 1993 constitution. But presidential candidates were made to sit Kyrgyz exams and politicians continued to ignore demands from the Uzbek, Dungan, Uighur and Tajik minorities, which they couldn't understand anyway.

I wondered whether to stick to English. But when I got lost, again, because I tried directing a taxi driver in Arabic, I decided things had to change. Despite the lure of an advert in the Bishkek Observer: *'Congress of Women of Kyrgyzstan offers Language Courses for Foreigners: We are waiting for you!'* – I chose Russian, because then I'd be able to understand what baddies said in Bond films.

Ulla recommended her teacher, Valentina, who arrived punctually at three the following Tuesday. She looked Russian rather than Kyrgyz with thin gold-rimmed glasses and light brown hair cut carefully around a pudding basin. I decided to delay the questionnaire about parentage until I was less scared.

"Zdrastvooytyeh Safi, ya zavoot Valentina. Ya oocheetyelneetsa."[8]

"Er, hi. Come in. Cup of tea?"

"Nyet spaceeba."

Valentina was a real teacher who taught Russian at School Number 14 around the corner. My Arabic teacher had been Matthew's secretary's aunt and we'd grown very fond of each other and spent more time arguing about how much salt to cook with beans than learning verbs. With Valentina there was no time wasting because she was serious. She had text books and exercises and even homework.

My first lesson was interesting because I didn't get past the pronunciation of 'hello' –*'zdrastvooytyeh'* – an impossible combination of all the letters you don't want to be left with in Scrabble. I thought I was copying exactly what Valentina said, and even mimicking the sounds the men outside with no teeth made when clearing their throats, but she still laughed after my fiftieth attempt.

Next lesson we recited "la, lee, loy, loo" and I learnt to flick 'lus' from the back of my mouth. I wondered how this would help me buy carrots. Next was the Cyrillic alphabet. You could tell its creator was a tenth century Byzantium Bishop; it looked like something you'd dream up praying in a cave all night. Deliberately designed to confuse those using the Roman alphabet (which is what we write English with), 'ш' is 'sh', 'п' is 'p' and 'p' is 'r'. I decided that Russian is a sadistic psychometric test for enemies of the Cold War: *'if 'ш' reads 'sh' and 'п' reads 'p' what does 'шапка' mean?*[9]'

---

[8] Hello Safi, my name is Valentina. I'm a teacher.
[9] It's pronounced *shapka* and means 'hat.'

I was just mastering the use of 'c' as 's' and trying not to giggle because we'd had *сок*[10] for breakfast when Valentina revealed that in lower case 'M' is written as 't'. I wanted to cry. Instead I pleaded intense prenatal exhaustion and we adjourned until Monday. I'd not be reading Tolstoy by bedtime but I might be able to buy carrots without disgrace – by Christmas.

---

[10] It's pronounced *sok* and means 'juice.'

Chapter Eight – Quiches and Quilts

During the months I'd lived in Bishkek I'd learnt that life for the ex-pat wife was hectic. With Playgroup, Craft Group, Mahjong, coffee mornings, lunches and Bridge there wasn't much time for housework. But that didn't matter because you didn't have to do anything you didn't want to. There were armies of housekeepers, cooks, nannies, gardeners, drivers and even a man who'd clear dog poo from your garden, all waiting to serve for minimal wages. The only worry was how to lose the weight gained from eating too many homemade cakes. Although I didn't 'do' many lunches and to everyone's horror chose to manage without five staff, the Women's Club network was a crucial part of survival. Without it I wouldn't know when Beta Stores had baked beans in stock or whether the Craft Fair was in the State or Fine Arts Museum.

I was good material for an ex-pat wife because I thought having a good time was knitting three rows without dropping a stitch. But thank God I'd been to the Aswan Finishing School; our home in Egypt where I'd morphed from City Lawyer to Housewife. With no tins, packets or takeaways to prop me up, old-fashioned cookery had been a necessity. Alone for hours I'd taught myself basic domestic skills and learnt to make bread, jam and pastry which didn't involve an afternoon in tears.

If Bishkek had been our first posting I'd have been terrified of ex-pat society where having a quilt to 'show and tell' at the start of Craft Group was obligatory and afternoon tea an unofficial bake-off. Thanks to my Egyptian survival training I could discuss Round the World without thinking it a travel ticket[11] and contribute quiches for a pot-luck lunch without fear of being ostracised or ridiculed – and still have time to paint my toe nails.

Craft Group was held at Marjorie's house and was an excuse for Mary-Lou to recount Quilt Camp anecdotes without anyone objecting. Tina and I usually shared nicotine-stained taxis to get there, it being too far north of *Chui* to walk. I'd have rather hiked for an hour than spend five minutes in a Kyrgyz taxi but Tina had bad knees from running too much with the Hash House Harriers. Once we'd explained to the driver which unpronounceable street Marjorie lived on, we settled onto the brown plastic upholstery and prayed we'd arrive alive.

Journeys were like sitting in matchbox cars being steered by invisible hands, swerving around corners and screeching up to lights with the reckless excitement of a child's game. The feeling of claustrophobia was enhanced by black, plastic tint which drivers smeared across windows in an attempt to make their Ladas trendier. It was like travelling in an anchovy tin waiting for

---

[11] It's a quilting pattern

someone to peel the roof off. Our feet were so close to the ground I felt sure we'd get there faster if we all paddled with our legs like Fred Flintstone.

Marjorie didn't live in a shoebox. She had a real house with a garden and swimming pool, hidden within a warren of streets where Slavic cottages were holding out against bulldozers and modernisation. Most ex-pats, I was learning, lived in houses. We hadn't been given the option. If we'd started somewhere more comfortable we might have taken time to look around and I would have spent my days chatting over the fence with Kyrgyz neighbours rather than puffing up fifty-eight steps.

A security guard opened the gate and a maid showed us to a modern, open-plan sitting room on the first floor. It had a thick, cream carpet and large windows overlooking the garden. Mary-Lou, Gina, Ulla, Penny, Anthea and a lady in an emerald green shalwar-kameez were gathered on plush sofas and plump floor cushions discussing whether to embroider snowmen or santas for the orphans' Christmas party.

The house was a monument to Marjorie's itinerant life. African masks, Chinese calligraphy and Indian sari silk quilted into hangings competed for space on the walls. Inlaid boxes, family photos and wooden giraffes cluttered immaculately dusted sideboards. In a corner a spider plant draped from an ornately painted box which rocked if you nudged it.

"It's a cot," Marjorie explained, catching me looking, "a Central Asian cot. The hole in the middle is for babies' bottoms. They're strapped in so that poo collects in one place, they don't use nappies you see. These wooden pipes are catheters which go between girl's legs and over a boy's penis. Delightful isn't it, much better used as a planter."

With the first fundraising ball of the Bishkek International Women's Club only a week away, Craft Group was mobilised to prepare table decorations. In chattering teams we cut discs of voile and measured lengths of ribbon to turn after-dinner chocolates into twee gifts; 'favours' as they were known in the trade.

"Marjorie, these truffles are delicious, you must send me the recipe."

"Use lots of rum, that's the secret."

"Oh dear." Pakistani Mrs Shah, a devout Muslim, replaced a chewed truffle quietly on her plate.

"What colour do you think I should add into this Log Cabin pattern?" Anthea asked, holding up her quilting ring.

"My friend at Quilt Camp says she's still hunting for a perfect Round the World colour combination and she's been at it thirty years."

"Red," Marjorie said, and her decisions weren't to be challenged. "I have some beautiful cotton I picked up in Sierra Leone, I'll give you some of that."

Blinded by the glamour of Marjorie's house, her mementoes bragging of wild adventures in remote lands, I became sucked into the bonhomie. Tying ribbons around favours; discussing whether the cleavage on Penny's dress was too low; deciding who should sit at whose table while a mute maid cleared away tea cups. This was exciting!

"Is anyone gonna stay at the Hyatt after the ball?" Gina asked.

"Take your earplugs if you do," Penny interrupted caustically.

"Why, is the casino noisy?"

"No, it's the other guests. Larry and I were there at the weekend, it was our wedding anniversary."

"Congratulations!"

"Thanks Mary-Lou. Anyway, I was woken at 3am by this girl screaming."

"Was she hurt?"

"No, screaming in pleasure, you know, moaning like a porn movie."

"Is that for real?"

Mrs Shah started twitching her *shalwar kameez* and muttering something about Allah. She was an older lady, elegant with grey wisps of hair escaping from a bun which was hidden discreetly by a scarf when in the presence of men. Mrs Shah was a grandma you treated with deference. It was unlikely she'd ever watched porn.

"And I said to Larry, 'why's she makin' that noise?' And you know what Larry said?" The room paused with expectation. "He said, 'she's *paid* to make that noise'."

"Oh-my-gaawd!"

"Ladies, what is so funny?" Marjorie returned to the room having checked her maid was bleaching the crockery. Although the government were still saying SARS hadn't arrived in Kyrgyzstan, you couldn't be too careful when entertaining the international women. "Mrs Shah, are you alright, you look pale."

"They discuss sex at the Hyatt Mrs Marge."

"Sex? At the Hyatt? We want people to have a good time at our ball but we're not putting on a show. These favours will be quite enough. Now, how many have you done?" There was no messing around with Marjorie in charge.

At Playgroup the average age was closer to my own and conversations focused on children's swimming lessons at half-term rather than colours for quilts. We met every Wednesday afternoon in someone's home and I was very grateful to be welcomed, despite not having a child. For me it was reassuring to learn that contrary to Fiona the midwife's opinion, it wasn't considered reckless to bring a baby to Bishkek.

Although Playgroup's official purpose was for younger kids to meet and play, mums considered it gossip time, annoyed if children interrupted. For me it was a precious source of survival information and anecdotes, but with language misunderstandings and multiple topics crossing midair, it wasn't always easy to keep up. I usually stumbled from Playgroup dizzy with lost conversations.

"...I was riding..."

"...a really good hairdresser called Marat..."

"...for hours yesterday afternoon..."

"…so my fanny is real sore…"

"Your fanny?" Was this a suitable confession for a room full of three-year-olds?

"'Fanny' means 'bottom' in American," Birgit whispered. I tuned back in.

"…you can buy goat's cheese…"

"…for three *som* a metre…"

"…from the Blind Artisans of Kochkor…"

"Where can you buy goat's cheese?" I asked, getting out my notebook. The veterans sighed and rattled off cross streets while I struggled to spell Russian names. I looked forward to the time when I'd have useful information to share rather than always asking irritating questions.

The week of the Ball Playgroup was at Anthea's house, a palace in the foothills south of Bishkek. The guard let me into a terraced garden with white marble steps leading to the portico. Anthea was a US Embassy wife, blond, petite and always beautifully dressed in internationally hand-embroidered jackets. She'd had the advantage of being posted to countries famous for silk, rugs and wood-carving so her home was an enviable exhibition of some of the world's best crafts. She also had the advantage of a seven-ton embassy shipping allowance. Now I knew why she'd looked incredulous when I said we'd arrived with a hundred kilos.

Gina was there with her two boys, telling everyone about their next destination, which although a year away was already being arranged by the Embassy.

"I can't wait to leave Bishkek. Now we've done our hardship posting I hope our next tour is somewhere cool. I'm pushing for Tokyo, I love sushi." The US Embassy classifies Bishkek as 'hardship' because there's no McDonald's. I classify Bishkek as cosmopolitan because there are three Italian restaurants.

"Bishkek's not bad," Anthea countered. "You can buy most things, if you know where to look."

"Even a wife," Susi added sardonically. Susi was Australian, married to Pete, an American lawyer working for UNHCR.[12] Her nine-month-old son Alfie had ginger curls and a lot of energy; Susi wasn't often able to join in conversations as she was usually chasing Alfie.

"We only survive 'cos we have a $3000 consumables shipment," Gina explained. "It's all there in our cellar – Jello, Cool Aid, Oreos, although you can get those at the base right now."

Playgroup was better than any parenting class. I learned that it was very important to have a full range of vibrating baby accessories while noting the effects of various mothering techniques and doting nannies. I felt like Mary Poppins in a starched apron. Was I strict in believing that drawing on the walls and taking a bite from every biscuit on the plate was bad behaviour? Mentally I took notes of all the things I would *not* be doing because I was, of

---

[12] The United Nations High Commissioner for Refugees

course, going to be the perfect mother. In my pre-parental ignorance I believed it was possible to rear an angelic two-year old who always played creatively and never threw things or said 'no'. I was going to have a shock.

"You're starting to look really pregnant," Birgit commented. I put a smug hand on my belly, a hard ball straining under a pink floral skirt – maternity clothes were still a source of indecision; should I flaunt my bump or hide demurely under sailor dresses? For month five The Books showed a pink dolly dozing upside-down in the womb. I'd recently started feeling little taps, a silent hello deep inside me. It was very odd knowing that someone else was alive in your body.

"It's so beautiful growing a child," Anthea reminisced.

"Not so beautiful when they're out!" Alfie had just regurgitated cucumber onto Susi's shirt.

"I think I'll miss my bump when Baby is born." I was enjoying the companionship of Baby's constant presence.

"You won't have time to miss it!" Susi corrected, hurrying after Alfie who was crawling towards the stairs.

Sometimes Playgroup was a preview for a life I wasn't sure I wanted. What would it be like having no time of my own? Would I actually be a good mother? What would happen if I didn't love it and wanted to go back to paginating in windowless rooms? But confusingly, mewling babies at Playgroup also intensified maternal emotions stirring within me so that I felt impatient to meet my own child. Seeing two-month-old Isabelle made me broody with anticipation.

Her mother, Iona, lumbered up the stairs trailing a huge bag and crashing a car seat, which also vibrated, into the wall. A donut cushion was wedged under an elbow and she was nudging a dummy back into Isabelle's mouth with her chin.

"Hi, sorry we're late, took me ages to get ready." What had she been doing? She wasn't even made up. Iona plonked into a chair, plumped the cushion on her lap and laid Isabelle across it for a feed. Watching them my heart-rate quickened – in only four months I'd have one of those.

The conversation about whether to boycott Calypso pool because a workman had been seen using a drill while standing in the water was interrupted by Penny puffing up the stairs into the gallery where we were sitting.

"You won't believe what's happened. The ball's been cancelled!" My dream of waltzing with ambassadors ended.

"What!"

"Why?"

"But I've had Dilbar make me two dresses!"

"Let her explain."

"I've just come from an emergency meeting of the Standing Committee," Penny said breathlessly. "Because of terrorist attacks in Osh the Hyatt feels nervous about hosting a high-profile expatriate event."

"You know, I'm sorta glad because I was feeling real nervous about going," Gina admitted. "Everyone knows all the ex-pats would be there and *even* the American Ambassador."

"But cancelling the ball is giving in to the terrorists."

"I'd rather that than be dead."

"If they wanted to kill foreigners, the Navigator on a Friday night would be an easier target," I suggested.

"Who are these terrorists?" Birgit asked.

According to the Bishkek Observer the terrorists were the Islamic Movement of Uzbekistan (IMU), alleged brethren of al-Qaeda. The IMU, designated a 'foreign terrorist group' by America in 2000 due to their drugs trade, kidnappings, civilian murders and links with Osama bin Laden, was committed to creating an Islamic state in Uzbekistan and liberating the volatile Ferghana Valley.

The Ferghana Valley became contentious when Stalin deliberately divided it between Tajikistan, Uzbekistan and Kyrgyzstan. The IMU consider it the heart of Central Asia, the key to conquest of the region where they intend to spread their jihad. The people of Ferghana are believed suitable targets, made more susceptible to political alternatives and extremism by over-population and poverty. This threat is used by Karimov in Uzbekistan and Akayev in Kyrgyzstan to encourage foreign assistance to control the IMU as part of the War on Terror.

Fortunately for us the IMU hadn't yet found their way to Bishkek, spending most of their time torching American Express bureaux in southern Kyrgyzstan because they didn't like the exchange rate. They would probably be surprised to discover that a ball had been disrupted on their behalf. The people who would be most distressed by the decision of the Standing Committee were the hairdressers of Bishkek – distraught that hundreds of appointments would now be cancelled.

Chapter Nine – Penis, Scrotum

Even without the distraction of the ball, weeks zoomed by so that it was soon time to return to Dr Bucket. Matthew came with me, keen to see Bucket's clinic – and the baby. As all the seats were taken he stood outside watching expectant mothers chain smoke. This time I was relaxed, a veteran of proceedings. With a bulging bump above my trousers I felt authentically pregnant, at last confident that others realised I was not simply gluttonous. I was twenty-four weeks and swelling rapidly. This was creating logistical problems – the maternity bras I'd bought in advance were now too small and I couldn't find anything appropriate in Bishkek. Lectured by The Books about the importance of properly fitting underwear but unable to rectify it, being detached from Mothercare and on-line shopping, I was starting to panic.

A positive development was that Matthew had felt baby move. Until then the phenomenon of pregnancy had been mine, something which meant Matthew had to do the vacuuming because I claimed I couldn't bend. Now he too could communicate with the little person who would change our lives forever.

Men haven't entered the 'new age' in Kyrgyzstan and Matthew was conspicuous as the only father wanting to see his child. The stern *babushka* guarding the door tried to stop him coming through but Bucket just laughed and stuck a cigarette behind his ear in preparation for a break. While Matthew and I watched the pulsing jellyfish on screen, Bucket recited body parts and his assistant ticked boxes on a form. He'd wanted to see me after twenty-one weeks because by then all organs were supposed to have developed. As he was smiling I presumed all was growing appropriately, but without Gabriella's help we'd struggle to discuss the implications of any deformities.

Although Baby looked less like a blob in a murky pond I still had trouble determining cute features. Matthew, enthralled at his child becoming a visual reality, had forgotten his nerves about Kyrgyz medical facilities and was pointing to tiny feet and hands.

"Look at the toes!"

"You're sure they're toes?"

"And look how it's curled up. D'you think its asleep? It's so amazing that this little human has taken over your body."

Looking back in slow motion we reconstructed what happened next. Bucket had concluded his examination with a trademark thumbs up and I was starting to roll off the bed when the assistant called out from her dark corner, pen poised over an empty box. Before we knew what was happening Bucket pulled me back down and wiggled the transducer.

"Penis, scrotum."

"That'll be a boy then." Matthew and I exchanged looks, trying to work out if the other was upset. We'd been planning a surprise, not wanting to know whether to paint the nursery blue or pink as we didn't have a nursery. We spent the walk home trying to reassure each other of all good reasons for knowing the sex: 'it' was now 'he' and could be given his name.

We had to wait to cross *Manas* because a policeman in a ski-jump cap was barring our path with a light sabre. A patrol car screamed down the road, lights flashing, instructions blasting from a loudspeaker: 'Get out the way you bastards the President's lunch is getting cold!' Or something like that. No-one could ever determine what was being said, but we all got the idea. With lanes cleared of peasants a convoy tore past: black jeeps, an ambulance, a mini bus of soldiers. We wondered if we were supposed to salute. Ironically this ostentation made President Akayev easier to assassinate: you knew he was coming and he always travelled in the black Mercedes with no number plate.

The excitement over we crossed, narrowly missed by a Volga too impatient to wait for red lights to turn green.

"The scan photo is not exactly what I was expecting either," I admitted. Feeling that our child wouldn't survive primary school if he too didn't have a womb photo in his baby album we'd asked Bucket for a print. Pregnant friends had emailed theirs so I knew what it should look like – a cute, curled up baby, perhaps sucking its thumb. With an enlarged head, gaping eyes and wide laughing mouth ours resembled Jolly Roger's skull without its crossbones. We weren't sure if this was due to Baby's abnormalities, Bucket's inability to use his hi-tech machinery or the quality of photo paper, but we certainly wouldn't be sending it to everyone on our email list.

At the junction with *Moskovskaya* we kissed goodbye. Matthew was walking north up *Manas* to the office and I was meeting Tina: it was Friday so it must be Mahjong. Like many other ex-pat women before me I'd realised that the key to sanity was routine. There's no point sleeping until ten then swanning around in your dressing gown pondering what to do that day. It might sound like a luxury but after a week you stop getting dressed and after two weeks you stop getting up and wallow in being lonely and depressed and a long way from home.

My routine revolved around the Women's Club. On Monday I went shopping. I usually walked to Bishkek City Market, forty-five minutes away. I liked the exercise and the chance to observe the Kyrgyz. My American friends couldn't believe I walked when there were hundreds of taxis but then I couldn't believe they used cake mix when flour, butter and sugar were much cheaper and easier to find. Tuesday was Craft Group, Wednesday Playgroup, Thursday lunch at DaVinci's and Friday Mahjong. Mahjong is a Chinese game using tiles of four suits, winds and dragons. In China, Cantonese and Shanghai rules are played seriously for money and honour. In Bishkek, Mahjong involved more gossip and cake than concentration.

As the weather was now warm and sunny we were playing in Anke's garden, a sanctuary of roses and cherry trees. Anke was a chic German lady who'd also been a lawyer in her former life. It was only when I saw the enormous flag flying outside her house that I realised she was the German Ambassador's wife.

Anke didn't have any pretensions; she was quiet, unassuming and very patient at teaching new players Mahjong. Everything about her was elegant: her drawing room, her maid in a starched apron and even the way she smoked. Anke didn't use a packet; her cigarettes came from a silver pot by her side and were lit by a heavy, square marble lighter which you wouldn't want to drop on your toe.

Soothed by good coffee and home-baked strudel I narrated Bucket's revelation with a humour I hadn't felt earlier.

"Maybe it's a girl doing this," Ulla suggested holding a thumb-up against her crotch.

"At least you know what to ask for in your baby shower," Penny reasoned.

"Are you sure he's called Bucket?" Anke asked.

"I think the Kyrgyz name's Bakyt," Ulla answered.

"I was introduced to him as Bucket," I justified. It was fortunate for Gabriella that she'd returned to England as I was cross with her for making me look foolish in front of the German ambassadress. "It does suit him – mad doctor, mad name."

"Language misinterpretations are very common," Ulla said quickly to try and hide my embarrassment. "Last week I got *derevna* and *dereva* confused and ended up asking Mark's boss which tree he lived in." Gina looked blank.

"*Derevna* means village," Ulla explained. Gina still looked blank. "And *dereva* means tree."

"It's all foreign to me. It's no wonder we were enemies with these Russkies so long if they make their words sound the same."

We started to shuffle the Mahjong tiles, clattering them around the tables.

"We can't play next week because we're going to Lake Song Kul on a Hash weekend," Tina explained while Ulla dealt a hand to each player. In the taxi she'd suggested I go with them, knowing my frustrations about not seeing more of Kyrgyzstan – so far, apart from our picnic in Ala Archa, the furthest I'd been was Bishkek City Market. Confined to Bishkek reading explorers' books of journeys into the mountains I was increasingly envious; trapped and disappointed that I was destined to leave Kyrgyzstan without visiting a *yurt*, riding a Kyrgyz horse or swerving through mountain passes. I'd had to decline the Lake Song-Kul offer, knowing it was on a high, remote plateau seven treacherous hours drive from Bishkek.

"Why do you wanna go to that lake? It's cold, wet and the john is a stinking hole in the ground." Gina was in her usual xenophobic mood. "Gad I can't wait to get outa this country. I've had such a bad week."

"What's wrong? Were your children ill again?" Tina asked politely.

"No, although Svetlana's cooking is enough to make anyone sick. It's these supermarkets. I've been ta all three this week and none of them had the candy I wanted nor the cake mix I need. I mean, it's a capital city for gawd's sake, they're supposed to be selling groceries."

I concentrated on studying my tiles to stop my face advertising my disgust at Gina's sentiments. While she was complaining, *babushkas* throughout Kyrgyzstan were squatting next to fires frying sheep fat for dinner before helping the rest of the family harvest cabbages. In a country where 45% of the population are considered below the poverty line, who cared about cake mix? I decided to try and share some perspective I'd learnt from Matthew's experiences.

"At least the drinking water's clean in Bishkek. In one of the villages where Matthew is working everyone has hepatitis because the stream runs through the cemetery."

"What does your husband do again?" Some people found it difficult to understand Matthew's job. It wasn't easily identifiable like issuing passports or being a banker.

"He's a water engineer. He's on a project to try and improve drinking water supply in areas of rural Kyrgyzstan."

"What's wrong with the taps?"

"They don't have any, that's the point."

"So how do they fill the bathtub?"

"They don't have baths."

"They don't? So how do they keep clean?"

"They're dirty."

"Yuk!"

"And they drink water from dirty puddles."

"But that's so disgusting, what about diseases?"

After conversations like this I wondered whether I was really fitting in and would be happier at home reading books. Then I remembered how miserable foreign life is without a Women's Club. It frightened me to think that without Matthew's Internet research in Denmark I wouldn't have known such groups existed and could have wandered lonely through my time in Bishkek, unaware that in homes throughout the city ladies were companionably sipping coffee and stitching quilts.

Age wasn't the problem. Although I'd never consider going for lunch with five menopausal ladies in England, it didn't matter on the ex-pat circuit where being foreign united young and older. In a small community you befriend everyone but are close to few. Transient relationships are hedonistic; you need each other but you don't necessarily like each other. Acquaintances remain on the periphery of your life, changing as husbands' contracts start or end, their wives shipped to the next posting.

Fortunately there are always exceptions. Sometimes you're lucky enough to meet people you'd choose to know and foreign experiences are intense, creating lasting friendships. Once you've stayed up all night together worrying whether you're going to be evacuated there's a bond which transcends distance. But with most 'friends' you go to their goodbye meal, sign the card, think of them the day they fly out and swap emails until you run out of news. Then you return to the Mahjong table and teach rules to the new girl. It's the depressing truth.

I knew this would happen with Iona who I'd met at Playgroup. She was my friend because she had a young baby and lived round the corner, but she was leaving in September and I knew I'd never see her again. Therefore we enjoyed the companionship while we could, walking Isabelle under the trees of *Erkendik* boulevard, drinking tea in the sun at the Navigator and going to endless fittings with Natasha the tailor.

Iona had suggested Natasha when I'd confided that I was having trouble finding maternity clothes. I'd brought some things with me but shopping ahead for a body change I'd never experienced had been challenging. A helpful assistant at Mothercare had given me a round pad which I fastened to my waist with a large Velcro band. I'd emerged from the changing room with hands on hips, back arched in the 'I'm nine months pregnant' stance I'd seen on television. In a white skirt and pink t-shirt I'd resembled a wedding marquee and Matthew had run from the shop yelling "bring back my real wife!"

Iona told me that Natasha had made her some lovely maternity clothes, although admitted she wasn't very quick, taking on too much work then disappearing to Issyk-Kul when the sun shone for more than three days. You had to be careful that you didn't outgrow things before Natasha finished them, Iona warned.

Natasha lived in a micro-district in southern Bishkek. Her tenement was the ugliest shoebox I'd seen. Horizontal, grey and ten stories high, the architect had attempted to create decorative features from the rounded open balconies. Unfortunately, his design was flawed and the building looked like it was covered in warts. According to a headline in the Bishkek Observer the city was to become beautiful. What were they planning to do? Drop a bomb and start again using only Cotswold stone?

The stairwell stank of urine and I was surprised the international community came here, however desperate for ball gowns. Natasha's flat was number 9, the digit scratched into the dirt outside a door on the third floor. The bell rang, despite wires hanging from the socket, and a woman with brittle orange hair and grey leggings sagging at the knees answered.

"Zdrastvooytyeh Natasha," Iona said. *This* was Natasha! I thought tailors were supposed to be sleek and trendy, an inspiration to fashion rather than a bag lady. As we entered I saw a small ante-room full of plastic bottles: apparently Natasha *was* a bag lady, scouring bins for Kyrgyz social security when she wasn't sewing.

Natasha's workshop had two ancient sewing machines, a cutting table covered with scraps of fabric, an ironing board and a box of tangled cotton reels. On the walls were an Askar Akayev calendar, a gilded Orthodox icon and a poster of St Basil's Cathedral – advertisements for Natasha's split loyalties, a concept I still hadn't mastered.

Iona had explained Natasha's history: Natasha was Russian with Russian parents. They'd been sent to Kyrgyzstan in 1945 by Stalin because they knew how to operate ammunition-making machinery and the factory they'd worked in had been moved to Kyrgyzstan during the war. Both had died but Natasha stayed, not through affinity for Kyrgyzstan but because she had few living ties to Russia. What she did have ties to was a profitable niche making clothes for Bishkek ex-pats and Lake Issyk-Kul, only 200 kilometres away.

Ludmilla, a sister, thumped pink satin through one machine while Natasha reached around my waist with a tape measure. I had two metres of fabric – bought at Osh bazaar with great risk to my life – and a photo of a pregnant pop star in chiffon. I wanted Natasha to match the two. Natasha gabbled to Iona who had the advantage of six months embassy language training, despite only being a Trailing Spouse. From my lessons with Valentina I understood 'big' and the price but other than that Natasha could have been saying that I had terrible taste in clothes and Iona agreeing.

"She says we should come back on Monday for a fitting, but I'm sure she'll call and postpone," Iona translated as we walked back to the car, Isabelle's carrier still bumping against walls. I was reminded to enjoy life without children as accessories, to appreciate the freedom of only needing a small handbag. "D'you mind if we swing by the embassy and pick Todd up? What time's Matthew home?"

"He's away tonight, in Karakol."

"Oh man, are you gonna be okay? Would you like to come over for dinner?"

"Thanks but Karen's already invited me."

Karen was our neighbour and a Kumtor wife, used to being alone all week because her husband worked at mine-site from Monday to Friday. I left Iona with promises to call if I needed anything and arrived home just in time to answer the phone. It was Mary-Lou.

"Are you nuts letting him travel?" What was the problem: the arrival of SARS, dangerous roads, typhoid outbreaks, the IMU? "They should have an announcement when you arrive at Manas airport: 'Do not leave husbands unattended, they will be permanently removed!' These girls are predators, you can't trust them. All they want is to trap a western man. Why d'ya think they dress like whores and get pregnant quicker than a bitch on heat? They're not fussy but yours is a good-lookin' blond one, better 'n most they shack up with."

This wasn't something I'd thought to worry about and didn't like to tell Mary-Lou too bluntly that we had trust in our marriage.

"I don't think Matthew will have time to be trapped. They're visiting ten villages around Issyk-Kul to try and save the project." As is usual on Aid projects there was an unofficial crisis. Attempts to lay water pipes were being sabotaged by officials who insisted their construction companies got the lucrative contracts, despite assets of only one shovel and a wheelbarrow. Matthew and a team were visiting problem areas to select suitable contractors without using nepotism. If they failed DFID would withdraw the funding and we'd be heading home. I was trying to think positively about these surprise developments – at least we'd be back in plenty of time for the birth and might even fit in some tests and parenting classes.

Mary-Lou was determined to unsettle me.

"Well then there's vodka terrorism."

"What's that, rivals for the IMU?"

"You got a lot to learn about Central Asia kid. Nothing gets done here without a bottle of vodka, it's a Russian legacy. Locals terrorise you by makin' you drink and once a bottle is open you gotta finish it 'cos they throw the top away. Your man's gonna come back a lot later than planned, if he comes back at all."

I relayed the conversation to Karen when I joined her half an hour later. She was more philosophical.

"Aw, Mary-Lou's just sore because her first husband left her for the Filipino maid. My Pete's away all week and I'm not fussin'. You gotta be more worried about avalanches wiping out the road than some itsy girl takin' your man."

Karen's support was important. I was nervous about my first night alone in a strange city – but thought booking into the Hyatt an overreaction. Our block was supposed to be safe but yobs, tramps and beggars loitered outside, ringing our bells or accosting us in the stairwell, tugging shirts and pointing at mouths if they managed to get in. Karen had stuck a sign to the front door reminding residents to close it. Most people in the block were foreigners and liked feeling removed from Bishkek's problems, high in a tower. We'd become so fearful of strangers we were reluctant to admit anyone: it wasn't unusual to find the gasman crying on the doorstep because no-one would let him in to read the meter.

Matthew called just as I was checking the door was locked for the eighth time.

"How's Karakol?"

"Lovely. There's a rat in the bathroom and we're having a ceremonial sheep for dinner."

"Pretend it's roast chicken."

"I would if it were warm. But there are advantages to being junior because there's a strict hierarchy when it comes to eating sheep. As the boss Luigi is presented with the head to prepare for everyone else. He usually gives me the ears; it will make me listen better apparently. Then he has to cut skin off the scalp and put it in the soup." Female laughter spluttered in the background.

"Who are you with?"

"Just some local dignitaries and staff from the Karakol office."

"Sounds like you're having fun."

"They are. I'd rather be snuggled up under the duvet with you."

"I miss you too. It's lonely without you."

"I should be back tomorrow, but it'll probably be late as we've got to stop at a village near Balykchy where a member of parliament is insisting his brother has the best site for a borehole."

"I hope you're back by Thursday. It's my haemoglobin test and I'm nervous about having blood taken at that clinic."

"Don't worry, I'll be there."

The way things happened I was very glad he was.

Chapter Ten – Vodka Terrorism

Matthew returned late the next night with a hangover and litre of honey in a plastic bag.

"Vodka terrorism," he groaned as he clambered into bed. "Everything has to be done with vodka; saying hello, saying goodbye, saying thank you. That's a lot of drinking when you're visiting ten villages. Everyone has to make a toast and at dinner last night Kerimbek went on so long our soup iced over. It's not pleasant fishing for scraps of meat through inches of fat. I had to make the toast for women so after congratulating all the female workers on the project I mentioned you carrying our son, which got me a standing ovation."

"Where's the honey from?"

"It's tasty corruption. One of our site engineers is terrified I'm going to fire him so insisted I come to his house for vodka and bring back this honey for you. It's collected in the *jailoo* where his family spends the summer herding sheep. There's even a bee stuck in it, just to prove it's real."

"So were you able to appoint non-corrupt contractors or are we going home?"

"The funding is safe for now; at least until the review mission comes. But one politician admitted to me he'd built a five-bedroom *dacha* with the money he'd creamed from an aid project and at our feet a little girl was scooping water into a kettle from a dirty puddle. I was amazed he didn't feel ashamed about the damage his attitude is doing to his country and its people."

Corruption is cited as the main reason foreign investors avoid Kyrgyzstan – as Aid projects claim triumph if only 20% of budget is siphoned, that's understandable. Officials are above laws because they pay politicians to make them and politicians are above democracy because they pay people to vote for them.

"Corruption is a disease and we're doing all we can to fight it," the Prime Minister was reported to have said, stepping out of his black Mercedes. But in a country with a law stating policemen must inform bosses about bribes received each day, is there any hope of an honest future?

Early next morning I left Matthew snoring and raced to the clinic for my blood test. I wanted to be first in the queue so I wouldn't have to wait all day on a hard bench. The city was still waking. First rays of sun were tinting the highest peaks pink; children were walking to school with *komuz*[13] slung across their backs and trolleybuses rattled by packed with commuters staring blankly through the grimy windows.

---

[13] A small wooden guitar-like instrument with three strings

After a mimed conversation with the receptionists about whether I should have eaten before my test or not I was allowed to wait outside Room Six, the lab where my urine had been analysed. Behind the door a girl was screaming. I sat on my hands and thought about running away. I wish I had. When the door opened I meekly obeyed Gulzat the technician who pushed me into an anteroom where a woman in a stained lab coat sat behind a desk.

She gestured for me to sit in a chair at the end of the desk. In front of me was a tray of test tubes, most broken into viciously jagged peaks. With a long, thin glass pipette she transferred blood samples onto slides, pinching two together to make a red blob. Although she occasionally dipped her pipette in a clear liquid I wasn't convinced this was sterile or hygienic and started to fidget. I was just wondering how to mime 'I don't think I'll bother thank you, I don't fancy hepatitis today' when she grabbed my left wrist, pinning my hand to the desk. Before I could stop her she lanced my index finger, squeezing until blood oozed into the pipette. I gasped and squirmed, a chill of fear seeping through me.

"What did you use to cut me?"

"Eh?" She was busy spattering my blood onto a slide.

"That metal, was it clean or did you use it for the person before?" It looked like a broken razor blade. My voice was becoming shrill with panic.

"*Kak problem?*" She looked bemused by the ranting foreigner. Gulzat had come to watch, holding her wet arms up in front of her as if carrying an invisible stack of logs.

"WAS-THE-METAL-STERILE?" Even slow, emphasised shouting didn't work. "You could have infected me with hepatitis or HIV!" She looked at Gulzat who shrugged. "Why doesn't anyone speak English?" I wailed to the spider plant on a high shelf, its leaves browning as it died of neglect.

In 'Neither Here Nor There' Bill Bryson writes that he '...*can't think of anything which excites a greater sense of childlike wonder than to be in a country where you are ignorant of almost everything.*' He's obviously never had a blood test in Kyrgyzstan. For me there was no childlike wonder, just fear and frustration.

Usually the vague haphazardness of my international ante-natal care was annoying but this time misunderstanding had taken it to a more sinister level. In my own country I'd know where to go for help and comfort but here I was deaf and dumb. I felt scared and guilty, wondering if I'd endangered my baby's life with my misplaced sense of adventure. I'd thought I was doing the right thing by accompanying my husband but Fiona was right; I was foolish to have moved to Kyrgyzstan.

I ran out of the clinic and back through the park as fast as my bouncing bump would let me. I pushed through a platoon of marching soldiers and stumbled across roads trying to blank out the dreadful consequences beating through my mind. Grasping the banister I dragged myself up the stairs and crashed through the door, collapsing onto the sofa with the tears I'd suppressed. Matthew came out of the kitchen, cup in hand.

"What's wrong? What were the results? What's happened?" I couldn't reply and sobbed until I started hyperventilating.

"Stop crying. Breathe. Stop it!" Matthew ordered, shaking my shoulders. "Tell me what's wrong." Gradually I explained what had happened but I was too distraught to hear his comfort.

"What happens if I've got HIV?" Matthew didn't answer. He was trying not to be sucked into my depression but I knew he was blaming himself, blaming his work for bringing me to this moment. "I want to go home! I'm so tired of all this strangeness. I want to go home to modern hospitals and doctors in clean white coats who use syringes and talk English."

I longed for the comfort and familiarity of the NHS, an institution easily criticised until you've been to a Kyrgyz hospital and can appreciate what an incredible service it is. "I'll have to wait three months until a test can give an HIV result won't I? What happens to babies born with HIV?"

"I'm calling Dr Hilary."

"She's not at the clinic until Monday, I already asked." We called her home number, no-one answered.

"Why don't we go back and try and find out if the metal really was dirty? Ascertain the risk...make reasoned decisions..."

"But we can't understand them."

"We have to do something."

"Okay." I uncurled a little. Under my hands Baby wriggled. "I'm so sorry," I whispered. "What have I done?"

In Room Six Gulzat looked up from her microscope.

"Lena!" she called into the anteroom where the woman was still dipping her bloody pipette into test tubes.

"That metal," I pointed at the crumpled piece of blue paper the lancers were lying in. "Is it sterile or do you use the same for every patient?" She answered in slow Russian. Seeing my bottom lip start to quiver she took my hand and led me through the corridors to an office where a Kyrgyz man with black hair and thick glasses was bent over a book, jotting notes on scraps of paper.

"There is a problem?" he asked in carefully enunciated English.

As he translated my concerns Lena smiled, showing a top row of gold teeth. She waved her hands as she gabbled her answer, pointing at me then out of the window.

"She says each piece is new and then thrown away and her pipette is cleaned in bleach solution. She says she knew you were worried but you shouldn't be because they know proper medicine here." Relief warmed me like sun on a cold morning – I'd conveniently forgotten Hilary's anecdotes about archaic Soviet practices. I wanted to believe her because the alternative was too frightening.

Outside everything seemed brighter because I felt I'd been given a second chance at life. As we walked hand in hand up the road Matthew's mobile rang.

"Hi Marat...I'm just at the clinic with Saffia. No, we can't select a village just because the president's wife is from there...we're supposed to use socio-economic rules of sustainability...Have the villagers been asked?...If they don't want the scheme we can't impose it just because the First Lady wants taps...that's not the purpose of the project...tell that to the British taxpayers...yes, good luck...See you shortly." He looked at me and shrugged. "More corruption."

"I hope DFID stop the project because of it. I'd love any excuse to go home right now."

Crossing *Moskovskaya* we were disturbed to see a man face-down in the gutter.

"D'you think he's dead?"

"It's hard to tell. There's blood on his forehead."

"Why's no-one stopping?"

"Because he stinks of vodka."

"Should we help?"

"But what can we do? He won't understand us and there's no emergency number we can call."

"What are we doing in a country without 999?"

"Let's not think about it today."

Back in the sanctuary of our flat I lay on the bed and tried to ignore the image of Lena putting the piece of metal back into the cluster of blue paper. Despite her assurances I hadn't seen her throw anything in a bin and there could easily have been a mix up. Baby Tom wriggled, my internal comfort system. 'Cheer up, we'll be okay', he was saying. I wanted to believe him.

Outside the window a man called a slow litany of names. His tone was doleful and sad, as if searching for lost girlfriends. "Rehat, Gulnara, Aijan, come back to me, I still love you." Actually he was selling milk, cream and yoghurt, listing his produce for interested housewives. I turned on my side, trying to get comfortable, hoping I wouldn't feel as anxious as this for three months. At least Fiona, keen on tests, would take my blood without questioning why I wanted a full screen.

What would my friends say if I returned from Kyrgyzstan with HIV? They believed my life glamorous because I didn't squash onto the Tube to go to work, telling me I was lucky because I didn't have a boss, deadlines or timesheets. What they didn't realise was that I'd swapped a boss for the terrifying ignorance of an unknown language.

Looking in from outside there is an allure to ex-pat life: it's easy to be blinded by the trappings, believing that every wife spends idyllic days drifting from luncheons to cocktail parties. But having maids and coffee mornings can't solve everything. Marjorie's masks and Anthea's silks, the trophies we all bring home, are sweeteners to hide the pain of itinerant life. You're always a stranger: moving on and starting again just when you've become settled; making friends then leaving them; lost in new cities, beleaguered by ignorance and fear. These are the aspects of ex-pat life you don't boast about in emails.

"I lived in Delhi, Hanoi, Nairobi..." women chant in exotic lists, and I imagine bright saris and gins on verandas, even now so easily seduced by stories of the happy times. The reality is groped breasts and sweaty knees; nights spent in cellars hiding from rebels, homesickness for the NHS and irrational fears that your family will be run over just because you live four thousand miles away.

I must have fallen asleep because I was dreaming about a hospital. An alarm was sounding because they'd discovered I was infected with Vodkapox and Fiona was zipping me into an isolation tent. I awoke with a jerk. The telephone was ringing. It was Susi, calling to confirm that I was still going to 'Anatolian Breeze' that evening.

Anatolian Breeze was the much anticipated garden party being hosted by the Turkish ambassadress as part of celebrations for Bishkek's 125th birthday. The city was a beehive buzzing with preparations: soldiers with nothing else to do had been conscripted to plant marigolds on *Erkendik*; convicts were painting the fence around the White House and banners were being unfurled between the arches on Ala Too Square, becoming permanently drawn curtains in front of Matthew's office windows. Invitations to the garden party had been handed out at the last Women's Club meeting and there was great excitement about socialising at the Turkish residency.

Susi persuaded me that it was too beautiful a day to stay inside so later that afternoon I dressed my rounded belly and swelling ankles as smartly as I could and set off along *Moskovskaya*. It was hot; summer had come to Kyrgyzstan. Snow was creeping up the mountains and melt-water gushed through the network of ditches called *ariks*. Bins smelt of sweaty trainers and spittle steamed on pavements. And the rumours were true – summer fashion was miniscule. While Bin *Babushka* was still hesitant about removing her brown overcoat, girls wandered streets in skirts which made it difficult to bend with dignity.

"Central Asia – where wet dreams really do come true," I'd once heard a grateful marine say to his friend in the Navigator garden. When a girl passed me in a dress so low the tops of her areola peeped out like rising suns, I understood why.

In comparison I was huge and cumbersome, my white skirt a billowing sail as I rolled and listed over potholes like a ship in a stormy sea. I embraced the magnificence of my curves, unconcerned by stares from the skinny girls who thought I was disgustingly fat. The walk cheered me up. Bishkek almost looked beautiful, gleaming under a blue sky. Grey shoeboxes were decorated with pennants of washing which fluttered from balconies; pigeons cooed contentedly while they shat on it from the roofs.

The Turkish Residence was an oasis of green squashed between two vertical, brown shoeboxes. Its garden was fresh with roses and lush grass and the building, square and turreted, looked as though it had been designed by a child on a beach with a bucket and spade, apart from the bars on the windows. A wrought-iron fence was all that separated the castle from the street and I could see Bishkek's elite chattering over cocktails as I arrived. If the IMU wanted to kill a few foreigners and grab headlines, this was their opportunity.

I took a glass of fruit juice from a tray at the gate and waved to Anke who was admiring the ambassadress' lupins. The reception resembled an English fete, without the ice-cream van. Stalls were set up around the perimeter and a programme advertised that folk dancing would begin at 5.30. I strolled across the lawn over snakes of red flags, heading for the corner where Gina wasn't shrieking about how cute the table runners were.

I stopped to watch two ladies stitching woollen braid onto *shyrdaks*. *Shyrdaks* are traditional felt carpets, made by layering contrasting colours of felt over each other and cutting out symmetrical designs which are sewn together in a mosaic of geometric patterns. Rural Kyrgyz were hoping for a renaissance through felt. There were often presentations at our monthly meetings from enthusiastic co-operatives, their sub-text: 'we have a room full of desperate women sewing just for you'.

International experts were teaching Kyrgyz what foreigners wanted, so they were busy making mobile phone cases in unnatural colours. What foreigners actually wanted were pieces of old embroidery which hadn't been traded by their owners for a pittance. Unfortunately, families needed dollars more than nostalgia so readily sold their heirlooms, leaving a void of heritage and nothing but debts to pass to the next generation.

Seeing my interest the saleswoman dashed over. The Turkish ambassadress had promised that in return for free kebabs foreigners would spend lots of money.

"My name is Gulmira. You like our craft? Kyrgyz artisans are unique because their work integrates practicality of nomad life with spiritual world. In our ancient practice of Shamanism men use the spirit powers of earth, animal and heaven to guide their life. They lived in harmony with nature. Our problems started when man believe himself stronger than nature." She showed me a piece of patchwork. "This is *kurak*. Each pattern is a narrative; if you know the symbols you can read the design like a letter. This says, 'goats are grazing on high summer pasture'. You like?"

Every culture has a shape. In Kyrgyzstan it's the *kochkor muyuz* representing a ram, two curved horns with a prong in the middle, a Central Asian Fleur-de-Lis. You find it everywhere: on clothes and *ak-kalpaks*, stylised into square or circular designs on carpets and facades of government buildings, welded into gates, stamped onto leather flasks, imprinted on car steering wheels and stitched into the *kurak*. Alongside this most dominant emblem were hundreds of symbols, created by Kyrgyz craftsmen, Gulmira told me, to document the stories of their lives.

"In this transiting period women find satisfaction in learning and preserving the heritage and enchantments of our grandmothers. There is much magic in our *kurak* you know," she leaned forward, whispering her secrets. "You have to give babies *kurak* to protect them from the Evil Eye."

I dutifully bought two cushion covers, a red and black design of triangles sewn into a magic square for health, wealth and happiness – after my blood test that morning I felt I needed all the help I could get. By then the dancing had started and the ambassadress was scooping us up to admire men leaping around in dresses. After ten minutes of craning to see flashes of red between heads of the audience while sweat ran down my legs, I decided now was the time to use the excuse of pregnancy.

"I've got to sit down," I whispered to Mary-Lou who nodded understandingly. At a table in the garden I found Susi trying to stop Alfie screaming and distracting the musicians.

"You look fantastic! I love the skirt. Alfie, no, not the flowers."

"Thank you. How's Pete?"

"He's fine. He's in Osh at the moment interviewing hundreds of Tajik refugees to decide whether they can stay or have to be sent back."

Ulla snuck over to join us, grinning mischievously.

"Hope the ambassadress doesn't notice but there's only so much hopping around I can take in this heat. Still on for tomorrow Suse? We're going riding Saffia so I'd better not invite you." Horse-riding, another favourite ex-pat hobby, is a focal part of Kyrgyz life. The horse is revered for its strength and movement, the freedom it gives nomads to roam vast distances through their land. Manas is always depicted on his faithful steed Akkula and folklore is lyrical about the qualities of a horse; its loyalty, sturdiness, sure-footedness and speed. Unfortunately for the horse this glorification does not prevent them being eaten at funeral feasts.

'If a man's life is only one day long, he must spend half of it riding a horse',[14] instructed a Kyrgyz proverb – but not if falling might cause a miscarriage. I felt frustrated, again, confined to another weekend of knitting. Being pregnant in Kyrgyzstan was like going on an activity holiday with a broken leg.

"Hey Saffia." Iona sat at our table placing Isabelle underneath in her vibrating car seat. "How's baby?"

"Energetic."

"And look at those ankles!" Gina interrupted. They were thick and swollen, puffed to the same girth as my knees after too much standing in the heat. "They *really* show you're pregnant."

"Isn't the belly a giveaway?" My legs looked like fence posts, an inelegance of pregnancy I wasn't enjoying. I looked forward to having shapely calves again; it seemed strange to think that for that to happen a baby had to come out.

---

[14] Kyrgyzstan: The Word about Homeland – Imanaliev

"Did you finish that book yet?" Gina had seen me reading 'The Coming Anarchy' by Robert Kaplan and assumed it was about having children. "Does it advise you to just get a nanny?

"Actually it's concerned with political..."

But Gina had been distracted by spotting Franz, Anke's husband and hurried off to apprehend him yelling, "hey there Mr Ambassador, can I get tickets for the Chai-kove-ski concert you're organising."

When Matthew arrived from work, Penny was trying to persuade a Turkish musician to serenade our table and Mary-Lou was telling everyone she was going to recommend they served stuffed vine leaves at Quilt Camp. Matthew, unaccustomed to the pack mentality of ex-pat ladies, was stunned into silence, although he was impressed when I later explained who their husbands were. It always amused me that while we were having banal conversations over Mahjong our husbands were running businesses which accounted for most of the country's GDP, advising Akayev on the next year's economic policy, teaching opposition parties about government structures and tailing the IMU. Inadvertently I'd drawn us into a social group who were the powerful elite of Kyrgyzstan.

Most people left at seven, having another soiree to attend at the Indian Embassy. Matthew and I stayed for the last *baklava,* one Ambassadorial reception a year exciting enough for us. Local newspapers declared the capital 'hot' with a sequence of parties, concerts and functions. According to The Bishkek Herald, '*...the qualitative dimension of the local social life is increasing at an incredible speed...becoming a primary dimension with the participation of those that make the politic and the economy of the country with a due respect for cultural players.'*

Despite such enthusiasm, Saturday-night card games with Pete and Susi and Anatolian Breeze were the extent of our social life. Bishkek's restaurants and bars were too smoky to be comfortable when pregnant and we now avoided the Navigator on a Friday – deterred by weird ex-pats and local girls who'd bend any way for a Green Card. My evenings were spent deflating swollen ankles. American Ambassadors and famous conductors came and went without disrupting my routine of feet up, fluid down.

We walked home; it wasn't yet dark so we felt safe. Returning from Pete and Susi's one evening we'd learnt that the warnings on our first night at the Navigator were true: it *was* dangerous to walk at night – but not because of muggers. The danger was not being able to see where you were going. Without streetlights the city was pitch black and we'd groped along in the dark, stumbling over uneven pavements. Matthew had fallen into an *arik* and I'd narrowly missed plunging into a sewer, open and treacherous without a man-hole cover. We'd been relieved to get home unharmed.

The official 'Bishkek 125' celebrations were the following weekend. The celestial weatherman was smiling on Kyrgyzstan because it was the first Saturday without rain since we'd arrived. Saturday storms were as predictable as vodka terrorism; I'd not suffered from any oppressive heat everyone had been so anxious to warn me about. Each weekend skies were bruised grey and purple by lunchtime, sudden winds howling from the mountains so that trees bent in violent submission and open windows banged against frames. It would rain so hard water pooled on the floor in the minutes it took to rush around and close everything. This, according to Matthew's colleagues, was unusual for the time of year.

That day the sky was a dome of deep blue and so hot I wore a short sundress Natasha had finally finished. We decided to mingle with the Kyrgyz rather than hide at the Hyatt pool and walked up *Erkendik* boulevard where families were promenading under the oak trees, children dragging festive balloons over shoulders.

The Kyrgyz love nothing better than a party with a grandiose theme. As well as 125 years of Bishkek city it was also the 2200th Year of Kyrgyz Statehood, a designation no-one really understood since the country had only officially existed since 1991. According to propaganda, the Kyrgyz were among the earliest people to develop the concept of a state. Desperate to engender the national pride squashed by the Soviets there had also been celebrations for the 1000th birthday of the Manas epic, a wild few days of horse racing, vodka drinking and boiled sheep heads. Manas the hero was being used by the government to spur its subjects into patriotism.

We arrived in Ala Too Square to find women in national costume performing formation dances on a huge stage. They wore frilly white dresses, red velvet coats embroidered in gold and were balancing what looked like Christmas cakes on their heads.[15] These didn't seem convenient outfits for nomads on horseback.

There was something for everyone that day: pastel candy floss for children; Baltika beer tents for men; popcorn for women and even bins full of empty bottles for those on Kyrgyz social security. Dubovy Park was jammed with food stalls, the air pungent with fatty meat sizzling over hot coals. Sticks of *shashlik*, trays of *samsi*, basins of *plov* so huge you could bath in them once empty, charred sheep's heads and white tangles of gut: all were being consumed at crowded tables, washed down with shots of vodka.

In Panfilov Park the fairground was packed, revellers bouncing on dodgems or trusting their lives to the rusting Ferris wheel for a panoramic view of the city. Some stopped to sing: in Bishkek, karaoke was bizarrely performed on the street, customers singing to small television screens balanced on tables, their voices amplified to a metallic screech.

We bought ice-creams, another local favourite in winter and summer, and perched on a bench. Most of its slats were missing and the ground underneath was crunchy with husks where previous occupants had sat cracking sunflower seeds between their teeth.

---

[15] The Christmas cakes were actually traditional hats called *elechek*

"How are you feeling?" Matthew asked, looking concernedly at my pensive face.

"Fine." We'd not talked about HIV since our morning at the clinic. During daylight I kept myself too busy to have time to worry. It was at night when fears filled my sleeping mind and I often woke feeling sick, adrenaline racing round my body. I'd learnt to calm myself back to sleep by reciting Mary-Lou's favourite quilt patterns. "Don't worry, I'm not thinking about *that*. I'm wondering how Fred and Kate are doing."

Fred and Kate were friends from my childhood, marrying that day in the village church. It felt strange to be eating ice-cream in Central Asia rather than joining them. To provide a presence we'd emailed a ridiculous photo of Matthew in an *ak-kalpak* but missing weddings was another difficult part of ex-pat life: momentous things were happening to our friends and we weren't there to share them.

Surrounded by raucous Bishkek 125 celebrations I felt nostalgic for home. We'd been listening to Wimbledon over the Internet and the crack of tennis balls across grass was making me homesick for an English summer of seagulls and combine harvesters.

"I don't see any other foreigners today," Matthew commented.

"Americans are told to stay away from big gatherings, for fear of reprisals, especially after that Italian soldier from the base was beaten up last week. They're probably all on the golf course."

"So it's just us and the Kyrgyz."

Families wandered past, country folk with ruddy cheeks who'd ventured to the city for the festivities. Grandad, arms clasped behind his back, wore a traditional long black velvet coat with high leather boots and an *ak-kalpak*, despite the heat. Little girls tottered in stiff doily-dresses, huge puffs of white lace lifting high pig tails. Mama and *babushka* were in floral velveteen dresses with headscarves and hoop earrings. Papa had polished his gold teeth for the occasion.

We walked home through the park, tripping over weeds growing through cracks in the tarmac. It was sad to see how dilapidated municipal spaces had become since the Soviets had stopped maintaining them. Statues of forgotten heroes toppled into long grass, cannabis grew in high clusters and dry fountains stained green without use.

"Hello, where you from?" A man was running excitedly towards us.

"England." This was extraordinary. Kyrgyz never talked to strangers, their reticence a legacy of Stalin's purges. Maybe the festivities – or the vodka – had gone to his head.

"I like England, you have David Beckham." As our football anecdotes were lacking we chatted about Manas, mountains and his insistence that you must show respect to your *ak-kalpak*, never losing it or putting it on the floor or you'd be inflicted by the Evil Eye. It was fun to meet someone local – until we discovered his motive.

"If you want to lose your kilograms, call me." He handed me a piece of paper with a mobile number on. Matthew was coughing, trying to swallow laughter. I stared incredulously.

"I'm not fat, I'm pregnant!"

"Oh." He turned and walked away without embarrassment or apology, his shoulders slumped, despondent about missing what he'd thought was guaranteed business.

"Maybe I do need one of those 'Baby Under Construction' t-shirts," I said to a highly-amused Matthew.

The celebrations ended at ten with fireworks which cracked across the sky, waking Baby Tom. Strands of red, white, green and gold burst from each explosion, glittering globes of colour which dripped over the city.

"How much d'you think that cost?" I asked, our noses pushed up to our bedroom window. When your life is dominated by giving water and beggars eating your rubbish it's difficult not to reduce everything to dollars.

"More than the government spent on healthcare this year," Matthew replied. We climbed back into bed and watched Baby Tom swivel in his nest. Eventually he fell asleep. We tossed and turned under the duvet: Matthew plagued by scheme designs and me with fears of HIV.

Chapter Eleven – Lake Issyk-Kul

Ask a Kyrgyz where they're going on holiday and they'll reply "Issyk-Kul" in reverent whispers. For them there is no comparison with anywhere else on earth – because they've not holidayed anywhere else on earth. Valentina was the most animated I'd ever seen her when I asked if she'd had a pleasant break.

"Oh Safi! The air is so pure and the water heals your every problem." I was sceptical, having read that the Russians extracted uranium and tested torpedoes in the depths. This, combined with natural radon, allegedly made the lake the most radioactive place on earth. Maybe that was the key to its healing properties, for its health resorts and sanatoria were heralded throughout the Soviet Union. Today the hulking institutions aren't quite as fashionable and treatments too intrusive for most visitors. Penny reported that colon cleansing and gynaecological massage were included in her room rate. She'd stayed well clear of the spa.

'Everybody goes to Issyk-Kul!' was the headline in the Bishkek Herald. "Everybody except me," I said grumpily, disabled by pregnancy and a husband who said he travelled enough during the week. Boris Yeltsin was there as a guest of the Akayevs, Natasha had adjourned for the summer and I no longer had to queue at the clinic because I was the only patient. Kyrgyzstan was tipping east, emptying the population of Bishkek into Issyk-Kul on rusting *mashrutkas*.

"I want to experience the Kyrgyz way of life," I moaned to Matthew.

"What, sleeping in a mouldy *yurt* after a meal of sheep's eyes and vodka?"

"Well, yeah, if that's the real thing."

Matthew was unsympathetic so we spent our weekends at the Hyatt pool, when it wasn't raining. My watermelon belly was incongruous among tattooed biceps of marines, let off base once every three months to remind them what the world they were fighting for looked like. Americans played hip-hop, puffed cigars and tossed balls across the water and Danes smoked, drank beer and sunbathed into toasted almonds. I gazed at the concrete skyline wondering how warm the lake was.

It was small comfort that at least the American airmen had seen less of the country than I had. Someone once said that war was God's way of teaching Americans geography but despite a new Bush era of imperial colonialism, those posted to Kyrgyzstan still had a lot to learn. When Matthew told a captain he was off to Balykchy the guy asked if that was a casino. Matthew had given him a withering look.

"Sorry, we didn't learn a whole lot about Kyrjikistan at college."

"Kyrgyzstan," Matthew corrected, "Bishkek is the capital of Kyrgyzstan. Dushanbe is the capital of Tajikistan."

"Doo-shan Bay. Yeah, I heard'a that. What's the beach like there?" As Tajikistan was a land-locked country miles from the sea, Matthew gave up trying to explain anything.

My chance to join the exodus came the following Saturday evening over cards with Pete and Susi.

"We're going to Issyk-Kul next weekend," Susi announced, inspecting a strange black object she'd found in her food. We'd ordered Chinese takeaway and it had arrived slopping about in plastic bags, as if the chef had simply vomited and dispatched the courier.

"Lucky you. We'll probably be going to Beta Stores."

"Why don't you come with us?"

"I'd love to but do you think it's safe?" The responsibility of motherhood had already started. I'd given up my body to someone else and with it my freedom; another's needs would always come first now. "Matthew says it's a long, dusty journey on treacherous roads with huge potholes but no toilets. If something goes wrong, where will I get help?"

"If something goes wrong in Bishkek where d'you get help?"

"Good point."

"If you're brave enough to come to Kyrgyzstan while pregnant – and many wouldn't – you might as well see as much as you can. I'm not suggesting you climb Lenin Peak or go on a two-week horse trek but I think a trip to Issyk-Kul will be okay. You can't leave Kyrgyzstan without visiting Issyk-Kul!"

"You sound like Valentina."

Persuaded, I threw off my western paranoia about what was sensible for an expectant mother and threatened Matthew with divorce if he didn't agree to go. I was so excited about leaving Bishkek I spent the whole week telling everyone. Gina was full of advice.

"Take snacks!"

"Meals are included."

"Yeah but it's Kyrgyz food."

"We are in Kyrgyzstan."

"You crazy girl, should you be going on a five-hour drive across mountains in your condition?"

"But I feel fine."

My ankles swelled if I sat too long at the computer and I had occasional indigestion where Baby Tom was taking the place of my stomach but I suffered none of the ailments The Books listed for month six. By now I was supposed to have achiness in the lower abdomen, constipation, headaches, faintness, dizziness, nasal congestion, occasional nosebleeds, ear stuffiness, bleeding gums, leg cramps, backache, skin pigmentation changes, varicose veins and haemorrhoids. Who would get pregnant if they read that; what happened to advertising the joys?

I loved being pregnant; loved the curves of my round belly; loved feeling a baby moving inside me; loved not having to worry about a fat tummy bursting out of my bikini. I loved the silent presence of this baby so much I was still certain I'd miss it when he was born, despite what Susi said. I knew I was lucky because I didn't have to struggle with going to work. My only hardship was saggy boobs because without under-wires my breasts hung inelegantly under my armpits. I didn't pine for brie, oysters and pâté – fortunate because I couldn't buy them in Bishkek anyway – and after two years in Egypt, teetotalism was easy. Being pregnant was fun; nine months without periods!

I was unexpectedly grateful that in Bishkek I was protected from western pregnancy hype: reality would hit once I got back to England and started organising baby-gros, having to deal with the logistics I'd been sheltered from. During the insecurities of week twenty-four I'd taken a peek at a few websites and started to panic because I didn't have a Prenatal Yoga video, Before You Were Born book and double-sided bump pillow to allow maximum flow of oxygen to the placenta, all listed under 'Pregnancy Essentials'. Fortunately, in week twenty-five I realised Baby Tom wouldn't be retarded if I didn't strap a Wombsong Prenatal System to my belly and play stimulating music. I was happy and healthy and eating Mars Bars when I wanted to – far more beneficial, in my opinion, than disturbing Baby with The Marriage of Figaro.

Pete, Susi and Alfie collected us from outside our flat at 6.30 the following Saturday morning. As they'd been expected at 6am we'd had a chance to watch the dawn creep across the sky and listen to the first cries of *"ma-la-ko!"* from early milkmen. The streets were eerily quiet as we drove north to pick up the main road to Issyk-Kul, the only life signs from sleepy bakers piling round loaves of *lepioshka* next to clay ovens and a diligent *babushka* sweeping last night's debris from Ala Too Square.

The three towering smoke stacks of the power station marked the edge of the city and from then we moved backwards in the evolution of Kyrgyzstan, shoeboxes thinning until replaced by fields where farmers bent to harvest crops in the early morning cool. Looking back, mountains shimmered like a mirage above concrete high-rises. At last I was out of town, exploring new territory, heading east along an ancient silk route.

Sitting in the back next to a recalcitrant Alfie, who already wanted to get out of his seat, I started to worry about being in labour by Tokmok. Matthew was right; there were huge potholes. In 'Turkestan Solo' Ella Maillart describes the same problems on this route, writing *'At every hole in the road our lorry gives an enormous bump, and shoots us into the air...'* That she travelled in 1932 was a depressing measure of Kyrgyzstan's development.

I clutched upholstery and tensed limbs, my head hitting the roof as the jeep bounced over ruts and pits, wondering if the motion would cause my waters to break. I'd not spent much mental time on giving birth; it was something unknown and allegedly unpleasant that I'd hoped wasn't going to happen until October. When I saw women with young babies I felt jealous because they'd already survived the ordeal. It was a primitive sense of envy, the sort which grabs you when you see friends coming out of their last exam while you're still queuing for yours.

Baby Tom wobbled between my legs. Although, according to The Books, babies *can* survive outside the womb at twenty-eight weeks, I knew this was unlikely in rural Kyrgyzstan. Maybe Gina was right and Issyk-Kul wasn't such a good idea after all. I kept my worries silent, not daring to admit my discomfort to Matthew. He'd find out what was going on when baby's head started crowning. As a distraction I concentrated on the scenery; after all, this was what I'd come for.

The road ran through the floor of the Chui valley. To the north, foothills rippled into Kazakhstan. To the south, the jagged peaks of the Kyrgyz Ala Too serrated the horizon. The plains between were patched by fields of potatoes, cabbages and maize, smallholdings delineated by shacks where families sheltered from the hottest sun. At the roadside watermelons like boulders were piled into pyramids by traders hoping you'd stop for them rather than the fifteen other sellers in view.

"You can map the route to Issyk-Kul by the fruit for sale," Matthew explained conversationally, unaware that he might soon be a father. "First watermelons then red apples around Tokmok, there are hundreds stacked up in buckets on thin wooden trestles. As you come out of the pass women offer jam jars of tiny orange berries called *oblepikha* which Marat tells me every time are 'good for health'. You can tell you're nearing the lake when the apricots start."

Villages followed the road, strips of one-storey Slavic houses, attractively whitewashed with wooden eaves and window frames painted pale blue or green. *Babushkas* rested in the sun on wooden benches, leaning back against cottage walls. Chickens pecked the grass in the shade of poplars and children tied parsley into bundles to sell in Bishkek's bazaars. Fruit trees hung over fences and men stopped work and leant on hoes to chat to neighbours. As we passed, geese ran shrieking from the road, wings flapping wide, their orange beaks open in protest. It was a cine-film of rural life.

Having made it beyond Tokmok without my waters breaking I started to relax. We'd been driving for two hours. Alfie was asleep and the road was starting to incline towards the pass. Green hills were closing in, tumbling over themselves in smooth arcs. Tiny *yurts* were visible in creases where shepherds had led herds to summer pastures. As we started to climb behind huffing *mashrutkas,* rolling hills sharpened into ridges, rising like the spines of dozing dragons. Grass was replaced by shale which threatened to run down sheer cliffs in landslides. The sky was a slash of blue which we craned to see above the canyon walls. The road spiralled higher, curling precipitously around Soviet statues of stocky workers and elegant stags mounted on exposed promontories.

"Bloody hell! Are they trying to kill us?" Pete swerved and we skidded violently towards the precipice as a convoy roared past: wailing police cars, black Mercedes, jeeps of soldiers and an ambulance to scoop up those injured by their aggressive driving.

"I heard Putin was going to Issyk-Kul this weekend," Matthew remarked. "It looks like he'll be there before us."

Once Pete had stopped shaking enough to be able to steer we journeyed on, winding further into the pass until we could see white peaks glistening in the distance. On a bend *mashrutkas* had pulled over so that passengers could collect water from a spring and tie strips of rag to bushes around it. These were 'prayer trees', a shamanist custom asking the powers of life to heal relatives, protect them against diseases or save them from Russian presidents who drove too fast.

"Anyone want to stop and make a wish?" Pete asked.

"I'd like to stop for a wee," I said hopefully. "And I'm hungry; how far is the next service station?"

After the glut of fruit in the valley there was nothing offered for miles in the pass until we turned a corner and found the Kyrgyz equivalent of Little Chef, Welcome Break and Moto all pitched on the same bend. Opposite, ravine walls swung away, opening into another vast valley where shepherds ambled after their flocks. A road was snaking into the mountains.

"That goes to Naryn and on through the Torugart Pass to China," Matthew explained. "It's a wild road, blocked with snow in winter and broken-down trucks of scrap metal stolen from Bishkek in summer."

We stepped into the darkness of the round, greying *yurt* we'd pulled up outside. It smelt comfortingly sweet with wood-smoke. Woven reed mats of red, blue and green were wrapped behind the circular lattice frame which created the *yurt's* structure. Curved red rafters stretched up to the round roof vent known as a *tunduk,* its criss-cross pattern representing nomad belief in the wholeness, unity and reliability of the sun; this was the gold emblem on the red national flag. Strips of heavy felt were laid over the frame to keep the weather out and warmth in. It was surprisingly cosy, despite stinging wood-smoke, although I wasn't sure I was ready to move in permanently.

When my eyes became accustomed to the dark I noticed a woman pounding a stick into a brown barrel. She was wearing a red dress, long woollen gilet dragging down to her knees and a paisley headscarf. Her face was wide-boned and burnished, telling tales of a harsh life in the mountains. She handed Pete a sheet of paper which he translated.

"There's *koumys*, that's what she's stirring. It's fermented mare's milk, a very important part of traditional Kyrgyz life, one of the sacred white drinks which should never be poured away. Or dried fish, which we saw hanging up by the roadside so they'll be nicely seasoned with petrol fumes or *kurt*, hard balls of white curd cheese which I can confirm are disgusting. You can also order sheep's head but that takes an hour to prepare." Susi and I settled for water, Matthew ordered Coke; there is no escape from the Coca Cola franchise, even in remote *yurts*. Refreshingly the nearest McDonald's was in

Moscow. Pete chose *koumys*. The woman reached down into the barrel and scooped white liquid out with a bowl.

"*Spaceeba vam.*" Pete slurped then offered it to me, "try it."

Being cautious of strange substances, for Baby Tom's sake, I took a delicate sip. It tasted of rancid yoghurt and champagne bubbles. The Kyrgyz believe in the medicinal properties of *koumys*, claiming it will cure tuberculosis and indigestion; paranoid foreigners believe it will *cause* tuberculosis and indigestion. By custom it is the first drink at the table and is drunk in great quantities at feasts and festivals. Being mildly alcoholic this always creates a good party.

"She's stirring the *koumys* with a *bishkek*," Pete explained. It looked like the ladle you use in a sauna to tip water on the coals. "Rumour is the capital got its name after a woman left her *bishkek* behind when they'd camped by the Alamyedin River." I looked more closely at the woman's work. To my horror I realised the barrel was actually a dried sheep's skin, gaping open at the neck with four stumpy legs swinging as she stirred. I placed an anxious hand over my belly, wondering how I would explain to Fiona that I induced labour in a mountain pass by drinking stale mare's milk from a sheep's carcass.

It was down-hill to Issyk-Kul from there and we free-wheeled out of the pass, oscillating with a racing-green train running parallel with us. Its passengers were hanging from windows, waving enthusiastically. As Matthew had promised, ladies were squatting at the roadside with jars of tiny yellow fruit. We tried them and they burst juices simultaneously sweet and sour over our tongues. Ancient trucks were wedged into lay-bys, their drivers standing hopefully behind tables of golden honey. After three hours of wild driving Lake Issyk-Kul shimmered before us, mountains mirrored on either side, parched into reds and tans by the sun to the north and still gleaming with snow to the south.

Issyk-Kul was formed, according to one legend, by a father's tears after his daughter hung herself because he wouldn't let her marry a poor boy. It's 182 kilometres long, 60 wide and 1,608 metres above sea level, which sounds more impressive if you say that's a mile. No-one has got to the bottom of it yet, creating myths about its depth and what lurks there. Some say there are sunken towns, others unexploded torpedoes which the Soviets dropped when testing weapons.

To reach the lake you drive through Balykchy, a forgotten frontier town which reached its peak when the Soviets built boats and gathered fish there. It's better known today for prostitutes, vodka and a children's home sponsored by Kumtor. After Balykchy the main road skids along the north shore with nothing but a few cows chewing tufts of grass between you and the water. Here the lake is remote and untouched, everyone preferring to cluster around Cholpon-Ata where you can buy inflatables and ice-creams.

The Kyrgyz government is excited about Issyk-Kul's unexploited tourist resources and a Japanese team are undertaking *'preliminary for the preparations to the basic investigation'* regarding the area's development. Issyk-Kul is recognised by UNESCO as a biosphere reserve and it would be nice to think that in ten years time unfinished concrete monstrosities will have been bulldozed and the shore transformed into a haven of Central Asian charm: Slavic cottages offering beds and traditional breakfasts of warm *lepioshka* and apricot jam. Unfortunately it will probably have been destroyed by a predominance of ugly high-rise hotels, a Central Asian Benidorm: the dollar's lure is strong when you don't have running water or electricity.

Pete's driving was cautious by Kyrgyz standards and locals had overtaken us in teams of three, rocketing around blind corners in the pass and slaloming through herds of cows leisurely ambling along the highway. The only car we overtook was a Lada, weighed down onto its suspension by the hundreds of cabbages piled on its back seat and roof-rack, the boot wedged open by bags of potatoes. I remembered Gina's advice and commented that they'd brought snacks. Distracted, Pete nearly collided with a bus speeding past a donkey cart.

"Talking of snacks, I'm hungry again; I wonder what's for lunch."

Matthew answered. "It'll be salad of peas and diced carrots smeared with mayonnaise, followed by greasy soup with mutton, cabbage and potatoes floating in it then fatty chunks of chicken with rice, all washed down with apricots dissolving in water. Dinner will be whole potatoes and half a cabbage submerged in more soup."

"Don't get Matthew started on Kyrgyz food," I warned. "He's jaded by too many cold sheep heads."

"Sorry," Matthew apologised, "but I bet I'm right. Look, this is Kara-Oi, one of the villages I'm working on."

Slavic cottages were clustered around mazes of dusty tracks. Riding high above four-wheel-drive tyres, I could see apple, apricot and cherry trees so fecund with fruit the branches were bending to the ground, aping the backs of those who'd picked them for years. Red quilts were draped across bushes to air and axes were wedged into blocks next to piles of wood. "Those pegs are our site investigation markers, the water pipes will run alongside the road, I hope."

"Is it difficult working in the field?" Pete asked, tooting at a sheep which was wandering into the road after a clump of hay.

"It's definitely a challenge. Language is the biggest hurdle in remote villages as everything has to be relayed through English-Russian-Kyrgyz-Russian-English. Last week we caused a riot because our new translator got confused. The word *'som'*, Kyrgyz currency, means 'cat fish' in Russian and she told villagers they needed to provide ten thousand catfish to qualify for clean water. We couldn't understand why all these *babushkas* were lying in the road crying until a boy brought me a tin of tuna and asked if this would help."

"There are catfish in Lake Issyk-Kul."

"But I don't want ten thousand of them dumped on my desk. I don't know what the bureaucrats from the World Bank and DFID are going to think about all the craziness, especially if they're forced to eat sheep's eyes. I'll be here with them on a review mission in a couple of weeks. If DFID have been told by Whitehall to make a stand against corruption we might be closed down."

I sighed. "Another week wondering if we're going home early. Last week it was all over because the money was running out."

"That's always a risk on Aid projects," Matthew justified, "because policies, governments and priorities are always changing."

"How do you cope with the uncertainty?" Susi asked.

"Ignore everything Matthew says until he hands me a plane ticket," I replied.

Along the roadside women squatted on low stools behind buckets of apricots, the fruit merging into yellow lines like road markings as we flashed by. Deciding to stock up, just in case Matthew's menu was correct, we pulled over next to a stall where cherries hung like bunches of grapes from a wooden frame. Each stalk had been intricately tied into clusters with thread and wrapped around loops of wire. There were fat burgundy sweet cherries and small sour ones used to make juice; jam jars stuffed with raspberries; watermelons sugary with intense flavour; buckets of blackcurrants, buckets of redcurrants and baskets of strawberries. The summer fruit of Kyrgyzstan is addictive; juicy, flavoursome, tempting and cheap it's impossible to pass by without buying something.

Behind the stall an old man dozed on a bench, leaning against his rickety green fence. His house had a wooden balcony tucked under the eaves and his front garden was a dense orchard with chickens pecking among the trees. A boy in denim shorts was forking hay onto a donkey cart. Sensing a very big jeep with red diplomatic plates and four rich foreigners, grandpa pulled himself up and hobbled over to ensure his wife made sales.

"American?"

"American, English and Australian."

"Ah! Michael Jackson! David Beckham!" He didn't know any Australians. "You like my fruit? I also have plums." He dispatched a bare-foot grandson to fetch a wheelbarrow of them while Alfie, who was delighted to be out of the car, reached for a cherry, wiggling his toes in excitement.

Babushka gestured to us. She'd been sorting strawberries into sizes and her fingers were stained red by the juices.

"Why isn't the baby wearing slippers?" she asked. As Pete spoke fluent Russian he was able to explain that they didn't consider slippers necessary in thirty-degree heat, even at 1600 metres. The old man started to yell at her,

remonstrating that she'd lose them the business until Pete reassured him that we were used to being disciplined by *babushkas*.

We bought two bunches of cherries, raspberries and a watermelon and promised to return for crates of apricots on our way home. *Babushka*, who was now pointing to Alfie's head and muttering about him not wearing a hat, wanted us to take a bucket of blackcurrants. At only 30 pence this was a powerful illustration of how hard people had to work to earn a pittance; I knew from experience that there were hours of backbreaking picking in that bucket. I asked *babushka* if she'd harvested them.

"The grandson, Rustan, did," Pete translated.

"That's good of him," I said, smiling at the boy.

"She says she would have beaten him if he refused," Pete explained while Granny stared at Alfie who was whining because Susi wouldn't let him run into the road. He was quickly strapped into his seat and we took off for our last leg, through Cholpon-Ata.

Cholpon-Ata felt like a beach resort. People ambled by in shorts and sarongs carrying towels and sun-hats. Cafés spilled over pavements and a grinning Akayev welcomed us to the Kyrgyz Riviera from a roadside billboard. We'd decided against a Soviet sanatorium with sulphurous baths and were staying just outside town in Manas Village – formerly Lenin Village – chosen by Pete because it had flushing toilets. It hadn't been easy to find a hotel, the Central Asian obsession with Issyk-Kul meaning rooms were always full in high season and prices forced surprisingly high.[16] Unfortunately dollars did not always translate into comfort: 'value for money' meant 'no bed-bugs'.

We turned down a sandy track, passed a bazaar where people were buying impossibly big watermelons and bounced into our five-star resort. Manas Village was six bungalows scattered across a scrubby field where a dog was cocking its leg against the only tree. The proprietors were a Russian couple who'd decided to endure Independence and remain in Kyrgyzstan to cook cabbage for tourists. This meant we enjoyed a Central Asian mix of Russian and oriental hospitality, with a bit of communism thrown in.

Meal times were communist: all guests ate the same food at the same time, quickly consuming, without conversation and apparent enjoyment, whatever was thumped onto the table. Lunch was salad of peas and diced carrots smeared with mayonnaise, followed by greasy soup with mutton, cabbage and potatoes floating in it then fatty chunks of chicken with rice, all washed down with apricots dissolving in water. The chicken looked as though it had been regurgitated. Matthew chewed smugly.

After bowls of *chai* we walked down to the beach, a pleasant stroll through a landscaped wasteland which smelt of sewage. *'Visit the most beautiful places on our planet and swim in the purest salubrious lake…'* Kyrgyz media shamelessly boasts. To me a beautiful beach is secluded with white sand and

---

[16] A basic chalet was $30 a night

palm trees or rugged with rock pools and waves to play in. Issyk-Kul beach doesn't have any of those, but it does have its own charm. The water is a sheet of shimmering glass so vast that the mountains on the other side look like clouds to the uninitiated. Behind the huts and hotels, crescents of green foothills run up to white peaks which pass in and out of view as clouds rush by. It's a unique experience to lie on sand so far from the sea and sweat in the sun while huge drops of rain fall from a blue sky, turning to snow just up the road.

What the beach lacks in sand locals make up for with vodka. A holiday at Issyk-Kul is one long picnic for the Russians, Kazaks, Uzbeks and Kyrgyz who gather there. Red-raw limbs and bins overflowing with bottles and watermelon rind tell tales of all-day binges. From sunrise to sunset, with a brief siesta to digest lunchtime grease, huge gatherings of families slurp beers and raise vodka toasts, hacking chunks from watermelons they've dragged from the bazaar.

On our bit of beach, children stuffed discarded cigarette packets with sand and made castles with bottle tops while their parents got drunk. Young mothers dosed babies with beer after breast feeds, tipping inches into teated bottles. To sober up women ran into the lake, screaming about cold water splashed over them by randy pot-bellied males. Disapproving *babushkas* in towelling dresses sat in clusters, remembering their wholesome holidays in Soviet Pioneer camps which rejuvenated young bodies and minds.

This was where the rich of Central Asia came to play and I was fascinated. Despite 120 kilometres of beach I had a packed stage because, as we'd experienced in Ala Archa National Park, no-one could be bothered to venture far from the bus station.

While Pete and Matthew read action books borrowed from Fatboys, I decided to swim. The water was cool and smooth, invigorating and refreshing as it caressed hot skin, calming as I let it lap against me. All around flotsam emanated from the huge resort next door: pedalos, rowing boats and children leaping off inflatables. A Kazak oil baron in tight, leopard print swimming trunks strutted next to his sleek speed boat, admired by shabby men, women and children from poorer Tajikistan who hovered around it in awe. When he offered them a ride they shrieked with excitement and piled onto leather seats, the engine powering into life with a roar.

I didn't linger long in the water for fear of radiation sickness – although I had been comforted by an article in the Times of Central Asia stating that following recent tests, radiation levels at Issyk-Kul were reported to be within the norm. Walking back up the beach *babushkas* nudged each other and three men raised their glasses: I had my bump out, proud of my belly browning off between pink pieces of bikini. I felt wonderful. Having spent my life worrying about excess weight I'd expected to balloon in pregnancy, to lay down fat stores in my face, bum and thighs. To my delight the only bulge was in front and you couldn't tell I was pregnant from behind – unless you looked at my ankles.

"You can tell you're big because your boobs look small," Matthew commented, raising his eyes from his Tom Clancy. I kicked him and plonked down onto the towel to watch the vendors parade past. They were women and children from local villages, desperate to make a few *som* – possibly to pay for their contribution to Matthew's project. They sold ice-cream, beer, sweet pastries, bunches of cherries and dried fish strung from metal rods, stiff, orange and pungent. Their sales pitches were delicate songs which blended with the crash of water on the shore: "*samsi, samsi, who will buy my samsi.*"

Noticing my interest a lady approached with a huge tray of pastries, strands of calories twirled into figure-eights and dripping with honey.

"American?"

"English."

"Ah, David Beckham." She smiled revealing a gleaming top row of gold teeth. "Issyk-Kul beautiful yes?" She swung her arm encompassing fag butts and broken glass, snowy mountains, miles of water and snoring drunks.

"Very beautiful." I chose two pastries, Matthew deciding he'd stock up on carbohydrate before the evening's cabbage.

"Pete, you want one?"

"No thanks, the *koumys* is still repeating on me."

The afternoon drifted soporifically towards dusk as we lay on the beach, my ankles slowly inflating in the heat. Watching the tableau of Central Asians was the perfect antidote to my more traumatic experiences of Kyrgyzstan, my worries about the blood test being diluted with time. The drinking family behind us passed out, the rich Kazak started chatting up one of the beautiful Tajik daughters and the pastry lady went back and forth three times.

When my legs were so swollen someone tried to drag me into to the water and float on me, we returned to our room. Susi was entertaining Alfie on the steps with a huge piece of watermelon. He was holding it in his lap, lowering his head to bite the flesh and let juice run down his chin.

The restaurant manager walked past dragging a sack of wood. He waved enthusiastically.

"You have good time? You like our Issyk-Kul?"

"Wonderful. Is there a barbecue tonight?"

"Yes, we have sheep cook in spit."

"You mean *on* a spit?"

"Yes, on fire. They kill it now behind kitchen. You can see." I imagined a struggling animal held down by its legs while chef sharpened a knife. Maybe they'd use the skin for *koumys*. "It's party for rich Kazaks. We also have special show of Kyrgyz music. You want come?"

"Will there be a wailing fat lady wearing a Christmas cake hat?"

"Of course."

"Then no thank-you." Matthew and I had seen a show at Bishkek's Philharmonic Hall. The musicians had created soft haunting melodies on their *komuz*, small ceramic flutes and *kyyak*, stringed instruments played with a bow. Unfortunately a local diva had ruined the effect by screeching. No-one else had noticed, the rest of the audience dashing adoringly onto the stage to present bouquets of flowers between songs.

"What's for dinner if we don't eat sheep?" Pete asked.

"We have soup with cabbage."

"Can we have soup without cabbage?" The manager paused, thinking seriously.

"It cost extra."

Matthew and I watched the sun drop into Issyk-Kul from our balcony while my ankles slowly deflated. Pete and Susi chased a crawling Alfie around the garden, trying to stop him eating grass and throwing himself off walls. It was wonderful to relax after an afternoon on the beach, skin tingling from sun and sand, knowing that in a few hours I'd climb into cool sheets and sleep as long as I wanted. I wasn't sure I was ready to have my life dominated by someone who didn't understand what a lie-in was.

After dinner – we had the cabbage, it was actually quite tasty, seasoned with dill – Alfie slept and we played cards. The moon was a crescent in a cobalt sky and yodelling, nasal chants and strumming *komuz* drifted across from the restaurant, competing with Michael Jackson at the disco next door. This wasn't exactly the tranquillity of rural Kyrgyzstan I'd read about. We'd opted for the sanitised version, packaged up for those who've only a weekend to spare.

What you really need to appreciate Kyrgyzstan are endless days to explore random tracks to their ends; the ability to ride off the map through networks of hidden valleys and passes to remote pastures. I tried to be positive about all the amazing things I had seen, things I never dreamed I'd experience, to remind myself that sights I now took for granted would be admired in pages of National Geographic. Visitors are good for helping you recognise the extraordinary within your routine; it was a shame we hadn't had any.

But there remained niggles of dissatisfaction at the back of my mind, glimpses of scenery tormenting me about opportunities so close but unattainable. Although I was starting to understand the country better, I felt the real Kyrgyzstan was eluding me. The mountains were still one-dimensional façades, the mysteries behind them impenetrable.

This is the curse of ex-pat life – you're posted to amazing countries and yet see less than friends who come as tourists. With all holidays spent travelling home to see family and stock up on Marmite, there's no time to find isolated *jailoos* or hike across mountains to Kazakhstan without being late for work on Monday.

We got home safely, Putin having left the day before. As promised we'd stopped for apricots and I'd bought a bucket of blackcurrants and ten kilos of apricots for £1.50. I spent the week stewing, stoning, bottling and jamming apricots and blackcurrants, moving obsessively to strawberries, raspberries and plums because with fruit this gorgeous and cheap I couldn't resist buying something every time I went out and it seemed a shame not to use it. Unlimited strawberries, I decided, were the ultimate treat: Matthew and I felt decadent eating so many and homemade strawberry jam seemed the epitome of luxury.

The flat was pungent with sweet fragrance as I boiled vats of fruit, watching the edges of my jam kettle erupt into volcanoes of viscous red liquid. Whether we'd eat it was irrelevant; I was satisfying my nesting instincts, frustrated because there are only so many times you can clean the fridge and tidy your wardrobe when you live in a rented apartment.

In the haze of my activity, Matthew returned to Issyk-Kul with the DFID and World Bank review mission, hoping they'd look favourably on eating sheep's eyes and blatant corruption so he wouldn't be unemployed by the weekend. Collapsed on the sofa, surrounded by jars of cooling jam, I started to think beyond fruit and panicked – I'd offered to host Playgroup the following Wednesday.

Chapter Twelve – Finding Nemo

The problem with attending ex-pat socials is fear of reciprocal hosting. Unlike the palatial embassy homes, our flat was small with sofas that looked like a cat had vomited on them. I hated entertaining in a place which didn't reflect me. With floral crockery, mirrored ceilings in the hallways and a television which swivelled on a glass cabinet, I'd get a reputation for having no taste.

Most critically I lacked the one thing necessary for hostessing success – a large coffee pot. All experienced ex-pat ladies had tall, shiny thermal flasks which kept gallons of coffee warm all afternoon. All I had was a two-cup Bodum cafetière: stylish and shiny, but small. Nothing sold in town was appropriate. The flasks in Osh bazaar were too Chinese for any self-respecting member of the Bishkek International Women's Club and the flasks in Dordoi bazaar all leaked. I'd spent the afternoons I hosted Craft Group apologetically boiling the kettle every time the President took a slurp.

Coffee pots aside, Playgroup was definitely the scariest club to host. I didn't want teams of brats screaming around our flat but enjoyed my Wednesday afternoon excursions too much to drop out and English manners dictated I take my turn. Reluctantly I'd whispered, "I'll host next week," hoping no-one would hear.

"Awesome, we'll see you there."

"Where's your house?"

"I live in a flat."

"What?"

"An apartment."

"Oh okay, what number floor do I press in the elevator?"

"You climb stairs."

"Oh gee."

I spent Wednesday morning preparing. Any ornaments that we didn't want smashed were hidden in our bedroom and I begrudgingly removed sharp objects which might harm the little darlings. I cooked banana bread and chopped carrots and tried to coerce the coffee pot to hold more liquid.

At three the doorbell rang and Birgit and Anthea arrived, with empty hands despite my pleas that children bring toys because Matthew and I didn't own any. For the next ten minutes I scuttled between door and kettle, monitoring which corners of my home the kids were destroying while pumping gallons of coffee into every water-tight container we had.

Gina and nanny Natasha were last to arrive, her two boisterous boys complaining in nasal whine about the lack of an elevator.

"Sorry I'm late girls, I had my hair fixed."

"How nice." It hadn't looked broken to me.

"Go for it guys, go find your friends." They tore off into the kitchen and I counted silently to ten, persuading myself this was good training for motherhood. "Gawd, it's great to have a break." As she'd only been with them for the ten minutes it took to drive from the hairdresser, I thought this melodramatic. But I pasted a huge smile on my face, pretended I didn't care that five kids were rearranging the china cupboard and said "Come in, come in. Coffee or tea?" in a forced, jovial voice.

"Mom! Where's the playroom?" Gina's eldest, Bradley, was bored of jumping on the sofa. "They don't have one honey."

"Why not?"

"Because it's only a small apartment."

"And we don't have any children," I interjected.

"Mom, I'm bored."

"I don't wanna hear this, now go play."

"With what?"

"Anything."

"I'd rather you didn't. Why don't you draw a picture?" I pointed hopefully to paper and crayons I'd brought as damage limitation entertainment.

"That's boring. Mom, can I watch 'Finding Nemo'?"

"Of course honey."

"Actually we don't have it."

"Don't have Nemo! Oh my gawd, but you're gonna have a kid, you gotta have Nemo, they love it, he's so cute." Gina starting flicking her head back and forth like a Wimbledon audience, searching for something in our sitting room. "Where's your TV? Oh man, is your set ever small. You gotta get a widescreen fifty-two inch plasma television or you'll never appreciate Nemo."

"MOM! I'm bored!" I looked at my watch, only one hour and forty-five minutes to go.

If you ever find yourself searching for an alternative form of contraception, come to the Bishkek International Women's Club Playgroup. If the kids don't put you off reproducing, the mums will. Feeling the need to talk to someone, I made the mistake of confiding that I was feeling insecure about becoming a mother, wondering how I'd cope with an inescapable demand on my time.

"You gotta make the most of every minute you have left," Penny advised.

"I'm not terminally ill." But I knew what she meant. I had the feeling that sand was running quickly through my egg-timer. There was still so much I wanted to do before 'I' became 'we', although I was trying to see birth as a beginning rather than an end.

"Once the baby comes you'll never pee in peace again."

"And don't expect to read any books."

"Your breasts leak milk." Iona pointed to a splodge on her t-shirt.

"And you're so tired you just wanna sleep."

"But you can't because baby's crying."

"Or your husband wants sex." With such positive encouragement it was a miracle the human race hadn't become extinct.

The griping was interrupted by Lola, Penny's daughter, a precocious madam in a pink dress. She was holding dirty palms up to me.

"You need to tell your maid she missed a bit." She'd found two dusty stools we never used hidden in a corner of the balcony.

"I don't have a maid."

"Why not?"

"I prefer to do it myself."

"Why?"

How did I explain self-sufficiency to a four year old who thought Mummy couldn't lift a vacuum cleaner? These children were like princesses, moving from capital to capital, indifferently shedding tearful surrogate mothers in their wake. They lived in palaces, were chauffeur-driven to school and Daddy's best friend was always the president. How were they to know that normal people cleaned their own shoes and washed up after dinner?

It was a long two hours. The children whined because there weren't cookies, they didn't like the juice, there was no garden to play in and they couldn't find Nemo. The mums whined because I didn't have a nanny to distract the children while they gossiped undisturbed. My cheeks ached with false smiles and I collapsed on the sofa after I'd waved the last one off at five, trying to find some energy to welcome Matthew home.

He crashed through the door at six-thirty, finding me scraping banana off the walls.

"Six people; seven nights in the Hyatt; block-booked guesthouses in Issyk-Kul; two flights each, business class; endless celebratory and self-congratulatory dinners – I could have put water into the rest of our villages with the amount that cost!" It had been an expensive week with the review mission. "And what have we achieved from it? Nothing! I don't know what's worse, the vodka terrorism or the bullshit. At no time did they address the issue of corruption. They don't have the guts to say, "no, we won't keep sending you millions of our taxpayers' pounds if you spend it on black Mercedes and *dachas* in Issyk-Kul." Why not? Because it's politics, politics, politics. Thanks to oil and Islamic militants in Central Asia they're desperate to keep the Kyrgyz government happy and compliant and will let them get away with anything in the name of development. Makes me sick. Here they are toasting how wonderful the project is and *babushkas* are still walking miles to fetch water from contaminated rivers. None of these donors care about the beneficiaries." He paused to breathe. "What the hell's gone on here, why are there footprints on the coffee table?"

"I hosted Playgroup."

"Oh my god! How was it?"

"Great, I spent my afternoon talking in an enthusiastically high voice to other people's kids about Finding Nemo and my lack of cleaning." By now Matthew had pulled off his muddy site-boots and was giving me a hug.

"Sorry, I should ask about your week."

"It was fine until three this afternoon. By the way, Gina says we have to buy Finding Nemo and a widescreen fifty-two inch plasma television."

"What?"

"And I had a dream that Tom will be born on the tenth of October." He was due on the thirteenth but the tenth would be great. We just didn't want him arriving before the first when Matthew was returning. It was a race against nature, which wasn't always inclined to fit around flight schedules.

"Did your dream give any other details?"

"No, but then I had a nightmare…"

"Were you asleep the whole time I was away?"

"No, although Gina keeps telling me I should rest more. Anyway in my nightmare my sister was shot and I was upset because she'd never felt Tom move. So now I feel guilty because I'm denying my family the pleasures of my pregnancy."

"You'll be seeing them in three weeks, they can feel Tom then."

"Not if they're dead." I was always paranoid about my family's safety when abroad, as if something was more likely to happen to them because I lived 7000 kilometres away.

"Can we talk about something else?"

"How was the guesthouse?"

"I ended up staying with a family who were very nice. Zamira, the landlady, made *blinis* with home-made *kaimak* and apricot jam for breakfast which was delicious and a great improvement on the cold pasta and spam we were served in the Celestial Mountains in Naryn. I'm glad to be home though, what's for dinner?"

"Banana bread."

In contrast to Playgroup, my Russian lesson the next morning was a pleasure. I was fairly lazy about lessons. Most weeks I had a fight with my conscience about wanting to cancel them. Now I could buy carrots without humiliation I found it difficult to concentrate on reciting "I eat soup, you eat soup, he eats soup," when I'd rather have been strolling in the park. I'd soon be back in the land of Bristolian where it didn't matter what gender your noun was.

With advancing pregnancy my brain was starting to seize up and rust, my hormones prioritising blood for other parts of the body. But I was making progress, even though I'd given up trying to pronounce 'hello'. I could now say "get stuffed you cheating drunk, I always pay forty *som*," to taxi drivers, and that was an advantage.

Valentina was understanding about my failing concentration and even fell for my distraction trick: asking about her life. I now knew she had a *dacha*, holiday home, which cost $500. This seemed like a bargain until she told me it had no bathroom or electricity and was in a village outside the boundaries of Matthew's project.

That morning my plan was to discuss her genealogy – I was still trying to understand these Central Asians.

"My parents are Russian and I am Russian."

"But you were born here?"

"Yes."

"And you have a Kyrgyz passport?"

"Yes."

"So aren't you Kyrgyz?"

"No, Russian, that's what is says in my passport."

"It does?"

"Yes, ethnicity is Russian."

"Ethnicity!" That was the key. In Central Asia you have a nationality, which is arbitrary, and an ethnicity, which you cling to as your label.

"My husband's mother was German but he is Russian. We stay here because we have jobs and we like the Kyrgyz, although the country is so corrupt, I know this. When I go home to Russia I notice that we have more expensive cars in our country Kyrgyzstan, even though it's poorer. How do you explain that without corruption?"

Her speech was full of contradictions – 'home' to Russia but Kyrgyzstan 'our' country. She was like me, an ex-pat who used the word 'home' confusingly to describe the place where I wasn't at the time, pledging allegiance to two teams.

"Stalin sent my parents here in the 1950s to educate Kyrgyz because they were teachers. Then Russians believed they were better than Kyrgyz and got the best jobs and the best wages. Now the Kyrgyz believe this and they have the best jobs and best wages. One day we'll go home to Leningrad, I don't know when."

"St Petersburg."

"To us it will always be Leningrad. My daughter, things are difficult for her. She is clever and studies at your LSE in London. She doesn't want to stay in Kyrgyzstan because there are no good jobs for young people if they're not corrupt or having an uncle who is a politician. Maybe she will try and work in London for one of your big accountants, if they will let her."

"Is she Kyrgyz or Russian?"

"She is confused. All the young generation are. They have seen societies outside Kyrgyzstan so they question all the problems we have. Maybe they will start a revolution. Maybe they will just shrug their shoulders and leave. It's easier to walk away when your homeland is a stranger."

After the lesson I walked to the *bazaarchik* on *Bokonbayeva*. Ulla had recommended this small bazaar so I now shopped locally rather than hiking all the way to Mo-Soviet to be ripped off. I'd made friends among the vendors, who didn't hassle me to buy from them. They called me '*dyevooshka*', young woman; a compliment, Anthea told me, who was now referred to as '*jenshcheena*' meaning 'woman' without the 'young'. This was my High Street where people smiled and waved to me. With only weeks to go until I left I realised I'd miss them; I'd found warmth in unlikely places.

First stop was the bakery, a hole in a brick wall, where Umarzak was scooping hot *lepioshka* from his domed clay oven with an implement which looked like a Scold's Bridle on a stick. He wore a bandana over his black hair and his face was shiny with sweat. Cooling round loaves were laid along the ledge so I picked two, put ten *som* in the box, grinned at Umarzak and walked on along the street.

Mary-Lou was stepping out of a taxi.

"Hi honey. My you're lookin' bi-ig." I felt big. Matthew had measured me the night before and I was 45 inches round, which sounds disgustingly huge, and looks disgustingly huge if you hold a tape measure open at that diameter. I could feel Baby Tom growing daily, stretching my very stretched belly. It was going to be a shock for my parents; they'd put a slim (well, relatively slim) daughter on a plane and a Weeble was going to wobble off.

There were only nine weeks to go until I became a mother and I still wasn't sure I was ready for it. According to The Books my pelvic joints were expanding and Baby was head down, ready for birth. Before long Tom would be clutching my finger saying "mama." But that was the easy bit. I was terrified how I'd cope when he grew up and got bullied at school, raced down motorways in a sports car, broke his neck playing rugby or got stabbed in a nightclub. Could I handle the traumas of motherhood? He was better off in there, safe from all the terrible things that happened in the world. I patted my tummy absentmindedly.

"Are you okay honey, you're looking rather pale. Shouldn't you be resting?"

"I'm fine, absolutely fine."

Wanting to deflect attention from my preoccupations I asked Mary-Lou about herself – it worked every time.

"Me? I've come to try out a new hairdresser before heading off to Quilt Camp in At-laana. We're havin' a symposium on log cabin combinations."

"How exciting."

"It's gonna be great. I'll show ya what I make when you come back in January. You are comin' back right?"

"Unless DFID terminates the project by then." Or baby has asthma, a nut allergy or is blind. I must stop doing this to myself.

"What?"

"Never mind Mary-Lou, I'm sure I'll be back. I wouldn't want to miss the next ball would I."

"No siree. I've gotta run but I'll see ya soon. And get some more rest honey. Tadaa!"

"Bye Mary-Lou."

I walked into the *bazaarchik,* people staring because I'd just been jabbering in English with a woman wearing a green velour tracksuit. The market was in an open-sided barn with produce laid out on trestle tables. At the far end, flanks of meat hung outside a cubby-hole where a man was smashing thigh bones with a cleaver. At the entrance a woman sold cold noodles and bowls of grated carrot, beetroot and sauerkraut; salads folded into fresh-baked *lepioshka* for lunch.

I went straight to Mahabat and bought a kilo of potatoes, kilo of onions, kilo of aubergines, kilo of tomatoes, kilo of cucumbers, two cloves of garlic, some parsley and a four-kilogram watermelon, all for the equivalent of 90 pence! I placed it all carefully in the wheely shopping bag we'd bought in Copenhagen: it was black rather than tartan and made by Bodum but still aged me by five decades.

I trundled over to the flower stall where lilies, daisies, carnations and roses were rammed into buckets. Flowers were another Russian obsession adopted by Kyrgyz. They regularly bought huge bunches and displayed them still wrapped in the coloured cellophane and ribbons; compensating, I assumed, for the dreary concrete.

"Good morning *dyevooshka*, what would you like today?" the flower lady asked. She wore a floral tabard and sat with her thick, Russian, hairy legs splayed around a bucket of daisies.

"Those peonies look nice."

"They're 20 *som* a bunch." I handed over a grubby note and tucked the flowers under my arm. "Daisies, lilies, carnations? All beautiful." Even when you'd bought something Kyrgyz salesmen never gave up hope that you actually still wanted one of everything else.

"No, just peonies thanks."

"Never mind *dyevooshka*. Come again!"

I crossed onto *Manas* and headed home. The sun was warm on my back and everyone seemed to be smiling, even the *babushkas* who'd changed into summer uniforms of floral dresses, socks with flip flops and white cotton headscarves. I felt so happy and relaxed I barely flinched when someone projected a large missile of gob towards my feet.

"Nice bag!" The retort was full of English sarcasm. "And you're so big! Are you smuggling a watermelon?"

"Hi Ben." Ben was English, married to Nicky who Marjorie had introduced me to because we were 'both young'. They lived off *Manas* in a homely Slavic cottage with a cat called Kyzyl. Nicky often invited me for tea and I loved going to visit because we always had lots to talk about and she served decent tea from a teapot.

Nicky was Country Director of a Non-Governmental Organisation (NGO) trying to persuade the Kyrgyz government to close Soviet orphanages and spend the money on creating stable family environments. Orphanages weren't full of orphans but children whose parents couldn't cope.

Ben was the Trailing Spouse, looking for work when he wasn't cycling to the Suusamyr valley and back in a day, 140 kilometres up and down mountains. He'd been for an interview with KTR, a Kyrgyz television station who were advertising for a 'normal looking foreigner' to read the news in

English. He'd not got the job. Instead he'd done some marketing for Franco Maccaroni, Italian owner of Tzum and was now setting up his own business to deliver sandwiches to offices. He was wearing a red cap declaring him 'Mr Sandwich Man' – and he dared criticise my bag?

"It may make me look eighty but it's very practical when you're pregnant."

"I'll have to get Nicky one."

"Is she pregnant?"

"Shit, I'm not supposed to tell anyone, she's not twelve weeks yet."

"Don't worry, I won't gossip."

"Why don't you come round for a barbecue? I'm sure that now I've told you Nicky would appreciate discussing birth plans with someone who's interested."

"That would be great. Will we have *plov* or *lagman*?"

"Burgers I should think. Gotta dash, lunchtime rush on chicken rolls today. Careful getting that bag upstairs. Shouldn't you be resting?"

"Shuddup!" But they were all right; I did need to rest more, especially after a bad night's sleep induced by the traumas of Playgroup. I spent the afternoon reading with my feet up – a luxury I was enjoying while I could.

On Friday morning I walked across town under the cool shade of oak trees. There was no Mahjong because Anke was hosting a ceremonial banquet and was busy preparing the Residence. In Ala Too Square Lenin was having a pedicure, scaffolding wrapped around his pedestal while men polished his boots. With Lenin unavailable, business was slow for the photographers waiting underneath.

In Kyrgyzstan it's tradition to have pictures taken in front of statues and monuments. Photographers set up stalls in the most prestigious places; each one the same so that rows of wooden boxes and red and yellow beach umbrellas litter municipal spaces. Hung on each umbrella are a mirror and a board displaying previous shots. I liked to stop and peer at the photographs: loving couples with arms around each other in the dusk, their images bordered by flowers and butterflies; groups of friends standing under banners made for *Nooruz* or May Day and formal family gatherings. One of these was being taken behind me that day, three generations standing rigidly in front of the flag pole, arms pinned to their sides in fear of the occasion. Their faces were solemn under *ak-kalpaks* and headscarves, despite the photographer's best efforts to engender some cheerfulness.

The motionless soldiers guarding the red flag continued to stare straight ahead, not distracted from duty by Lenin's pedicure or being photographed. They probably have the most boring job in Bishkek. From 9 'til 5, teams of two men stand either side of the flag pole, ancient guns with bayonets ready to defend its honour. Every two hours the guard is changed, relief soldiers marching into the square. At 5pm the national anthem is blasted through loudspeakers, they take the flag down and go home.

My destination was Edgar's pizza restaurant where Tina was having a goodbye lunch. She was leaving on Saturday, going home to Australia while Brian braved a posting to the Finance Ministry in Kabul. I had three more weeks in Bishkek and my emotions were already pitching into the turmoil I feel before leaving a place. Half of me couldn't wait to go. Now my departure date was imminent I'd lost patience with the city's foibles and looked forward to life in the first world. But the other half of me was sad. Four months ago I'd just wanted to do my time and leave. Now I felt affection for the streets I walked and faces I saw, the concrete softened by the comfort of familiarity I hadn't known in April.

I was worried I'd feel a stranger in England; it was two and a half years since I'd lived there. When we'd left no-one used credit card pin codes and you had to lick postage stamps. Cut off from television, radio and newspapers there was a huge hole in my knowledge of popular culture. I'd feel like a nerd.

I paused on the corner of the square, waiting to cross, shifting my swollen feet in my sandals. Gina would tell me off for walking but I still enjoyed the exercise. The lights turned red and traffic stopped. I looked both ways, just in case, and stepped out.

Blaaaaaaaaaaaaaaaaam! A car blasted its horn as it skidded to a halt.

"Translate this!" I flicked him the international sign of displeasure: it would be nice to be in country where red lights weren't just for decoration. Who would run over a pregnant woman? Didn't he realise I'd do more damage to his Lada; it would crumple on impact, being only held together by string and duct tape.

It was a perfect summer's day; clear blue sky, warm sun, light breeze, hovering smog. According to Sky News everyone in England was complaining about heat, empty reservoirs, sweltering Tubes and hosepipe bans. In Bishkek it was still raining every Saturday; so much for summer being so hot I'd melt.

"Don't tell me you walked!"

"Hi Gina." I took a seat in the shade next to Tina while Gina berated me for walking in my condition, Mrs Shah nodding her head in agreement.

"You need to order quickly because the restaurant's filling up."

"Yes Gina."

"And what's this about a constitution for the Women's Club?" Penny asked accusingly. "I heard you're writing one and we're going to have elections. Why?"

It was all Marjorie's fault. She'd left at the start of August, her husband exhausted after two years of trying to teach Customs officers they couldn't charge people extra because they were Uzbek. She'd bequeathed me her supplies of Bisto and custard powder then, while I felt indebted, made the request which was to draw me inextricably into the executive heart of the Women's Club.

"You're a lawyer aren't you?" Marjorie had said.

"I was in my former life."

"I think the Women's Club needs a constitution, to set out how we vote in the executive."

"Marjorie, you're leaving next week."

"I know, but I'm worried that it seems dictatorial, me appointing my successor."

"Not in Kyrgyzstan."

"We should set an example and rise above such nepotism. What's needed is a document stating the aims of the club, membership rules, election procedure etcetera. Can you do it?"

I hadn't liked to confess that I'd spent my time as a lawyer paginating. You didn't say no to Marjorie so I'd struggled for hours to create a legal document which told a bunch of international women how things were to be done from now on. So far I'd written the heading.

"Are there gonna be rules and stuff?" Penny quizzed.

"Yes, but hopefully helpful rules, just so everyone knows what's going on." A surly waitress with dyed-blond hair arrived to tidy the table, despite the fact we were still eating. She collected the used napkins, replacing them with fresh. I didn't know why she bothered. Kyrgyz napkins are small, thin and useless. One dab and they disintegrate leaving you with pizza sauce dripping off your chin.

"Maybe I'll run for president." Ulla held two fingers up to her head in mock salute.

"But you're leaving in September," Tina objected.

"And Marjorie's already appointed Claudia From, wife of Gerhard, the Hyatt manager. Ilke's the secretary. My constitution will be ready to elect the next president."

"Who's Ilke, do I know her? Is she a Playgroup mom?" Penny asked.

"She's Danish, her husband Soren is the cigarette baron of Central Asia..."

Ulla interrupted, "they've got a factory here which has the capacity to produce twelve billion cigarettes. The company's the third biggest private investor in Kyrgyzstan, after Kumtor and Hyatt." I stared at her, eyebrows raised. Ulla laughed and shrugged apologetically.

"I read it last week in the Times of Central Asia."

"Must be true then."

"So her and Claudia are gonna know all the important people?" Penny asked.

"Yeah, they're always at Hyatt brunch with the Prime Minister and his wife."

"So d'ya think the Women's Club is gonna get, like, glamorous?" I could see Gina calculating whether she had enough cocktail dresses for all the functions.

"We might even get in the newspaper, especially if we've got a constitution," Penny reasoned. I missed Marjorie and her sensibilities. What had she started?

111

I walked home with Tina, stopping at Tumar Art Salon to view the latest creations of the Blind Artisans of Kochkor. Someone had persuaded them that ex-pats use tea cosies and they'd mass produced oval offerings in reds, greens and yellows which looked rather sadly like squashed *ak-kalpaks*. I said goodbye to Tina at the junction of *Isanova* and *Moskovskaya*. I'd attended Craft Group and played Mahjong with her every week for three months but I knew I'd never see her again. It gave me a hollow feeling of displacement, enhanced because soon it would be my turn to say goodbye to everybody.

I'd just entered the flat, huffing because fifty-eight steps are hard work when a five kilo watermelon-baby is restricting your lung capacity, when the phone rang. It was Matthew.

"Hello dear. Foof. Sorry, bit out of breath. What do you want for dinner?"

"I don't care about dinner, something incredible is happening. You've got to see it. They're ripping Lenin down!"

Chapter Thirteen – Goodbye Lenin

When I arrived in the square Lenin was on his back at a 90-degree angle, his outstretched arm reaching towards the sky. From Matthew's agitation I'd imagined a frenzied mob tearing at his feet, reminiscent of bronze Saddam in Baghdad. Instead there were two cranes and five languid engineers, watched by an apathetic crowd.

"The Communists are protesting," Matthew justified.

"Where?"

"Over there." He pointed to three people standing defiantly at the edge of the square with a red flag. "According to Kumashai they say this is disrespectful to Lenin who the government promised to protect."

"I wonder what everyone else thinks."

"The only people who look bothered are the photographers." They were seeing their most profitable backdrop being removed.

"It wasn't a pedicure after all."

A screech of metal on metal interrupted our conversation. Lenin slipped. The crowd gasped. The engineers ran out of the way. But there wasn't a dramatic crash to the ground; Lenin had just shuffled down a bit onto the steel girders which were buckling under his weight. He was being lowered by a crane holding a rope around his chest, which looked inadequate for 25 tons, tipping him back from his feet onto three struts leaning against the plinth which had been his home since 1984.

"I can't believe he's going," murmured Matthew.

"I can't believe we didn't have our photo taken with him."

"I assumed he'd always be there, he's lasted all these years, I thought the Kyrgyz didn't care." According to one guidebook, Lenin's survival was, *"testimony to a philosophical decision on the part of the Kyrgyz not to obliterate their Soviet heritage but to grant it a place in their people's history."* According to everyone else it was testimony to not being able to afford to remove him.

I looked around at the audience, trying to work out who I could quiz for opinions. There were only about sixty people watching, squatting along the kerb in quiet contemplation. There were no cheers or tears, just a group of youths blasting pop music from their car stereo so that Lenin was being reclined to the irreverent cadence of Christina Aguilera.

An old peasant couple sat on the wall and watched in silence. Perhaps they were remembering what Communism had meant for them, simply grateful that they had lived to see this day.

"History, history," said one Kyrgyz man with a wrinkled brown face, white goatee and worn *ak-kalpak*.

"Are you pleased?" I asked. He shook his head.

"We hate Lenin," the lads in the car said. I could understand their sentiment: Russia had taken over and told them everything in their country was crap, dismissing centuries of culture, religion and clan loyalty.

"So you're pleased?"

"No, no, very sad." Their attitude was as contradictory as their national identity.

"I will tell you the story," said a young man dressed in the international uniform of jeans and leather jacket, accessorised in Kyrgyzstan with pointed black shoes and a mobile phone dangling from his neck. "Why is Lenin coming down now, after twelve years of Independence?" Soviet infrastructure had crumbled quicker than the decision to remove him. "The newspapers say it is because this year is celebration of 2200 years of Kyrgyz statehood and we must look forward as independent nation, not back to time with Soviet Union. But I think there is something else." He looked around, checking no-one was eavesdropping. I leaned closer. "I think President Akayev is nervous because the economy is being slow to develop and hospitals and schools and roads in Bishkek is falling apart and people are saying, 'where is the Switzerland he promised us?'"

Twelve years before, the great hope for Kyrgyzstan was to be the Switzerland of Central Asia, a comparison derived more from geographical similarities than banking comparisons. No-one was going to be rushing to Bishkek with their millions: the city only had two cash machines and one of those froze in winter. But the idea had formed in people's minds and they were still waiting for the affluence and Milka chocolate.

The man continued, giving his conclusion in a whisper. "I think Akayev doesn't want Lenin in centre of Bishkek reminding people of life under Soviet Union because, you know, for us, it wasn't so bad."

This was a view taken by most Kyrgyz. If you discount collectivisation and a few purges, Kyrgyzstan did well from its seventy year sentence. It didn't suffer food shortages and endless queues, which the West considers synonymous with Communism, but gained schools, roads, hospitals and a love of vodka and synthetic cakes on festival days. Many pined for the good old days when every citizen had a job, roads were smooth and doctors knew a pancreas from a penis. With high unemployment, nurses nannying for foreigners, cars rutting through pot holes and *babushkas* selling the contents of cutlery drawers to survive, Independence was harsh.

"If people happy, no-one cares about Lenin but people in Kyrgyzstan is angry about being poor and President Akayev is," the man paused again, looking round, "becoming more dangerous to keep control. Maybe he not want people to start to say he a dictator like Lenin. He is squashing opposition. He puts leaders in prison and closes newspapers who say he and his family run lots of businesses. There is even a new law saying he can live in his big government houses and have his cars and big salary, even when he's not president. People are saying this is wrong when children and old people are starving. They don't understand why America say Kyrgyzstan is democracy." Someone coughed behind us and our companion jumped nervously.

"It's just the loudspeaker," Matthew reassured, "it's five o'clock." We stood in silence while the national anthem marched around the square. It sounded like a Sunday School hymn played by a kids' brass band at their first concert. Three guards in ski-jump caps, olive uniforms and white gloves marched up to the flag, tugged it down then retreated in exaggerated goose-step, legs swinging waist high in perfect rhythm, right arms smacking across chests, left hands clutching the butts of gun. I turned to ask my new friend what he thought of such pomp but he'd gone, merged back into the crowd with his treasonous ideas.

We left Lenin standing on his head. The girders had bent again so that he'd lurched in his imposed bindings and turned towards us, his arm flung out in a final plea. By now the evening sun was low, skimming tops of buildings and forming shadows with the contours of Lenin's face. He looked pitiful and I felt he was aware this was his final sunset, his visual reign over Bishkek ended.

I was sad to say goodbye. It was Lenin who'd welcomed me to Bishkek on that wet April dawn and Lenin who'd formed a landmark in my first explorations of the city. I liked his authoritative dependability and wasn't sure the Kyrgyz had anyone suitable to replace him.

Local spectators stayed on, wanting to see him safely into the flat-bed truck. They stared in silence, smoking, spitting and cracking sunflower seeds between their teeth, pyramids of husks forming at their feet. Maybe older Kyrgyz were apathetic about politics because having been pawns in someone else's game for so long they no longer cared who was in power as long as they could drink *koumys* and ride horses.

Ulla's husband Mark, who was writing a college text book on politics and economics, was excited about his hopes for the next generation.

"Everyone over thirty is paranoid, still looking over shoulders for the KGB, and everyone under thirty is angry," he'd told me animatedly over dinner one evening. "Change didn't hit Kyrgyzstan in 1991, the real change is generational, and it's happening now, initiated by those who haven't grown up in the Soviet Union. They see stifling corruption and are frustrated because their votes are worthless and political expression has gone underground. I'm just waiting for the explosion."

"Maybe it will happen during the parliamentary and presidential elections next year? I read they're being heralded as Central Asia's first potential peaceful handover of power."

"Maybe," he'd said, deflated because Ulla had just reminded him all the promising students left for America, "or maybe it will just be another farce of rigged votes and bribery."

The big question – among ex-pats, locals weren't bothered – was, where had Lenin gone? We discussed it with Ben and Nicky at the promised barbecue. I hoped he'd been retired comfortably into a nice museum where he could live out his days under the gaze of curious tourists. Ben was convinced he was on a scrap-metal truck bound for China.

"Why did they have to take him down? In London there are still statues of colonialists and warriors whose politics are now out of favour."

"But this is the new Kyrgyz Republic with something to prove."

"It's taken them twelve years to prove it."

"It's taken them twelve years to scrape the money together to afford it!"

The second question was who would replace him? President Akayev? His wife? George Bush? If it had taken twelve years to get Lenin down, how long would we be looking at the gaping hole on the plinth?

"More importantly," Nicky interrupted, "have you found anywhere to buy baby car seats in Bishkek?" Buying car seats and buggies, I had discovered, involved exhausting options of styles, colours, folding techniques, weight and car compatibility. Was it relevant whether a buggy had 'soft air-filled tyres and innovative adjustable three position rear suspension system' when baby was only going to puke in it? Kyrgyz parents didn't have such problems. They carried their children and didn't bother with car seats, probably because there weren't any seat belts. Kids sat in the front with foreheads pressed to windscreens; one emergency stop and they'd splatter like eggs dropped on stone.

It was hot, stiflingly hot, oppressive, sticky and intense. The temperature had been rising for days, the city pulsing with heat like an oven ready for baking, hushed in waiting for the explosion which had to come. It happened as Nicky was serving coffee. A hot wind burst from the mountains and lightening cracked above us, preceding huge, slow drops which stung bare flesh as we ran for the house. Irrigation ditches, blocked with rubbish, were unable to absorb the onslaught and overflowed across pavements so that we waded home through a flotsam of ice-cream wrappers and fag packets, breathing in the refreshing smell of hot dust dampened by cool rain.

Time for me was a paradox. Although my last weeks were flying by I drifted calmly through them, made languorous by my swaying belly. Pregnancy had formed another body and I'd swollen into lumps and curves, creating places I could no longer reach. I was ugly but beautiful, distorted by nature but content with my body's performance as I submitted to the purpose it was designed for.

Even without the gravity of late pregnancy I never enjoy final weeks of a posting, wishing I could sneak onto the plane early to avoid their contradiction. Mentally I'd moved on so that all the quirks I once enjoyed had become nuisances I couldn't wait to escape. Physically I was clinging, sad that I wouldn't walk to Bishkek City Market again or hear the call of the *malako* man, craving more days to do everything one last time. But the pressure of 'last' taints everything with artificiality, tarnishing happy memories. The last bowl of *plov* always seems greasier and for the last stroll up Erkendik, leaves don't shine as green. It's best just to yank at your emotions and leave quickly while everything feels good.

I was even nostalgic about my last appointment at the Family Clinic. Needing check-ups and a doctor to write my letter for British Airways, I'd been forced to return to the clinic after my blood test, although had gone no-where near the lab. I was trying not to think about the HIV test I'd have in England, irrational thoughts about the result only surfacing when I lay awake late at night.

Dr Hilary had left in July, referring me to her American colleague, Dr Gideon, a softly-spoken, diligent doctor who carefully checked blood pressure, heartbeat and swollen ankles while trying to coax answers from dopey students.

"Why do we monitor blood pressure?" Gideon asked, wrapping the strap around my arm.

"Because if it's high it means she's having a boy." My Russian had progressed to the point I could understand conversations, even if I couldn't join in.

"No." Dr Gideon quietly explained, again, about pre-eclampsia.

A student advanced towards me with a thermometer, wiping its end with a tissue. I was just about to tell her that she could think again if she assumed she was sticking that dirty thing in my mouth as I was already high-risk for HIV and didn't fancy adding tuberculosis to the list, when she took out a packet and rolled what looked like a tiny condom down over it. I dutifully opened wide. "And what else are possible signs of pre-eclampsia?" Gideon continued. Blank faces.

"Come on!" I willed silently, lips clamped onto mercury. "We've been doing this for four months and I can't be your only pregnant patient." I didn't want them to fail; they were my friends now, even if they were stupid. I tried to provide clues by hopping surreptitiously, pointing to swollen ankles. I failed and fell over. The student removed the thermometer and pinched each end with her fingertips while she read it so that my body temperature was recorded at the level of her freezing fingers.

The quiz finished, all students scoring badly. Gideon signed my letter reassuring BA that at thirty-four weeks I wouldn't explode on take-off. I didn't think health was the problem – as Baby Tom had grown two centimetres in two weeks I wasn't sure I'd fit into a seat. I called Iona as I was leaving the clinic. She'd phoned just as Gideon was squeezing between my pelvis to see if baby's head had dropped – not conducive to discussing walking to Playgroup.

Playgroup was at Chitra's house that afternoon. Chitra was a gentle Indian lady with a secluded garden tucked behind the Navigator. I was looking forward to the snacks; they were likely to be exotic because Chitra travelled with a chef who rivalled Madhur Jaffrey.

We wandered along *Moskovskaya,* Isabelle dozing in her pram. Looking around I realised I was sad to be leaving. I'd not miss kamikaze drivers, struggling to make myself understood, dodging blobs of gob and putrid bins, now creating a heady scent of high silage and vomit. But I would miss *babushkas* selling fruit on every corner, huge bunches of flowers for 50 pence, rattling trolleybuses and the unique combination of Soviet concrete and shading oak trees. Why do we only appreciate things when it's too late?

We stopped at *Panfilov* for the lights to turn red – and drivers to notice. On the other side of the road was a pregnant woman. It was incredible how many had appeared with the sunshine, testament to what happened in Bishkek on long winter nights. Most wore denim pinafores and teetering stilettos and we grinned shyly at each other, sisters of the same sorority. This woman, however, was leaning on a tree in a dirty red tracksuit with a sleeping infant cradled across her bump. When cars stopped she wandered between them, cupped hand held pleadingly up to windows.

Although all ex-pats bought lots of raffle tickets at Women's Club fundraisers and supported the bin *babushkas* outside our blocks, it was difficult not to feel guilty about the huge gulf between us and the indigent Kyrgyz. Every day street children and beggars reminded us that people could live for months on what we spent each week at Beta Stores. Warned off giving cash by Nicky, who said they spent it on vodka and mafia protection, I was still searching for a suitable way to help.

At the gate of Chitra's garden I noticed balloons tied to trees and a table covered with presents.

"Oh no! Whose birthday is it? I haven't brought anything."

"It's no-one's birthday, it's your baby shower," Iona announced, flinging out her arms. I stopped walking, choked by tears I hadn't expected to shed. All the women were there, smiling and pushing their children forward with presents for Tom – clothes, ducks for the bath, felt animals and a blow up breast feeding pillow from Iona, ordered on-line from America and delivered to her PO Box at the base. I was very envious of her Internet shopping facility. She and the other embassy Americans didn't seem as separated from home as the rest of us because they could still buy anything which would fit in the post. To get the larger maternity bras I desperately needed I'd resorted to coercing Matthew's boss into bringing them when he came over for a review mission. He'd coyly handed them over with the cornflakes.

As I unwrapped gifts I felt touched. Caustic, cynical me, softened by the generosity of these women. I'd been welcomed into the sisterhood, won over by their kindness which transcended endless fussing about nannies and pedicures. The reality was that the ex-pat women of Bishkek had ensured my emotional survival. They'd comforted me when I was new, lost and scared by pregnancy in a strange land and told me what *kaimak* was and where to find broccoli. Understanding fears without having to ask was the advantage of a small community. They'd taken me under their collective wing and protected and helped me. Now I had to leave them.

"Will you be back with Matthew in January?" Chitra asked. We were sitting round the table eating chocolate cake which Iona had made, courtesy of Betty Crocker.[17] Chitra would be in Bishkek for another year with her husband who headed up the IMF – that's the bankers not the terrorists.

"I hope so," and I finally did. I felt braver about the idea of starting motherhood in Bishkek with these women to support me. I didn't want our new family to be pulled apart when we'd only just formed and I could even imagine myself heaving a buggy with soft air-filled tyres and innovative adjustable three position rear suspension system through snow drifts.

There was still so much left undone for me in Kyrgyzstan. In my roly-poly state, scared about damaging my first, precious baby, I hadn't stayed in a *yurt* or climbed to Lake Song Kul. But would it be any easier with a child in a car seat rather than my tummy? Would I want to travel across a country where there are no service stations, no nappy-changing facilities, no roads?

"Lots of us will still be here you know," Susi reassured, "Penny, Anthea, me!"

"I know, and that's great. But what do you do in a medical emergency?"

"Pray!" Iona could afford to be cocky. She was leaving in September, moving to a country which had 999 call centres staffed by people rather than answer machines.

Birgit smiled apologetically. "My husband is making some progress training paramedics, but with only one ambulance it makes little difference."

Gradually the conversation turned to organising children's swimming lessons the next week. I listened, detached because these were days for which I'd be irrelevant. Life was going to carry on after I'd gone and no-one would really notice I wasn't there. My Kyrgyz persona would be suspended in eternity while the Bishkek International Women dashed between beauticians and swimming lessons in a universe parallel to mine. I felt as if I had two lives: one in Kyrgyzstan where I played Mahjong and stitched quilts, and one in England where I'd huff and puff and expel a baby. To return I'd just swig the bottle marked 'drink me' at Heathrow airport and be transported back to the Mad Hatter's Tea Party of the Bishkek International Women's Club, reconvened as if I'd never left, my English family now suspended in the other time-zone.

Matthew loved my tales of the baby shower, fascinated by the tiny clothes I'd been given, both unbelieving that our child would actually fill them. At eleven that night we feared that Baby Tom might be wearing them sooner than planned. I had terrible stomach cramps and crouched in the bathroom, wondering if the sisterhood were capable of assisting at home births.

---

[17] A brand of cake mix, not a member of the BIWC

"Fatboys Bill says don't give birth here because the paperwork's a nightmare," Mathew called through the bathroom door. "The Kyrgyz won't give a birth certificate because they think you'll claim citizenship and ex-pats have been trapped here for years with unregistered babies."

"Sod the paperwork! At the moment I'm more concerned about dying!"

But Bill was right; I didn't want to give birth in Bishkek. I wanted to give birth in white NHS sheets in Bristol with a competent midwife and my mum holding my hand because Matthew said he wanted to watch at the bottom end. "Hang on baby, only another six days," I willed. My stomach gurgled, rumbling and bubbling so much Tom must have thought he was in a volcano. Another spasm gripped me. Maybe it was time to call Birgit's husband.

I emerged from the bathroom half an hour later, pale and sweating.

"Are you alright?" Matthew asked. Do we need to sort travel plans?"

"I think the panic's over."

"What? You're not in premature labour?"

"No. False alarm. I don't think Betty Crocker's cake frosting agreed with me."

Tom was awake with me more often now, dancing while he laid down fat stores in preparation for leaving his safe cocoon. He kicked and thumped his way through my last Mahjong, the ladies shrieking when they saw my belly move, dents in my dress where a foot took impact.

Claudia From joined us, not because I was leaving but because she wanted to discuss the constitution. This was a frightening prospect. Claudia From and husband Gerhard were German, both representing archetypes of their race. Claudia was tall, blond, chic and efficient, determined to elevate the social and financial status of the Women's Club on behalf of the orphans. In contrast Gerhard was a caricature of a tuba player in an oompa band with a round belly, guffawing laugh and walrus moustache. It was admitted, however, that he was an excellent hotel manager; able to make missionaries feel important at Sunday brunch, flatter politicians when necessary and impress international businessmen with his insight into Kyrgyzstan's economy.

"In zis constitution it must be clear zat ve don't have a bank account or pay anyvun vages," Claudia From instructed, pulling on a long, thin cigarette. "Othervise ze government vill say we must register as legal entity and tax all our money."

"We don't have a bank account? Where's all the money then?"

"Under zee mattress in my spare room. But you must tell novun zis!"

"No, no, of course not."

The constitution had become an unwanted burden. I couldn't sleep at night worrying about whether the procedures I'd created were workable and what everyone would think of my dictum. Fortunately it was to be presented at the September meeting. By then I'd be in Bristol, out of earshot of criticism.

It's difficult to draft a succinct legal document when your body is slowing down. With six weeks until due date movements were lethargic and with a swollen body came restlessness, my nesting instincts unsatisfied by the jamming frenzy. I cleaned out my wardrobe, again, bagging up clothes to be donated to Bishkek's homeless: a good purge at the end of every posting is a satisfying advantage of itinerant life.

I was unsettled, agitated because I was about to be uprooted again, walking out on a home which I wasn't sure I'd return to. Where is home when your life is nomadic? Was it the building we owned in London or my parents' house where all our possessions were piled, waiting in boxes for the day we settled or inherited a seven-tonne embassy shipping allowance? Or was it this brown flat in Bishkek where we'd nested for the past four months? When you're an ex-pat 'home' is a confusingly moving concept. 'Home' is where Matthew is, I'd learn while we were apart.

Goodbyes are an unpleasant aspect of expatriate life: public tears at airports, regrets, reminiscences and extended absences from family, not to mention the relays of farewells you sign up to when joining Bishkek International Women's Club. Hugging friends one day only to see them next morning at Beta Stores is exhausting.

For someone who hates goodbyes I'd chosen a lifestyle which involved rather a lot – and they don't get any easier. At my last Russian lesson Valentina cried and said she loved me, which made me feel guilty for all the times I'd not done my homework. At my leaving lunch Nicky said the next time we saw each other we'd both be mothers and Iona said in her mind I'd always remain pregnant because she'd never known me otherwise. Gina sniffed and said she hoped I'd have an epidural because she couldn't stand the idea of all that pain.

The last goodbye was with Matthew and although only for a month, was the hardest of all. I was worried about leaving him alone in Bishkek, not because I was expecting him to hit the Navigator bar the day I left but because he was depressed. After what had seemed like a jolly, positive review mission, the World Bank had sent a report criticising the team for delays. Matthew was livid.

"Us cause delays! It's the department who don't authorise a design for three months and then refuse to sign because they don't like the colour of the fencing. Were they drunk the whole time we were in the field?"

It was depressing to think that the millions of dollars were being wasted. Aid projects, heralded with such enthusiasm for better lives, were hampered by bureaucracy and politics. The premise was simple: you need help, I have money, but the execution was complicated. Good intentions were weighed down by terms of reference, memoranda, proposals, rules, policies and statements of intent. It would be much easier to just take a pick axe into a field and get on with it. But everyone had to have their say and while officials, who showered every morning in hot water, pontificated about ministerial decrees, children were still contracting Hepatitis A.

Matthew also had a new friend, Mr Kalashnikov. Mr Kalashnikov had been big in The Party before hammers and sickles had fallen from fashion. He still called everyone 'comrade' and wasn't used to people saying no to him, or at least not used to people who said no to him staying in town.

I was worried that if I left Matthew unattended he wouldn't be at the birth because Mr Kalashnikov would send him to Siberia. Mr Kalashnikov was angry because Matthew said his niece's wedding wasn't a suitable reason for putting At-Bashy at the top of next season's construction list. Mr Kalashnikov had retorted that Matthew was too young to know anything and that he was writing to the president to complain about the project. President Akayev hadn't responded yet.

"Do they want a water system or not?" he asked me every night. "They're not looking a gift horse in the mouth, they're poking its teeth out. International contracting systems will never work while securing bribes is more important than getting a job done. And the villagers aren't any better. You'd think they'd be grateful but all they do is complain which street the pumps will be on and say their contribution is too high. I'd feel sorry for them if they didn't spend much more money on vodka. Don't worry about bringing Baby Tom back; this project will be long over by January."

Within all this conflict I dreamt about leaving Matthew. He was going into battle, an old fashioned battle with bloody hand combat and two huge, violent armies, dragged from me to fight. I woke in a sweat. Sensing my distress Matthew flung his arm across my belly, his hand warm on my curves. I lay awake in the dark, comforted by his regular breathing, trying to cauterise anxious thought-processes with shopping lists and decisions about which tent-dress I'd wear the next day. How would I recover from nightmares when Matthew was sleeping in Bishkek and me in North Bristol?

Matthew turned over so that our noses were touching. He traced patterns on my face, stroking his finger across my eyes, cheek and mouth. "What are you doing?"

"Touching something I won't see for a while." Tears stung the back of my eyes and my nose tingled. I'd thought about this moment for so long: the anticipation was so painful the goodbye would be a release.

"Don't be too nice to me or I'll cry."

"We can handle long distance. We've done it before."

"Doesn't make it any easier. And this time I'm taking your son with me." We murmured in the dark, listening to dogs barking and engines revving outside, the city sounds lulling us back to sleep for our last Bishkek dawn together before we multiplied into three.

Next morning I flew home to become a mother.

"Bin *Babushka* watched from her low wooden stool, legs crossed and hands clutching grubby *som*."

"The people were an interesting mix: big-nosed Russians, oriental gypsies, Mongoloids with flat eyelids; round faces, broad faces, brown faces; gold teeth, brown teeth, no teeth."

123

"Tell Mummy you'll be fine because I'm your *Droog* Dema."

"I loved being pregnant."

"Gulzada grabbed Tom and hoisted him onto the horse."

"Tanzilya was Tatar with Russian parents, her fore-fathers part of Genghis Khan's Great Golden Horde."

"Curved red rafters stretched up to the round roof vent known as a *tunduk*."

"In the distance, perched high on the second tier of mountains, were two white yurts, so small they could have been button mushrooms in the green."

"I watched two *yurts* being erected on the snow outside our block, helpers blowing on freezing fingers as they fumbled to tie red rafters to the circular frame."

"I started to appreciate that tenements had different architectural styles; curves and crosses of concrete repeated over facades to create striking geometric patterns."

"Beta Stores had been annihilated. Smoke drifted from broken windows leaving black scars up the walls."

"An *aksakal* in an *ak-kalpak* leant against the fence, his poster asking 'Akayev, did you forget about the people?'"

"Peeping around a pillar I saw an incredible sight: men climbing the fence, swarming into the sacred White House."

"Making felt is hard work. I know because I went on a felt-making day."

"It was difficult for Matthew to gain the respect of *aksakals* when he looked as though he were only 21."

"Children were collecting water, dragging heavy churns on handcarts."

"Umarzak was scooping hot *lepioshka* from his domed clay oven with an implement which looked like a Scold's Bridle on a stick."

"The meat hall at Ortosai bazaar is not somewhere to visit if you are verging on vegetarianism."

"Farmers converged on the city to sell surplus from their gardens."

"Three guards marched up to the flag, tugged it down then retreated in exaggerated goose-step."

"Matthew's office was in an impressive building with a colonnade of arches."

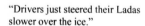

"Drivers just steered their Ladas slower over the ice."

"Vendors paraded past. Their sales pitches were delicate songs which blended with the crash of water on the shore."

"Cherries hung like bunches of grapes from a wooden frame. Each stalk had been intricately tied into clusters with thread and wrapped around loops of wire."

"I stopped to watch two ladies stitching woollen braid onto *shyrdaks*."

"The horse is revered for its strength and movement, the freedom it gives nomads to roam vast distances through their land."

"Women were balancing what looked like Christmas cakes on their heads."

"Men proudly wore their *ak-kalpaks* all year."

"Ulak involves two teams of four wild men on four wild horses wrestling a dead goat from each other."

"The Kyrgyz are proud of their celestial Tien Shan, said to symbolise 'the high spirit of our ancestors, their striving for freedom, wisdom and philosophy'."

"We'd taken Tom to Ala Archa National Park for his three month birthday, he wasn't impressed."

From top right: Nicky, Saffia, Matthew, Dirk holding Tom, Michael, Kay, Lucy with a snowball over her face and Jenna.
From bottom left: Ben, Siana and the twins, Tim and Ben.

"Bishkekers lived in shoe-box-blocks with three variations: grey or brown; standing horizontal or vertical; balcony open or closed."

"Our new home was in a vertical, brown shoebox."

"The Tien Shan skirted Bishkek's southern districts on their journey from the Pamirs into China."

"There were no cheers or tears, just a group of youths blasting pop music from their car stereo so that Lenin was being reclined to the irreverent cadence of Christina Aguilera."

134

Part Two – Baby in Bishkek

Chapter Fourteen – Droog Dema

I was convinced I'd drop him. I was standing alone in Heathrow's Terminal Four with hundreds of people pushing trolleys and shoving past me with chunky suitcases. Matthew had disappeared to investigate which huge queue we were supposed to join. I felt vulnerable and exposed, as if everyone could tell how raw my motherhood was.

When my arms started to tremble with fear at what we were undertaking, I placed him in the buggy and smiled reassuringly, even though I wanted to cry. Tom kicked his legs inside his white baby-gro and reached for his toy, a fluorescent bug with dangly legs. He hadn't seemed to notice that everything in his short life was changing.

Tom was twelve weeks old, an age that had seemed so distant when he was one week old, new and still uncurling. Tom had blue eyes, chubby wrists and dark hair, thinning at the sides where he left it in his cot. His face was a happy collection of curves which fattened when he smiled. He smelt of hot milk and clean washing. He'd just learnt to suck his thumb and the current challenge was to roll towards toys tantalisingly hanging above him. Every day was an adventure, an exploration of knowledge. To him Heathrow was just another kaleidoscope of colour

Leaving home again had been traumatic, even though I'd been preparing since Tom was born healthy, giving me no excuse to stay. The project still hadn't folded, despite all Matthew's gloomy predictions. I'd blocked out thoughts of departure with frantic packing, asking friends what I'd need for a baby aged three to seven months and trying to stay calm when they said how brave I was because they had enough trouble leaving Chiswick. Four months of western comforts had quashed the love I'd felt for shabby Bishkek and hormones, exhaustion and the awe of birth and early parenthood had culminated in tearful goodbyes.

Now we were on the way my pain would be numbed by the journey. My parents had to return to the empty house where their first grandson no longer lived and try not to miss him when they found stray vests in the washing. All I had to do was survive in a country without sensible medical services.

To my enduring relief my HIV test had come back clear so I felt able to trust the Family Clinic again, although I would *not* be having any more blood tests. I'd had more trouble with my clinic in England: it had taken weeks of hard negotiation to be allowed to take Tom's last set of immunisations to Bishkek and my health visitor had become irrational about water.

She imagined me boiling vats of it, straining out bugs and beetles each night until I reassured her that drinking water for paranoid ex-pats came in bottles. Then she became obsessed with the mineral content of these bottles, providing me with a leaflet – any question you ever asked her resulted in a leaflet rather than an answer – listing the safe amounts for each element. This was not helpful. Not only did it panic an already nervous mother but it presupposed I could do something about it if there was a problem. Unlike the Americans at the airbase, I wasn't going to start importing water into a country full of mountain springs. I believed ex-pats had a duty to support the local economy – and it was improbable I'd get anything through Customs before Tom died of thirst.

A lone female traveller leaning up against her backpack smiled sympathetically at me. I tried to respond but it's difficult to smile when you're biting your lip in an attempt not to cry. I knew what she was thinking because I'd thought it so often in the past: 'Why are you flying with a baby! Why don't you just stay at home?' At that moment I agreed. Why was I leaving safe territory with my first child? I wouldn't be able to survive in Central Asia with a three-month-old baby; I still had trouble collapsing the buggy.

"We're never flying again with Tom after we get back from Bishkek," I told Matthew when he returned from his recce. The backpacker's pity had convinced me that all future holidays should be spent in Cornwall and I must NEVER fly on my own with a child.

"Shall we just get through this flight before worrying about the next," Matthew said patiently.

Early motherhood is full of panics. My first happened about two hours after Tom was born. Matthew and my mother were evicted from the ward leaving me with a baby curled asleep on my chest. I didn't dare move because I wasn't sure what would happen next – just because I'd given birth to him didn't mean I knew what to do. Tom had inconsiderately been born before the parenting class about bathing. I'd hoped an hour of dunking a doll in a washing-up bowl would teach me everything I needed to know about looking after a baby. I felt intimidated by the packed ward, tensing when other babies cried. I'd fumbled through my first nappy at 3am and managed to change his vest without snapping an arm. Going home to my mother's support had been comforting. Now I was on my own again.

Apart from wanting to cry when a drunk gold miner yelled at me for taking too long in the toilet with Tom, the flight wasn't as painful as I was expecting. Tom behaved impeccably; feeding, sleeping and only pooing when it was Matthew's turn to change the nappy. He listened diligently to the safety demonstration, following the stewardess's movements with serious eyes, and had only cried when we taxied so long at Baku I thought we'd taken a wrong turn and were headed into town.

At Manas airport I sat on a plastic sofa in the VIP lounge and wallowed in déjà vu while the sense of foreignness closed in again. Britney Spears was still entertaining smoking men in fur hats, blond women with fake boobs were wrapped in cellophane and Dema the driver was even wearing the same cream cable-knit jumper.

"*Zdrastvooytyeh.*" And the basic greeting was still unpronounceable.

"Tras-voo-dya Dema. How are you?"

"You will not see me again." That sounded terminal.

"Why not?"

"I go home to Russia to find better life. We are not welcome anymore. Kyrgyz take best jobs and only look after each other and now government has new law which will make discrimination for people who don't speak Kyrgyz."

I didn't know why Dema was worried. According to President Akayev, while promoting Kyrgyz language as the symbol of Kyrgyz statehood, the strategic task was to 'form a common national space comfortable for ethnic self-realisation', his favourite slogan 'Kyrgyzstan is our common home'. But despite this encouragement Dema wasn't the only one leaving. The Bishkek Observer reported that 40% of ethnic Russians had already migrated, unhappy at their role reversal. Soon there'd be few Slavs left in Kyrgyzstan who remembered the good old days of Soviet mastery, everyone would have been born Kazak, Kyrgyz or Turkmen, whatever that meant.

"How is your baby?"

"Very well considering he's just flown 7000 kilometres." Tom was looking around from the sling across my stomach, taking in Britney, porn and fur hats with big, blue eyes.

"He looks like Matthew. Little bit happy, little bit serious. I hope one day to have a son, one day when I have enough money in Russia." I hoped he would find what he was looking for in his surrogate homeland and not return disappointed.

Walking into the flat after sixteen hours of cars, planes, airports and jeeps was such relief. Tom, who'd fallen asleep in the car, continued to doze in the cot Matthew had prepared for him so we were able to climb into cool, fresh sheets and stretch our cramped limbs. It was such bliss. This travelling lark is easy I thought as I drifted to sleep.

I wasn't thinking that at 1.30 the next morning when Tom, who'd gone to sleep beautifully at the usual time of seven-thirty, was screaming with confusion because I wasn't pleased to see him. When people say travelling with children is hard work, they don't mean the journey. Carrying fifteen kilos of nappies, muslins, rattles, toys, clothes, a set of immunisations in a thermal flask and basic medication, just in case, stopping baby yelling during take off, changing nappies through turbulence and eating a meal with a sleeping child on your shoulder, are all easy compared with jet lag.

Tom and I spent the whole of our first week battling against sleep and insomnia, lying to Matthew that we hadn't dozed until ten then paying the price with the midnight scream session. In the mornings Tom looked like I felt, head lolling, blinking eyes straining to stay open, bemused as to why he couldn't stay longer under the cosy blankets. I felt my body was in Kyrgyzstan but insides somewhere else; contentment lost in a void between North Bristol and Bishkek. I missed home; missed the lopsided tick of the grandfather clock, missed the crackle of the fire and my attic bedroom with dark beams and childhood mementoes, a piece of my past frozen in time.

I plodded through days, stepping over half unpacked suitcases spilling across the floor, wondering if I'd ever feel happy again. I felt off-balance because our comforting routine had been left at Heathrow. I knew I should take Tom out into the city, introduce him to Umarzak the baker and Soviet architecture but I dreaded the return to bilingual shopping and wondered how I'd get back up the fifty-eight steps with a buggy. Without sleep I was swamped by loneliness and worries about what I'd do if I discovered I was missing something crucial which I couldn't buy in Kyrgyzstan.

It was easy to blame Bishkek for my depression, fooling myself that life would be perfect if we were still in North Bristol. Standing at the sink in the camping kitchen I thought, 'just get through January, then February's a short month. Your parents are coming in March and by April you'll be packing then out of here'. I don't know how I'd have reacted if someone told me then I'd still be there 18 months later.

Bishkek hadn't changed much. Bin *Babushka* was still wearing the same woolly tights, the contents of dairy counters were still a mystery to me and Playgroup was still on Wednesday afternoons. I'd promised Gina I'd bring Tom to meet them all, hoping talk of *kaimak* and pedicures would make me feel less isolated. We travelled to Playgroup with our new driver, also called Dema. I wasn't sure about having a driver, it sounded too colonial, but not wanting to trust Tom to the anchovy-tin taxis or drive myself I'd been left with little choice. Having someone to help carry shopping up fifty-eight steps was also useful.

Dema was Russian with Russian parents, a trucker with dark, weathered skin, gold teeth and smudged tattoos along his knuckles. His parents had moved to Kyrgyzstan as part of Stalin's Virgin Lands policy, farmers resettled to increase agricultural production. Dema had grown up on the shores of Issyk-Kul, starting out as a professional boxer and gymnast – very Soviet – before becoming a long distance truck driver ferrying clothes and refrigerated goods between Leningrad, Kiev and Moscow.

Five years ago he'd had a heart attack and lost his lorry license so now resorted to ferrying Tom and I between Playgroup, Bishkek City Market and home. Unlike Matthew's office Dema, my Dema didn't show any signs of wanting to leave, despite criticising Kyrgyz driving skills every time we went out. Although he had the Russian mentality of superiority I decided he was secretly passionate about his native homeland. Dema was a hunter and snuck off at weekends to fish or shoot fluffy creatures, returning with tales of snow-crested mountains and lush gorges which were so beautiful he thought he was in heaven. Well that's what I thought he said: as Dema spoke no English and I spoke terrible Russian I could never be sure. Directing him around town was awkward – until he realised I only went to three places.

I felt sad that we sat in silence for most journeys, polarised because the way the world had developed we used different grunts to communicate. Tom was our bond, a mutual link where language didn't matter. Dema adored Tom, fussing over him like a *babushka,* insisting on carrying him from the car to the door. As the only belts were in the front Tom sat next to Dema, facing back in his bucket seat. When Tom cried Dema crooned and reached over to stroke him, paying so little attention to the road so I felt sure we'd crash. Dema was proud of his tiny friend, yelling "meet my *Droog* – Friend – Tomas" to anyone he knew when we stopped at traffic lights.

We eventually got to Playgroup with the help of a map, much hand waving and a few u-turns – Dema wasn't used to someone saying right and pointing left. My first legitimate Playgroup, legitimate because I now had a child to play, was at Gina's. Her house was new, large and square with a scarlet roof because architects had decided this was the only was to inject some colour into the grey city. It looked like a toyshop had exploded in the playroom, the floor covered with discarded bits of plastic, all of which had vibrated at some time in their lives. In the sitting room brightly coloured fish were swimming across a television screen bigger than our kitchen – the ubiquitous 'Finding Nemo'.

Tom was sleeping angelically in his car seat which I lugged through the hallway, crashing it into the doorframe because I wasn't very good at steering with it yet. I sat at the end of the sofa, tucking Tom behind the arm in the hope no-one would stamp on him or spill tea on his head. When Tom was asleep it was easy to forget I had a baby, his waking cries always surprising me back into motherhood.

It felt bizarre to be back with the sorority as if I'd never left. In five months a few details had changed. I no longer had swollen feet, Susi had cropped her hair short and Alfie was walking, able to reach a new level of mischief. Sheela, Chitra's eldest child, had started at the International School, being dragged from innocence to the world of precocious princesses by Lola, Penny's daughter.

"Does anyone have any tips to combat jet lag? I'm so tired I just want to lie on the floor and cry."

"You'll be fine once you've got a nanny," Gina said soothingly. She spoke with such assurance it was obviously something they'd discussed. "Ilke, she's the new secretary of the Women's Club, has the list and there are lots of good ones available because a few families have just finished their tours."

"I don't want a nanny." There were audible gasps of horror.

"Not want a nanny? Why not?"

"Because I won't be going out to work."

"But you might as well take advantage of cheap wages," Penny reasoned.

"It's not about money." I had an image of motherhood and it didn't involve a stranger warming bottles while I went for a pedicure. I resented the assumption that a nanny was a requirement of living abroad. I was too jealous to share Tom. He was my baby and seemed too small and vulnerable to be left with someone else. I could imagine his face crumpling as I walked out of the door, bottom lip jutting, looking up at me with sad, wide eyes as if saying, 'mummy, what are you doing?' like he sometimes did when I placed him in his cot.

I felt strange enough when Matthew suggested I go shopping on my own, sad to be parted from Tom even for an hour, despite spending the morning wishing he'd go to sleep. Maternal emotions are complicated. Even after a difficult day when I'd craved my own space I often watched him sleeping, impatient for the morning when I'd be greeted by a gaping gummy grin and excited wiggle. I didn't feel quite the same at 5am.

"How are you going to shop if you don't have a nanny?" Anthea asked. I hadn't sussed shopping logistics yet, but wasn't about to admit it. In my world I was self-sufficient and proud. I wasn't about to hand over control of Tom's life to someone else, it felt strange enough passing some of my independence to Dema.

Feeling persecuted by the incredulous criticism I changed the subject.

"What's new in Bishkek?"

"Bey-da now stocks lasagne."

"And marmalade."

"And baby car seats!"

"Wow!" Had Bishkek's status as a capital city finally been recognised or had some entrepreneur reopened the Silk Road so that we didn't have to import everything we needed from China via England?

"There's even a new supermarket called Narodne." I'd already been there. It was modern, large and well-stocked but still intrinsically Kyrgyz – condoms called Stinger were sold at Narodne's checkouts. Apparently the chain was owned by Aidar, President Akayev's son, which was why it was smart and profitable and putting Europa out of business.

With the news that Birgit had left for Lima and Mary-Lou hadn't been seen since Quilt Camp, Tom started to wake up, little squeaks rising from behind the sofa. I lifted him onto my lap where he hunched, chin on jowls, watching four girls wrap sarongs around their heads, dictating parts to each other in endless games of 'let's pretend'.

"How old is he?" Anthea asked.

"Just over three months." He'd been born on 10th October, as foreseen in my dream. I didn't want to be psychic; it would be extremely tiresome to predict everything. Every time I dreamt Tom fell off a cliff we'd have to cancel family holidays to Cornwall. "And he weighs six kilos."

"How fascinating." I had yet to realise that only I was interested in the details of my child's life. I was however desperate to explain how we'd weighed Tom, proud of our resourcefulness.

"We put him in a bucket which we hung from sprung scales like the ones vegetable sellers use." Anthea looked bemused, Gina horrified. Tom had participated calmly in the procedure, peering over the edge with placid perplexity while Matthew hoisted him into the air and I made the nonsensical noises of encouragement you learn on becoming a parent.

"Why didn't you go to a clinic, why d'you wanna do everything naturally?" It was something Gina asked me frequently, unable to comprehend why I thought terry nappies preferable to disposable and ironing my own clothes preferable to moaning about how someone else did it. She certainly couldn't fathom living in an apartment without an elevator.

"Why d'you make your life difficult? I mean, how do you get up those stairs?"

"Slowly."

It had taken a few attempts but I'd finally worked out how best to leave the building with a baby. I'd started by carrying Tom down in the sling and erecting his buggy in the street, but by the time I'd unclipped all the straps of the sling, wrapped him in enough hats and layers to stop *babushkas* yelling at me and tucked him into his blankets it was time to go back up for the next feed.

A neighbour had offered use of their garage to store the buggy. I'd been excited about this solution until I'd tried to open the door and realised I needed muscles, a spanner and two hands, which wasn't something I had while carrying Baby Tom. Finally I'd resorted to loading up in the flat and bumping the buggy down the stairs, carrying it back up with Tom safely in it. I could cope with this solution as long as he didn't put on too many more kilos before we left in April.

Despite the fifty-eight steps I liked to take Tom for a walk every day. It eased the sense of loneliness and claustrophobia and helped me lose unwanted fat. I'd assumed I'd remain huge forever following pregnancy but the breastfeeding diet was the best one I'd ever been on: I indulged my cravings but weight dropped off, Tom sucking out calories at every feed. It was wonderful. I was now 'back in my jeans', the goal we all strive for, but I still had a flabby belly. In the mirror my midriff was a 'before' picture in an advert for liposuction. 'More walking, less Mars Bars' had been my New Year's Resolution, so Tom and I took to the streets of Bishkek.

Winter Bishkek was grey, so grey that sky and pavements merged and there was a risk of getting lost on the way home because every block looked the same. Iona had promised that winter Bishkek was sunny and beautiful, its imperfections hidden under inches of glistening snow. I'd been excited and nervous about snow. Excited because it would be novel to live in a country where there were extremes of seasons and winter meant blizzards, minus temperatures and wrapping up in furs. Nervous because if there were metre high drifts I'd get the buggy stuck and have to stay inside for three months.

I needn't have worried because so far we'd only had English snow – flakes which fell with such promise but melted by lunchtime. Everyone in Matthew's office said, again, that the weather was unusual for the time of year. Hadn't they realised that thanks to carbon emissions and El Niño there is no 'usual' weather any more?

On our excursions I re-familiarised myself with Bishkek's one-way grid system, practising my Russian by reading road signs in Cyrillic. On every corner were new apartment blocks. Clad in tiles of pink and yellow plastic, the latest architectural craze from China, they looked as though they'd been dropped from outer space.

The familiar Bishkek was still there. Old women with scales offered to tell you your 'correct' weight for 1 *som* – and a lower weight for 2 *som* I imagined. Hospital patients wandered around in velour dressing gowns and slippers. Newspaper shacks unashamedly sold porn magazines and children's toys; wind-up cars and fluffy blue kittens interspersed with naked women lounging back with legs spread, mobile phones covering their intimacies. Drivers were still maniacs, refusing to slow down even if a mother and child were crossing the road inches in front of them. I had to remind myself that zebra crossings were just for show and trolleybuses were allowed to drive both ways down *Moskovskaya,* even thought it was a one-way street.

Gradually I realised I must feel at home because I didn't flinch when people spat on my feet and no longer thought men in *ak-kalpaks* looked like overgrown Smurfs. I took Tom to see the New Year tree in Ala Too Square, a metal frame twenty-three metres high with 4000 fir branches slotted into it. I was relieved to discover that Lenin hadn't been scrapped. I found him relegated to a patio behind the museum where his face was in permanent shadow.

On his plinth was Erkendik, a bronze winged lady balancing on a huge ball. She'd been erected in time for August's Independence Day and waving her *tunduk,* was heralded as a symbol of freedom and Kyrgyz identity. But would she be enough to mend the north-south divide and unite tribes in the Ferghana Valley?

According to one Central Asian philosopher, 'no sovereignties can separate our peoples and our common culture', but in reality Kyrgyzstan is divided into the Russian north and Islamic south. Southerners believe northerners take all the prestigious jobs and northerners believe southerners are militant troublemakers. This image is not helped by disagreements between clans in the overpopulated Ferghana Valley, lacerated by Stalin's provocative cartography.

On the map Kyrgyzstan's Jalalabad, Osh and Batken *oblasts* pincer Uzbekistan, the gap closed by Tajikistan. The Ferghana Valley is the fertile heart of Central Asia. Not wanting it to become a powerful region of opposition, Stalin deliberately divided its assets giving Uzbekistan the cotton fields, Kyrgyzstan the water supply and Tajikistan the access, leaving controversial pockets of foreign land near the boundaries and large portions of ethnic groups in the wrong country – about 40% of the population of Kyrgyzstan's Ferghana is Uzbek.

During the Soviet Union no-one noticed, everyone crossing between Republics to visit family without problems. Independence turned administrative borders into international borders, exact positions of which are still contentious. Customs officials foment racial prejudice with indiscriminate rules and prohibitive visa prices. Families fight over land and ethnic supremacy, covertly planting apricot trees to claim ownership, cutting off water supplies and tearing down frontier posts. Tensions are exacerbated by poverty, the angry and displaced people more susceptible to the advances of Islamic militants.

If they ever invent Buggy Olympics, anyone living in Bishkek will have the best chance of winning. There are three categories: 'slalom' – how fast can you steer around piles of gob; 'off-road' – get in and out of ruts and potholes without ejecting baby across the pavement and 'assault course' – enter shops and apartment blocks while retaining dignity. I was relieved we'd rejected three large wheels in favour of four conventional ones: if Tom's buggy had been any bigger I'd never have fitted anywhere. As it was I had to stand like a starfish to force the lift doors wider at Susi's flat.

Bishkek is *not* wheelchair or buggy friendly. There are pits, bumps and pavements corrugated by protruding tree roots. Every shop door is perched above fiddly steps. Those who have built ramps fail to realise that their purpose is to ease the transition to a different level, not make them so steep baby would end up in Beijing if you let go at the wrong time.

But the buggy was useful for one thing – by the time I'd been to Beta Stores and back I finally knew how to identify every tribe in Central Asia. Kyrgyz silently helped carry the buggy up steps, apart from the *nouveau riche* living in the block next door who strutted to their black Mercedes with the arrogance of wealth in a poor country. Uzbek women clustered on corners pointed and laughed at the rain-cover as if they'd never seen such a contraption before.

Russian women were rude, barrelling me out of the way with mammoth bosoms. One gargantuan matriarch was so desperate to leave Bishkek City Market she stepped over the buggy I'd wedged across the threshold while I struggled to open the door. The door banged against Tom's feet while I stared after her in incredulous silence. I thought she was the woman who'd interrupted my timid enquiries for tofu at the deli counter with imperious demands to taste a picked mushroom. But then they all looked the same, these Russian matrons with brittle orange hair escaping fur hats, mouths puckered in disapproval of everything and hips the size of a Lada's boot, built to survive harsh winters.

Once I'd mastered pavements, doors and massive Slavs the last challenge was to work out how best to shop with a baby in Bishkek. Tom hadn't yet learnt to poo, sleep and eat at times regular enough for me to be able to book Dema without panicking we'd be ready so our shopping trips usually started with Dema waiting outside while Tom guzzled milk and I prayed he wouldn't projectile vomit it across the car.

The next problem was how to transport Tom. I started by taking him in the sling, heaving cartons of milk over his head onto the counter. He soon objected to this so I unclipped his car seat and wheeled him around with me. Realising I was having trouble steering a buggy and a trolley, Dema insisted on accompanying me, pushing Tom and advising which sort of honey to buy. This made me feel *really* colonial and uncomfortable about the slightest extravagance – Dema would never spend extra *som* on soft, white toilet paper when scratchy grey stuff did the job. It also prolonged homesickness. I felt I'd lost control because I had to shop at prearranged times and pretend not to want things Dema disapproved of.

Sensitive to this it was Dema who found the solution. The next week he announced that '*Malinki* – Little – Tomas' would be staying in the car with him.

"Tell Mummy you'll be fine because I'm your *Droog* Dema." When Tom grinned at him I realised I had no choice. It felt very odd walking into the supermarket without Tom. Dema could easily drive off and trade him on the black market for a set of new tyres – a healthy, blond baby would go for a fortune. Was I being completely irresponsible I wondered, freezing with panic as I reached for the butter?

Twenty nervous minutes later I cautiously peered around the shop door with my carrier bags. The jeep was still there and Tom was in it, smiling at Dema who was wiggling the fluorescent bug with dangly legs above his head. It was the start of a wonderful friendship. From that day Dema became Tom's Russian grandfather and his wife, Galena, Tom's *babushka*. She knitted him bootees, fussed about whether he wore hats and gave him jars of pickled vegetables – which I had to throw away because they were truly disgusting.

Chapter Fifteen – Nyet Balshoi

After a month I was happy to be in Bishkek again, the period of adjustment over. Tom and I were friends because he'd recovered from jet lag and I only had to get up once in the night to feed him. I'd sit on the sofa watching his cheeks bulge with effort and his eyes roll as he got drunk on hormones while the pink flush of dawn warmed the mountains. By the time Tom finished, peaks had transformed from soft grey to a jagged flash of white against a pale sky. Dozy with contentment I'd snuggle back into bed, marvelling at how huge Matthew's ears seemed after staring at Tom's dinky features.

I was proud and amazed by how much Tom had grown and developed purely on milk taken from me. According to The Books it was time to start weaning but I was tempted to just carry on breastfeeding. I wasn't planning on being one of those hippies who let their children suck when they get home from school but didn't think a few more months would hurt.

My reluctance to wean was as much about the psychological tear of Tom losing his utter dependence on me as it was about the hassle of sterilising bowls and spoons. Breastfeeding was portable and convenient; blending carrots was not. It was also due to nervousness about *what* to feed him. Everyone offered different advice – savoury first, fruit first, cereal first. I was confused until remembering my new tactic: follow your instincts. This was the key to motherhood. I'd discovered that if I relaxed I knew intuitively when baby should sleep and when I should eat Mars Bars. Once I'd learnt to trust this inner knowledge everything was less scary.

My instincts told me to buy baby rice and I eventually settled on a Russian brand, despite there being a demonic child wearing a bunny costume in a cornfield on the box. I had the instructions translated, just in case, but even I could work out that you just added water.

When I put a tepid spoonful of pulp into Tom's mouth he looked at me and frowned. I'm sure he would have said 'blurgh' if he could. Instead he spat it out: weaning was going to be challenging.

"Weaning in Kyrgyzstan is especially challenging," Susi told me, "because the range of food is so limited." Selfishly I'd felt only relief that I was going home to Tesco before Tom's dietary requirements became more complicated.

At the February Women's Club meeting Tom was accepted as an honorary male member, although no-one really understood why I wasn't leaving him at home with a nanny. There I met Ilke, new secretary of the Women's Club. She was blond, petite and, being Danish, an avid smoker: the perfect advertisement for her husband's cigarette company.

I sat next to a Kyrgyz woman. She satisfied the constitutional definition of 'international' because her husband was Welsh but exhibited prime Kyrgyz tendencies. Throughout the presentation about Tokmok Orphanage she lectured me in whispers that Tom had hiccups because he was cold.

"You don't get hiccups because you're cold," I hissed back.

"He should be wearing a hat," she persisted.

"It's hot in here. It's dangerous for babies to overheat."

"But he has hiccups, he needs more blankets." I didn't sit with her again.

Now I'd settled into Bishkek life with *Malinki* Tom and even survived an excursion – we'd taken him to Ala Archa National Park for his three-month birthday, he wasn't impressed – the ultimate test of coping with a baby outside safe 'home' territory was Mahjong at Anke's house. I hoped Tom wouldn't do an exploding poo and embarrass me in front of the German Ambassador.

Dema was impressed with our latest destination where a huge flag fluttered in the garden. A porter carried the car seat deftly into the house while I took off my shoes – you always remove footwear in Kyrgyzstan because no-one wants gob trampled across their carpets. Tom was placed in the middle of the drawing room where eleven ladies stopped playing to coo over him. He looked across at me and frowned at the attention.

While I transferred Tom to his bouncy chair, play resumed. I was to join the table of three where Anke and Mrs Shah, resplendent in pale blue shalwar-kameez and thick glasses, were teaching Ilke the rules. The room was elegant, furnished with Anke's trophies of her itinerant life; small Syrian inlaid tables, Persian rugs and sepia maps of countries where she'd lived. An open fire crackled in the corner, stoked by the porter. Its orange glow and soft hint of wood smoke gave the room a cosy feel.

Mrs Shah won the hand with a swift 'Windy Chow' and I helped shuffle the tiles.

"How's the newsletter going?" Anke asked. Ilke had started a monthly Women's Club newsletter and persuaded me to help. The first month they'd written about where to get pedicures. This month we were researching the more grisly issue of medical care. It was going to become an ex-pat bible. Ilke stubbed out her cigarette, promising she'd smoke the next one in the dining room away from Tom.

"We've collected lots of information but it's all rather scary. One American mission doctor told us that if you have a medical emergency in Kyrgyzstan it's best to be at peace with God."

Working on this newsletter wasn't helping my nerves. The lack of an emergency service was my biggest worry about returning to Bishkek with Tom, something I'd played down with the mineral-water-obsessing health visitor. For weeks I'd had recurring nightmares, dialling 999 to discover the telephone wasn't working or being told the ambulance wasn't available that day. I'd realised these dreams were manifestations of my fear that there was no-one to help. We were walking a tightrope and every day was another step without falling off.

"We're fine because we have a doctor at the embassy," Gina called helpfully across the room. "Although she's a little over cautious, she sent Abigail to London because she had stomach ache."

"This I can understand," Anke snapped, dealing thirteen tiles to each of us. "The Ambassador is furious because a consular officer had a burst appendix at the weekend and he was turned away from the clinic at the American base. They have the most modern equipment in the country and they won't share it!" Oh dear. Running to the base for help was Plan A if Tom was ill. We didn't have a Plan B.

"It's because he's a security risk," Gina said knowledgeably.

"So if I turned up at the gates with Tom they'd turn us away because we were a security risk?"

"Yep."

"How can a hysterical mother and dying baby be a security risk? What about the UK's special relationship with America? Won't that get me a dispensation?"

"When you're a US marine you can never be too careful."

The conversation was interrupted by a metallic version of 'Twinkle Twinkle Little Star' causing everyone to scrabble in handbags.

"Whose phone?"

"Sorry, it's Tom's musical bee." I looked down at him and he smiled, enjoying the power he'd discovered over a room full of gossiping women.

"So where are you suggesting we go Ilke, apart from church?" Anke asked tersely.

"I have found a very good hospice where they practise alternative therapeutic medicine," Mrs Shah said calmly. "I'll send you the details."

"Kyrgyz medicine is certainly alternative," Anke retorted. "Our consular officer had to have emergency surgery at the German Hospital, which I'm ashamed to say is like an abattoir. He was medi-vacced out yesterday."

"Tom has some real cute toys," Gina said passing with a fresh plate of *Apfel Strudel*. "I can't believe that bee also plays the Star-Spangled Banner!"

"Actually I think that's your mobile."

"Oh gee, you're right!" She grabbed at the phone clipped to her belt. Tom grinned again.

"There's a hospital on *Jibek Jolu* which is supposed to be alright," Chitra said, "but no-one's allowed in with the patient..."

"You can't even accompany children?" I interrupted. "I'd have to abandon Tom on the doorstep?"

"It has an infectious diseases ward, so they're nervous of contamination," Chitra explained.

"But you're hardly likely to want to go there if you'll come out with tuberculosis," Anke added.

"Is there no-where safe to go?" I asked, my voice growing shriller in my panic. "Penny, where do you take Lola?"

Penny looked apologetic: "to the Kumtor clinic."

I realised what immense corporate support some people had: security patrols checking your front door was locked, company doctors, PO Boxes, even drivers who'd do your shopping if you didn't want to go out. As Matthew was not attached to a huge international office in Bishkek I was starting to feel very isolated and vulnerable. Should we leave before anything happened? I felt ashamed even considering it, a failure because I wasn't tough enough to survive in a less developed country. But it was Tom I was worried about. How would I feel if he died from something a modern hospital could have cured?

It occurred to me to feel guilty about the Kyrgyz: we all had million-dollar medical insurance, hoping a high-tech aeroplane would arrive in time to rescue us in an emergency. Sheltered from modern developments, Kyrgyz have no expectations. In England we believe we have a *right* to be cured; when someone dies, doctors can be accused of negligence, the hospital sued. In Kyrgyzstan they accept the frailty of human life. When someone dies they bury them and kill a horse to feed the village at the wake, not demand a public enquiry. Although I wasn't condoning the lack of spending on Kyrgyz healthcare, I did wonder if we had become too precious and immortal in the West.

On Saturday 14th February the elite of Bishkek attended the International Women's Club Valentine's Day Fundraising Ball. We stayed at home because we didn't have a babysitter. Although plenty had been offered I wasn't leaving Tom with a stranger and didn't see the point in him getting to know someone when we were leaving in two months.

I could remain a recluse because I wasn't an A-lister wife. Not being married to an ambassador or banker, just a mere water-engineer on an Aid project, I wasn't expected to attend charity balls or embassy drinks receptions. I wasn't summonsed by the First Lady to attend compulsory lunches in the chalet at Ala Archa. In the Bishkek caste system, I was right at the bottom.

I was content with my social position; relieved I didn't have to dress up every night and remember to be polite. I'd only been coerced into one official World Bank dinner. It had taken place during one of the thunderous storms of our first summer. I'd spent the evening trying not to scoff at self-congratulatory toasts from useless but arrogant bureaucrats while rain hammered the roof and my pregnant ankles swelled under the table. I wasn't very good at propriety; I'd rather stay in and watch pirate DVDs from Tzum.

Ben spent the evening of the ball with us. Nicky was still abroad, having given birth to Siana, pronounced See-ah-na, in January. She was due back at the end of the month. Ben had returned early because he had an office job. 'Mr Sandwich Man' had become so popular that the local mafia had asked for protection money. Scared by their muscles and handguns, Ben had closed his business while he still had all bones intact. He'd found a safe job with an American NGO helping small businesses. His boss was an ex-pat who'd confided to Ben that he hated Bishkek. He'd had to bribe his wife with expensive gifts before she'd agree to relocate with him.

"It's not uncommon," I said authoritatively. "Gina was given a widescreen fifty-two inch plasma television as compensation for moving to Kyrgyzstan."

"My boss gave his wife breast implants."

1st March is officially the first day of spring in Kyrgyzstan. Dema had informed me of this and I replied by asking whether this meant people would finally remove their fur coats. For the past few weeks the sky had been clear and twenty degrees by lunchtime. There had been none of the ice Tina had warned me endlessly about slipping on; I'd not used the shoe chains Father Christmas had given me and felt cheated out of my Soviet winter.

Being English and accustomed to stripping at the first sign of sun, I enjoyed the warmth and wore t-shirts when promenading with Tom along *Erkendik*. This attracted stares of horror from locals who considered a display of bare arms in February reckless. Seasons are still Soviet in Central Asia. February is winter and in winter you wear fur, even if it is twenty degrees.

You also have the heating on. On the few occasions when it had been cold I'd been impressed by Soviet engineering. They may have sent artists and objectors to the gulag but they knew how to pipe hot water around a city. With district heating our flat was cosy day and night, wonderful when it froze outside but stifling when it was summer by mid February. With no thermostats to adjust I'd opened all the windows and felt guilty for letting expensive hot air escape when Kyrgyzstan was one of the poorest countries in the world and racking up huge gas bills with Kazakhstan and Uzbekistan. But I reasoned with myself that they did have the choice to turn it off. According to the Bishkek Observer the heating would be turned off on 31st March, whether or not it was snowing. This was the procedure in the former Soviet Union.

March was a bonus month for me. First there was Women's Day, celebrated in Kyrgyzstan with the passion Brits save for Christmas. Kyrgyz love national holidays – another remnant of Soviet times when anything was used to brighten drudgery. In Matthew's office they stuck rigidly to this protocol and there was always an excuse for a vodka party after work – Women's Day, birthdays, Wednesday.

On Women's Day everyone wandered around with bunches of flowers and synthetic cakes in huge boxes. Matthew made me breakfast in bed and Dema coyly presented the traditional gift; a carnation wrapped in cellophane. I felt like a princess.

The feeling persisted because a week later it was my first Mother's Day. Tom bought me a pendant from Tumar Art Salon and we went for Hyatt brunch. Sipping espresso I thought about being a mother. In all my daydreams I never imagined I'd be bringing up my first child in a third floor flat in Central Asia. For years I'd recited words in church service sheets about motherly love, sacrifice and hard work but I'd never really understood.

Now I knew what it meant to give yourself entirely to a child and my message to my mother that year had been drafted with sincere thanks for all the things I'd never appreciated. I imagined us as Russian dolls, she coming from inside her mother, I from her, Tom from me, our genealogy and bond of maternal love inherited through generations.

On 21st March it was *Nooruz*, 'НООРУЗ' in Cyrillic, a hippy celebration of the spring equinox, awakening of natural life and Muslim New Year. It was fêted with vigour in Bishkek. This meant more vodka, banners across Matthew's office windows and celebratory dancing in Ala Too Square by women wearing Christmas cake hats. You could smell the *shashlik* from our flat. The day ended, as always, with expensive fireworks which woke every baby and dog in the city.

The next day was my birthday. I was thirty, a monumental occasion marked by a tame tea party at the Hyatt because we didn't have a babysitter. I didn't feel thirty, but despite the Mother's Day pendant I didn't feel like a parent. Sometimes I'd look at Tom examining his fat knees in the bath and think, '*I* am *your* mother! It doesn't seem possible, I'm still too young and irresponsible and fond of loud dance music. How can I be a mother?'

At the end of this festival month of celebrating my parents, Bruce and Sue, arrived. I'd been worrying about their visit, concerned that by mixing my two parallel lives I'd violate a space-time continuum. Penny didn't help by warning that family vacations were stressful because having not seen each other for months you were together for an intense period in a place where you were at home and they were on holiday. Penny said her parents' stay had reminded her of the complications of family life and that there were advantages to only seeing them for half an hour a week on a web cam.

Despite such fears our week passed peacefully, a happy time which assuaged some of the guilt I felt for taking Tom away from his relations. Bruce and Sue were impressed by Tom's development. When they'd last seen him he was horizontal. Now he'd moved on to vertical life, eating in a high chair, drinking water from a cup – although he sometimes frowned in confusion at how he could be sucking and drinking when I was on the other side of the room – studying cloth books intently and sitting up straight in his play nest. The adoration was reciprocal: Tom loved having two more devoted play mates.

Contrary to Penny's moaning it's easy to entertain visitors in Bishkek. By the time you've been to Ala Archa, Sunday Hyatt brunch and Playgroup, got a crick in your neck studying the huge and violent pro-communist-anti-American ceiling mural at the museum, bought vegetables at the *bazaarchik*, walked across Ala Too Square to find Lenin, admired the latest creations of the Blind Artisans of Kochkor and met Bin *Babushka*, the week is almost gone. For my parents' visit nature contributed extra entertainment by offering three-out-of-four seasons in one week. On Wednesday it snowed, Thursday was a spring thaw and by Friday we were eating lunch in the Navigator garden worrying about Tom getting sun burnt.

On Saturday we went bargain hunting at Dordoi bazaar. Although I'd shopped weekly in the market in Aswan and was therefore a veteran of having my bum grabbed and carts rammed at me, I'd not been a regular customer at Bishkek's many bazaars. I'd been put off by trips in the rain with Leyla, stumbling after her through miles of narrow alleys hoping no-one would mug a pregnant lady.

Dordoi bazaar was hyped by ex-pats as being one of the most dangerous places in the world. At first I scoffed at this but with Leyla chanting "hol yo bag clo coz dey steal ev ting" on every corner and Playgroup gossip about which diseases Penny might have caught from the rusty blade which slashed at her bag, I'd stuck to Bishkek City and Beta Stores. To me this was a failure because Dordoi was where the locals bought everything.

Allegedly the biggest market in Central Asia, Dordoi sold everything you wanted and everything you didn't want but would buy anyway because the prices were so cheap. But you had to be able to find the right stall. It was a maze of shipping containers, stacked up and overhanging each other to create a medieval city with damp muddy streets, pick-pocketing urchins and the risk of slops being thrown on your head.

To get there we drove north towards Kazakhstan. Leaving the familiar streets of Playgroup and Mahjong the city became low-rise and bedraggled, dilapidated cottages and shacks lining side streets rutted with thick mud. Surrounding the market was a gypsy encampment of rusty caravans and hovels made of corrugated iron. Women hunched over cooking fires, the smoke collecting above the dwellings in a smog of stale fat, body odour and human excreta. Dema muttered as crowds pushed around the jeep and I wondered whether it was sensible to include Dordoi Bazaar in the Bishkek tour.

Our goal was to find a winter coat for Sue because Dordoi was rumoured to offer a large, well-priced collection. I knew that the coat section was in the top left corner of the market so we pushed through the main arterial street, shoved mercilessly by shoppers, ladies selling *samsi*, boys pushing carts loaded with jeans and young men hustling fake Rolexes. We burst from this melee into an open yard of stalls surrounded by containers stocked with fur, sheepskin and leather coats from Italy and synthetic copies from China. As we wandered round, poking through the stock, vendors shouted their sales pitch, a rapid fire of why we should choose them above the hundred others.

Eventually Sue chose a caramel coat all the way from Spain. While she turned left and right by the mirror, I looked nonchalantly at leather jackets, the container bursting with styles because leather was the spring fashion once winter fur was discarded. Tentatively I tried one on. It didn't fasten across the chest so I hurriedly hung it back up. Ruslan, the owner, had spotted my interest.

"You want coat, we can find big." He stepped out into the yard and yelled, "ALL SELLERS MOBILISED TO FIND THE LARGEST COAT IN CENTRAL ASIA FOR THE HUGE ENGLISH!"

Stall holders ran in and out with samples, discussing just how enormous this coat needed to be to zip over my boobs. I was used to such indignities: whenever I ventured near Bishkek clothes shops, teeny assistants would greet me with 'nyet balshoi' – 'nothing big' while I struggled to drag Tom's buggy up the steps.

"Actually, I'm looking for a bag," I snapped at one girl. "Even fat people can use those."

Thanks to Ruslan's perseverance I did buy a coat. It was three-quarter-length black leather, fitted and very elegant – size XXXXL. I wasn't upset: as an assistant in a bra shop once told me when I was crying over my measurements, "they're only letters, it's how you look that matters."

We recovered from the Dordoi experience at Twelve Chimneys, the restaurant in Alamyedin valley which I'd heard about at my first ladies lunch. It was a favourite with the local mafia. They sat on sheepskins in booths around open fires – hence the name – drinking vodka while waiting for the rabbits they'd chosen from the cage at the entrance to roast.

We sat inside the log cabin and chose more conventional Kyrgyz food; shashlik, lepioshka and soup with bits floating in it. Outside a river roared over boulders and a plume of smoke rose like a pillar from a wooden shack where an old woman was curing dead squirrels. The sky was a strip of blue between towering grey mountains and a huge eagle swept low over the valley. His wingspan was longer than Dema's jeep and he flew so close, talons outstretched, that I worried he'd pluck Tom from his buggy, mistaking him for a rabbit in his fluffy coat.

My parents left early on Tuesday morning. I was sad to see them go, plunged again into loneliness and the necessity of bumping Tom down the fifty-eight steps to find entertainment. The end of their holiday reminded me that soon we'd be saying goodbye to Bishkek, Dema, Valentina and our little flat which was doing its best to be a home.

We'd become accustomed to brown and Tom loved the grotesque chandelier in the sitting room. He lay under it watching light gleam through the crystals. Matthew and I assumed this chandelier was where the National Security Services bug was hidden; they were bound to be listening, this was the former Soviet Union. One of Matthew's engineers had been threatened after mentioning on the telephone that he would not be favouring a contractor just because he was related to the governor of Talas.

With my parents gone I started my 'last few weeks' routine. I was busy purging my wardrobe when Matthew phoned from the office. Ken had collapsed with terrible stomach pains and they were worried he had a burst appendix. I was being consulted as a contributor to the Bishkek International Women's Club medical newsletter. We'd headed it 'What would you do in an emergency' in the hope our provocative editorial would prompt someone to rectify the situation. Unfortunately someone was now expecting me to answer this rhetorical question.

"So what was the conclusion, what do we do in an emergency?"

"Pray."

"Ken's atheist."

"Call the ambulance."

"We did, they said it was busy."

"Initiate international negotiations to get into the Kumtor clinic."

"Kumashai wants to take him to Hospital Number 4."

"Don't go there, that's the one with the infections diseases unit."

"So where do we go?"

Ken ended up at the German clinic, rushed into emergency surgery as the sun set over Bishkek. Lakshai, his wife, wailed with despair because this was where the Korean man had died and the German consular officer had been medi-vacced from a few weeks before. We all wondered; would Ken survive the night?

Chapter Sixteen – Colostomy Bags

Ken survived the operation. It was the after-care that nearly killed him. The doctors reported that it wasn't his appendix but a perforated colon and they'd operated, just in time, in accordance with their *precass*. The problem was that they didn't seem to have a *precass* on what to do next.

"A few more hours in that clinic and he'll be dead," Matthew announced after visiting with Luigi. "They're giving him oxygen straight from the bottle so he'll have pneumonia by morning and shit is dripping all over the floor because they've given him a colostomy but don't have any bags. Luigi's considering calling the medi-vac team and Bill's trying to remember what he did last time a British citizen was ill."

This was the emergency we all prayed would never happen. Selfishly I was glad it wasn't happening to us and that within the month we'd be back in the care of the NHS – until our next posting. For months the company had been seeking Matthew's permission to include him on proposals for new projects. Every day Matthew came home talking about a new, exciting destination and we'd start to imagine ourselves living there.

The problem was that Matthew was asked whether we'd go to a country at the beginning of the tender process. This meant that even if the company won the project, by the time the tender had been evaluated by central committees, local no-objections obtained and personnel approved by beneficiaries and donors there had usually been a military coup. The Pakistan guidebook never made it out of the cellophane. To avoid disappointment we made a rule – no guidebooks or gazing at enticing pictures on the Internet until all contracts were signed.

Then there was the tantalising idea we'd had that after Bishkek we might settle in England. Although many ex-pats advise that once you start travelling it's hard to give up the adrenaline rush and go 'home', I wasn't convinced I wanted to spend my whole life packing, unpacking, finding new supermarkets and friends and dragging children between schools.

I'd grown up under the scrutiny of a village community which, although intimidating at times, had given me a safe feeling of belonging. My friends were children of my parents' friends and I wanted Tom to enjoy that security of history and the commitment of generations. But it's easy to forget the difficulties of itinerant life with the lure of a new country. When Matthew said "how d'you fancy a year in Cambodia?" I didn't think "oh, we'll miss the village fete" or hesitate remembering the miseries of transition, but "fantastic, I've always wanted to go to Angkor Wat."

Some were incredulous that we even considered settling.

"Are you sure you want to go West? Back to traffic jams and over population and doing your own ironing? Where's home anyway? I've been gone so long I feel more foreign in the country of my birth." This was the opinion of Lauren, a new friend I'd met on the newsletter committee. American, single and restless, I envied her lack of ties. She didn't feel obliged to settle like I did because she had no family; no grandparents waiting to get to know their grandson.

"And I hope you realise how hard it will be. Reverse culture shock is much more painful. From crazy places like Bishkek it's easy to assume the first world is perfect but when you get there you realise that they have power cuts too. The difference is no-one will come to fix it for three days and when they do it costs hundreds of dollars. It drives me mad when women here moan about how hard life is. They don't realise that they'll never have it so easy as being rich in a poor country. Okay, so you can't buy haloumi cheese or ready meals but we never have to wait at bus stops in the rain or save money for anything. We don't have to cook or clean if we don't want to and there's even someone to paint our toes if we can't be bothered to bend. You really wanna give all that up?"

But I was tired of everything being temporary, of borrowing Aigul's tasteless crockery when we had beautiful wedding presents sitting in boxes in Bristol. When we went to England I stared enviously at every house we drove past. I was jealous of front gardens, washing lines, cosy conservatories and sitting rooms lined with shelves of books I could see through the glow of bay windows.

At the age of 30 I'd never had my own home. I craved somewhere to unpack all my belongings so I could stop wondering which country I'd left my jacket in. I wanted normality; cats, chickens, a vegetable garden, milk delivered to the front door, a bathroom with a bath in it and stairs I'd only climb to go to bed. Secretly I was hoping that none of the projects with Matthew's name on would be won so we could slink back to England and retire into routine. Maybe I was naïve to trade short-term travelling misery for regular misery of traffic jams and expensive food shopping, but I felt ready to try.

Ken's colon couldn't have perforated at a worse time. With scheme designs completed and approved by the thirteen signatories around the world, contracts tendered and won by whoever paid the biggest bribe to Mr Turdibayev, the ground thawed in high villages and risk of landslides lessened, the construction season was about to begin.

It was Ken's job to oversee the reservoir building, chlorination system installation, well drilling, pipe laying and pump fitting in the seventy sites in Naryn, Talas and Issyk-Kul oblasts, but neither the insurance company or Lakshai were keen on letting him travel across Kyrgyzstan with his colostomy bags. Ken was desperate to get back to work, insisting he was healthy between bouts of vomiting. When yellow puss started oozing from his wound the medi-vac team was finally summoned. Horrified by the condition of their

155

patient he was air-lifted to Helsinki leaving the project short of a chief engineer. Matthew was asked to step in and our departure date started to slip.

While we waited for news of our future I concentrated on enjoying the gorgeous spring April had turned into. The heating had gone off as promised on 31st March but as it was thirty degrees on 1st April no-one cared. Winter – not that we'd really had one – had left for good and we were appreciating a spring which had leapt into summer. Skeletal trees swelled into avenues of rustling green and the city smelt sweetly of lilac – until children picked it all. Playgroup was hosted in shaded gardens across the city, Susi and I spent afternoons promenading on *Erkendik* and Anke was once again serving coffee and strudel under cherry trees fluffy with blossom.

We went for walks and picnics in the foothills with Ben, Nicky and Siana. Shepherds watched their herds as they grazed slowly along the hillside. One leaned on a staff, another hunched over a thick leather saddle, his *ak-kalpak* low on his forehead. The meadows were spotted with scarlet poppies, delicate forget-me-nots and tulips. Fresh mornings of cornflower sky and the smell of cut grass made everyone smile because they could taste the summer ice-creams at Issyk-Kul. If spring had been like this a year before I wouldn't have spent my first three weeks in Bishkek wanting to leave.

Matthew's new duties started almost immediately and on the anniversary of our arrival in Central Asia he went up the mountains to investigate site delays. This time he went to Naryn, a town two thousand metres above sea level, pit stop to the Torugart pass and invitingly labelled the coldest town in Kyrgyzstan.

I asked him not to be too harsh on the Kyrgyz engineers, remembering they'd not had the benefit of years of expensive training in international contracting methods. He replied he was always fair but claiming two thousand dollars for delays due to the curse of the Mountain Ghost was straining even his patience – and unlikely to be reimbursable under World Bank rules.

In the remote village of Kyzyl-Jyldyz it transpired that the delays were not so much to do with the curse of the Mountain Ghost as the curse of home-brewed vodka. By the time Matthew arrived on site, the adults who were supposed to be working lay comatose in ditches while trenches for pipes were being dug ineffectually by five-year old boys.

"Why aren't you at school?" Matthew snapped.

"Because we don't have any shoes and these men pay us 1 *som* to dig."

The elders, withered men with gnarled brown faces and straggly white goatees,[18] tried to console Matthew with *besh barmak*. *Besh barmak* is a prized national dish made by boiling a sheep and hacking it into huge pieces. The best meat is shredded, placed on noodles, sprinkled with eyes and brains and served with a cold broth. The head is passed round separately so that

---

[18] hence their collective name, *aksakals*, white beards

diners can slice off pieces of scalp and ears. Unsurprisingly, this gesture did not improve Matthew's mood.

Back in Bishkek my week wasn't going any better. I felt vulnerable without anyone to share parenting anxieties and Tom morphed into a horror baby, sapping the dregs of my energy with incessant grizzling. Much as I loved him I wished he had a pause button. In Soviet Kyrgyzstan parents who couldn't cope enrolled children in institutions. I considered taking Tom to the Tokmok orphanage where I knew he'd be cared for by donations from the International Women's Club.

It might have helped if there'd been a friend to talk to who wouldn't think me mad for not having staff. I felt pressurised because all around me women were relinquishing their roles to paid help then complaining when their children called nanny "mom". Although I now understood why parents succumbed to tactics I'd ignorantly disapproved of, I clung stubbornly to the standards I'd set myself when Motherhood was just an idealistic image, afraid that if I let go just a little my principles would clank past like a heavy anchor chain gaining momentum.

Walking to Playgroup I was cheered by the sight of a woman whose hair matched her pale pink outfit. She was buying Shoro. Shoro was a local drink; a brown, fizzy yeast drink, almost as disgusting as *koumys*. During summer women wearing blue caps and aprons sat for twelve hours a day behind barrels of Shoro. Normally I thought it a desperately boring job but that day I had a terrible realisation – I wanted to swap. I wanted to sit behind a barrel reading a book and turning a tap every ten minutes rather than deal with Tom's demands, cries, nappies and lunch refusals. Was that any way for a Good Mother to feel? What I was yet to realise was that a couple of hours off wouldn't make me a Bad Mother but a happier Good Mother when I was with Tom. That concept was still forming somewhere in my subconscious.

Gina spent Playgroup hassling me about hiring a nanny so I could go on Women's Club excursions. I tried to explain about breastfeeding and being at the centre of my child's upbringing, despite the desire to institutionalise him sometimes. Gina just frowned. "But these excursions are fun. Last week we visited the Blind Artisans in Kochkor and next month we're going to Burana Tower." Burana Tower was the oldest monument in Kyrgyzstan. In fact, it was the only monument in Kyrgyzstan, unless you counted Tzum. It was made of bricks, rumoured to date from the eleventh century and leaned slightly to the right. I'd taken my parents and Tom had thrown up all the way home.

To compensate for my maternal and social failures I busied myself with household jobs, calling Aigul to say we'd had another electricity bill and could she please pay it before we were cut off. Unfortunately this just served as a reminder that I still couldn't communicate in Kyrgyzstan because an hour later Larissa our caretaker was on the doorstep with Igor the Master to fix our electricity. 'Master' is the Soviet term given to those with a skill. What Igor's skill was I never learnt, it took him all day to change a plug.

"It's a Soviet attitude," Kumashai explained when I called to ask her to translate. "Without competition there was no incentive to work well or quickly. You wanted an electrician, you got an electrician. My Uncle was a Master. He told me, 'the government pretends to pay us so we pretend to work'."

Igor shrugged when Larissa explained there wasn't any work after all. I was relieved he didn't come in because it usually took the rest of the week to exorcise the smell of his body odour. Matthew returned late that night from Naryn. Exhausted by the strain of sulking and being alone I wasn't very welcoming.

At times like this Matthew and I played what's known in the parenting trade as Martyr Poker, competing for the hand filled with most hardship.

"I've had two days bumping up and down in a car, being shouted at by villagers who want their free water faster, firing contractors who only got jobs because their daughters are married to Mr Turdibayev's cousins and then being forced to eat cold sheep's intestines."

Matthew wasn't feeling well. He'd drunk fourteen shots of vodka because there were fourteen people at the meeting and they all had to make a toast. Engrossed in my own woes I was unsympathetic.

"Well poor you! While you were driving through beautiful valleys seeing what this country is really like…" I was still very resentful that I'd not been further than Bishkek City Market in months "…I've been picking tuna vomit from the cracks of Tom's buggy."

"It serves you right for feeding him tuna."

"I'm trying to give him a balanced diet which isn't very easy because tinned tuna is the only fish I can find." Weaning in Kyrgyzstan was tricky – I remembered with regret the smugness I'd felt when I thought we were going home before Tom's dietary requirements became more complicated. Friends in England recommended avocado, Petit Filou, sweet potato and cod loin, which didn't help because I couldn't buy any of those and was left trying to convince Tom that cauliflower was delicious. Kyrgyz children were brought up on *koumys* and mutton fat.

"If that's the worst of your day then I don't know why you're complaining."

"Will you let me finish my hand! While the buggy was drying I walked to Beta Stores with Tom in the sling. They took so long at the checkout trying to find out how much pasta costs because the bar codes weren't working, again, that Tom started screaming because he was late for a breast feed so I ran home with him and he did a sloppy poo which smeared all up his back and out over my top. How's that!"

"I've had to eat two sheep heads in one day."

"Serves you right for bringing us here in the first place."

"And I've eaten *besh barmak* three times in two days."

"But you've seen real *yurts* lived in by nomads rather than tourists."

"I'm still at work."

"I work longer hours than you with your vodka parties and *besh barmak* lunches. Maybe one day I'll go out and see amazing things and you can stay here and purée apricots for your son." Eventually we decided on a draw and went to bed. People who have kids to 'save their marriage' are idiots. A third, demanding, irrational dependent person puts huge strain on even the strongest couple.

The next night it was my turn to go out and drink vodka because it was Ladies Night. I've never been good at girly things. At school and university most of my mates were rugby players who I cheered from the touchline on Sunday mornings, surrogate boyfriends for the ones I couldn't get. I felt more comfortable around lads and although of course I did have some female friends, half the women at my hen night were wives of male friends.

In Bishkek that changed and for the first time in my life I was part of a pack of women. Although I often found this oppressive I had the sense not to exclude myself. The Women's Club was a fraternity: we might not always like each other but we needed each other and at no time was that more evident than when Kyrgyzstan disintegrated into political anarchy and revolution.

Going out in Bishkek was a novelty for me, possible now because Tom was growing up and I was no longer completely tied by the link between nipple and demanding mouth. My first night out was Celebrity Bartender at the Hyatt where Ilke was mixing cocktails to raise money for the Tokmok orphanage. I'd felt socially inept and insecure; out of practise at small talk, standing around holding drinks and dressed-up glamour.

I always looked less groomed and glossy than everyone else. I'd intended to be a Yummy Mummy but never seemed to have time to ensure I left home with immaculate clothes and matching lipstick. Instead, while Dema waited patiently on the doorstep, I'd be desperately wiping yoghurt off my shirt and scraping wild hair into scrunchies. For Celebrity Bartender I'd managed to style my hair without a scrunchie and Ilke noticed.

"Your hair, it's so long! And no glasses! You look so much better!" I'd resolved never to leave the house in a scrunchie again, an ambition which lasted until the following Wednesday when Tom projectile vomited macaroni cheese across the kitchen ensuring there was no time left for hair styling and make-up.

Ladies Nights were initiated by Jenna in the hope she'd find some fun in Bishkek. Jenna, an American, had just arrived from Almaty in Kazakhstan with husband Dirk and girls Eleanor and Lucy. Dirk was tall and dark with a cheeky grin and only managed to be sensible when he was at work as head of a development bank. Jenna was tall and slim with wavy blond hair and wore all the clothes you see in Vogue but never think to buy. She had an enviable ability to dress and accessorise naturally so that she always looked glamorous and poised and never as if she'd just dashed out of the house ten minutes late having lost her car keys. Despite feeling small and frumpy when I stood next to Jenna, I liked her and Dirk. They were fun and funny and most importantly, having lived in London for eight years, appreciated the subtleties of sarcasm and didn't misuse the word 'fanny'.

Dirk and Jenna loved nothing more than a huge party, so it was unfortunate for them that they'd moved to Bishkek where the most exciting social event since Anatolian Breeze had been a *shyrdak* exhibition in the museum. Matthew and I weren't bothered by this somnolence; we were still excited about the range of international restaurants in Bishkek compared to Aswan. It also saved us addressing the conflict of wanting to be young and dance all night but needing to be in bed by ten-thirty.

The turn out for Ladies Night was impressive: Nicky, Penny from Kumtor, Ilke and Gina. Chitra and Anthea were special guests; as they were soon to leave Bishkek this was billed as their farewell party. The evening turned into a club crawl. Not because we were decadent but because we couldn't find anywhere we liked. With hundreds of clubs and bars Bishkek should have had a thriving nightlife. Unfortunately there was an undercurrent of seediness. Bars were filled with male ex-pats seeking compliant companions and club proprietors had yet to realise that some people liked to go dancing without sex involved.

At every disco we visited someone was pole-dancing in the middle of the floor. At Equinox a pouting blond with huge breasts rubbed herself up and down the pole. At Pyramid an effeminate man dressed as a Boy Scout stripped down to red hot-pants. At Arbat a petite oriental girl twirled upside-down in a diamante g-string. When she finished a *babushka* in a floral dress shuffled out to wipe down the pole.

We ended up at First Club, allegedly owned by Aidar Akayev, playboy son of the president. The music was good, the lasers were good. It was a huge space and in London it would have been full. Unfortunately we were the only eight people in it, apart from a barman and three girls dancing apathetically on the bar in bikinis and stetsons. Clubs were too expensive for most people in Bishkek. Nightlife for them meant promenading though Ala Too Square, eating popcorn, having group photographs taken in front of the White House and performing bad karaoke songs under *Erkendik's* statue.

Conversation at First Club was predictable. We'd discussed our children, moaned about our husbands and were now dissecting any interesting relationships in Bishkek. Next we'd talk about Zarema, Jenna's housekeeper. We'd not known Jenna long but we already knew a lot about Zarema.

Did you hear about the new young Kumtor engineer?" Penny asked. As a Kumtor wife she always knew their gossip. "He's been forced into marrying his local girlfriend because she's pregnant."

"That girl was with a marine last month," Anthea said disapprovingly. "As he went home without her I presume she wasn't going to let this foreigner get away."

"And then there's Paul from Holland," Penny continued. Paul from Holland had arrived six months ago with a wife and family, employed a young nanny and was now moving the nanny in to his house and the family back to Holland. This was further incentive not to get a nanny, if any more were needed.

"Mary Lou always said it was hard being a spouse in Bishkek because you never knew when someone was going to try and lure your husband away."

"I suppose Paul's wife would agree."

The song changed and one of the girls jumped down to the floor and started gyrating against a bar stool, undeterred by the improbability of eight gossiping women tucking fifty dollar notes into her thong.

"You'll never guess what I caught Zarema doing," Jenna said sensationally

"Feeding strawberries to the dogs?"

"Arranging the fly swats in a vase?"

"No, that was last week. Today I found her washing oil paintings with soap and water, about to chip the lumps of paint off. I feel awful about firing her as her wage supports the whole family, but I'm nervous about having her in the house. On Monday she let the plumber into a room where I was naked on a table having a massage! She's gotta go."

Nicky's mobile beeped. "It's Ben. He says he's won fifty dollars and wants to know which club the blond with the big boobs was dancing at." Dirk had taken all the husbands to a casino.

"We should never have let them go out alone!" Gina said hysterically. "They're probably being hassled by prostitutes."

"I had an email from Birgit," Anthea said. "She's in Lima and wrote how nice it was being in restaurants without prostitutes."

"Is she a prostitute or going to a costume party dressed as one?" We turned to look where Jenna was pointing. A girl had just arrived wearing white hot-pants so tight her g-string made a VPL. A black shirt was tied under her boobs and plastic shoes with a wedge heel made her bottom wiggle. I assumed she was making the most of her figure before bloating into a *babushka* and commented that I was jealous of her flat tummy.

"Being that ugly she needs something to compensate," Gina sniped. Our insecurity was making us bitchy. "What have these girls got to offer apart from skinny legs and sex?"

"Yesterday I saw a girl wearing a chiffon skirt and no underwear," Ilke announced scandalously, stubbing out another cigarette. "It was disgusting. You could see *everything*, bum cheeks behind and dark triangle in front."

"Was she Russian or Kyrgyz?" Penny asked.

"I don't know," Ilke shrugged. "I wasn't looking at her face!"

During the next pause in the music the dancing girls wiggled down off the bar, pouting swollen lips so good for their trade. Their gyrating friend let go of the bar stool and stalked after them, looking contemptuously in our direction.

"These girls are all fanny, we could do much better," Gina said defiantly. "C'mon Saf-fee-ya, let's dance." She grabbed my hand and I climbed self-consciously onto the bar, dancing awkwardly until I realised there was no-one to witness our disgrace. Ilke, Penny and Jenna got up too while Nicky, Chitra and Anthea laughed and took photos. Could I still dance on bars and retain my dignity or was I just 'Tom's mum' embarrassing herself? I'd never felt more like an ex-pat wife, making a fool of myself in an empty bar while my driver waited outside. Being an ex-pat was fun when you got used to the strangeness. Maybe I would miss the craziness if we settled in England. Maybe we should consider another posting, if offered, after all.

Chapter Seventeen – Learning to Love Soviet Concrete

"What would you think about staying here longer?" Matthew had returned from work loquacious with the joys of Kyrgyzstan after another office vodka party and a letter from grateful village elders thanking him for the wonderful water system which meant their children didn't have Hepatitis and women had more time for cooking. Ken had been forbidden to return to Bishkek by the insurance company and Luigi was looking for a replacement.

I looked out of the window. The mountains were clear against a blue sky, clouds suspended between glistening peaks. It was a good Bishkek day so I didn't say no immediately. But I did have reservations.

"I'll never get Tom up the stairs."

"He'll be able to walk soon."

"Two more summers without a garden."

"We could move to a house." I imagined myself sunbathing in a paradise like Anke's and started to feel less objectionable.

There were advantages to staying; we had friends and I knew where the supermarkets were. And I might get to stay in a *yurt* after all. Tentatively I said yes. Nothing was definite because DFID and Mr Turd had to agree to Matthew taking the position. Ageism is rampant in the engineering profession so as Matthew wasn't a bearded octogenarian in a tank-top they might not think him capable of Ken's job. Ageism is also rampant in Kyrgyzstan – it was difficult for Matthew to gain the respect of *aksakals* when he looked as though he were only 21. But, on being told it was likely we were staying for two more years, the words of Diana Shipton, diplomatic wife of the 1900s, rattled in my head: 'Mentally, I began immediately to pack and to plan.'[19]

For Matthew the extension just meant sitting longer at his desk, for me it was a question of logistics. My inventory for Tom was only relevant until April. Compiling, purchasing and packing what we'd need for two more years in Bishkek was going to involve a lot more questions and research.

After the scare of Ken's illness there were also the medical considerations of staying. We now knew there was no safety net under our tightrope and I woke at night sweating cold fear about Tom being taken ill and us helplessly watching him die. I reasoned with myself that life is all about balancing risk, finding a compromise between safety and reality, caution and sense. Staying in England wasn't necessarily the answer. According to some statistics the most dangerous occupation there was driving your children to school,

---

[19] Quoted in Daughters of Britannia – Katie Hickman

something I'd do without questioning. Maybe the safest place was a *yurt* in the mountains – apart from the risk of tick encephalitis.

In Aid work there's rarely a definite answer to a specific question so rather than Matthew receive a contract and start date for his new position, he just drifted into the role because we didn't object too strongly to staying.

After evenings of listing the pros and cons of moving to a house or staying in our flat, we'd decided to stay, as long as Aigul renovated the kitchen. I felt safe up here when Matthew was away and we didn't have any of the worries plaguing those in houses: mould in cellars giving children strange chest infections, strangers peeing in gardens and endless deliberations about whether to employ a security guard. No-one was quite sure whether they offered protection or acted as billboards advertising where the rich foreigners lived – everyone had heard the story about the guard who told his friends when to come and steal the television.

We traded simplicity for the freedom of a garden and I learnt how to manoeuvre a buggy up fifty-eight steps. If we'd known when we first arrived that Bishkek would be home for three years rather than four months we'd have done things differently: bought a car, made more effort to learn Russian, found a house we felt safe in and shipped out more possessions. But living with the insecurity that the project and our stay in Bishkek might end abruptly, we didn't want to be financially entrenched. We made the right decision for our circumstances and I tried not to look back with regrets. We were hybrid ex-pats, not entirely committed to a life of displacement so leaving most of our belongings at home base. The trick was to make our temporary life seem as permanent as possible without spending too much of the money we were saving for our future permanent life.

For comfortable long-term occupation Matthew's priority was broadband Internet, probably the most advanced technology available in Bishkek. Technology has changed the isolation of living abroad. Unlike my diplomatic heroines from the past, I didn't watch the road for the post chaise, yearning for contact with home. I didn't have to yearn because I had fax, email, web cams and Skype. In modern ex-pat life letters are just nostalgia, which was fortunate in Bishkek because the post chaise rarely arrived. Letters took about four months from England – probably not hastened by someone writing 'RUSSIA' across the address – and were dumped unceremoniously in the stairwell.

The only annoyance of this, apart from feeling unloved on birthdays, was not being able to reliably receive supplies from home. This was a problem I shared with my diplomatic heroines; for us 'any small luxuries...assumed an almost agonising importance'.[20] They'd wanted fashionable clothes; Catherine Macartney in Kashgar was most distressed when her brown velour

---

[20] Daughters of Britannia – Katie Hickman

winter hat trimmed with ostrich feathers arrived squashed. I wanted the latest Harry Potter book. I had to re-learn patience and ask courier favours when friends travelled. This was a valuable lesson in wanting but having to wait; something we no longer do in the West with the expectation of immediacy cyberspace has given us.

My priority for comfortable long-term occupation was removing more brown from the flat, an aim usually made more urgent when I returned from Playgroup at Jenna's house. Jenna lived in the most gorgeous house in town, a large, L-shaped wooden cottage with a veranda running the length of it, overlooking a secluded garden of apple trees. Inside, colourful rugs, eclectic furniture, travel curios, modern art and children's drawings were arranged with Jenna's inimitable sense of style. Everyone wanted to move in with Jenna.

As that wasn't possible I made pathetic attempts at mimicry. I bought cushions and lamps from the Blind Artisans of Kochkor and went on a Women's Club trip to see some artists, returning with a large oil painting. I even paid a huge amount of dollars to have cream sofa covers made. Someone at the American Embassy had told me the seamstress was cheap but her bill was as much as Matthew's engineers earned a month. Money was difficult to quantify in Bishkek: rumour was waitresses were paid 4 *som* an hour, which wouldn't even buy a *lepioshka*.

Our joint priority for comfortable long-term occupation was learning Russian and we'd started taking lessons together. This was a mistake. While I'm a reluctant linguist, Matthew revelled in the obscure points of grammar.

"Note that the neuter third person singular accusative form is like the masculine accusative form not like the neuter nominative," he read from the text book during a homework session.

"How does that help me buy carrots?"

"It's just like Latin declensions." It sounded like a painful disease to me, but then Matthew had been reciting verbs at a posh school where you were rusticated if naughty while I'd been peeling gum off tables at my comprehensive. As I'd never even been taught English grammar how was I to know that, *"when used with masculine inanimate, feminine or neuter singular nouns and with any plural inanimate noun, special modifiers take the same endings in the accusative as are taken by nouns."* Russian was so complicated we'd already learnt five forms of the word 'one' and we were only on tutorial eleven.

Tom thought our lessons were marvellous. We often had them in the morning before Matthew went to work and Tom would listen to our pronunciation exercises, 'uz, uzer, zoo, zee, zoo, zare', delighted that we were finally learning *his* language.

Valentina, who'd grown out her basin haircut, was delighted to be with us again. I'd warmed to her since she told me she loved me so just smiled placidly when she said Tom had hiccups because he was cold. She encouraged us to read propagandist dialogues in our Soviet textbook, conversations between Anna Petrovna and her friend with my favourite patronymic, Ivan Ivanovich, about whose concrete shoebox was the most modern with hot water *and* gas. Life in the USSR, we learned, was perfect. Everyone had jobs in factories or institutes, enjoyed playing chess and regularly took *adehayet*, rest holidays at sanatoria.

Anna Petrovna and Ivan Ivanovich belonged to the generation of true Soviets, patriots born Soviet and grateful for education, sanitation and healthcare. Through their enthusiasm I realised I was missing an important facet of Bishkek: I was living in the former Soviet Union, a formidable power which had covered nearly one-sixth of the earth's land surface but remained cut off from the world for a lifetime; the old enemy demonised for eternity by Bond films. The key to happiness was grasping the magnitude of history and looking beyond drunks in the gutter and street kids sniffing glue.

If, like Anna Petrovna and Ivan Ivanovich, I could be happy in my surroundings it would be easier to overcome the problems. I might even get over the horror of seeing Bin *Babushka* defecating behind the skips, searching through the rubbish for a piece of wiping paper with her grey pants wedged on white, flabby thighs. Bishkek was now home for the next two years rather than a novelty interlude and I knew I should maximise the experience rather than wish it away. Inspired by my textbook heroes I set about learning to love Soviet concrete.

I started to appreciate that tenements had different architectural styles; curves and crosses of concrete repeated over facades to create striking geometric patterns. I became obsessed with photographing shapes, enjoying their oppressive greyness as imposing symbols of the Soviet era. Rather than complaining that Bishkek's buildings were depressing and dismal, I sought out designs to add to my collection.

Behind the stalls in Comfort bazaar selling taps, plugs and coat hangers was a huge horizontal, grey shoebox: criss-crosses of concrete over each enclosed balcony made it look like a giant sieve. On *Kievskaya-Manas* was a long, squat horizontal shoebox. It ran the length of a block and had open balconies where people kept ovens and bits which had fallen off their Ladas. At the end of a road I'd not taken before I found a shoebox estate, blocks gathered together in a towering community. They stood at right angles to each other and were decorated with arches in concession to Islamic architecture.

On the ground floor of one I found the only clothes shop in Bishkek which sold something other than disco tops the size of a duster. Unfortunately the changing room doubled as the manageress' office and she watched impassively while I wedged an allegedly size 16 t-shirt onto my shoulders and wiggled inelegantly to release myself. Despite such humiliation it was an excellent find; I wrote about it for the IWC newsletter and everyone was delighted. Learning to love Soviet concrete was proving very useful.

I received a flattering reaction at Playgroup to the news that we were staying. Nicky was pleased because Tom and Siana were just learning how to make friends and Gina was pleased because I helped her with Mahjong hands. Gina had been due to move but, discovering that wages were so high in Tokyo she'd have to chose between a housekeeper and a nanny, decided Bishkek was the best posting in the world and insisted her husband extended a year.

Unfortunately Playgroup was now even scarier to host. With the ex-pat community swelling and Bishkek classified a family posting by the American Embassy, Playgroup was now an enormous conglomeration of huge kids rampaging through small apartments. We were multinational with Germans, English, Americans, Swiss, Indians, Croatians, Australians and even a house husband from Mexico, but he only braved one session.

With size Playgroup got nasty; something had to be done. Penny suggested reinstating the age limit but those with older children didn't want to leave. When Ilke mentioned that it was affiliated to the Women's Club and membership was necessary to attend, an American Embassy clique took offence and boycotted playdates, slagging off the rest of us around town.

Matthew said it was like 'Lord of the Flies'. I re-read the book and discovered some worrying comparisons: we were thrown together in an unknown place; some wanted rules, some wanted anarchy; some wanted to blow the conch and have assemblies, others preferred hunting. No-one had been murdered yet but spiteful words were spoken. A pack of grown up women should have known better than a pack of school boys. Withdrawing from ex-pat society and becoming a hermit had never looked so appealing.

"I'll be a hermit with you," Nicky said.

"You can't be a hermit *with* someone. Anyway, if the rest find out they'll all want to join and before we know it Ilke will be announcing that Hermits meet on Thursday mornings."

Fortunately there was a way off our island – holidays, or home-leave as Americans call it. We went first, avoiding end of term mayhem because it didn't matter to us. Ironically, having been desperate to leave in January, I now wanted to stay. I'd settled happily into routine and was sad to miss the best cheap strawberries and the Queen's Official Birthday Party, billed as the largest annual event in an embassy calendar. We'd not been invited to the party the year before because Bill at Fatboys didn't have us on his list, despite our having registered with him – with organisation like this I didn't rate our chances of being rescued in a crisis. This year we'd received an invitation embossed with a gold crest and I was disappointed I wouldn't discover what really happened at ambassadorial receptions.

This home-leave was a necessity. We needed medical tourism: bi-annual visits to doctors, dentists, opticians and health visitors so that we only had to rely on health care in Russian for emergencies. We were also stocking up for the next two years, packing the two-hundred kilo shipment allowance we'd been given as a bribe for staying in Kyrgyzstan. I couldn't decide whether to take my wedding china or all my shoes and was receiving plenty of advice on what I'd need for Tom.

While we were away Igor the Master was going to renovate our kitchen. He had two weeks to install a tiny L-shape worktop, fit a new sink, plumb a dishwasher and lay a miniscule amount of lino. This would just be enough time, if he worked twelve hour days. I was looking forward to having a dishwasher; I just hoped it didn't kill us. Electricity was haphazard in Bishkek: sockets were known to overheat and melt if you boiled the kettle at the same time as making toast.

Most importantly, both Tom and I needed rehabilitation time in England. Tom had started making worryingly Kyrgyz noises, hawking at the back of his throat. He'd spent most of his life in Kyrgyzstan and needed time-out before he started spitting and wiping snot on trees. I needed fashion rehabilitation. Surrounded by wannabe prostitutes my sense of style was starting to warp. I'd mentioned to Clorise that I'd seen some nice clothes in the new shopping mall called Dordoi Plaza.

"Honey, when you start thinkin' clothes here are nice you gotta get out and take a good look round the real world," she'd advised.

Going 'home' was always traumatic, unsettling because weeks of my life were lost in the void of travel, jet lag, repatriation, goodbyes and homesickness. Despite the practise I still couldn't move efficiently between my parallel lives. Three weeks before leaving I'd start displaying obsessive-compulsive pre-travel behaviour and had to take hundreds of photos and buy one of everything on the craft floor of Tzum, just in case we didn't come back.

On re-entry I was hit by reverse culture shock, emerging from Central Asia blinking at the speed of the first world. I spent the first week wondering whether I could ever live again on an expensive, overcrowded island of traffic jams, yob culture and MRSA, disillusioned that it wasn't the haven I thought it to be. Clothes shopping was intimidating because there were so many shops selling so many nice clothes in my size I didn't know where to start and ended up getting stressed and buying nothing. At the supermarket I stared at car parks full of shiny new vehicles, none held together with duct tape. Inside I had panic attacks – forty types of pasta, what to choose? I could only think of Bin *Babushka* eating rubbish.

'Reverse' culture shock is much more significant. When you arrive in a new country you expect everything to be different. When you come home you expect everything to be the same and it's disturbing when it's not. I was embarrassed by my ignorance, picking up a friend's cigarette packet in amazement at the huge 'SMOKING KILLS' sticker, unaware these were now required government health warnings. Living abroad you miss out on cultural nuances which, although seemingly unimportant, form your national subconscious. There should be repatriation classes for confused ex-pats so you can reabsorb into society without humiliation.

We spent a week in Cornwall with a group of friends. They had babies Tom's age and listening to the mothers I realised that hawking would be the least of Tom's expatriate problems. Without attending gym clubs, music groups and swimming lessons I worried his development would be stunted. Would Tom be teased in the English playground because he couldn't swim underwater at three months and didn't have a plate with an imprint of his baby feet moulded in clay? I wasn't sure the fact he'd win the 'who's got the most stamps in their passport' competition would be sufficient consolation. Kids are bitchier than groups of ex-pat women. Was Tom going to be a misfit?

Living away you appreciate 'home' and I soon rediscovered the luxuries of western life – baths, junk food, trashy magazines, pubs without strip shows, cinemas and television. Before I could stop myself I was reliant on Tesco, had lost my fifty-eight step fitness and was reluctant to return to the privations of Bishkek – although part of me was looking forward to our own space and the tranquillity of Kyrgyzstan compared to England's oppressive consumerism. I was also bored of answering the 'are you happy in Bishkek' questions and explaining where the country was.

Matthew was leaving before me to attend a World Bank mission. This meant I'd be flying on my own with Tom. I've learnt my lesson: the cliché's true, never say 'never' to anything. I'd said I'd never fly with a baby, never fly *a lot* with a baby and never fly *alone* with a baby. My non-programmed life as an ex-pat was teaching me that nothing was ever as expected and the more challenges I accepted, the stronger I became at coping with them.

One week later – a week spent practising peeing with Tom on my lap – my parents dropped us at the airport. I was nervous, although felt pathetic to admit it when remembering Catherine Macartney who in 1903 had trekked through the Tien Shan to Kashgar with a five-month-old to get to her posting. Fortunately Tom was having an 'I'm a model child day' and looked so cute Japanese tourists took photos of him with their phones. I looked so pitiful the grumpy BA steward let me through with excess baggage and gave me a 'fast-track' sticker so I didn't have to queue at the security check.

Somehow I managed to buy lunch, change Tom's nappy and make it to the gate without crying. We were shown to our seats and I prayed that it wouldn't be a drunk miner sitting next to us – I didn't fancy dealing with alcohol breath and incomprehensible insults as well as breast-feeding with minimal nipple display.

God answered. I've become increasingly religious since becoming a mother; you have to believe there's someone out there helping or you'll go mad with responsibility. God gave me Sister Kathy. Sister Kathy was an American nun who'd lived in Bishkek for years. During the flight, while Tom sat on her knee and played with her crucifix, I learnt how she and the Sisters ministered in six poor villages. Every week they taught the Catholic faith in someone's home, discovering the physical and emotional needs of villagers and trying to help.

"Last month we found four young sisters living alone because their mother had gone to prison."

"What did you do?"

"We moved them to our compound where they'll stay until she's out. In another village we provide a hot lunch for the children once a week. They're so skinny and dressed in rags it really breaks my heart."

"Do you worry that your aid isn't sustainable, that people need more long term solutions?"

"Of course. What upsets me is that the government isn't helping its people. It gets $7000 for each take off and landing from the American airbase and yet none of this is benefiting the poor of Kyrgyzstan. I like to think that we help by offering the personal touch. Often problems are solved just by talking them through."

In the West we're weak. We moan if the electricity goes off in the middle of a favourite television programme. How would we cope for six months in snow without heating?

"We wouldn't tolerate what these people endure. If our hospitals were in such condition we'd write to politicians and newspapers in disgust. But these people know nothing more, they've had no chances for their life to be better."

"How do you cope emotionally?" I asked, explaining to Kathy that I often felt overwhelmed by the need in Kyrgyzstan. There was so much poverty I didn't know where to start and felt frustrated that whatever I did would have so little impact I ended up doing nothing.

"I find the process of these people sharing their lives with me humbling. Sometimes I just want to walk away and cry but I have to go back or what will that say to them, that I am too weak to even hear about their problems? Just a pair of winter shoes can change a child's life. Think how we value small things, how something insignificant can make us happy. For these people small things are also fundamental needs."

Listening, I realised I'd finally found a way to give something back to the community I was living in. God hadn't just sent Sister Kathy so that I could pee alone – although I took Tom with me when Kathy was asleep and succeeded without making any mess, even during turbulence. God was telling me to forget trying to rehabilitate the whole of Kyrgyzstan and concentrate on how I could realistically help. I couldn't solve all Sister Kathy's problems, and certainly not alone, but I did know some people who could make a difference to the lives of poor villagers. My role was intermediary; my role was to introduce Sister Kathy to the Bishkek International Women's Club.

Sister Kathy exuded peace and calm so that Tom and I drifted off the flight feeling relaxed and happy. It was a shame she hadn't been on the World Bank Review Mission. Matthew had spent a frustrating week in Naryn with economists who were more concerned about IMF PIPs being exceeded by the MOF's spending plan than clean water. When proudly shown children using a *kalonka* the Bank Bureaucrats had muttered, "is that all we get for our millions?"

"Yes, when you only allocate $50 per person," Matthew had replied. "Don't you read the paperwork we send you?"

"Then we're wasting money." They wanted guaranteed output, specific results for their millions as well as institutional development, training and sustainability. They needed Kathy's gentle reminder that development, however small, is an improvement. Although they expected hot running water and uninterrupted electricity, life was much easier in Naryn with a *kalonka* every half a mile.

It got worse. At a community meeting an *aksakal* criticised the practise of lining old pipes rather than laying new ones.

"Why's he complaining? It's free," the Bureaucrats retorted, struggling to appreciate that even poor, oppressed peasants could have opinions. They were not mollified by the hospitality. As one of the economists was a woman she was presented with the boulder of fat from the sheep's bottom at every banquet. She went home vegetarian, glad to hide in the safety of her Washington office. Matthew went home exhausted, glad to return to the comparatively easy task of exorcising the curse of the Mountain Ghost in Kyzyl-Jyldyz.

Inspired by my encounter with Sister Kathy I began recruiting people to my cause. I started with Susi as we walked together one afternoon. Susi was an incredibly generous person, finding time to give baby massage to disabled children at an orphanage and sending clothes and toys with Pete to a group of asylum seekers stranded near the border with Tajikistan. Susi agreed that Sister Kathy sounded unique, someone who truly knew how to give help where it was most needed. She would add her to the agenda for the next Women's Club Charity Committee meeting.

We were walking east on *Moskovskaya,* heading for *Maladoy Gvardia,* another strip of green where locals liked to promenade. We passed bored soldiers marching to another day's gardening and a Lada so laden with watermelons its exhaust scraped along the ground. Young children sat behind tables selling cones of sunflower seeds and individual cigarettes. Most customers were little girls who skipped home in floral dresses clutching Daddy's Marlboros. An old man shuffled up with a *som* he'd saved to buy a treat. He lingered over each brand, fingering the individual sticks laid across the gaping lids of open packets as he made his choice.

"Don't you *love* that building?" It was a favourite of mine, a horizontal grey shoebox with tessellating arcs of concrete decorating enclosed balconies. Susi wasn't impressed. They'd just moved out of town to a diplomatic compound, new-build houses with red, blue and green roofs nestled against the foothills. Matthew said it looked like Legoland. Susi liked the fresh air, complaining that Bishkek was hidden under a cloud of smog.

On *Maladoy Gvardia* men were scything the long grass, swishing their blades listlessly through buttercups, dandelions and thick clumps of marijuana. The name means 'young guard' and refers to the memorial on *Chui* commemorating young Kyrgyz who were lost in the Soviet Union's wars. Being close to Osh bazaar and the less salubrious end of town it is known locally as *kulbazaar*, slave market, because groups of men stand around waiting to be offered a day's manual work. If they fail they resort to vodka and loll on benches. Walking by you get high on fumes.

On alternate blocks were small playgrounds, rumoured to have been built with generous donations from Soren's cigarette factory. We stopped at one and Tom sat on my lap, swinging under a canopy of oak leaves while Alfie chased pigeons. Opposite an old man in an *ak-kalpak* was reading from newspapers pinned up on huge notice boards, arms clasped behind his back as he concentrated on the latest propaganda.

"I've got something to tell you," I said to Susi.

"What? Pregnant?"

"No."

"Leaving?"

"No, no threat of that yet this week, despite the review mission."

"What then? Getting divorced?"

"No, nothing so dramatic." Well, not for anyone else. For me it had been a momentous decision. While home I'd done some serious thinking and decided to relax some obsessive principles: I was going to get a nanny.

Chapter Eighteen – Tanzilya

For weeks I'd fought a confusing tussle with my emotions – the desire to be what I considered a Good Mother against my desire to write. As a mother you have such responsibility, the power to create or destroy happiness, to raise a balanced human being or an adult who'll end up in therapy. I didn't want Tom to feel the emptiness of rejection but I still couldn't quash my urge to write. I needed more intellectual stimulus than shape-sorters and brick towers. I craved cerebral silence, an academic escape from every-day practicalities. Writing, I felt, gave me a purpose and identity. But admitting that made me feel guilty – wasn't being Tom's mother enough?

My mother, Sue, a qualified nursery nurse, encouraged me that I wouldn't be a failure by leaving Tom with someone else for a few hours. "A child should have four people in his life," she told me. Normally the extra two would be grandparents; in our ex-pat life those roles were taken by staff. I assuaged my guilt by convincing myself that any nanny – or babysitter as I preferred to call her, it sounded less official – was only coming during the day so that Tom would know her if he woke at night when we went out. My writing was an incidental bonus.

The hardest part was finding someone suitable. I'm very fussy about who I let into my home, I didn't want someone criticising me and telling me what to do, I had enough of that on the street. Nicky had a Kyrgyz nanny and a Russian gardener who, both middle aged, gave daily advice when she returned with six-week old Siana. She was instructed to wrap a hot towel round her belly to tighten the muscles and put breast milk on her spots. I'd have fired them.

Then there was the matter of trust. Not only was there the 'Paul' factor – you didn't want someone stealing your baby and your husband – nannies learnt the intimacies of a family's life and swapped them at Playgroup when bosses weren't listening.

Ilke kept a list of nannies and mentioned a young student called Tanzilya who babysat for lots of ex-pats. This meant she was already tied to the community and therefore less likely to abscond with the DVD player or Tom. She also spoke English – useful because Anna Petrovna and Ivan Ivanovich hadn't had a dialogue about how to care for a baby while writing in the study. They were stuck on how wonderful it was to live in Academy City in Siberia. Apparently Tanzilya was also pretty. Gina thought this disqualified her immediately; she only employed nannies with acne.

As Matthew would be at work when nanny was in the flat I chose the risk of divorce over bossiness and eventually found the courage to call Tanzilya. The next day an attractive girl, smiling shyly, arrived on the doorstep. She was slim with dark glossy hair and high cheekbones. I checked out her clothes: her top covered her midriff and jeans weren't cutting her up the middle, this was a good start.

Tanzilya was Tatar with Russian parents, her fore-fathers part of Genghis Khan's Great Golden Horde. She'd been born in Kyrgyzstan because her grandparents had moved to Osh to escape the worst effects of the Great War – that's the Second World War to Russians. When her parents returned to their Tatar village in south-west Russia, Tanzilya had stayed to look after her grandfather and study. She was supporting herself by babysitting for ex-pats.

I'm not very adept at handling 'staff'. I'm apologetic and flustered when trying to instruct and then feel guilty if they're cleaning while I'm reading, assuming they're thinking, 'lazy bitch, why can't she do this herself'. The first ex-pat wife I ever met was old school, a miserable Scottish woman who never left her bedroom without full make up. She was happy to be patronisingly nice to me until she realised I had a mind of my own. Her advice was to be firm and distant, but that wasn't my style. I'd rather staff were friends.

My first employee was Mary, a tiny Coptic Christian lady in Egypt, the hardest worker I've ever met. I have no idea how I communicated with Mary as she spoke only Arabic, but we loved each other and cried a lot when I left. Having someone look after your baby was different to cleaning. I looked at Tanzilya, trying to suss out whether she had obsessions about cold and hiccups. I was supposed to be interviewing but didn't know what to ask. "Have you ever shaken a baby and given them a brain haemorrhage?" seemed a bit excessive.

Before I could change my mind I found myself explaining what Tom liked to do and retreating to the study. It felt odd listening to Tom giggle for someone else. I sat there gripping the desk with jealousy, even though all morning I'd been craving time to myself. I was scared to let go of control even just a little because I worried about sliding away from the pinnacle of perfect motherhood I'd set for myself. If I handed Tom over successfully for an hour what was to stop me thinking, 'he's happy with Tanzilya so I may as well go and shop without him'. If that worked I'd start taking riding lessons, playing golf, having massages and pedicures before going for lunch. Before I knew it I'd just be petting him at bedtime, having become the sort of mother I disapproved of.

Summer was quiet in Bishkek. With school finished most families had gone home to stock up on vibrating toys, making Playgroup a pleasure to host and leaving more free sun beds round the pool. Summer is traditionally the time postings end, coinciding with the academic year. So many people left I had to acclimatise to the gaps they'd created in the life which had become familiar; no Anthea to chat to while quilting, no Anke to play Mahjong; no Karen next door or Chitra to host exotic dinners created by her expert chef. More international friends made and lost.

I was fortunate that none of my really close friends had gone. Susi was due to leave in December and I knew I'd miss her terribly. One career ex-pat told me she'd given up getting close to people because they always moved. That saved heartache but made for a lonely life.

During the summer, because the members of Bridge Club went away, Bishkek International Women's Club officially closed down. Those of us staying were pitied by the others who wondered what we'd do for two months without them and their playdates. 'Playdates' was a new phenomenon for me. When I was growing up no-one pre-arranged anything, we just hung out at home with our neighbours who we loved one week and fought the next. In Bishkek, unless there was a birthday party, swimming lesson or movie showing at school you needed a playdate because otherwise you were considered an outcast. The international children had a busier social life than their parents.

Tom and I managed without playdates. We went to the pool where Tom learnt to drift in a rubber ring, smiling and proud of his independence. We played at home, Tom happily exploring the intricacies of his toys and talking in sentences of gibberish emphasised with an earnestly pointed finger. In the afternoons we walked, searching for the best examples of Soviet concrete and the tightest trousers in Bishkek.

Wandering around town was always entertaining, once you'd mastered gaping manholes and uneven paving slabs, rutted like bad teeth. I liked to walk; it gave me thinking time and the chance to notice the details of city life. At *shashlik* grills men fanned flames with pieces of cardboard, the meat spitting and hissing over the fire. Girls gazed into bridal shops called Lady Gold where mannequins wore puffs of lace and open-mouthed looks of astonishment as if to say, "someone's marrying me in this dress?" Drivers squatted by roadsides cracking sunflower seeds between their teeth while boys washed their cars, spilling pools of foam across pavements for me to steer around. Looking south down cross streets I would, if lucky, see the mountains rising in vertiginous peaks, snow glinting in the sun.

I was often asked directions. This was good practise for my pathetic Russian and flattering – until I realised that if I was blending in that much I must have been dressing terribly. I looked so at home American tourists started discussing me in a bazaar.

"These people have kids as cute as Christmas," a woman said, raising her camera.

"*Nyet!*" I stopped her in my best accent, not wanting a photo but reluctant to completely ruin their sight-seeing afternoon. It was disturbing to discover how easy it is to make people feel like zoo animals with innocent traveller's curiosity.

Unlike last year's season of weekly rain this summer was hot, so hot that Tom rode in his buggy with his legs spread over the arms. Girls laughed at him and I glared back. How dare they ridicule my precious baby, especially when they were wearing pink pumps with 'Love Me' written in Tippex across the toes. Trips in the car were sticky, Tom sweating in his seat and complaining when we stopped, usually because the city jammed into gridlock to let Akayev's convoy pass.

Most mornings it was thirty degrees by 8am. If the trees were still I knew it would be stifling by lunchtime; shimmering heat radiating from tarmac, pollution from exhaust fumes hovering in a haze and the smoke plumes of the power station rising straight up into the bleached sky. On other days the cool mountains, where snow still clung to the tips, sent a gentle breeze. This refreshed stale air in our rooms but covered every surface with fine dust. Outside our block it smelt hot, an olfactory déjà vu of Bishkek summer: putrid rubbish, vodka breath, ripe strawberries and soft tarmac. When I threw bags of rubbish into the bins, clouds of disturbed flies swarmed up around me. I longed for swaying cornfields and Cornish cliffs; the city could be claustrophobic in the heat.

Evenings were sultry. Myna birds chattered outside the window. Lazy music and the smell of grilling *shashlik* drifted from restaurants where clientele relaxed in the dusk. Nights were less sultry. Cats yowled as they mated painfully and outdoor discos thumped monotonously through the same songs. Two blocks away trains rumbled through the city, their horns slow and deep like ships leaving port. I imagined them speeding across the dark steppe, packed with sweaty bodies oozing vodka. Tanzilya was going home for a holiday on one of these trains. It would take her two days to cross Kazakhstan into Russia.

Summer was wedding season. Undeterred by the heat, brides squashed into polyester and lace hired from Lady Gold and planned their day according to custom: marriage at the wedding palace; bouquets laid by a war memorial and videos of romantic promenades under oak trees while guests picnicked on *lepioshka*, salami and vodka from the bonnets of cars. I learnt not to cross in front of wedding convoys; they paid no attention to red lights as they roared around town. The bride and groom travelled in the lead vehicle, a long, white ostentatious limousine or crappy Lada, according to budget. Everyone else followed in cars and *mashrutkas* decorated with ribbons and plastic flowers, horns blaring and bridesmaids hanging inelegantly from windows, recorded conscientiously by cameramen filming from sunroofs. It was amazing more brides weren't lost to road-traffic accidents.

August 5th was a momentous day: Tom bottom shuffled off the *shyrdak* and we had an earthquake. Apparently there was an earthquake a day in Bishkek but you didn't usually feel them. I felt this one. I was sitting on the sofa when the room started to shake. At first I thought it was the noisy upstairs neighbours returning from holiday and dropping suitcases on the floor, but the room kept shaking. It trembled and shuddered and the whole building seemed to sway.

"Matthew!" If we were going to die in a crush of concrete – I didn't believe for a moment the block would stay up – it would be nice to die together. He didn't come, maybe he was already pinned down by the computer. The room shook again. In my fear I managed to feel amazed that three floors up I was experiencing the effects of tectonic plates rubbing together deep inside the Earth. I just hoped I'd stay three floors up.

"Matthew!"

"What?"

"Didn't you feel the earthquake in the study?"

"No." I couldn't believe it had only been in the sitting room. He must have been too engrossed in his latest spreadsheet. I read later that it had measured 4 on the Richter Scale which, when there are only 9 levels, seemed quite high to me.

Tom's bottom shuffling had more long-term effects than the earthquake: he was finally mobile. He'd never crawled; if you put him on his front he'd mewl helplessly until you turned him over. Now I watched in amazement at my baby propelling himself, dragging his bottom with his legs, exploring the edges of the *shyrdak* before venturing out into the sitting room. Occasionally he'd lose balance and fall back onto his head with a thud. He'd cry "mama" and cling so desperately I felt loved beyond all others – it was tempting to push him over whenever I wanted to enjoy that unique cuddle of unquestioning love.

Although Tom had mastered independent movement he still didn't travel well. This meant we spent weekends in town rather than touring mountains. I couldn't help feeling dissatisfaction at what I *wasn't* seeing, especially when Matthew returned from Lake Song Kul with tales of huge valleys bordered by mountains, vast plains, remote *jailoos*, herds of yak and women milking mares – only after he'd finished moaning about terrible roads, *besh barmak* and spam for breakfast. To me such things were still guidebook myths. How could I live in a country described as having 'Central Asia's finest mountain architecture'[21] without seeing any of it? All I did was talk to women about babies.

Dema knew my ambitions and tried to help.

"Come fishing with me," he pleaded. "It's magnificent. We'll camp on a crest high in the mountains with clouds drifting below us and the river crashing at our feet." I was tempted. My 'Kyrgyz Style' calendar was teasing me about what was out there. Each month was a glossy image of pastoral Kyrgyzstan: meadows of poppies, hidden glacial lakes, ancient mausoleums on the high Silk Route, ruddy-faced children peeping out from *yurts*, nomadic domesticity in alpine valleys. My aim was to get myself into at least one of those scenes before we left.

---

[21] Lonely Planet Central Asia

August's picture resembled one of Matthew's photos, a view taken from the roof of the world looking back across miles of jagged peaks. A road climbed the nearest mountain in switchbacks, an insignificant zigzag within the immensity of the scene. I was about to accept Dema's offer when I remembered baby Tom.

"How cold will it be at night?"

"Oh, not bad, maybe five degrees. You can wrap *Droog* Tomas up like a Kyrgyz baby."

"Where are we sleeping?"

"In a tent, or the car."

The adventurer in me had to give way to the mother. Much as I trusted Dema to drive us round town I wasn't sure if he'd really considered the logistics of taking Tom fishing at three thousand feet. I knew Dema had one son but he lived in Ukraine so I'd never met him. He might have no fingers, lost to frostbite on a fishing trip. We compromised with an expedition to Kegeti, a waterfall which Dema promised was an easy hour away.

The journey was all I'd dreamed of. We drove inside the first layer of mountains to find huge valleys with steep slopes of pines and snow caps in the distance. We looked down on small villages straddling a river, the banks chequered with cultivated fields, lanes delineated by rows of tall poplars. We passed toothless men on horseback herding sheep along the road, bleating animals eddying around us. Colourful birds sang from telegraph wires.

Unfortunately Tom vomited on every bend. By the time we arrived at the waterfall, which really wasn't worth the effort, I'd resolved never to leave the Hyatt pool again, tortured with guilt at the pain I'd selfishly inflicted on my son. There's nothing like a retching baby to dampen your adventuring spirit. Defeated, I put guidebooks away, accepting that Bishkek City Market was my geographical limit from now on. I'd come to Kyrgyzstan at the wrong time of my life. To really appreciate its rugged opportunities you should be fit, healthy and adventurous, not pregnant, breast feeding a car sick baby or paranoid about the inadequacies of healthcare.

Summer was a confusing warp of time, weeks drifting by in bewildering lurches. With people leaving and returning and normal routines interrupted I could no longer remember what day it was and which month we'd travelled to England. Time has a different meaning when you're a parent. There's someone to remind you of the consequences of passing days. Weeks fly by in routines of motherhood and you're too busy to work out where each day goes as you crawl exhaustedly into bed.

Tom was no longer a baby with sweet milk breath but a little boy with curls at the back of his neck whose burps smelt of stale cauliflower. He was also getting teeth. I discovered this by peering in his mouth during a scream. On his bottom gum two white points were ripping through the flesh with a red tear. He whined like an insistent mosquito, obsessed with mouths, poking in mine as if he could take the teeth and avoid growing his own.

Nibbling exploratory fingers and trying to block out the baby-noise torture, I thought about my previous life in London when Friday afternoons were full of anticipation about which pub we'd go to, carefree days before babies and greater responsibilities weighed us down. My lawyer friends were now aspiring partners: I just aspired to make an edible dinner. They were buying fast cars and eating in famous restaurants: my hobbies sounded like Girl Guide badges. While I thought learning to pee in an aeroplane toilet during turbulence with Tom on my lap was an achievement, they were negotiating high profile takeovers impacting the Stock Exchange. The modern career-girl 'Saffia Farr' who'd worn suits, amended contracts and had stimulating conversations with adults had been replaced by 'Mummy', fully domesticated and machine washable.

Did I want to go back? Not that there was much for me to go back to as I'd abandoned my career years ago for Matthew rather than to have Tom. At least this meant I'd had the advantage of getting used to being a housewife so there wasn't the double shock of being at home and having a child.

Being a mother was the hardest job I'd ever done. I was sometimes overwhelmed by the oppressive sense that wiping up and changing nappies was all that lay ahead for years. I felt trapped, my life made claustrophobic by Tom's incessant needs: there was no escape, no coffee breaks, no end of shift, no weekends off. Workers and fulltime mums have differing perspectives of freedom. When you're at home with a child's demands, going to work seems like freedom. When you're at work with a boss's demands, looking after a child seems like freedom.

When Tom grizzled "mama-mama-mama" all day, the constant repetition of my name drummed into my head, the cloying, needy love becoming suffocating. At those times, returning to the relative silence of an office would be a reprieve. Fortunately the motherhood job was redeemed by good moments. When Tom blew raspberries on my cheek, clung to me like no-one else mattered and smiled a raw, gummy smile all drudgery was forgotten and I wouldn't swap time with him for any lawyer's salary.

Tanzilya now helped a couple of times a week and I was gradually getting used to relying on her. Being sensitive I watched every change in Tom, blaming any signs of spoilt behaviour on too much time with Tanzilya. If he ever called her "mum" she'd have to go. It's difficult to let someone else have influence over your child when you've done everything yourself for so long.

One afternoon Tom was restless so I let Tanzilya take him to the park. It felt odd watching her wheel him away. It felt even odder when two hours later they'd not returned. Never before had I not known where he was for such a long time. I imagined baby snatchers lurking in bushes, *mashrutkas* swerving into them, their unidentified bodies now lost in a Kyrgyz hospital. When the phone rang I assumed it was a kidnapper calling with a ransom demand. It was Matthew. He told me not to be paranoid, reminding me that

Tanzilya worked for lots of other ex-pats who trusted her. But I couldn't write and paced the flat looking out of each window. In the shoebox opposite a woman was hanging grey towels and sheets to dry on the rail outside her balcony. Bin *Babushka* was licking a yoghurt pot I'd thrown out that morning. Two men were skinning a goat on the grass next to the swings.

Eventually I checked whether Tanzilya had left her bag – she'd taken it and I knew she'd never come back. I should have demanded collateral for my baby. This was probably the chance she'd been waiting for, an opportunity to slip out of my sight and sell my healthy baby to people traffickers. At the May Women's Club meeting I'd learnt this was the second largest industry in Kyrgyzstan after drug smuggling.

Was Tom crying for me? Would they harm him? Would the police help? Should I call Bill at Fatboys? The *malako* man returned for his evening rounds, calling dolefully about having milk, cream and cheese for sale. A woman bought her rugs out to beat, rhythmically whacking them and dispelling clouds of dust. I stared out of the window, waiting for my baby to come home.

Chapter Nineteen – Social Climbing

"How did you get through the long hot summer?" Gina was back. It was mid August and as the heat started to fade, families were returning so that children would be over jet lag in time for the new term. The Playgroup reunion was in Jenna's garden, a child's paradise of toys laid out under fruit trees; ball games, a slide, bikes and a selection of 'dress-up' clothes more impressive than my wardrobe.

I was there with Tom. Tanzilya had returned him after three hours. They hadn't been with people traffickers but in the park making friends and spotting squirrels. I'd felt relieved, ashamed, then jealous. It should have been me pushing Tom on the swing not some stranger.

In Jenna's pool Tom showed off in his rubber-ring. I tried to hide my flabby figure from the toned bodies in string bikinis and sarongs. Amongst these glamorous women I felt I was back at primary school, still the tubbiest and last in every race on Sports Day.

Having stuck out the summer I felt like a Bishkek veteran, qualified to welcome people home with a proprietary 'how was your trip?' Next I'd be telling new recruits what *kaimak* was and rattling off cross streets as directions while they looked confused. It was easy to forget how alien it had all seemed until recently.

"So what *did* you do for two months without us?" I told Gina about days at the pool, picnics in the mountains and that actually Bishkek parks were quite pleasant for a stroll and an ice-cream.

"Last weekend we went to Issyk-Kul again, this time with people from Matthew's office."

"Oh my gawd, where did they make you stay?" Gina wasn't an Issyk-Kul fan. She'd never forgiven me for swimming in the allegedly radioactive lake when I was pregnant.

We'd had a truly Soviet holiday in Bereke *pensionnat*, sleeping in mouldy wooden chalets with dank, dripping bathrooms, brown wallpaper and shot glasses by the bed. Meals were lukewarm cabbage soup in a refectory so huge you got lost on the way from the door. But Tom had survived the trip without vomiting and Matthew's colleagues, who were drunk the whole time, thought him wonderful because he swayed in time to their singing and guitar playing.

Only Kumashai had remained sober. She was pregnant and disdainful of Russian excesses – Kyrgyz claimed Russians drank the most and Russians claimed Kyrgyz drank the most. Kumashai had spent most of the weekend in tears because her sister had been kidnapped.

Gina was horrified at this news. "Oh my gawd! I thought the IMU only went for foreigners?"

"They do, she was kidnapped by her husband."

In Kyrgyzstan 'bride kidnapping' is more common than officially admitted and not just limited to remote rural areas. Nazira lived in 'modern' Bishkek, but she'd been snatched by her boyfriend because he felt threatened by another suitor. He'd taken her to his parents' house where she was confined for the regulatory three days, emerging sore and hobbling, officially his wife. Gina was disgusted. "Why doesn't she leave him?"

"Now she's spent a night away from home she's tainted and no-one else will want her. In this situation many women consider their best chance is to stay."

"Your weekend sure sounds stressful."

"It gets worse. The translator's husband drank so much vodka on Friday he dropped dead of a heart attack on Monday. Matthew was at the funeral yesterday."

"Oh my gawd! I'm so glad we just went to Florida Keys, although I couldn't wait to get back to the nanny. Talking of which I hear you have a nanny now. Good job, one of us at last."

"Well, I haven't had a pedicure yet."

"And you sure need one."

"Thanks Gina." You could categorise women in Bishkek by the state of their feet. I was a woman who walked, despite dusty pavements, and didn't have time for pedicures. Most were women who drove and spent two hours having toes painted – beauticians in Bishkek were like Masters and took their time. At Playgroup I had to sit on my feet or surreptitiously cover them with Tom's muslin to spare the shame of Gina staring at my black soles and yesterday's chipped colour.

Summer officially ended on 31st August, Independence Day in Kyrgyzstan. This was the time Kyrgyz celebrated pulling away from the Soviet Union by dancing in Ala Too Square in Christmas cake hats. Ethnic Russians stayed at home and sulked. We walked through the festivities on the way to the pool. Apparently the temperature would drop in September so our swimming days were running out. Fortunately Bishkek International Women's Club were preparing alternative entertainment. Committees were busy organising sponsors and teams for the BIWC 2nd Annual Charity Golf Tournament and the fashion was to spend weekends at the club practising. As Clorise told me, in September, golf was the new sunbathing.

Although we weren't yet invited to functions with the Akayevs, I was expected to support Women's Club socials. Because I'd written the constitution the president, Claudia From, assumed I should be on the Standing Committee. I attended meetings with lawyers to check we weren't breaching any local laws, was newsletter co-ordinator, second assistant to take subs at meetings and generally part of the administration. All this meant that I had to 'volunteer' for the golf tournament, despite having never played a round. This was Soviet volunteering, perfected by Claudia From: "I need two volunteers, you and you." Not wanting to disgrace myself I took up Ilke's offer of a lesson and joined the A-listers at the golf club.

Maple Leaf Golf Club, the first and only golf club in Kyrgyzstan, was opened in 2002 by an ex-employee of Kumtor gold mine. It had nine holes and five artificial lakes and was bordered by wrinkled foothills which grew into mountains. To get there you drove south-west out of town, through villages where *babushkas* sat behind stalls of end-of-season apricots and men laid out maize to dry in the exposed triangles of cottage eaves.

On my first visit I stayed off the course and hit balls on the driving range. Ilke's six-year old son advised on my swing and stance and a donkey brayed with laughter in the next field. Tom played with Dema under a Marlboro sun-umbrella and clapped when he thought I hit a good shot. I asked him if he thought I'd embarrass myself at the tournament. He answered, "ooh".

While I was improving my social leisure pursuits, Matthew was in Karakol attending the funeral of an engineer who'd died suddenly of liver disease. Although diagnosed months before he'd died suddenly because he'd stopped taking his conventional medicine in favour of a snake skin, frog spawn and vodka concoction prescribed by the local *shaman*. A *shaman* is a messenger, interpreting the powers of animal, earth and heavenly spirits in the ancient practise of shamanism, followed and truly believed in rural Kyrgyzstan. According to the engineer's wife, if her husband had seen the *shaman* earlier he'd still be alive and she wouldn't be sitting beside his body in a draughty *yurt*.

It was in her interests to keep him alive because Kyrgyz funerals are expensive. Shamanism and nomadic traditions have been grafted onto Islam to create the unique vodka-drinking-hippy-hybrid Muslims of Kyrgyzstan. The result is a costly mourning period which lasts a year and involves a lot of eating and vodka. Although laws have been passed limiting the amount to spend and imams preach that the Qur'an does not require a dead horse for a funeral feast, it is tradition to kill one. At $800 a horse, when the average wage is $30 a month, it makes an expensive wake.

Matthew attended the first stage of mourning when the body is laid out in a *yurt* for three days and friends and relations gather to keep it company. He wore a white armband and sombrero – he'd forgotten his *ak-kalpak* and needed a hat and this was all Dema had in the car – drew his hands over his face repeatedly in sorrow, ate plaited horse-intestine sausage and drank lots of vodka. Eventually the corpse was driven to a cemetery in an old bus and dumped in the ground in a shroud. For a week someone would read the Qur'an to it because it wasn't used to being alone.

Only after forty days would it be accepted that the man was actually dead and in recognition of this there'd be a cake and more vodka. A year later there'd be another feast with another expensive horse and more vodka to finally say goodbye and erect a headstone. Then the widow could start paying off her bills. Matthew didn't enjoy his trip to Karakol. He'd found the process ritualistic and the mourning false. He came home feeling depressed, and slightly sick.

Now that I'd learnt to love Soviet concrete and considered Kyrgyzstan 'my' country, I started to take more notice of what was going on. Election fever was gripping the world – Bush and Kerry in America, Blair and Howard in England and Akayev in Kyrgyzstan. Parliamentary and presidential elections were announced for February and October 2005 respectively. With a combination of revolution in Georgia, an increasingly belligerent Russia and America escalating its influence in Central Asia, the run up to those elections promised to be fun.

Controversies were already building. A man called Felix Kulov had announced his intention to run for president – from prison. This was brave because when he'd declared candidacy for the 2000 elections he'd been arrested and imprisoned on charges international human rights groups were condemning as politically motivated. Conveniently his sentence was due to expire in November 2005, a month *after* the presidential elections. What would they do to stop him this time? Could he run from Siberia?

Feeling confident about his position, Akayev was busy handing out science prizes and promoting his fourth book, 'My Optimistic Vision of the Future: Reflections on Foreign Policy and World Order'. According to sycophantic editorials, it was full of acute political and philosophic reasoning and answered the world's grittiest problems. With beheadings in Iraq and the Beslan School siege, there were plenty of those.

I wasn't convinced Akayev had the answers – don't you have to make sense to solve problems? That week he'd been quoted in the Bishkek Observer as saying, *'I think that any global structure will be sustainable if it is based on the diversity of poles, but, at the same time, striving to ensure the sustainability of tasks and goals in all countries of the world and to provide smaller countries with an equal say in decision making.'*

Maybe he was getting nervous because the Kyrgyz constitution prohibited anyone being president for more than two five-year terms: Akayev had governed for fourteen years. In 1998 the Constitutional Court ruled that elections *pre* the new 1993 constitution didn't count and therefore the 2000 elections initiated only his second term. As to allowing him a third, the Constitutional Court had just decided that it wasn't them but Parliament who should interpret the constitution on this matter. This, according to the opposition, was why the parliamentary elections were so significant: Akayev was going to stack the chamber with supporters so that he could change the constitution allowing him to stand for a third term.

Electioneering and the decision of the Constitutional Court was discussed on the golf course at the BIWC 2nd Annual Charity Golf Tournament. A lot of important men with influential jobs were playing. Under the presidency of Claudia From the BIWC had morphed from a quilt-obsessed WI to a significant social force in Bishkek. Matthew and I were mingling with men who helped Akayev run Kyrgyzstan. There were publishers, gold miners, ambassadors, bankers and managers of companies pumping millions of dollars into the country. For them election results were not of curious interest but fundamental to the success of investments and businesses. If it all went wrong they might find they'd spent the last few years befriending the wrong people and would have to start networking with a different clan.

The big question was: would Akayev run again? Franco Maccaroni, publisher and owner of Tzum, had written an editorial opining that there wasn't much of an alternative to President Akayev and hinted that the country might be better off letting him stay. The head of an international bank playing on my team thought Akayev should go quietly.

"Although there's no doubt Akayev has done a lot in modernising Kyrgyzstan in the short time since it became independent he's also broadened presidential powers at the expense of the legislature. I think a new way is needed," the banker told me while we watched Jenna line up for a putt. "He has a lot of responsibility on his shoulders. There's no doubt the outcome of the elections will depend on the way the executive branch influences them. The results will have an effect on the whole of Central Asia, and in turn the world because Russia and America are taking such an interest." I nodded sagely. Jenna tapped the ball across the green and missed. The banker didn't know how prophetic his comments were.

It's appropriate to network on a golf course. On the next hole my target was head of Kumtor. I wasn't after his gold but his clinic, thinking he might be a useful contact in a medical emergency. We'd had a near miss the day before. I'd put Tom in a high chair which clipped to a table. I hadn't wanted to use it but my host was insistent. I should have followed my instincts: the chair unclipped and Tom fell in an arc, still strapped to the chair, onto a tiled floor. I screamed, he screamed and the shocked ladies who were playing Mahjong stared in horror.

Eventually we both calmed down and miraculously there was no damage. After ten minutes Tom was smiling and I felt much better after a brandy the ladies insisted I drink. If I'd been in England I would have taken him to casualty, just in case. Being in Bishkek all I could do was glare at Penny until she called the Kumtor doctor for advice. I'd spent the night watching Tom sleep to check he didn't fall unconscious. He was fine; I had the headache all weekend.

Back on the golf course I surprised myself and my team mates by hitting some good shots. There were none of the protocols which make golf so stuffy and elitist in England. The sun shone, people chatted on mobiles and ambassadors called comments and competitive taunts to friends across fairways.

By each tee, sexy girls in red mini-dresses offered free cigarettes. This was healthy family entertainment in Kyrgyzstan, to which we were acclimatised because most of the twelve billion cigarettes produced by the local cigarette factory were dumped on IWC fundraisers. Dirk confessed he was tempted to take up smoking just because it was such a value-for-money hobby. The cigarette girls loitered in most restaurants and supermarkets and even if you bought cigarettes they only cost 16 *som* (20 pence) a packet.

While I played, Matthew entertained Tom under a Marlboro umbrella outside the clubhouse. He ended up running a crèche with Tom surrounded by Playgroup girls playing make-believe in squeaky American accents they learnt at school. "Let's pretend we're a family. I'll be mom, you're baby and Madeline's the nanny."

From there Matthew was well positioned to watch the dynamics of all the important men. We were still trying to work out who was undercover CIA, intrigued by what covert operations they might be running in Kyrgyzstan. Our prime suspect was the headmaster of the International School because he'd gone to Bratislava for a mysterious conference coinciding with a visit by George Bush. Our other suspect was Clorise's husband. He was involved in anti-drug smuggling activities, although no-one really knew in what capacity. We'd decided that Clorise and her noisy gossip were part of his deep cover.

After nine holes I joined Tom and Matthew on the rugs. Ilke was already there happily chain-smoking free cigarettes.

"You must meet Delphine. French, husband Philippe works for OSCE[22], here to monitor the elections." She called to a slim, dark lady, dressed in a chic skirt and jacket.

"'ello Saff-ya. You're the one I 'eard about who used to go to Playgroup without a child." I didn't like the thought of being discussed but supposed there were worse reputations to have in a small community.

"Yes, but now I have Tom. Welcome to Bishkek. How are you settling in?" An obligatory question, one often regretted.

"This country ees sheet. I 'ate it 'ere. I 'ate the food, I 'ate the people, I 'ate my 'ouse. Ze power is always out. How can I cook proper soufflé when the oven goes 'ot cold 'ot cold?" I tried to calm Delphine with Lauren's perspective, that the West had power cuts too.

"But in your 'ome country you can call someone for 'elp and they understand you. 'Ere I am 'elpless." She had a point. Ilke reached for a cigarette from a passing girl and sidled away. She must have heard this before.

"Philippe said I must make sacrifice but life is so 'ard. I can't get what I need for my French cuisine."

I wasn't sure this was an appropriate time for my "define 'need' in Kyrgyzstan" speech. It was basically: *"'Need' is kids who can't go to school because they've no shoes to walk two miles. 'Need' is mothers who die in childbirth because there's no clinic in their region. 'Need' is teenagers sold as sex slaves because the family can't afford to feed everyone. It's not a lack of vanilla pods in the supermarket. Any time you're depressed in Bishkek just go and stand by the nearest bins. Watching people forage for food will*

---

[22] Organisation for Security and Co-operation in Europe

remind you what a hard life really is." I'd tried it once on Gina who'd concluded I needed a nanny because I was so stressed. Instead I made banal pacifications, trying to be patient, remembering the blinding misery of first weeks.

Desperate to change the subject I trawled my mind for something more interesting.

"What does your husband think will happen during the elections?"

"He says the 2000 polls were the most fraudulent elections he'd ever monitored anywhere in the world. 'E has warned the Kyrgyz leadership that if they don't take note of what 'appened in Georgia and ensure elections aren't violated again, similar events will knock them from power."

The Kyrgyz opposition were hoping that this was their big chance. They were delighted by the Georgian Rose revolution, sending excited letters to the new president saying it was an inspiration and would influence democracy in other ex-Soviet republics.

Akayev stalwarts were adamant that Georgia wouldn't happen in Kyrgyzstan. They reassured voters that their president was creating the best reform programme in the former Soviet Union. Akayev himself dismissed events as a coup d'etat initiated by western powers, orating repeatedly against the export of democracy which had brought the people of Georgia nothing. "It will not be possible for anything like this to happen in Kyrgyzstan," said the chairwoman of the Democratic Party of Kyrgyz Women, adding more curtly, "and we must not allow it to happen."

Akayev's confidence was helped by there being no significant opposition. As a reaction to the dominance of the Communist Party under the Soviet Union, political parties weren't developed in Kyrgyzstan. Akayev's opponents were politicians who ran as independents and about forty opposition parties who appeared to have used Monty Python scripts as inspiration for names. The People's Unity Movement, the Democratic Movement of Kyrgyzstan, splitters from the People's Congress of Kyrgyzstan, New Kyrgyzstan, Fatherland and New Direction were attempting to unite into the People's Movement of Kyrgyzstan. They hoped that lots of noisy rhetoric about free and fair elections might win them some international financial support – and eventually some votes.

Kurmanbek Bakiev had been elected chairman but they couldn't agree on a manifesto, apart from that everything must be free and fair, and continued to confuse themselves and voters on what they actually stood for. The OSCE and USAID[23] sponsored democracy programmes were desperately trying to assist them in time for the elections but it looked as though Akayev and his Alga Kyrgyzstan party would walk easily to victory again.

Clorise won first prize in the raffle – two boxes of cigarettes and a flight to Istanbul. Delphine won second prize – two boxes of cigarettes and a trip to

---

[23] United States Agency for International Development

Kumtor mine site. We won two boxes of cigarettes and a leather collage of Manas donated by the outgoing Turkish Ambassador who was benevolently bequeathing all the crap he couldn't fit in his suitcases. I gave Dema our cigarettes. In return he presented *Droog* Tomas with a pheasant he'd shot. It stank and the head lolled over my arm. I grimaced gratefully and gave Tom a feather.

"Saf-*fee*-ya!" Clorise yelled as I strapped Tom into his car seat. "Would Tom like a playdate on Monday? My Tula would love him over to pet." Tom had suddenly become popular with the little girls. They thought he was cute with his fat cheeks and dribbly mouth; they said he was "dripping."

"Would you like a playdate Tom?"

"Yeah." I stood back in surprise. I'd been asking rhetorical questions for so long I didn't expect an answer. Parenting was going to get much more complicated if he started expressing opinions.

"So you'd like to be petted by Tula?"

"Yeah." He nodded earnestly.

"Thanks Clorise, we'd love to."

"Good job! See you Monday at 2pm." I looked forward to an afternoon of Clorise discussing Tzumingdales while Tula tried to wedge Tom into her dolls pram and tie ribbons in his hair.

A week later we all met again, this time for a Fun Run in aid of Alpine Fund. It was organised by American Lauren, who I knew from the newsletter committee. Lauren worked for USAID, co-ordinating school construction projects across Kyrgyzstan. She spent evenings in the Hyatt gym training for the New York marathon so was, according to Alpine Fund, the obvious choice to set up a Fun Run.

Most runners had no idea that Alpine Fund arranged days out in the mountains for underprivileged children. I only knew because I'd helped Lauren publicise the run. Ex-pats were happy to support whichever charity was stuck under their noses. Wise fundraisers knew this and pestered Ilke to allow them to talk at Women's Club meetings: once your charity was befriended by the BIWC your dependents were saved.

Dirk and Soren, Ilke's husband, insisted it was an oxymoron, a run couldn't be fun, but dutifully chased children on bikes and roller blades round the five kilometre course. We'd advertised that the route would prestigiously follow Bishkek's main streets. Unfortunately, because Alpine Fund refused to pay bribes, the mayor refused to close roads and the alternative non-corrupt route took us past a mosque, through a bazaar full of bemused locals, over a bridge in the red light district and back to Dordoi Plaza.

Matthew and I were excused from running because we were pushing Tom. Ben, intent on showing off his fitness, was running with Siana in a jogging buggy. Matthew's achievement was going to be getting round the course without dashing for a toilet. The plaited horse-intestine sausages were still having a detrimental effect on his bowels, despite, or possibly due to, the huge, scary pink pills Kumashai had bought from a local pharmacy.

We'd used our dictionary to try and decipher the crackly piece of paper in the box but couldn't work out whether the 'horse' mentioned was the intended recipient or specific cause of illness. The incident confirmed that our practise of bringing one of everything from an English pharmacy was sensible and I made a note to ask on our next trip what was recommended for severe diarrhoea as a result of eating plaited horse-intestine sausage.

Apart from members of the Bishkek International Women's Club, the run was supported by Hash House Harriers who wanted to show off the benefits of Sunday running (and drinking), a few muscled marines who'd been let off base and some do-gooders full of praise for Alpine Fund. There weren't any Kyrgyz. When we'd tried to sell them tickets they'd frowned in confusion. They were happy to give money but could not comprehend the concept of paying to run around Bishkek.

Tom enjoyed the run, peering round the side of his pushchair to stare at people who interested him. It made a change from bottom shuffling. He'd become so adept I was considering spraying polish on his shorts and hiring him out to clean floors. For us it was interesting to see ex-pats who didn't go to Playgroup or Mahjong. Slowing our pace on the steep incline up to the bridge we met Chad, a Peace Corps volunteer who told us he was walking because he'd injured his knee climbing Lenin Peak.

Peace Corps is a group of enthusiastic Americans braving adventures in dangerous lands without McDonalds so they can save the world. In Kyrgyzstan they do understated work in villages, speaking Kyrgyz and often really helping at a basic level. Their only problem is public relations as people assume they're soldiers in red berets looking for terrorists.

Chad was a typical volunteer, hoping to succeed in the foreign service and therefore evangelical about America's international role.

"How long have you been in Bishkek?" This was always the first question asked when ex-pats met.

"I came for four months and eighteen months later am still here," I replied.

"I've met lots of people who say that. Kyrgyzstan is the Bermuda Triangle of Central Asia. I suppose that's because it's such an amazing place to live."

"Or because there are so many problems no-one gets to leave."

Chad's enthusiasm wasn't dampened by Matthew's cynicism. "Where d'you live before here?" This was always the second question. Matthew rattled off his travel CV and waited for the inevitable response.

"Laos! I lived there in '92. Where did you stay? The Parasol Blanc? Wow, then you must know Tony who always had afternoon tea at the Lao Plaza." Of course Matthew knew Tony; he'd often joined him for tea. It's a small ex-pat world so you have to behave or whispers of indiscretions will precede you to new postings. "I was in Laos on a landmine project. Man, what a country. I'm so glad to see America doing so much good there."

"Because they destroyed it in the first place." Tact isn't Matthew's greatest skill. Fortunately Chad had been distracted by a prostitute and didn't hear.

"Before here I was in Doo-shan-Bay, Tajikistan. There are some fantastic USAID projects happening there."

By now Matthew's patience had run out. "Don't you feel uncomfortable that ultimately the US is helping for its own benefit, giving Aid to counties in return for political favours?"

Chad leapt to his country's defence. "Does that matter if the effect is the same? I mean, who cares about the reasons for our Aid if we're improving schools and hospitals?"

"Just a question of ethics. How do you justify millions of dollars given to an Uzbek dictator for example? Should certain countries dictate world politics just because they have money? Is it ethical for rich countries to use Aid to influence domestic policies? And by the way, American Aid is tied so America is actually the greatest beneficiary. USAID only employs American companies to use American products."

"I maintain that who cares if you're giving some benefit?"

"Aid makes countries dependent on donors. Aid gives the impression that donors' values are right and should be aspired to. Many developing countries still respect core values that *we* should learn from *them*, like the importance of family for example."

"What's wrong with progress?"

"It's not always progress but westernisation and that's dangerous. People get the wrong image and think life's unbearable without a mobile phone. Why do you think there's such an immigration problem in the West; people think the streets really are paved with gold."

"The US promotes freedom."

"What you teach isn't freedom but the ultimate in bullying. The US uses Aid to buy obedience. It doesn't care whether it's paying dictatorships or democracies or whether the dollars are spent on black Mercedes or school classrooms. All that matters is gaining the political influence."

"That's bullshit! We're making a difference."

"So why, despite millions of dollars and hundreds of NGO's, do 45% of the population in Kyrgyzstan still live below the poverty line?"

We were saved from fighting on family fun-run day by the arrival of Gina, looking ridiculous in cerise lycra shorts. A small rucksack was fastened round her waist and dangling over her bum.

"Have you seen my Bradley? He zoomed off on his blades and I'm worried he'll fall down a manhole." He probably had. "I don't wanna stop, I'm getting momentum. If you see him, can you tell him I've got his water in my fanny pack." She dashed off pumping hand weights.

We found Bradley back at Dordoi Plaza, eating cookies while watching the circus entertainment. There were mini Cossack dancers, clowns dancing on unicycles and a female acrobat wearing fish-net tights but no knickers – Soren and Dirk were glad they'd joined in after all.

Being part of the social set was hard work. We were now recognised around town and had to stop and swap golfing anecdotes and remember to ask how the meeting with Akayev had gone. Tanzilya spent more evenings at our flat than we did and I sometimes longed for the old days of anonymity and nights in watching pirate DVDs from Tzum. At Playgroup we talked of what dress to wear and what Claudia From had said to Mairam Akayev when they'd met at an orphan's benefit.

The autumn social calendar was hectic. There was a Rotary Ball, which the Bishkek Observer described as 'nice' and the unveiling of Dilbar's winter clothing collection. Now being a regular customer I sat in the front row with Jenna and Ilke.

The climax of the season was Dirk and Jenna's Halloween party. Everyone was going to be there: the American Ambassador, the German Ambassador, even cool people from Almaty. Costumes were obligatory and Dirk and Jenna were hiring caterers and a DJ. It was going to be huge.

We missed it because we went home, again. This time it was to work on our house in London and celebrate Tom's baptism and first birthday. Poor Tom, unlike his embassy friends who hosted lavish parties with clowns and puppet shows, he had to endure being dunked in a font and passed round relatives for his birthday. I felt it was important for him to learn that life wasn't always society glamour and golf tournaments, even when you lived in Bishkek.

Chapter Twenty – In Akayev's Village

We left in t-shirts and returned in coats, that's the difference two weeks makes in Kyrgyzstan. It was cold in Bishkek and the city was full of rumours about when the heating was being switched on. Some said 1st November, others said 15th, some said after three consecutive days at eight degrees and others said there was no coal or gas or money to buy it so there wasn't going to be *any* heating.

When the 1st November passed without any warmth I began to despair. I was already wearing so many layers my arms stuck out stiffly from my sides like a child's toy. It was difficult to remember how we'd sweated under a fan in the same flat. Clothes wouldn't dry and we smelt because we couldn't shower – the risk of frostbite coming out was too great. And we had *more* jet lag. I'd lost half the year to erratic sleep patterns and jet lag when you're cold is the epitome of misery. In desperation I'd followed every piece of advice available on children and time zones; so why was I still playing skittles with an insomniac baby at 1.30am?

In an attempt to rehabilitate we walked to see Nicky and Siana. Everything was in soft focus, the city's grey tinged pink by hazy autumn hues. I kicked through leaves, smelt bonfires and wanted to sit in front of a fire eating fruit cake.

Siana, at ten months, was now crawling. Tom was fascinated, thinking her an exotic sort of cat because he still shuffled on his bottom. The alternative stimulus of England had made him grow up, new people teaching him different things. He knew how to comb his hair, eat chocolate and stroke cats so he and Siana formed a tactile friendship, passing toys, telling stories and hugging when Siana stayed still enough for Tom to lunge. He was now a little boy, independent of me because I'd dropped our final breastfeed. It felt strange to no longer have that ultimate connection but it was wonderful to swap nursing bras for under-wired ones and be reunited with my cleavage.

While Tom and Siana chased Kyzyl, Nicky updated me with all the gossip. Elections had been held successfully at the October Women's Club Meeting, in accordance with my constitution, and Ilke and Claudia From had both held their positions for another term. Clorise was telling everyone about a Hyatt guest who'd written to complain that he'd caught an STD from one of the croupiers. Jenna had a new housekeeper called Almajan who'd knocked the drainage pipe out of the washing machine, flooding the house, causing the electrics to fuse and a cable to catch fire, scorching a Kazak rug and killing a budgie from smoke inhalation. She was on a final warning.

"How's Playgroup?"

"Bigger than ever. We've got some new members – missionaries. Some from the Sacred Church of the Bleeding Heart and some from the Jesus Loves

You Foundation. Although they're both selling the same God they don't quite agree on how, so there's not always an abundance of Christian love. One told me off for perpetuating 'Soviet mastery' by speaking Russian. She's learning Kyrgyz, to 'get to the heart' of the Kyrgyz people."

"What did you get up to?" Nicky told me about their latest expedition to Karakol where they'd taken an old Russian helicopter to see the Inylchek glacier. "With Siana?"

"Yes, of course."

I had my usual moan about not being able to go anywhere remote because Tom was so travel sick. This time he'd thrown up on the flight and screamed through landing. The Scottish miners weren't amused and I worried Tom's first word was going to be 'fook'. Nicky listened patiently and watching her face I wondered if I were being too cautious. Should I just pack loads of wet wipes and take Tom puking through the Tien Shan to satisfy my desire to see hidden Kyrgyzstan? Was I being a Good Mother or pathetic?

Nicky and Ben were intrepid explorers, not afraid to take a new road, turn a different corner or trust that a Tupolev wouldn't crash into a precipice. In comparison Matthew and I were timid, constrained by our poor Russian. Ignorance brings fear and loss of spontaneity – I was too scared even to try ordering pizza. Nicky and Ben were rewarded by discovering new valleys, the best picnic spots and quirky places to stay.

Their latest find was Ashu guesthouse in Chong Kemin valley, the area where President Akayev had been born. As it was only 120 kilometres away, down relatively straight roads, we decided to go in mid-November when Matthew had a long weekend for the Eid festival at the end of Ramadan. His colleagues would be celebrating in true Kyrgyz Muslim style by drinking lots of vodka

We went with some American friends, Michael, Kay and their twin two-year-old boys, Tim and Ben. Michael was a journalist working for a charity who ran an independent printing house, publishing newspapers who dared to criticise the ruling family. Son of a former American ambassador, he'd been brought up an ex-pat in Vietnam and China. Kay was quiet and thoughtful, interested in alternative aspects of Kyrgyzstan like the fledgling wine industry and organising a team to swim across Lake Issyk-Kul.

They'd arrived in the summer and Kay said she'd never forget her first Playgroup. It had been Jenna's glamorous pool party and Kay, dazed with jet lag, had walked into the walled garden to find gorgeous women with immaculate pedicures and string bikinis drinking cocktails. It was the stereotype of ex-pat life, everything her mother-in-law had warned her about, a disturbing contrast to the old men scavenging bins outside. To Kay's relief the following Playgroup had been more normal.

We travelled to Ashu in a mini bus, all three boys sleeping until the driver had to stop to clear his filter because he'd been sold dirty fuel. It was a golden autumn day. Along the roadside poplars created flaming avenues. *Babushkas* sat in patches of sun, podding peas into enamel basins while they chatted. Strings of red chillies were looped like Christmas garlands under eaves to dry and children rubbed the husks from maize, creating huge piles of orange cobs and dried stalks, stacked into ricks for winter fodder.

In Kemin the mountains softened into round hills, egg boxes of curves with brown sheep grazing in the dips. A huge bronze horse reared with its rider, Shabdan Batir, 19th century chieftain and patriotic hero. The Kazak border veered away from the road, curving respectfully around Akayev's birthplace.

The entrance to the valley was marked by a ceremonial arch and guarded by a mountain shaped like a huge sleeping dragon, its head turned towards its tail. We followed a winding road along the river, twisting deeper into the pass. On the other side it was a different country. A huge, whitewashed school was set in immaculate gardens and red-brick mansions were tucked into the hillside behind high walls. There were evidently advantages of living near Akayev's home.

Ashu guesthouse was in Kalmak-Ashu village on the opposite side of the river. We crossed a bridge under which water crashed in white crescents, overtaking a horse and cart laden with cabbages. Tom had turned silent as the road started to twist then whined and squirmed in his seat. I got him out just in time and he puked under the sign which read, 'Ashu, 100 metres'. We walked the rest of the way down a muddy track splattered with horse manure. For Matthew it was déjà vu.

"I told you Kyrgyz villages were nothing special. They all smell of cow dung and are scruffy and depressing." In comparison I thought it was wonderful. I could smell wood-smoke and hayricks and, pressed between the huge silence of the mountains, the only sounds were chickens clucking and the thud of an axe on wood as someone chopped fuel.

Ashu was run by Yuristanbek and his wife Guljamal, the syllables of their names evoking ancient folklore narrated around camp fires. The guesthouse was a success because it combined modern comforts with Central Asian heritage. Usually in Kyrgyzstan you forfeit any sign of local culture for a flush toilet. At Issyk-Kul the choice was damp huts at the expense of sanitation, vast sanatoria at the expense of atmosphere or *pensionnats* like Bereke where you felt you were in a low budget Soviet film set rather than Kyrgyzstan.

While most places were still trying to remember the culture the Soviets had drummed out of them, Yuristanbek embraced it. *Tush kiz*, huge velvet drapes embroidered with nomad symbols, hung above beds. Bright *shyrdaks* muffled wooden floors. Pendants once worn on the end of hair braids, long links of silver medallions stamped with Kyrgyz curves, chinked decoratively against walls. It amazed me how luxurious and intricate traditional crafts were when Kyrgyz were credited only to have roamed steppes with their sheep. They didn't believe in travelling light.

From our bedroom we looked across the road to a large hayrick, three beehives and bumpy brown hills with a patchwork of shadows in their creases. We weren't going to be kept awake by traffic. On the wall

Yuristanbek's great grandparents stared at us severely from a large oil painting. *Babushka* wore a white headscarf and *dyedushka* his *ak-kalpak*, both sitting stiffly in heavy velvet coats of green and blue and Order of Lenin medals. They looked so real I felt sure I'd hear tutting if I didn't wrap Tom in enough blankets.

We ate lunch around an open fire which blew soot into our *lagman*. Black tea was sweetened with raspberry jam, rumoured to have curative properties.

"Do you think the water's safe?" Michael asked Matthew.

"Yuristanbek says it's from a well."

"That should be clean."

"Unless there's a dead cow in it."

Afternoon entertainment was a horse and cart ride. I watched it arrive across the muddy field, a chestnut mare pulling an open cart fastened to her by a wooden yoke. We crowded onto the wooden benches, Michael and Kay with a twin on each lap, Tom with Matthew, me with the camera, all wrapped in fleeces and hats against the chill.

We bumped through the village of Slavic cottages and muddy farmyards. Children leant on fence posts to watch us and a boy looked up from filling his churn at a *kalonka*.

"*Zdrastvooytyeh.*" I was keen to try out my Russian on locals. Altynbek, Yuristanbek's teenage son and our guide, smiled, used to being seen with city folk. No-one replied. Where was the legendary Kyrgyz hospitality? According to guidebooks they should be dragging me to their homes for tea, vodka and more food than I'd eat in a week by now.

"I don't think they understand," Michael said. He spoke fluent Russian.

"I know my accent's bad but…"

"No, it's not your accent, they speak Kyrgyz." Looking at the blank faces I felt clumsy and rude, insulting these people by perpetuating colonial disparities.

Language was a big political issue. According to rumour Akayev had only introduced the Kyrgyz exam for presidential candidates because he knew his grades would be better than Felix Kulov's – in case throwing him in prison wasn't enough. The Kyrgyz language had suffered a tortuous past, its history symptomatic of the region. With the arrival of Muslim conquerors it had been drawn into the Arabic alphabet but switched to Roman letters in 1928, until the Soviet government decreed it should be converted to Cyrillic in 1940. Generations of history and literature were lost because the communists only translated what they deemed appropriate. Since Independence there'd been a campaign to return to the Roman alphabet, which would take one linguistic struggle away from ex-pats.

In the Times of Central Asia I'd read that a new law required all advertisements to be in Kyrgyz. The Bishkek Observer was running a promotional feature, 'Let's Speak Kyrgyz!' With useful phrases like, 'I think none of us is a vegetarian. A good cutlet is much tastier than plenty of vegetables' and 'in my opinion, your producer likes only slim actors and actresses', we'd all be trilingual in no time.

Dema, like many ethnic Russians, didn't show any signs of wanting to learn his country's language: when all the signs changed he'd be as disabled as me by his ignorance.

We clopped back over the bridge and turned left. Children were scooping water from the racing river, a stubbly field was transforming into deep brown troughs behind a horse-drawn plough and leaves were red, gold and brown in the orchards. I felt we were riding through a fairy tale. In a moment Little Red Riding Hood would appear, waving her basket as she walked innocently to Grandmama's house.

Our destination was Akayev's birthplace, a pilgrimage Michael was keen to make. Being a journalist, Michael knew things. Being an avid reader of the Bishkek Observer, I knew things. As the horse trotted through the village we swapped notes. Tom slept on Matthew's lap and Ben and Tim practised new words with Kay, narrating what they saw – cow, sheep, tractor, defunct Soviet factory.

We talked about the elections and what they meant for the region. The date for presidential elections had been announced as 24th October 2005 and the international community was excited at the prospect of watching the first Central Asian leader leave office voluntarily. Unbelievably, four out of five Central Asian presidents had been in power since the fall of the Soviet Union, countries controlled by men who just happened to be the local Soviet boss in 1991.

This didn't give the area a very good reputation. In oil-rich Kazakhstan, Nazabayev was rumoured to have banked sixty million dollars of bribes in Switzerland. In Uzbekistan, Karimov was intolerant of any opposition, controlled the media and tortured prisoners, although he was still America's latest ally in the War on Terror, receiving unquestioning support and millions of dollars in military Aid as gratitude for hosting an American airbase.

In Turkmenistan, Turkmenbashi had written a spiritual code of conduct and renamed days of the week – 'Monday' was now 'Turkmenbashi'. It was unsurprising that compared to these men Akayev was star pupil of the West, regularly patted on the head for his reforms and sent cheques as rewards. Did he realise they only loved him for his borders?

The press was full of election news. Akayev had promised to 'do his best' to hold parliamentary and presidential elections in accordance with the Constitution. He'd assured the American Ambassador and Deputy Secretary of State that he wouldn't stand for an unconstitutional third term. They'd promised that this would make him and Kyrgyzstan a 'showcase model of democracy'. Michael and I weren't convinced this was enough to ensure he and his family gave up money, power and influence. Was Akayev really going to retire into obscurity or was the golden boy about to play truant?

We pulled up outside his childhood home. It was a squat pale blue house with small windows, now hidden behind a high wall and gate. Compared to his Uncle's mansion down the road it was a dump, the perfect public relations image to demonstrate that the esteemed leader came from humble beginnings. The cottage was so nondescript we couldn't be bothered to get off the cart and look inside. Months later I regretted our lethargy, another piece of history we'd lost the chance to see.

On the other side of the road a family had gathered in their gateway. *Babushka* was hunched over a stick with a grey woollen scarf wrapped over her head. A fat baby, with cheeks so round she looked as though she'd been inflated, was squirming in her mother's arms. She had a down-turned mouth, probably depressed by what she was wearing: red booties, pink jumper, brown woollen trousers, floral jerkin with red buttons and a blue bonnet, a traditionally Kyrgyz combination. I couldn't help imagining young Askar Akayev kitted out like this, playing in the dirt with the other urchins and learning about Lenin at school like a good Soviet boy. Did he dream he'd one day be the country's first president, flying the world, writing books and living in palaces?

Homeward bound, and worrying about whether Tom was going to be sick again, we passed a group of women kneeling over a roll of carpet.

"Altynbek, is this a special form of Kyrgyz Ramadan prayer?" Michael asked.

"No, they make felt," he replied. We stopped to watch.

Making felt is hard work. I know because I went on a felt-making day. First you wash and dry the wool. Then you whip it with long willow sticks on an outspread hide, tease it into fluffy mounds and dye it in boiling cauldrons of roots and leaves. Next lay the wool thickly on *chiy*, mats of woven reeds, sprinkle it with hot water and roll it up. The roll is bound into Hessian cloth with rope and hot water then dragged up and down by a small boy or horse, while others stamp on it. Then you unravel the bundle, rub the wool with soap – to seal the felt and brighten colours – and get on your knees.

With forearms, in the motion of Islamic prayer, you and friends roll and press, roll and press, more hot water, roll and press until the felt is smooth and thick. Felt making takes days, a completely unsuitable occupation for lazy foreigners. You have to be stuck in the mountains with no winter clothes or struggling to survive on post-USSR wages to have the patience to make felt. I'd tried for an hour and had blue hands and a sunburnt forehead as a result. But I'd also gone home with a felt 'bag' which I could proudly say I'd made, and that's rare satisfaction in this modern commercial world.

"Do you know how they discovered felt?" Altynbek asked as we continued home. "In the legend a poor boy had holes in his shoes so stuffed them with wool. After a few days of walking he'd made felt."

"And his discovery made him a rich man?" Kay asked.

"No, a rich man stole the idea. That's how it is in Kyrgyzstan."

We returned to afternoon tea with more raspberry jam and fresh *borsok*, diamonds of dough fried into small donuts which Guljamal cooked outside over a fire. *Borsok* are a traditional Ramadan food. According to custom you have to make so many your house smells of them, so the dead can enjoy them too. Guljamal was frying hundreds, piling them up on a cloth in a bedroom. Fortunately Jenna, Dirk and their two girls Eleanor and Lucy arrived to help us eat. Stepping out of their jeep they looked city clean, we were already countrified with mud splattered up our jeans and hair smelling of wood smoke. Tom was delighted; more people to shuffle after him and fetch the ball he pushed with his feet.

"Ee-i-ee-i-oo!" Tom yelled at Jenna through the window.

"That's good singing Tom." At the age of one he couldn't walk, or barely stand, but he could dance in time to a beat and 'la' the first line of Twinkle Twinkle Little Star. He was also a modern art critic with expensive tastes: Shigaev, who we'd visited recently with Jenna, was his favourite. I assumed the abstract shapes and colours communicated with him in a way we couldn't understand.

"We've been listening to nursery rhymes," I explained. "Old MacDonald seems appropriate when there are cockerels yodelling outside the window."

Singing the lyrics I realised how violent children's songs are, refreshingly untouched by political correctness: atheists thrown down stairs, farmer's wives mutilating mice and strangers playing nic-nac on little boys' knees. We'd had translation problems during 'Polly Put the Kettle On'. Altynbek was convinced we were singing "the bitch took it off again" as 'Suki' means 'bitch' in Kyrgyz. He'd been so adamant that even Tom had picked up the word and was now shuffling round Jenna's feet saying, "beech, beech!" This wasn't a greeting I wanted him using at Playgroup.

I loved staying at Ashu. It offered sanitised rusticity; a unique but comfortable experience of rural life. From the fireplace the village felt like paradise, until you screwed up your eyes and saw how hard people worked, just to survive. I enjoyed living with a Kyrgyz family, learning how they cleaned their teeth with pieces of wood, slept on the floor on quilts and watched loud television at mealtimes.

Over dinner they watched KTR, mesmerised by flicking pictures while sucking mutton bones. KTR was Matthew's favourite channel because he often saw himself inspecting chlorination chambers – there wasn't much news in Kyrgyzstan. That night there was great excitement because Dirk appeared on screen, chairing a banking conference held at the Hyatt the previous Friday.

"It's our guest, it's our guest," Guljamal squealed excitedly, dashing off to tell the neighbours they had a celebrity staying.

"Was Askar Akayevich present?" Granny asked breathlessly.

"Not this time."

"We love him because he gives school to our children."

"What about everyone else's children?" Michael muttered into his *plov*.

"He is handsome man of our valley," Granny said proudly.

"He's got funny eyebrows," Dirk corrected.

Matthew and I wandered out into the yard. We could see stars and hear individual noises: Guljamal gossiping in lyrical Kyrgyz with the neighbours, a cow mooing, someone tapping a metal bucket to call animals in for the night. In a city sounds are lost, melding into an incessant hum.

"It's so peaceful here, can we stay?" I asked Matthew, leaning my head on his shoulder.

"I wish we could. I'm not sure there's much peace in Bishkek. Luigi's just sent a text saying there's a demonstration outside the White House."

The apathetic Kyrgyz were finally complaining and it appeared that the handsome local boy wasn't quite as popular in the capital any more.

Chapter Twenty-One – Black Mercedes

The demonstration was disappointingly small. I'd expected huge crowds and *yurts* filling Ala Too Square. In Kiev, thousands of Yushchenko supporters were packing the capital, waving orange banners and accusing authorities of ballot rigging. I'd assumed revolution was infectious and the Kyrgyz were joining their former Soviet brothers in complaining about corruption.

Twenty men were silently holding posters accusing the National Security Service of organising the disappearance of the Kyrgyz human rights defender, Tursunbek Akunov. Michael told me that his charity was investigating: they were concerned because Akunov went missing during activities opposing the current administration. An *aksakal* in an *ak-kalpak* leant against the fence, his poster asking, 'Akayev, did you forget about the people?'

'*If Akayev appoints his successor and makes state machinery work in his favour, Kyrgyzstan will see a repetition of the Ukrainian scenario*', newspaper articles screamed. They likened Ukraine's East-West split to Kyrgyzstan's North-South divide. But Kyrgyz didn't have the stamina of Ukrainians. The Ukrainians were camping in orange tents in blizzards. The Kyrgyz all went home when it started snowing a few days later, despite Tursunbek Akunov not being found.

We woke to huge flakes floating gracefully past the window. They settled on the sill, crystals so crisp I could see every delicate filament of ice in the starred hexagon. Unlike last winter the snow kept coming, rushing down thickly toward your face when you looked up. Winter suited the city. Its imperfections were covered with a white mantel, ramshackle Slavic cottages were romanticised by deep crusts of snow on roofs and screeching car horns were muffled by drifts.

The snow continued all week, settling gently onto ice packed hard by feet and car tyres. Temperatures plummeted to minus three by day and minus eight at night and I'd call Matthew every morning for a report on whether it was safe to go out. I wasn't worried about slipping; I had chains for my boots. I needed to know if other babies were being pushed around town as I didn't want to be attacked by *babushkas* for irresponsible parenting.

Walking on Bishkek's pavements was actually much easier – although open manholes and ditches were more treacherous, hidden by snow like animal traps; ruts, potholes and loose slabs were iced over into a smooth rink. I drifted along using the buggy like a zimmer frame. For local girls stiletto heels were crampons in the ice, leaving tiny holes like animal tracks.

It was cold but at least the heating had been turned on, despite Kyrgyzstan owing Kazakhstan $13.5 million for gas. The flat was cosy. Soviet heating was a credit to communism and it was wonderful to climb from the shower into a warm bathroom. Centralised hot water was also flowing again, having been turned off for maintenance. It amazed me how the authorities were able to calmly announce that there would be no hot water for a month, knowing that only ex-pats and drug dealers could afford separate heaters. Raised as obedient communists, no-one complained. In England there would be riots, strikes and calls for public enquiries if a service went off for a day.

Nicky had been inviting me horse riding for months and I finally agreed to take the risk and go. On the day of our trek she phoned for a weather report. The Tien Shan outside the kitchen window were my horoscope, telling me what conditions to expect next. Techno Matt preferred his weather station which displayed temperature, humidity and phases of the moon. Nicky just wanted to know if there were blizzards in the foothills.

It was three degrees when I left the flat and I hoped I was wearing enough layers. It felt odd to close the door on Tom and Tanzilya. Usually I was home, able to intervene if Tom became demanding, although I made an effort not to jump up every time he whimpered or Tanzilya would be justified in telling me to look after him myself. Tom was happy with Tanzilya and I trusted her so I felt *able* to leave them, just nervous at relinquishing another level of control.

My favourite bin scavenger was sitting on the edge of a flower border when I went down. He was an old man with short grey hair covering his round head and wrinkled chin, baggy black trousers tied up with string and shoes split at the toes. He always had a large checked plastic bag slung over his shoulder, one of many beggars who trawled the city's bins looking for empty water bottles.

"Afternoon. Cold isn't it." I wondered how he survived the weather. The man stared unresponsively at me. I wasn't a friend, just a rich foreigner with interesting rubbish.

"What did you have for dinner last night?" he asked.

"Roast chicken."

"Leave any for me?" He held out his hand for the bag.

"You're not emptying it here." I didn't want the neighbours coming home to my debris strewn across the drive.

He followed me round the corner like a devoted puppy, sticking closely to ensure no-one else took his prize. Other beggars dashed towards us, drawn by the magnetic force of my potato peelings. By the time I reached the road he was tossing tampons over his shoulder in his haste to find the carcass and from the other side of the road I saw him licking bones which I thought I'd picked clean. Next to him an old woman swigged dregs of coke from a bottle. An image of Mairam Akayev in furs flashed before my eyes. How could she justify shopping trips to Europe when hundreds of Kyrgyz lived like this?

The riding stable was in the same village as Anthea's house. It was run by Stanbek, Kyrgyzstan's most famous stunt rider who starred in films about galloping nomads. He looked like Sean Connery with a bulge in his jeans and grey stubble on a sunburnt face. Although I'd had lessons as a little girl I wasn't a proficient horsewoman. Having not ridden for five years I was feeling cautious and asked for a slow horse. They put me on a black stallion called Mercedes.

I hacked nervously through the village, trying to distract myself by peering into farmyards from my vantage point. Brown discs, dung cakes prepared for fuel, were piled up on the walls of animal pens and stacked next to clay ovens. Fat hens pecked in the snow. An old woman wearing layers of woollen clothes hobbled back from a wooden privy, leaving the door hanging crookedly off its hinges.

We rode up into the foothills through orchards muffled with snow, ducking under laden branches as we trotted through avenues of trees, the horses' hooves kicking up puffs of white powder. Out of the cover of trees Nicky's horse broke into a canter. When Mercedes decided to follow I clung on and tried not to think about falling.

After five minutes I stopped feeling scared enough to appreciate I was galloping along a ridge in Central Asia on a black stallion, hooves thudding on hard ground. In front of me mountains crested majestically in peaks of white, magnified against the blue sky. As I rode closer it was as if curtains were opening wider until a whole panorama was laid out before me over the edge of the plateau. The hills dipped to the valley floor where villages studded the plain, dwarfed by the huge mountains which glittered in the sun. My cheeks were flushed with cold and hair whipped my face where it had escaped the band.

I reined Mercedes to a walk, exhilarated by the speed and relief that I'd not fallen off, breathing in dung, sweat and leather. Now I'd ridden a Kyrgyz horse, all I needed to do was sleep in a *yurt* and I'd be content to leave next time Matthew warned the project funding was running out and our departure imminent.

Turning back I could see Bishkek, the three chimneys of the power station pumping smoke into the still air. Below them were Bishkek's landmarks: arterial roads running north bordered by towering blocks of Soviet concrete. They were no longer ugly to me and I felt affection for the capital. Living abroad magnifies the highs and lows of life. Catching my breath from horseback it was difficult to remember the utter desolation I'd felt when I was new and lost in the city below me. Now Bishkek felt like home.

This didn't mean there weren't bad times: days when my back ached from carrying Tom upstairs; days when I was tired of being foreign and misunderstood; days when I longed for our own house because kids outside constantly rang our doorbell for a joke; days when I was scared by the volatility of Kyrgyzstan. Matthew was warned he might need a bodyguard because unscrupulous contractors had realised only he was standing between them and thousands of dollars. We wondered whether it was safe to stay.

The difference was that I now felt able to deal with these lows because I'd realised running home to England wasn't necessarily the answer. Life there wasn't as simple as it had first looked from Aswan, Copenhagen and Bishkek. It had taken me three postings to appreciate that every country has problems, they're just different. I didn't want to spend my life searching for utopia so had learnt how to be content with where I was.

I took a taxi home because Nicky was visiting a friend in the village. The car was an ancient Lada, its plastic dashboard covered with large dials, none of which worked. The gear stick had a clear knob with an ornamental red rose inside. The front seats leant back, secured only by seat belts slung behind them and tied around the handbrake. A cicada squeaked in the heater. The driver drove aggressively, blasting his shrill horn if people didn't pull away before lights turned green. He swerved across ice, swinging his steering wheel wildly to keep control. He wore a big, fur hat and wanted to talk.

"How much would that car cost in England?" he asked as we turned into *Sovietskaya*. Being a woman I'm not very good at pricing cars but I knew it was a black Mercedes and guessed at a huge amount of dollars. Matthew and I liked to exaggerate prices, our way of trying to educate people that not everything was free in England. He let out a respectful slow whistle.

"England very expensive. But one day I have car like that."

Driving home in the pink ethereal glow of a snowy winter afternoon it was difficult not to feel festive: as it was mid December, this was acceptable. An advantage of living outside the commercial west is not being expected to start buying tinsel in August. Being a Muslim country – albeit a tight-trouser-wearing-vodka-drinking-shamanistic Muslim country – no-one cared that 25th December was Jesus' official birthday. However, some enterprising Chinese were cashing in on western traditions and selling flashing lights and trees so that in tiny corners of Bishkek, with a bit of imagination, you could feel you were on Oxford Street if necessary.

I was quite happy without oppressive commercialism because working with Sister Kathy had given me a new perspective on true poverty. I'd written an article for the Women's Club newsletter and organised for Kathy to talk at a monthly meeting. With this publicity and Susi's encouragement on the charity committee, some dollars raised at the golf tournament had been spent on medical equipment for a mobile clinic Sister Kathy was organising for her villages. She was also inundated with bags of unwanted clothes and vibrating toys from affluent ex-pats.

Hearing about life in forgotten Kyrgyz villages I felt sick about the greed, waste and gluttony of western Christmases. Sister Kathy talked about people living in empty houses: we already had so much stuff we'd have trouble finding room for more presents. She told us about children who'd be grateful for a *lepioshka* on Christmas Day: we'd eat so much food we'd complain of weight gain and indigestion. That year, more than ever, I longed to reject commercialism in recognition of Kyrgyzstan's poor, but I didn't think

Matthew's family, who we were visiting in France, would appreciate my cashing in the turkey and giving the money to Sister Kathy.

The big Christmas event of the Bishkek social scene was Lauren's 'Cosmopolitan' party, only possible because the American airbase had allowed her to buy their entire stock of cranberry juice, not available in town. It was held at Lauren's boss's house, because it was big, and hosted by three other single girls who loved Sex and the City and aspired to be that glamorous.

The guests were an eclectic mix. Looking out from the bar, waiting for my first Cosmopolitan, I wondered who all the foreigners were and where they'd been hiding. I didn't expect them all to join the Women's Club but it's normal to see most people at least once at Beta Stores. I queried this with Lauren.

"You never see them at Beta because they shop on NetGrocer and have everything sent from the States. Their houses are entirely equipped with American furniture and white goods and their fridges are bigger than your kitchen. They create isolated islands of America, only going out to visit other Americans in similar houses to eat imported Oreos. I don't know why they bother moving here."

I'd arrived alone and short on Christmas spirit. Matthew was at an office party to celebrate signing the hundredth contract. He'd be drinking a lot of vodka and giving his 'Children of Kyrgyzstan' toast: *'we have a young son and every time I look at him I'm reminded of the children of Kyrgyzstan and how much he has and how little they have so I hope that our project can help create a better future for those children and I drink to them and Kyrgyzstan.'* It always went down very well in the villages.

My Christmas spirit was lacking because I was feeling ostracised. I'd caused an international incident at Playgroup by telling Tom off for throwing cheese across Susi's kitchen. I thought it was normal to teach your child manners but I'd heard them whispering about me, incredulous that I'd been cross with him. They'd said I just didn't realise how real kids behaved, but I was considered 'proper' by Playgroup mums and called 'Earth Mother' because I used terry towelling nappies. I'd made my excuses and left early.

I was trying to avoid Gina. I'd not forgiven her for announcing a cookie swap to raise money for a playground at the American embassy, straight after Sister Kathy's presentation. By choosing that moment to ask for contributions towards something only spoilt embassy children could use, I felt Gina discredited the whole club, making us seem ignorant and insensitive. Gina was completely unaware of the discomfort she'd caused.

"Hey, have you seen Clorise's Gucci bag? Is it real or a fake?"

"It's fake." I was expert at spotting them now.

"I'd love one for Christmas, I must tell Marty. What are you hoping Santa's gonna bring? I hope my Bradley and John aren't too disappointed. We're staying here you see and I could only order them three Pokemon computer games each to arrive in time and they already asked for five." I 'hmmed' non-committally and looked around the room for someone more interesting. An image of a Kyrgyz boy beaming with joy at the sight of a *lepioshka* wouldn't leave my head.

Delphine joined us. She was stressed because her parents were on the delayed British Airways flight. Most of the ex-pat community were waiting for relations on that plane. It had been circling between Almaty, Bishkek and Baku for two days, unable to land because there was a blizzard and Manas airport didn't have the necessary radar equipment to guide it down safely. We were due to leave the next night and had already warned family that we might be snowed in for Christmas.

"This country ees sheet," Delphine said cheerfully. "How was the Egg-Nog evening Gina?" The American Embassy had organised a Christmas party to raise money for the playground.

"Real quiet, no-one came."

"Because zere was no advertisement!"

"But if you advertise you're telling terrorists where to strike, I mean, the Ambassador and all those Americans in one place..." The Embassy was so inflated with its own importance, *I* sometimes felt like bombing it.

"Gina, is there really a terrorist threat in Bishkek?"

"There are lots of things going on down south with the IMU."

"Like what?"

"I can't tell you." Gina loved to be mysterious, believing only her husband, head of security at the Embassy, knew how to save us. "But it's bad. Kyrgyzstan is classified on the same danger level as Iraq, Iran and North Korea."

"That's ridiculous. Someone gets blown up every day in Iraq."

"Hmm, well."

"Gina, if there's a tangible risk, please share it. If not, stop scare mongering."

"I wouldn't worry about safety." Dirk had come to join us with a jug of Cosmopolitan. I could understand why the Sex and the City girls were always in such trouble; these things were toxic fruit juice. "At yesterday's UN security meeting the first item on the agenda was a banana seller who'd parked his cart in front of a UN vehicle outside Fatboys. I don't think that's a catalyst for world disorder."

We finished Dirk's jug of Cosmopolitans and Gina excused herself to 'go get the Ambassador under the mistletoe'. The dance floor was now busy, a snapshot of Bishkek society: foreign men drooling over local girls in hot pants and frustrated foreign women dancing with each other. Chad from Peace Corps was entwined in the arms of an adoring Kyrgyz girl.

"I hate the dynamic of this country." Lauren had joined Dirk and I with more cocktails. "Old guys chasing young girls and clubs full of prostitutes. There was even an editorial in the Bishkek Observer explaining how to have an affair. I think I need to move somewhere more balanced, there are no normal men for me to meet."

I noticed a besotted Chad gazing at his girlfriend as she headed for the bar. After our intense Fun Run conversation I expected him to blank me. Instead he came straight over.

"Here's one for you, what's better, morality by effect or morality by intention?"

"Hi Chad! Happy Christmas. What's your friend's name?"

"Aigul. I've been thinking since we last talked, and I wonder why it's a problem that donors have selfish intentions."

I decided that if Chad didn't want to swap banal seasonal greetings, neither did I and launched into the debate.

"Aid won't help alleviate poverty while it's distributed according to political agendas rather than need." People like Chad justify this with arguments that it's only realistic for governments to give money if it achieves their objectives. If so, why pretend otherwise? Why not be honest and admit that the primary purpose of Aid is actually achieved when the *donor* has benefited, the humanitarian goals are just a secondary bonus?

"Is it better to stand back and let the Kyrgyz learn their own way?" Chad asked.

"Possibly. The big dilemma – is Aid patronising or necessary? Are we helping or imposing our own mistakes on another country in the name of assistance? Do we have a duty to interfere because we are richer or should we let countries learn in their own way and time?

"Where's your husband?"

"Work do." Chad looked more relaxed. "He's not always so belligerent, it's just that working with Aid can be frustrating when you see so much need but so much money wasted on corruption, pontificating, reports and case studies and nothing actually *done*." Chad glanced across the room where Aigul was being chatted up by a marine.

"Hm, and so many people are still desperately poor."

"Exactly." I could tell that Chad was now more concerned about keeping his girlfriend than altruism.

"I gotta go, I'll think on this some more and get back to you."

"Happy Christmas!"

Dirk and Lauren had moved on, bored by Chad's evangelism. Rather than stand on my own I followed a sign saying 'Restroom' which pointed into the main bedroom with an en-suite. It was occupied so I took a peek at the bookcase while I waited. It contained an eclectic mix. As well as the complete works of Tom Clancy there was 'How to Teach Your Baby Math', '365 Manners Kids Should Know', 'God and Ronald Reagan: A Spiritual Life' and 'The Great Game', staple reading for anyone coming to Central Asia it appeared from my review of people's libraries. I was just peering closer to look for 'How to Behave When the Ambassador Comes to Tea' when the door clicked and the host walked out.

"Hi! Great books!" I blurted, trying to cover my nosiness.

"Sure thing. That math book has really helped my Brady. Do you have kids?"

"Just one, Tom, aged one year and two months."

"Good job! How's he doing?"

"Fine. He keeps me busy shuffling round on his bottom."

"I heard about him at the Egg-Nog party. You do know that all the books say a child should be crawling at nine months and walking by twelve?"

"Yes, but I didn't walk until I was twenty-two months and I can get around fine now." I was tired of Americans being paranoid about Tom's alternative development and the look of incredulity on this man's face was making me angry. How dare someone who owned a book called 'How to Teach Your Baby Math' criticise my son. It was worse than being confronted by an interfering *babushka*: as I was drinking this man's cocktails and needed to use his loo there were rules of social decorum.

My father taught me that comparisons are odious but sometimes it's important to defend your child. Shamefully, I entered the Competitive Parent Zone.

"Are you calling Tom retarded? He may not be able to walk but he's been pooing in a potty since he was eleven months old, can say 'aubergine', pronouncing all three syllables, and is a discerning critic of modern Kyrgyz art."

"What's an aubergine?" I'd forgotten Americans say 'eggplant', that didn't sound quite as impressive. It was time to end the conversation.

"Thanks for the party, great cocktails." With an apologetic wave I stormed into the bathroom and calmed down reading 'Excuse Me Your Life is Waiting'.

We drove to the airport the next night in minus fifteen degrees. The city was deserted, frozen in suspension. Outside town the road was lined with ghostly white skeletons of tall poplars, their branches iced into stems of delicate glass. I had no expectations of any planes leaving in these conditions. The airport was in chaos, everyone whose flights had been cancelled that week hoping to get on ours. A power cut plunged us into darkness for ten minutes and through the window we could see icy-blue fog creep across the runway. Somehow, miraculously, we all got on a plane which took off. Matthew and I prayed hard for journey mercies while Tom lolled across my lap. I hoped the difficulties would be worth it. I was looking forward to western luxuries in France: *pain-au-chocolat*, decent wine and a bath.

Chapter Twenty-Two – A Soviet Winter

January was even colder than December. The morning we flew back it was minus ten degrees, but with clear skies we landed without incident – unless you count Tom vomiting then falling asleep as we taxied. There'd been no thaw for a month and only *Manas* was gritted, to save Akayev's convoy the indignity of sliding into ditches on the way home. Roads were thick with shiny black ice and the back end of Dema's jeep skidded in arcs as we turned corners.

As a 'welcome back to Bishkek' treat I took Tom to the hairdresser. I'd already trimmed baby curls, weeping as I snipped golden strands from the nape of his neck. As my mother had commented that his fringe looked as though a mouse had chewed it, I decided it was time for a professional cut.

With hundreds of hairdressers in Bishkek I asked Tanzilya's advice – I didn't want Tom given a pudding basin or shaved head in local infant tradition. Tanzilya took us to Altynai where her Uzbek friend Nargiza worked. Nargiza was gorgeous; slim with coffee coloured skin, long dark hair and tantalising glimpses of midriff when she reached for a comb. Unsurprisingly, Matthew and Ben decided that taking Tom and Siana for haircuts was definitely a daddy's job.

With Tom looking very smart and grownup, I decided I should find a hairdresser rather than wait until our next trip home. Since a girl called Sharon 'thinned' my hair until it resembled a well-used Brillo pad I've had trouble trusting hairdressers, so selecting a salon in every new country is always stressful. In Denmark I chose the salon closest to our flat – less distance to run home crying. In Egypt I chose the stylist the other two ex-pats used, a crazy Lebanese man called Mahmoud who turned out to be the best hairdresser I've ever had.

In Bishkek Tanzilya chose me Irina, who also worked at Altynai. I sat nervously in front of the sink. To avoid a bad cut it's important to communicate precisely with your stylist – that's what makes me anxious about nomadic hairdressing. Anna Petrovna and Ivan Ivanovich never discussed haircuts so asking a hairdresser for a trim wasn't one of my stock phrases. I muttered something about 'little-little', making an inch between thumb and forefinger and holding up a frizzy clump of split ends. Irina nodded and slathered shampoo which smelt like bubblegum across my scalp before leading me to the chair.

The worst thing about going to the hairdressers, once you're there, is sitting in front of the mirror. You have plenty at time to study blemishes and work out that neither you, nor your new cut, are as gorgeous as the posters around the walls. While Irina tugged a comb through my hair I gazed at the bags under my eyes, crescents of blue deepening at the sockets and curved over my lids so it looked as though I had an X charcoaled across my face – Tom had a cold and wasn't sleeping well. I felt old. At least I didn't have grey hair.

Irina pinned up layers with a clip then jabbered at me. In panic I realised she was asking a question. It wasn't safe to resort to my catch-all answer "*da*" – I might emerge with Orang-utan orange high-lights. I wished my life was a DVD so I could change the language setting. My Russian knowledge was eclectic, confined to what was in the textbook. Although I could add the correct genitive ending onto fish, milk and eggs when they *weren't* in the fridge, take me outside my limited zone and I was clueless. Irina asked again. I smiled apologetically and explained I didn't understand. She shrugged and started chopping.

I'd almost dozed off when Irina pulled a clump of hair back from my temples. I sat up in horror. There, hidden under the brunette, were strands of grey, proof at last that I really was a parent and too old to go clubbing without feeling foolish. Noticing my distress Irina pointed to the colour sheet of dyes. Maybe I would have to succumb and by the time the next intake of young mums arrived in Bishkek, I'd be advising them on where to get the best colour. The greatest insult would be when locals started calling me *jenshcheena*.

Walking home the fresh-cut tips of my hair froze – I was too distressed to sit in front of that mirror long enough for Irina to dry it. It was snowing again, flakes falling slowly as if suspended. This was the real Soviet winter I'd craved the year before, extremes of weather I'd only seen in films. In bazaars vendors covered vegetables with eiderdowns to stop them freezing but every potato in town was still black. The city was grey with cold, people sliding along pavements, pulling children in sledges, stamping feet at trolleybus stops with scarves wrapped over heads, each expelled breath a cloud. Long daggers of ice hung from gutters and roofs, glittering fangs falling from each corrugation.

Outside the *banya* old women sold bunches of dry birch leaves, ready for citizens to warm themselves with steam and self flagellation. In Ala Too Square the photographers had built igloos to shelter in. Anyone who had a spade had been out shovelling so that piles of snow were in mounds on every corner. When it thawed I was sure they'd find lost *babushkas* frozen inside.

I was worried because Bin *Babushka* hadn't appeared all week and I'd not seen my favourite homeless man since the riding trip. For me this cold was a picturesque novelty but it killed those without homes. Tramps huddled around the eternal flame in Dubovy Park and chilled families sat outside Beta Stores, one child in a wheelchair while the baby suckled at a breast drooping from a ragged coat. How could I worry about whether Tom was absorbing enough iron when these children survived on whatever scraps strangers put into raw, outstretched hands?

"Don't feel too sorry for them," Nicky warned. "I know it looks tough but they probably have a flat to go to. They're allocated a patch by the Mafia, who take a cut, hire that wheelchair at Osh bazaar for a hundred *som* a day and make a good profit from sensitive foreigners. They might even hire the baby and they certainly drug it with vodka. I'm not saying they have a great life but it's not as bad as it looks and by giving money you're not necessarily helping."

I still felt uncomfortable walking by with my eyes forward as if blinkered. Even chanting "you're rented, you're rented," under my breath didn't help when the eyes of the woman pleaded with me mother-to-mother. I felt callous and went straight home to find more clothes to give to Sister Kathy as recompense.

The cold had even started to kill those who did have homes. Kyrgyz tradition came to the modern city when an elderly politician died in the shoebox opposite. According to folklore the *yurt* should be the last home of a Kyrgyz and I watched two being erected on the snow outside, helpers blowing on freezing fingers as they fumbled to tie red rafters to the circular frame. Hay was spread on the floor and thick felt thrown over reed-mat walls but it would still be sub-zero in there without a stove – alright if you're dead but miserable for the widow who was expected to sit in one of the *yurts* with female friends and relations for three days. Snuggled under my duvet, warmed by extra radiators because it was so cold even the district heating couldn't cope, I wondered if she was still out there, shivering as she kept her vigil.

Next day mourners visited, wrapped in furs and grateful their spouse hadn't died mid-winter. Bereavement was a mechanical process, expressed communally, openly and loudly. Tanzilya told me that in villages women were hired with soap or tea to come and wail. Outside our window I noticed that people would be chatting happily around the samovar until someone new turned up. Then, as if a director had called, "cue, sorrow!" they'd howl, bow their heads, sniff and dab eyes for five minutes before returning to cigarettes.

They were still weeping outside in minus twelve the following morning when I passed on my way to meet Susi. She was taking me to Ortosai bazaar, keen to introduce me to her favourite vendors before she left at the end of the month. Tom was staying at home with Tanzilya in the warm.

I'd been trying to find a bazaar where I felt comfortable shopping, attracted by rumours of bargains and useful treasures you couldn't find anywhere else. Osh bazaar, the place Luigi had shown us on the first morning as we drove into town, was closest to our flat so I'd walked there with Tom. After five minutes I'd been so intimidated I'd run away.

Osh bazaar was a magnet for the desperate of Kyrgyzstan: muddy, dirty, grey and mouldy with the crushed flotsam of human capitalism. It was full of beggars with no legs strapped into makeshift wheelchairs, their faces swollen into caricature features. Stalls were squeezed into narrow alleys: old women selling curd cheese, men selling rancid milk and sullen girls selling chicken heads. Grubby urchins rammed metal carts into your legs. A peacock waited patiently under an eiderdown to be photographed with shoppers. Next to him stood his dead brother, tail pinned to a board.

I'd resigned myself to failure until Susi introduced me to Ortosai. Smaller and therefore less aggressive than Dordoi and Osh it was a place to shop without feeling scared. It was also where Susi had discovered smoked ham. For this reason alone I was willing to risk a mugging.

The meat hall at Ortosai bazaar is not somewhere to visit if you are verging on vegetarianism. It's raw and wet and smells sweet and metallic with decaying blood, even in minus twelve. Every piece of every animal is displayed somewhere in its rows, a blunt reminder of what meat we happily buy packaged into sterile cellophane really looks like.

I concentrated on taking photographs – I wasn't really there to buy anything, I didn't want liver flukes. I just wanted to stare and take pictures to shock people at home. There were skinned rabbits, splattered like road kill, geese with stretched necks, yellow gall bladders, huge pigs' heads and the regular hearts and brains.

At the entrance a smiling man in a jumper was dismembering sheep carcasses with a hacksaw, knocking back shots of vodka to keep warm. Opposite him a grumpy woman in a grey bobble-hat sat behind a stall of plaited intestines and white guts which hung like sacks. There was a man scraping cow's tongues and a noisy group of women stacking cow's hooves. On their table were charred, black sheep heads, rows of them with ears sticking stiffly out, glistening eye balls staring blankly and dirty teeth bared into rigid grimaces. They did not look appetising.

Despite the gore I did buy some ham, vouched for by Susi. The *babushka* took my money and touched all remaining joints reverently with the notes.

"First sale of the day," Susi explained. In the next freezing hall two chatty ladies in headscarves and thick coats were stirring pails of yoghurt.

"You must try it. Fresh and delicious..."

"...and tuberculosis guaranteed," Susi murmured. The buckets didn't look terribly clean but the ladies wouldn't accept "*nyet spaceeba*" so I leant forward to have a spoon shoved in my mouth. It was surprisingly tasty; creamy and fresh with splinters of ice.

In the vegetable warehouse potatoes were wrapped in their eiderdowns and parsley and coriander were kept in glass boxes, prevented from freezing by lit candles so that they looked like tiny shrines. There were oranges, carrots, and turnips, jars of honey, boxes of nuts and pyramids of dried apricots glowing in the weak sun. Outside in the icy alleys *lepioshka* sellers hid cold chins in roll-neck jumpers and traders took money quickly with chilly fingers. By the time we'd finished shopping my toes were numb, despite the extra pair of socks.

"Great, isn't it," Susi enthused as we walked to the car, treading carefully down steps made narrow and treacherous by ruts of ice. "I'm going to miss Ortosai." Susi was moving to Geneva, Pete posted to UN headquarters. As Susi was a friend who I saw or chatted to every day I was trying not to think about the gap she'd leave.

Driving back through the wintry streets I felt a sense of achievement – at last I could shop with confidence in a bazaar where I didn't think I'd be stabbed. Now Bishkek felt like home I was emerging from the attitude of survival, wanting to try unfamiliar foods in supermarkets, braver about experimenting. Kumashai had translated everything in the dairy counters so I even knew what all the weird packets were. I was gaining control: it had only taken me twenty months.

The next day was Susi and Alfie's last Playgroup. It was held at Penny's house, a huge building in the centre of town barricaded behind a high wall. To honour the occasion I bought a synthetic cake in a square box tied up with string – I was starting to assimilate Kyrgyz tendencies. I was obsessed Tom wore a hat, liked neat vodka and had even retrieved something from a bin. I'd know it was too late to go home when I started spitting.

The cake was round and chocolate with pink flowers and looked better than it tasted. Siana enjoyed it most. Tom was too busy showing off new skills, pointing at Nicky's tea and saying "cup". He did circuits of the ground floor on his bottom, wheel spinning on rugs and door ledges. Outside it was snowing again, adding another layer to the frozen crust. "How beautiful" we all said, forgetting the homeless, villagers with no heating and mourning widows in felt tents.

Susi left Playgroup early. She'd already reached the miserable stage of limbo when you're desperate to be gone and ease the pain. Once your home's been ripped apart you feel too displaced to be comfortable. As I left I dreaded the day when I'd say goodbye and walk out of Playgroup forever, listening to people organise playdates and knowing life would go on without me.

We'd formed routines and relationships that would be hard to break. Tanzilya might visit us to practise her English, but I knew that we'd probably say goodbye to Dema forever. He'd watched *Malinki* Tomas grow up and adored him like a grandchild. The separation would be distressing. I could picture the scene at the airport: Dema's desperate hands pressed up to the glass and Tom screaming for him.

Thinking about leaving I felt an oppressive melancholy, as if a good holiday was ending. Images played in my mind, flashbacks I'd watch as we took off from Manas airport for the last time: Dema in his jeep; walking to the *bazaarchik*; Bin *Babushka* sitting cross-legged on her stool. Don't cry, your tears will freeze, I told myself. I knew that gradually those memories and the pain would fade as I became subsumed into a new life in England, but that wouldn't make parting any easier.

We were walking home because Dema was away on a hunting expedition. Tom growled at stray dogs and grubby bin scavengers. Tiny flakes of snow were falling gently as if someone was waving a giant sifter over the city. Pigeons huddled on blue, wooden window ledges for warmth where plastic had been taped over glass as extra insulation. It was minus ten degrees, the cold biting my cheeks and pressing against temples. The park was muffled in silence, made smaller and enclosed by branches bending under the weight of snow. The statue of Togolok Moldo was wearing a white bowler hat and the trees looked as though fluffy balls of cotton wool had been stuck to them. I could see the cold as darkness fell. Delicate flakes settled like dandruff on my collar. Outside our flat the *yurt* was quiet, the samovar being stoked for the final night's vigil.

On the third day of mourning a crowd of men in fur hats and coats arrived in old Soviet buses. They gathered outside the *yurts*, passed their hands in front of their faces with a roar of reverence and escorted the body to the frozen cemetery, leaving the widow behind because women aren't allowed at the burial.

The *yurts* were down by teatime. All that was left of the man were dents in the snow and a pile of stones, a memorial of where he'd lain which would remain for forty days.

"One less politician to contest the elections," Larissa the caretaker told me when she delivered a 4 *som* gas bill she'd found on the stairs – 6 pence for three months' cooking. The elections were only four weeks away and campaigns were in full rampage. Politicians proclaimed their honesty on KTR broadcasts, cruising cars blasted policies from megaphones and posters overlapped on lamp posts, torn down by the opposition then re-pasted by supporters.

Tom and I studied the candidates in our area. We had the choice of a bald man who leaned on a walking stick or hugged a child – he was wealthy because he also had a billboard on *Manas*; a scary military man with a green uniform and black moustache; a woman with a black bun, thick glasses and magenta blazer and a young, pretty, intelligent-looking girl in a black suit and white shirt whose poster read 'hard work and honesty'. This was Bermet Akayeva, the President's daughter.

According to one brave newspaper, the Caspian Business News, Bermet shouldn't have been running because she breached a controversial law stating that candidates must have lived in the country for the past five years – she'd been in Geneva. One candidate had already been denied registration under it; Roza Otunbaeva, who'd been abroad serving as deputy representative of the UN secretary general in Georgia. Roza was chairwoman of the Ata-Jurt party, a very popular opposition politician, formerly Akayev's Foreign Minister. She was the lady in the magenta blazer, due to run against Bermet.

Her supporters had taken to the streets in yellow scarves and ribbons, picketing parliament to amend the Election Code so that diplomats could run. Akayev's press secretary responded with scare mongering. "People wearing yellow shirts are pushing this country into an abyss," he warned. "An attempted velvet revolution may trigger off a civil warfare…The people who aim to re-enact last year's Ukrainian events may make it into a Tajikistan of 1992…yellow stands for treachery with us Kyrgyz."

An amendment to the Election Code was made, but rejected, because Akayev forgot to sign it. With Roza disqualified and no-one else daring to mention Geneva, Bermet was free to contest her first seat in parliament against a bald, old man and army general with a dodgy moustache. Her constituency was known as the University District and Bermet's supporters were thousands of students who screamed and mobbed her for autographs at every appearance. Rumour was they'd been threatened with expulsion if they didn't vote the right way.

Apparently, no-one was predicting that the elections would be calm, but then no-one predicted what actually happened either. Rumours were buzzing around the ex-pat community, the latest that barricades were being set up around Bishkek to keep any rowdy, protesting peasants out. The American Embassy were advising their staff to stay within city limits, not wanting Gina trapped in a village where there was no water, electricity or widescreen fifty-two inch plasma television.

Ilke was annoyed because she'd been planning to ski. We were annoyed because we'd be planning to watch *Ulak-tartysh*. We both decided to go anyway.

"See you at the demonstration," I told Ilke. "Bring a bottle, preferably broken."

There are many popular horseback games in Kyrgyzstan: 'kiss-the-girl', wrestling, racing. *Ulak* includes a headless goat; those of you who are squeamish should skip to the next chapter.

Ulak is the Central Asian national game, called *kökpar* in Kazakhstan, *buzkashi* in Afghanistan and "that gross goat game" by Gina. It involves two teams of four wild men on four wild horses wrestling a dead goat from each other and chasing up the pitch to dump it on a goal. It's fast, it's bloody and it's violent, but the winners get a good meal afterwards because the prize is the goat, tender after two hours of pummelling.

Nicky and Ben had discovered that *Ulak* was being played every Saturday in a village south of Bishkek called Koi Tash. I was delighted; raw and traditional Kyrgyzstan only half an hour's puke-free drive away. Matthew and Dema were less excited.

"What d'you want to go and watch these idiot peasants for?" Dema asked, picking us up. "And it's freezing today." I thought it was warm; it's amazing how your perspective changes. I'd woken up thinking, 'wow, it's hot, Tom can wear shorts and t-shirt and we'll go to the pool'. It was minus five.

We set off to the mountains, Tom wearing bootees Galena, Dema's wife, had knitted him and clutching a measuring jug – toy of the week. He was babbling about what he saw, the occasional word decipherable; car, cow, keys. I'd always wondered what was going through his mind, now I was starting to find out. Outside Bishkek, a few hundred metres higher, it was colder and snowing – again.

The game was due to start at twelve but when we arrived at 12.15 men in fur coats and hats were standing around drinking vodka, some chatting casually from horseback. It had the feel of a hunt meet: an evocative equestrian smell of worn leather and manure, the anticipation of a gallop across the countryside, men restless for a kill. On the way Dema told us he'd shot a fox on his hunting trip and asked us if we killed them in England. Unfortunately our Russian wasn't quite advanced enough to discuss the English and their feelings for foxes.

The village was on the edge of the mountains which were hidden in a sky so white only black silhouettes of poplars distinguished where sky finished and pitch began. A pale yellow sun strained through the clouds, mingling with wood smoke to tinge everything with a cold haze. It was bitter and oppressively grey. Without electricity there was no comforting glow of lights radiating from cosy homes. The houses looked bleak and chilly and I sensed the complete desolation of a Kyrgyz winter: no heating or hot water just ice and snow and inescapable cold.

We waited, horses getting restless and trying to bite each other. A funeral cortege processed across the pitch dragging spades and an empty stretcher, *babushka's* heads sagging into huge coats. I tried talking to a man on a grey mare. He was wearing black leather boots, an anorak and round fur hat, leaning along the horse's spine as if they were one body.

"Excuse me, what time does the game start?" He stared blankly. Maybe he didn't understand Russian – or my version of it. I tried extra polite phrasing, the type Anna Petrovna uses when she's trying to impress the ticket officer at the railway station.

Йзвйнйте пожалуйста – don't forget, in Cyrillic й is EE, в is N, н is N, у is OO and с is S. How are you doing? *"Eezveeneetyeh pajalsta, vas skolka nachenayetsa igra?*

He grunted an answer, which I understood because the week before we'd learnt about Russian double negatives and I'd excelled because they translated directly into Bristolian: "I don't know nuffink."

I was saved from prolonged 'look at the absurd foreigner' embarrassment by an enthusiastic boy who trotted over with a friend clinging on behind. He was keen to practice the English he learnt at school.

"Game start when goat come. My father gone to buy." We swapped names and countries of origin. He was Talibek, born in the village. His friend was Osmanakun, also born in the village.

"I have dream," Talibek leaned closer, pressing his weight onto the Adidas trainer wedged in his stirrup. "I want live America." He sat back up, looking at me triumphantly.

At times like this I tried to give my lecture on how the streets of America weren't paved with gold but hand guns and that if he gave up everything to move there he wouldn't live in a clapboard house with an SUV and satellite dish but a bedsit with hundreds of other immigrants. He'd get a job cleaning MacDonald's toilets, if he was lucky, and befriend an Uzbek crime lord because he'd be the only one who'd understand his language and love for sweet apricots from Issyk-Kul. He'd end up smuggling drugs from JFK to La Guardia, be caught, arrested and buggered in jail for being a foreign peasant.

If his father was rich enough to buy the goat – at $50 that was more than a month's salary for most – he'd be more comfortable in Kyrgyzstan.

My Russian failed me and I bleated a pathetic, "it's very expensive in America."

"But everyone rich!" Our conversation was interrupted by the arrival of a tiny, white Lada from which the goat was pulled.

"Oooh," said Tom, who was busy driving Beebob's – as he now called Dema – jeep. The goat was still alive. Were they going to chase it around the field until it died? I wasn't sure I'd stay for that.

We watched nervously as everyone jumped onto horses and followed the goat to the centre of the field. Slung across a saddle it looked around in bewilderment, wondering what it was doing there. Its last view was ankles and hooves as its legs were grabbled and with a roar from the crowd a man bent over and cut its throat. The onlookers passed both palms down over their faces in Kyrgyz genuflection, thanks for the meal they'd eat later. While we watched in horror the head and feet were severed and tossed into the field. Then one of the players heaved the warm corpse onto his saddle, bloody neck flopping, and the game began.

Bellowing and waving whips, four men on stringy horses chased after the goat. They clashed further down the pitch and the crowd pressed in to watch, those on horseback galloping closer for a better view. The eight players were locked in a scrum, bent over each other as they grappled for the goat, whipping horses and opposition in the frenzy. The horses snapped and reared, baring teeth as bridles were jerked. They snorted steam into the cold air, kicking up snow as they swerved to the commands of their riders.

Eventually someone broke away with the carcass dangling by a leg. The pack gave chase as he headed for the goal and scrummed again until, with screams and yells from the crowd, the goat was dropped onto the target. Then the next team charged onto the pitch and the ruck began again.

It was primitive, violent, passionate and bloody freezing, truly reflecting the rawness of Kyrgyz life. Unlike huntsmen in smart red coats and shiny boots, this was played in everyday clothes on scraggy horses which stumbled and sweated and threw their riders. No-one flinched at the goat's head tossed into the crowd or the carcass fought over while still warm and dripping because in rural Kyrgyzstan there's no place for pomp and sentiment when your life's a fight for survival. If this was how Kyrgyz men liked to relax after a cold, hard week under the mountains, I wouldn't back the politician who tried to tell them to leave the poor goat alone and chase a stuffed pillowcase around the field.

A ruck spiralled in our direction and I staggered back as a horse stamped off the pitch with bleeding mouth and steaming flanks. It tossed its head and shied sideways, reluctantly pulled into another gallop. It's hard work being a horse in Kyrgyzstan. Although revered by your owner as a hero of legends, you have to be prepared to play *Ulak*, tow anything – we'd seen a horse pulling a broken down Lada on a cart – and be eaten when it's your turn to be sacrificed for a funeral feast.

I snapped a few more photos, hoping I'd capture the force of the impact as, whipped by its rider, the horse crashed into the scrum.

"*Amereekanka?*" The question came from two policemen who'd pulled over to watch. They were wearing their winter uniform of grey fur hats and overcoats and squatted down next to me, eyes on my camera, smoking and spitting.

"*Nyet, Angleechanka.*"

"She lives in Bishkek, her husband's a water engineer," Adylbek explained protectively. He was Talibek's uncle, an old man with terrible teeth and a grey moustache who'd been explaining the rules to me after Matthew had retreated to the safe side of the ditch with Tom: Stanbek at the riding stables had cheerfully warned me that a few spectators were killed each year. Adylbek hawked noisily, clearing thick green mucus from the back of his throat and projecting it into the white snow. "He's helping to improve our country."

Unimpressed, the police moved away, put off by Adylbek's teeth. I returned to the game, my camera clicking as the carcass was dropped onto the goal.

"*Oopala!*" shouted Adylbek. Another team raced onto the pitch.

Chapter Twenty-Three – To the Polls

The Bishkek International Women's Club St Valentine's Charity Ball was held on Saturday 19th February, a week before parliamentary elections. I'd been waiting for this event for two years and was grateful to the IMU for postponing terrorist activities so it wasn't cancelled again. There were a few protests going on in Osh, roads blocked and the courthouse picketed because an opposition candidate had been deregistered. According to the Russian Communist Party the protests were orchestrated by Britain and America who were destabilising the situation as part of a master plan to remove Akayev and Karimov and alter the geo-political balance in Central Asia – which was why no-one in the international community was concerned and the ball proceeded.

That night we were staying at the Hyatt so I could have a bath and didn't have to struggle home through snowdrifts in party shoes at 1am – snow between the toes is not comfortable. Tanzilya was coming to stay with Tom. I'd been worrying about the ethics of this for weeks. I wasn't worried about Tom being safe or happy: Tom loved Tanzilya. When we went shopping after she left on Thursdays he'd turn away from me in his car seat, cross because I'd sent his best friend away. I was worried that he might be permanently traumatised if he woke in the night and Tanzilya arrived in a nightie rather than Mummy. My greatest worry was that he wouldn't miss us at all.

I hovered by the door with last minute instructions, prolonging goodbyes until Matthew pushed me out. Insensitive to his mother's trauma, Tom waggled his fingers as a wave and said a dismissive "bye." I felt better once we were underway. A glow was settling over the cold city, car headlamps and shop windows gleaming yellow in the purple sky. It was still freezing. You had to be impressed with Kyrgyz stamina. In England everyone would have perished by now, hidden inside since the first snow, closing schools and roads and complaining about not being prepared. In Bishkek they really weren't prepared – there was one gritting lorry and that just went up and down *Manas*. But nothing closed: at school they kept coats on and drivers just steered their Ladas slower over the ice. You couldn't cancel life and stay at home for three months.

Being a wimpy foreigner I was bored of winter. The novelty of blizzards had worn off and I was tired of having to allow an extra twenty minutes to layer up before we could venture out. Life felt heavier under the weight of snow, coats and jumpers. I longed for the lightness of spring. It served me right for whining about wanting to experience a real Soviet winter. I felt like saying, "it's okay God, you can turn the heat up now, we've seen enough."

In our posh room at the Hyatt I had my expensive bath and Matthew opened the complimentary bottle of Moldovan champagne from Gerhard. We had a panoramic view of the Tien Shan, Opera House and chimneys of the power station if we leant out far enough. For the social event of my year I wore a long, red chiffon dress with the black kitten heels I'd fortuitously packed two years before. Irina had straightened my hair and I'd thought scarlet lipstick a good idea until I saw the photographs afterwards.

My first job of the evening, as a member of the Standing Committee, was to sit by the door and check-off guests on the Kontroll-Liste provided by Claudia From. I was assisted by Sandy, also on the Standing Committee. Sandy was American, a teacher at the International School and wife of the headmaster, who headed mine and Matthew's list of possible CIA agents.

The Kontroll-Liste read like an extract from the Bishkek Observer. Any politician with social standing or fond of free fags – the ball was sponsored by the cigarette factory – was attending. Highest ranking was Djoomart Otorbaev, Deputy Prime Minister.

"Where are your boobs?" Dirk arrived with his usual level of decorum. Mine were on ample display – Matthew said I confused people, Mary Poppins by day, cleavage-showing-bar-dancing-hussy by night. "You looked so good last week with your hairy chest!" Ah, he was talking to Matthew. The previous week the German Embassy had hosted a carnival party and Matthew had starred as Larissa in my red leather mini skirt. His balloon breasts were so round and firm everyone spent the whole night groping them. He was now more famous than me in Bishkek.

That night Matthew was sedately dressed in a polyester dinner jacket and bow tie which, after a lot of research, we'd found in Beta Stores. We'd made the effort thinking this was required for a Black Tie event hosted by Claudia From. We were wrong. Although women had kept hairdressers, tailors and beauticians busy for weeks, male guests had paid little attention to the dress code, one American wearing a diamond-patterned jumper and trainers.

The ballroom was decorated, unintentionally, like a giant womb. Fronds of pink and red chiffon were draped across walls and ceiling. Heart-shaped helium balloons floated above tables, drooping lower throughout the evening. At our table were Ben and Nicky, Michael and Kay, Dirk and Jenna and lots of free fags. Soren and Ilke were entertaining the Deputy Prime Minister at Table One with the new American and German Ambassadors.

The American Ambassador was a young, single man, elevated early to his status through connections with the Bush clan. He was delighted to be in Bishkek with so many aspiring wives to choose from. In contrast the German Ambassador looked as though he'd been found at the back of the airing cupboard, wheeled out to attend balls and open retirement homes for ethnic Germans. There was a large community of these in Kyrgyzstan as many had been deported from the western USSR by Stalin as Nazi sympathisers. His wife still had all her faculties and own hair colour. Unlike Anke she didn't play Mahjong but had been invited into the elite Bridge set. She was being groomed for an executive position: the Bridge group was a self-perpetuating oligarchy from which all Women's Club presidents emerged.

After Claudia From officially opened the event everyone dashed for the buffet. A lot of business was conducted across the hors d'oeuvres that night; phone calls behind the salmon, whispers over sushi, muttering about the inadequacies of the new Tax Code when Djoomart Otorbaev wasn't listening. At our table we were more interested in politics.

"Have you seen the bitching in the Bishkek Observer this week?" Michael asked excitedly. Akayev had been accusing the West of interfering in democracy. He'd said, *certain forces in the West are trying to bring to power in Kyrgyzstan their own people...We oppose to foreign observers turning themselves into supervisors and becoming organizers of colour revolution...international organisations want to carry out a 'Tulip Revolution.'* [24] The US Ambassador had taken some stick, accused by The Assembly of People of Kyrgyzstan of interfering in international affairs and Alga Kyrgyzstan of sponsoring opposition groups. "I wonder what Philippe thinks about all these allegations?"

"We talked about it at Playgroup this week. Delphine said Akayev was an arrogant fool and needed removing because he's been in power too long."

"Interesting. Can I quote that as the official OSCE line do you think?"

"Akayev's just cross because Bakiev from the opposition was invited to a conference in the States this year."

"But you have to wonder what all these American civil society projects are up to," Dirk interrupted, leaning across the table waving his fork. "Why are they so concerned about opening centres where locals can read newspapers, watch CNN, surf the Internet and basically learn how things are done outside Kyrgyzstan if they don't want to stir up trouble?"

"They're promoting democracy," Ben said informatively.

"But what sort of democracy? Is it the West's role to dictate how things are done or should we let countries find their own way, which is what Akayev is basically saying?"

"What he's saying is 'butt out and let me keep siphoning off my millions'," Ben corrected.

"But why would the US want to replace Akayev?" I asked. "Akayev *loves* America, he's competing with our prime minister over who's Bush's best friend."

"Because he's also best friends with Putin," Dirk explained. "As in Ukraine and Georgia, the US wants a leader who'll look primarily its way."

"The US is also hoping to upset Kyrgyz relationships with China," Michael continued. "China is getting far too pally with Russia through the SCO[25] for their liking. The rhetoric about Akayev being a corrupt despot whose family is raping the country is just a cover. America's concerned with helping states

---

[24] It's unclear who first used the label 'Tulip' but it was given because tulips originated in Central Asia
[25] Shanghai Cooperation Organisation

not individuals, just look at Uzbekistan. The UN says that torture is widespread and systematic there and yet America happily signs military agreements worth millions of dollars with Karimov."

The conversation paused while Dirk stood to greet Djoomart, returning from the buffet with third helpings of vol-au-vents. He sat down looking sheepish.

"I'm surprised he stopped to talk. Our relationship's not been the same since I got my Russian verb endings muddled and suggested we pee on a document instead of sign it."

"Maybe he's trying to keep influential friends happy in these turbulent times?" Kay suggested. "Akayev's become increasingly outspoken against his benefactors, which is unusual because he's normally so compliant."

"He got mad when Transparency International classified Kyrgyzstan as the 122nd most corrupt country in a list of 146," Michael explained. "I went to his conference and he was whining about Kyrgyzstan taking lots of measures against corruption and the report not being objective. He doesn't seem to realise that organising conferences about corruption isn't enough, you've actually got to stop stealing the money."

"Maybe he senses momentum is against him so is lashing out as a last resort?" Matthew suggested.

"He'd better be careful; the Paris Club of creditors is deciding how to restructure Kyrgyzstan's debt in March," Dirk explained. "They're not going to feel inclined to write off $450 million if Akayev keeps slagging off our Ambassador."

The Ambassador didn't seem bothered about what was being written about him in Akayev's press. He was too busy flirting with his date who could see 'visa application granted' written all over the evening.

"So, what's going to happen on Sunday?" I asked. "According to Akayev, if foreigners don't meddle the elections will pass calmly."

"But corruptly," Ben added authoritatively.

Michael was despondent. "How can there be free and fair elections when opposition candidates are heckled off stage, denied access to voters, their cars smashed and microphones unplugged mid speech. Students are terrified that the new finger-inking system to stop multiple voting is actually a way for the KGB to monitor them. The more I learn the more depressed I become that it's still a Soviet system, there's no democracy."

"Mr Turd commandeered all our project cars last week to go to Issyk-Kul and secure votes," Matthew explained. "He's panicking because the government borrowed heavily from the World Bank, pledging clean drinking water. Villagers want to know where it is."

"According to one of our surveys, water is the biggest election issue after corruption and the economy," Michael explained.

"What's Mr Turd promising in return for votes?" Nicky asked Matthew.

"Free medical checks I think."

"Something healthy at least, in Talas I heard it was free vodka. Voters are having a wonderful time collecting these bribes."

"I think you'll find they're known as 'presents'," Ben corrected.

That was the official line. Akayev was rumoured to have sanctioned the practise, telling people, "take what candidates give you but vote with your heart" – easy when your heart was owned by the most generous. The opposition were more caustic: "take the presents, they were bought with stolen money so belong to you." In Osh people were being given carpets, shawls, bowls and teapots or having leaking pipes repaired. In Bishkek the price of a vote was a bag of coal and bottle of vodka.

"Hey Michael, did you get your instructions on how to report the elections?" Dirk asked, passing the Moldovan wine.

"Yes I did! What a farce. There's no free media in this country. Anyone interested in losing their job just needs to provide impartial analysis of the parliamentary elections. As most of the media is owned or controlled by the ruling family, these instructions weren't really necessary. All journalists have been told by the presidential administration to be responsible and patriotic and remember that democracy in Kyrgyzstan is immature so we shouldn't just criticise but also find positive things to write about."

"Akayev sounds worried. Do you think he's expecting a revolution like Georgia and Ukraine?" Nicky asked.

"There won't be a revolution," Ben scoffed. "These people are too well-trained in submission after seventy years of Soviet rule."

He must have yelled 'revolution' because Djoomart turned round and started fiddling with his belt. Had he brought a handgun? Sandy and I had forgotten to ask guests to check firearms into the cloakroom – normal practise in Kyrgyz nightclubs. Fortunately he was just checking his mobile for CNN news alerts, worried what might be happening in his country outside the BIWC Valentine womb. I heard Soren trying to calm him with promises of free cigarettes and another tour of the factory once it was all over. Gerhard came over to reprimand us.

"Your table is upsetting our honoured guest with serious talk." A grin was hidden under his huge moustache. "We will distract him with the raffle. Saffia, please assist."

While Gerhard commentated, I hauled a huge goldfish bowl of tickets around the room, choosing people to pull them. Djoomart wanted every turn and sulked when I wouldn't let him. He wasn't used to being scolded like a schoolboy by a woman with a huge cleavage. We'd sold hundreds of tickets, coached by Claudia From to remind people of starving orphans and pensioners without toilets.

"Sod the orphans," Clorise had replied, "I want another flight to Istanbul!"

The flight was won by the head of a Turkish bank. Clorise won two boxes of cigarettes wrapped up with a red ribbon.

"Lucky Vladimir," she commented, collecting her prize. Our drivers loved fundraising events.

After the last cigarette had been given away it was time for dancing. Unfortunately I wasn't going to get my tango with an ambassador – one was incapable and the other distracted. And the music was unsuitable. The band was *Altyn Gul*, Gold Flower, famous for their international hit 'Issyk-Kul Girl' and Bananarama cover, 'I'm your Wenus'.

"Where's Djoomart?" I asked Dirk, ducking to avoid an arm flung out by Gina who was jiving with Marty. "I wanted a dance."

"He's been cornered at the bar by Geoffrey from Tien Shan Gold."

"The stumpy man with the florid, red face?"

"Exactly. He's telling Djoomart he'll be herding sheep by Monday if their mining license isn't signed, in between lecturing the barman on how to pour a whisky."

"Obnoxious git."

"People like him seem to think that just because this country is less developed they can bully everyone."

"Why don't you go and rescue him?"

"Djoomart?"

"Yes. My Russian isn't good enough to ask him to dance."

Claudia From climbed onto the stage and took the microphone. "Is she going to sing?" Dirk asked.

"No, she's been counting money."

"It vaz a success," she reported, "ve made thousands of dollars. Zank you on behalf of the orphans." As the band started an encore of Issyk-Kul Girl she left to stash it under her mattress.

As if in answer to my prayers, the sun came out on Monday, blasting Bishkek with its rays so that according to Matthew's high-tech weather station it was sixteen degrees. The city dripped as two months of snow started to melt. Water poured off roofs and you had to be careful where you walked to avoid being brained by a falling icicle. It didn't take long for winter's hold to lessen. By afternoon you could see grass and the previous year's rubbish preserved by the ice. Bin *Babushka* hobbled out with her stool and I was so excited to see her I rushed over and took her photo.

Meanwhile, unbeknown to us, a court in Kochkor *Rayon* was disqualifying Akylbek Japarov and Beishenbek Bolotbekov as parliamentary candidates, allegedly to make way for 86-year-old Turdakun Usubaliev who'd formally served as first secretary of the Communist Party of Kirghizia. The response was a blockade by 3000 protesters calling for justice.

They were feeling feisty in Kochkor that week because the next day 5000 demonstrators blocked the Bishkek-Torugart Highway, closing the trade route to China. They demanded the reinstatement of candidates and the resignation of the governor, kidnapping the district head when their conditions weren't met. In Jalalabad they were storming administration buildings, vowing to continue misbehaving until officials stopped harassing opposition nominees.

The demonstration which gained most coverage was one in southern Issyk-Kul. There, objecting to more de-registrations, villagers blocked the road to Kumtor's mine site so that no-one could get up and no gold could get down. The Kumtor wives at Mahjong were incensed. "How can they do this? Our men are trapped and it's dangerous?"

"Don't you have a helicopter?" I asked.

"And they might have to close the mine and stop production. It's a disgrace." Quietly I disagreed. I supported the protesters who'd got Kyrgyzstan its first international headline since the American airbase was opened. At last the apathetic Kyrgyz were rousing themselves to fight for democracy.

We discussed the excitements that night at our lesson with Valentina. She'd been stressed for weeks because her school was in Bermet's constituency. She'd been instructed by her headmaster to knock on doors telling people to vote for Bermet, expected to provide lists of those who had committed to vote the right way. Valentina was considering defecting somewhere liberal – like Russia.

Despite enthusiastic student-supporters, Bermet was rumoured to be in a close race, man with a bald head and walking stick proving tough competition. Her brother, Aidar, also running for parliament, was having an easier time standing in Kemin, the family seat. Bermet's tactics were aggressive: accusing the opposition of having a single policy – criticising the president; condemning the current parliament for being a circus and claiming that her pro-Akayev party, Alga Kyrgyzstan, was the only one engaged in real work. But Michael credited her with being an eloquent speaker and she looked impressive on the front page of the Bishkek Observer, staring determinedly at the camera, hands crossed in her lap. She had her mother's grooming and elegance, but happily *not* her father's eyebrows.

In the days leading up to Kyrgyzstan's free and fair elections, Alga Kyrgyzstan claimed that 'if they didn't retain power there would have been a coup orchestrated by foreigners'. Some factions of the opposition threatened massive protests if the elections were rigged; others said they didn't want a revolution. Electricity to the independent printing press (US funded) was cut; Radio Liberty (US funded) lost their frequencies and Akayev told the youth that the fate of Kyrgyzstan depended on them rejecting the 'orange' and 'rose'[26] viruses being pushed on them by outsiders.

Law enforcement agencies were on 'state of emergency' training, the head of the Interior Ministry insisting the timing was purely co-incidental. Parliament introduced new rules to outlaw street protests and Akayev said that unrest would be met with the full force of the military, which sounded threatening until you remembered that the army were conscripted kids who spent their time weeding rose beds on *Erkendik*.

---

[26] In Ukraine the revolution had been named 'Orange'; in Georgia 'Rose'.

Gina told me embassy advice was to stay indoors on election Sunday with passports ready and an extra supply of water. This was not a stable environment in which a country should go to the polls.

Chapter Twenty-Four – Tulips or Daffodils?

Sunday passed quietly, so quietly you wondered if *anything* was happening, let alone an election. It was a beautiful warm spring day, mountains ice-clear against the blue sky. To celebrate we took a rebellious walk. I felt sorry for the Americans huddled by their front doors but the trade-off for corporate support was conforming to company policy.

The trouble started the following week. The Kyrgyz went back on the streets, this time protesting that their contestants hadn't won because elections were rigged. They demanded an emergency session of parliament and Akayev's resignation.

"Irresponsible candidates are trampling on democratic principles by their anti-constitutional actions," Akayev retorted, president-speak for Bad Losers. The election wasn't over: most constituencies had to hold run-offs on 13th March because no-one had obtained an absolute majority. Aidar Akayev was one of few who'd secured his seat. Bermet had failed to win by 6% and had to try again. Her constituents had rebelled: there were going to be a lot less naughty students at university next term.

In Bishkek we heard fuzzy reports, gossip about the governor being kidnapped in Talas and administration buildings being occupied again. No-one took it very seriously, especially when Akayev accused the opposition of inciting civil war. Observers from Russia said they were happy with voting while Delphine's husband at the OSCE claimed elections fell short of international standards. The Bishkek Observer headlined *'No violations in polls'*, but they always wrote what Akayev wanted to read.

I called Michael for the scoop. He'd been reporting from Batken in the south and had snuck into a polling station disguised as a Finnish election observer.

"I can understand the Kyrgyz anger. As I feared it was a complete farce, Akayev's machine had total control. I watched voters tick ballot sheets, take them over to the transparent boxes[27], show them to the returns officer who'd let them post their vote or tell them to try again. Free and Fair! These elections weren't free and fair."

Into this chaos flew Musharaf, moustachioed military President of Pakistan, come to befriend Akayev, promote trade and influence and so stake his claim in the New Great Game. The administration ensured the General didn't feel threatened by revolting peasants by closing *Chui Prospect* and stationing highly-trained Special Forces at regular intervals along *Manas*. They were easily spotted by their red berets as they dozed diligently against trees. Very

---

[27] flown in from Europe to prevent cheating

quietly, in the background, the Paris Club announced they'd write off a quarter of Kyrgyzstan's debt.

"It shows and proves the world accepts our adherence to the maximum principles of democracy," a victorious Akayev claimed, declaring a vote of confidence in his rule. But it was too late, no-one was listening.

For once I wasn't taking much notice of politics because I had other problems: Tom was ill. He'd caught a cold which lingered, keeping him awake at night, coughing until he vomited. Without sleep I felt exhausted and strained, pushed to an extra edge of fear because there was no help for a midnight emergency.

Tom didn't improve. He whined and clung to me, each plaintive "mummy" pulling me to him as if the umbilical cord were still attached. I felt helpless because I didn't know what to do. On the morning he had a temperature of 38.4, hot and flopping against me, I bundled him into the buggy and went to find Dr Gideon. Fortunately he was still working in the grey and decrepit building, guarded by obdurate receptionists.

Gideon listened to Tom's chest, tapped his knees and looked in his ears while Tom tried to grab his pen.

"Yes, there's a problem." My tired mind spiralled into panic imagining a serious ear infection, deafness and emergency evacuation, all because I hadn't cared for Tom properly and brought him to the doctor earlier. Gideon left the room and returned with some pink powder. "Antibiotics. Tom has a minor ear infection. Mix with water and take three times a day until the course is finished."

That night Tom screamed with pain until 3.30am. The neighbours must have thought we were torturing him. He continued vomiting and refused to take his medicine so I fought to dose him until Jenna lent me a pipette. When he wasn't being sick Tom was adorable, pouring imaginary tea from his pot and mimicking me on the telephone, lifting the receiver saying, "yes, yes, okee, bye," and scribbling notes in the diary. It's disconcerting to see your mannerisms acted back at you. I was relieved I didn't say "bugger off, it's still the wrong number" more often.

There's no psychological aspect to childhood illness. When they feel pain they yell, when they feel better they grin at you, oblivious you're on the verge of mental collapse. No-one ever tells you how your life is going to change with children. I cleared up puke on Monday, diarrhoea on Tuesday, snot on Wednesday, listened to coughing all night Thursday and cleared up puke again on Friday. My clothes were a map of motherhood, stained with his pain. At 6am on Saturday, Tom was sitting on my knee after his morning vomit. He was leaning against me, head under my chin. His hair smelt like a favourite teddy bear. He moved suddenly, knocking a glass of water onto the floor.

"Oh dee-yah," he said, looking up at me with serious eyes. I laughed instead of crying. Children have the capacity to bring you to the edge of despair one moment and unprecedented joy the next.

While I'd been nursing, Bermet had been harassing students and won her seat in the run-offs. Bakiev lost. Akayev now had seven family members in a new single-chamber parliament of seventy-five. The opposition had six representatives.

The population went crazy, finally woken from lethargic oppression by Bakiev's calls to rise up against rigged elections. In Jalalabad, Talas and Osh administrative buildings were surrounded then stormed by excited students waving sticks and petrol bombs, and angry *babushkas* in headscarves. At the Jalalabad police station terrified officers fired a few shots then fled, leaving the masses to burn the building and celebrate. They placed rocks on the runway to keep reinforcements out and claimed control of the south. Akayev asked protesters to be tolerant and act with wisdom but they had momentum and were enjoying international fame, camping out under Lenin who still stood in Osh's main square, singing songs and passing round the vodka.

In the capital was surreal calm, everyone shopping at Tzumingdales as if nothing were amiss. Symptomatic of the north-south divide, Slavic Bishkekers dismissed protests as the sort of behaviour you'd expect from drug-dealing peasants in the Ferghana Valley.

The Ferghana Valley has a history of unrest. In 1990 ethnic Uzbeks and Kyrgyz fought over land, culminating in violent clashes in Osh during which hundreds died. In 1999 the IMU kidnapped Japanese geologists, then American climbers in 2000, the captives used to barter for ransoms and safe passage in drug and weapon trafficking operations.

Neighbouring states argue about how to deal with the terrorists, Karimov accusing Akayev of being weak and placing land mines along the border. The Ferghana Valley is considered a 'hotbed' of Islamic fundamentalism, gaining worldwide prominence and drawing oil-rich Central Asia into the War on Terror. Some say this is convenient for local dictators: confident America won't contradict them they label any unwanted dissidents 'Islamic militants' and arrest them without further justification.

Bishkekers, ashamed of their rebellious south, were grateful the Tien Shan formed a natural barrier to keep troublemakers out. No-one believed these riots would spread to the capital, despite rumours of huge convoys heading north.

"They'll never get here, it's miles away," Dema pronounced dismissively. "Anyway, there's been a landslide, the road's blocked."

Monday 21ˢᵗ March was *Nooruz*. In Ala Too Square there was no sign that the country was falling apart at its extremities. As usual *shashlik* sizzled, vodka flowed and ladies in Christmas cake hats twirled on the stage. It was only when I noticed red berets surrounding the White House, awake for once and guns ready, that I wondered whether we should be packing an emergency bag. I wasn't scared; it seemed too surreal that danger could erupt in sleepy Kyrgyzstan. Akayev wasn't worrying either. He was busy blaming western powers for inciting discontent, claiming his subjects wouldn't know how or what to protest about if they hadn't been wound up by meddling foreigners.

"What d'you think Bill's emergency plan will be?" I asked Matthew, trying to distract Tom from Kalashnikovs pointing through the White House fence.

"I don't suppose he has one. We'll know things are serious if we actually hear from him."

While Bishkek was partying, down south things were going mad. Rioters burned effigies of Akayev and nasty rumours floated up about police officers being beaten to death. Women yelled their complaints to the few international reporters who'd bothered to turn up.

"Everyone you see here is unemployed."

"Try to find anyone who has enough flour or bread." Southerners were angrier because they were hungrier.

"Akayev doesn't care about us, he's for northern clans. Instead of people we trust, his children were brought in. We've had enough of him."

Political commentators remained unexcited, advising that although the situation was 'finely poised', another colour revolution was unlikely without an icon the opposition could unite behind. Calmly, they discussed contenders. The favourite was Felix Kulov but unfortunately he was in prison. Being incarcerated by Akayev had done wonders for Kulov's image. Once just mayor of Bishkek and Minister of Interior Affairs, he'd been martyred into the people's hero.

Other contestants were Kurmanbek Bakiev, darling of the south, visitor to America and persecuted election candidate. Roza Otunbaeva, who'd been disqualified and led the first protest, was also a figurehead. But would any of these be enough to coalesce the anger which seemed to be boiling out of control? Protesters couldn't even choose an emblem, wearing yellow, pink and green and waving daffodils and tulips; symbols of different factions with different agendas. Bermet was right; the only thing the opposition did agree on was dislike of Akayev.

On Tuesday evening Akayev went on KTR and said he was ready for civilised dialogue. Bill from Fatboys called and asked for our passport numbers. I packed emergency bags. I was a veteran of this, having been ready to flee from Egypt in the hours after September 11th when everyone thought the world was ending. You learn something about yourself when forced to choose what to take in ten minutes. In Egypt my priorities were journals and negatives, Matthew's his childhood teddy. This time we had to replace them with nappies and beakers.

I packed for three levels of escape. A small bag if we had to run for our lives – passports, water and a nappy. Two backpacks if we escaped by coach – journals, negatives, clean underwear and a couple more nappies. Huge holdalls in case Bill organised for us to be airlifted from the base – included in these were my Bishkek Observer archive, after much arguing with Matthew about priorities.

The whole city went to bed tense, no-one sure how this would end. I thought I heard a crowd chanting in the distance. It was dogs barking.

Rebellion came to Bishkek on Wednesday. By 11am Ala Too Square was packed with students waving banners declaring 'No to colourful revolutions!' and 'We love Akayev!' Where were the angry students Ulla's husband Mark had talked about, the new generation who were supposed to explode?

"We were told to come," they explained apologetically, "under threat of expulsion. We don't love Akayev, he's got ridiculous eyebrows."

Despite the apathy Matthew's office closed for fear of stray Molotov Cocktails. He and Luigi evacuated with computer hard drives and the contents of the safe in a plastic bag. I went shopping with Tom, whose new word was 'Kalashnikov'. It didn't look like there was about to be a bloody revolution. People were strolling in the sun eating ice-creams and pushing kids on swings.

It was my turn to host Playgroup, a small, controllable gathering because most were away for half term. Penny was on a Thai beach, Jenna was in Istanbul and Delphine was in Paris buying vanilla pods. Bored of discussing riots and revolution, Ilke, Kay, Nicky and I swapped the exciting news that aubergines had been sighted at Narodne and optimistically bought tickets for a concert hosted by the First Lady at the Opera House on Friday.

On Wednesday afternoon Akayev started sacking ministers and announced he was sending Tanayev, the unpopular Prime Minister with a huge grey quiff, to Osh. Michael reported a protest opposite Fatboys, symbolically under the Monument to Fighters of the Revolution: not a wild mob but civilised northerners asking Akayev to go.

"Dear and respected Askar Akayevich, you have been our president for fifteen years and we respected you but do you see what is happening with the people, what is happening with this country? Please leave and let the people elect their new parliament."

The protest was short and violent, quickly crushed by riot police in white helmets who demonstrated the benefits of their recent state-of-emergency training by dragging young girls away by their ankles in teams of eight. The new Interior Minister, hard-man Keneshbek Dushebayev, appeared on television reassuring everybody that they weren't going to shoot at women, old people and children. I didn't feel reassured.

On the morning of Thursday 24th March thousands gathered in Ala Too Square: aksakal in ak-kalpaks, irate young men, peasant women with headscarves and smiles of gold teeth and enthusiastic students from the newly formed KelKel movement. The curious, the angry, the hungry; some with pink armbands, some with yellow; some holding daffodils as symbols of peace, some waving huge Kyrgyz flags or carrying banners saying 'Get Out Thieves'. All yelling and raising fists in response to the zealous rhetoric of Kurmanbek Bakiev magnified through a megaphone.

"The people of Kyrgyzstan will not let anybody torment them. We must show persistence and strength and we will win!"

In their minds flashed images of injustices: Akayev shopping for penthouses in Moscow, children studying without books; Mairam greeting orphans in furs and pearls, *babushkas* eating from bins; Bermet skiing in Europe, thousands dying of tuberculosis; Aidar cruising in one of his black Mercedes, eight families living in one room.

International news networks were blaming poverty and endemic corruption for the social explosion. Finally it had become apparent to the masses that Kyrgyzstan was not going to be the Switzerland of Central Asia and Akayev, once hailed as a liberal in a region of dictators, was becoming entrenched as head of a ruling family.

Watching Bermet and Aidar swearing oaths as parliamentary deputies while protesters shouted 'Akayev Go!' outside Fatboys had been final clarification: one of them was being groomed as successor. For years the population had accepted that every profitable business in Kyrgyzstan was owned by an Akayev while nothing had improved for most of them in the first fifteen years of Kyrgyzstan's life. But the youth had started to question why Aidar, aged twenty-seven, was in government, owned chains of shops and a phone company and had a different black Mercedes for every day of the week when they could barely afford a new pair of trainers.

The protesters would probably have gone home quietly had someone not sent in the White Caps – Akayev supporters impatient for a fight. They charged into the defenceless crowd brandishing billy clubs and shields. There was chaos as *babushkas* fled over rose borders and students scattered across Ala Too Square. The White Caps pursued, beating bodies into submission with sticks, aiming for heads with thick army boots.

"We are all Kyrgyz, we shouldn't be fighting each other," one bloodied man generously said. But years of anger at poverty and increased oppression had been unleashed and aimed unstoppably at Akayev. The crowd turned and hurled bottles and stones at police who cowered under riot shields in the centre of the square like scared tortoises. Baying, the pack pressed forward, pushing police lines back towards the White House, only momentarily impeded by the cavalry sent in on horseback. A rider was dismounted, his horse captured by a protester who galloped down *Chui* as if playing *Ulak*, banner streaming behind. The frightened horse reared for television cameras, symbol of the nomadic revolution.

Inside the White House compound police surrounded the building. The swelling mob bombarded them with stones, rattling at the gates before lifting them off hinges, pushing through towards the president's centre of power. Uninspired by their recent training and unwilling to risk their lives for meagre wages, the policemen fled.

Outside the tall wooden doors, carved with swirling sheep horns, the crowd hesitated, expecting the Father of the Nation to come out and give them all detention. But no-one came: Akayev hadn't been seen in public since his address on Tuesday evening and no-one was prepared to defend his honour. The crowd edged forward, tentatively throwing stones at windows to see what would happen. No response, no attack, no landmines under doormats. Heartened by the ease of conquest they surged up the steps, smashing windows and bursting into the building. This is when I arrived.

History was being made in Ala Too Square and I wasn't content just to see it on CNN. Dema had been booked for shopping so I went to Narodne, grabbing things off shelves because it's always better to have extra loo roll in stock when there's rioting in the main square. The assistants were blithely handing out application forms for loyalty cards, unaware there'd soon be nothing left to be loyal to.

There was a surreal atmosphere in town, a city polarised by ignorance. While CNN were broadcasting images of young men being beaten, a woman was dancing in a Christmas cake hat on KTR. On *Erkendik*, two blocks from the revolution, children were swinging and licking ice-creams, unaware that the helicopter roaring over them probably carried their fleeing president.

As we walked into Ala Too Square, Dema my self-appointed bodyguard, I heard a roar. Spectators were on the museum steps looking towards the White House. Incredibly, two soldiers were still standing guard beside the flag pole, staring motionlessly ahead as if this were just an ordinary day in Bishkek. Peeping around a pillar I saw an incredible sight: men climbing the fence, swarming into the sacred White House, waving flags victoriously out of windows and tearing up pictures of an unsmiling Akayev.

"*Ploha*," Dema muttered, "it's bad. No tourists will come now." I thought I might cry. People power always makes me emotional. Whether it's a Countryside March or men in felt hats climbing presidential fences, the fact people care enough to get up and wave banners chokes me. I bit my lip, I couldn't cry in front of Dema.

Any tears were dried by fear. We heard screams from the heart of the crowd and saw people running towards us. Was that shooting, was it not yet over?

"We're going," Dema announced, dragging me back into the square, out of the path of a pack of angry young men marching and chanting. We later heard they'd stormed Tzum and tried to loot it. Reluctantly I let Dema drive me home, crunching over broken glass and stopping to let students clutching bloody heads cross the road. Matthew was furious.

"I saw you on CNN. What were you doing? It may seem safe but all it takes is one shot and the atmosphere would change in minutes. You're a mother now, you have responsibilities!"

Duly chastised, although unrepentant, we left to toast the revolution with cups of tea in Ben and Nicky's garden. Matthew was in danger of submitting to disaster-television syndrome and I was desperate to get away from the telephone. It rang endlessly: the BIWC network on red-alert sharing news and advice; concerned family calling from England; Susi calling from

Switzerland; Danes calling from head office and Luigi calling from his bed, his blood-pressure dangerously high. We'd had calls from everyone apart from Fatboys Bill who was maintaining complete silence on behalf of the British government.

In Ben and Nicky's garden the last of the snow and ice had melted from shadows. Cherry blossom was out and the grass was dry enough to sit on. Siana tottered around, proudly walking since her first birthday. Tom still shuffled on his bottom, leaving paths in the long grass.

Next door, work continued on a building site and a drunk snored in the hedge. Sheltered from the bizarre events of the day it was easy to forget that a mile away a regime was being changed. No-one had mentioned evacuation. Now the White Caps had gone the revolution was seemingly good natured, a celebratory street party, extension of *Nooruz*. On CNN grinning youths were swinging in the president's chair and people were wandering around the White House compound hugging and smiling, full of hope for prosperous years they assumed would be theirs now the period of tyranny was over.

We knew all our friends were safe. Kay was in the square watching the festivities with Michael – maybe *he* was the CIA agent, he always knew what was going on; Ilke was sheltering Claudia From; Lauren was in the Hyatt gym and Gina was at home. All ex-pats were reacting differently, some were frightened, some were fascinated, some were enjoying the excitement as a contrast to what usually happened in predictable Bishkek. Clorise reduced the country's pivotal moment to just another item on her day's itinerary.

"My husband is stuck in meetings at the Embassy so I've been out around town. I did some grocery shopping, stopped by the revolution and took Tula to bal-let, although I was kinda cross because the teacher never showed."

"Aren't you scared?" I asked.

"Nah. I'm from the Bronx, this is mild behaviour."

Siana and Tom were playing with teddies. Tom cuddled a stripy bumble bee given to him by Matthew's colleagues. It had huge black eyebrows and a round head so we'd christened it Akayev. Siana's green Care Bear had a dodgy moustache and star and crescent on its tummy so we'd christened it Musharaf. With help from parents they were holding another summit. Akayev was wailing about being betrayed by his people and Musharaf was furious because he'd wasted a plane ticket befriending the wrong man.

"I can't believe Akayev's gone," I said as Tom hurled his bee across the lawn. "And so quickly, without any fight."

"I'll miss his eyebrows," Ben mused. "*Manas* won't look the same without those ridiculous billboards."

"Has he actually left?" Nicky asked. "I don't believe he'd give up power that easily."

"Ilke heard he was at OSCE's offices."

"Luigi's convinced he was in that helicopter."

"CNN say he's in a safe place."

"Called Moscow."

"Do you think Putin will support him?"

Nazabayev, Akayev's so-called ally in Kazakhstan, had already blamed weak leadership for the riots, saying Akayev allowed thugs to act as they pleased. He was nervous that he might be next to suffer as presidential elections were due in Kazakhstan the following year. There were undeniable parallels between the Rose Revolution in Georgia and the Orange Revolution in Ukraine, both uprisings the reaction to fraudulent elections. Journalists were using the phrase 'domino effect' to describe the way former Soviet republics were falling.

Human rights activists were already hoping that the Kyrgyz revolution would be a good lesson for Central Asian dictators, claiming an irreversible trend towards democratisation. Others were more cynical, saying it was simply the consequence of the Bush administration's aggressive democracy policies. In Uzbekistan Karimov had demonstrated that he was not intending to lose his power to democracy. After being deposed, Shevardnadze had visited Karimov, reportedly warning against interfering international NGOs. Karimov had responded by evicting an 'open society' institute and restricting NGOs. Civil society projects were viewed with suspicion, suspected of being the West's way of undermining regimes. Akayev had been afraid of the effect of foreign influence but, choosing a reign of perceived tolerance rather than torture, had been overcome by the momentum of change.

"Are you planning to leave," Nicky asked.

"Yes, if we have to."

"Why?"

"Because according to CNN there's been a revolution!" Ben and Nicky remained an island of calm, gardening through riots without thought of fleeing. Our bags were packed but there was no-where for us to go. The airport was closed and we didn't have Kazak visas to escape by road. Unfortunately we'd need Bill's help to evacuate, so that probably meant we were staying.

"Have you heard from Bill?" I asked Ben.

"No."

"I always knew he'd be useless in an emergency."

"He's probably got no idea what's going on."

"Most people have got no idea what's going on."

"Bin *Babushka* is still sitting on her stool like nothing's changed."

"Maybe by tomorrow she'll be knitting under a guillotine in Ala Too Square."

"But there'll still be no help from Bill."

"What are we going to do without "Words of Akayev"?"

We scurried home at dusk to discover the heating and hot water had been turned off. The official reason was the $13.5 million gas bill, but I knew timing was too much of a co-incidence. It was Akayev's final defiant gesture to his mutinous country. "Let the bastards freeze without me," he must have shouted over his shoulder to a sobbing Tanayev as he left.

No-one else cared. Bakiev was on the steps of the White House surrounded by a jostling crowd. He announced it was all over, the opposition had control.

"You have triumphed," he told the people, a look of bewilderment on his face as if he couldn't believe Akayev had been defeated before bedtime. "If the generals and police come over to our side, we will solve this problem peacefully." He called for an orderly takeover of power, for Akayev and friends to leave office, for new elections.

"We did this for our future," a young man said, flag draped around his neck. "We hope there will be change for the better, we want to be more like Europe." In Russia, Putin, his sphere of influence shrinking with every revolution, was silent.

CNN, still giving us live coverage, showed an emotional reunion with Kulov. The people's hero, hailed as the man to unify the country, had been released from prison by authorities scared he'd be busted out. He arrived at the White House in black polo neck and jeans, grey hair cropped unevenly by prison stylists. Judging by his belly the chef was better at his job. He and Bakiev embraced in triumph before a jubilant crowd.

"Kulov! Kulov!" they shouted as he waved from a window. Kulov raised a clenched fist as if to say, "yes, I'm free, I can go down the casino tonight!"

Peeling potatoes, I suddenly felt sorry for Akayev. I forgot about his swanky houses and wife's pearls and thought of him as a man forced to flee. In the last twenty-four hours I'd realised I didn't want to be rushed from my home before I was ready, forced to leave possessions behind and forfeit goodbyes. How must he feel, chased undignified from his job and country, the place he'd written all his books and speeches about. I wondered if he'd cried as he'd taken off, looking down at his lost homeland. Exiled, the Akayevs didn't seem like greedy tyrants, just a displaced family with no change of underwear.

Over dinner CNN reported that Beta Stores was being looted and the White House was on fire. According to the BIWC hotline, Tzum and the Hyatt were surrounded by screaming mobs; Kyrgyz intoxicated by their own success, clamouring for victor's spoils. We looked out of the window and saw smoke and our nouveau-riche Kyrgyz neighbours ramming possessions into black Mercedes. This was more serious. What had happened to the party?

KTR had been captured by opposition forces. They'd sent dancing lady and her Christmas cake hat home and were holding a political discussion about the day's events in the studio. Kulov had popped in on his way to the casino. He was asking people to stay calm and urging Akayev to meet with opposition leaders to peacefully and constitutionally transfer power. Exuding authority and strength, he made you want to obey. Felix Kulov was the Arnold Schwarzenegger of Kyrgyzstan. It was a shame the mob were too busy to listen and Akayev already out of KTR's transmission range.

Across the world Kyrgyzstan was headlining. International news networks were rolling footage of the riots while an eclectic collection of experts dissected the details. They weren't sharing the afternoon's euphoria. Akayev was being discussed in the past tense, reported as having resigned by Sky News – but as no-one else was announcing this we assumed it was Sky breaking news before confirming it. Allegedly the Supreme Court had already annulled the elections and Ishenbai Kadyrbekov, Speaker of Parliament, was interim president in accordance with the constitution.

Most commentators were focussing on the power vacuum, predicting who would take over the country because the kids swinging in Akayev's chair weren't an effective alternative. We were doomed without a leader, they reported. Thanks to Stalin, Kyrgyzstan was already divided – north, south, clans, ethnicity. The theory was that without a strong commander differences would escalate, allowing radical Islamic parties to gain influence. This would lead to a Tajik style civil war – Moscow versus mullahs. Experts were consulted. They sensationalised scenarios of Islamic militants manipulating angry young men and their desire for change, truckloads of Afghan drugs flooding over porous borders, oil supplies cut off and Central Asia crumbing under a 'domino effect' of revolution. All because a few kids stormed the White House.

Hearing shouting and breaking glass outside we turned off lights and moved to the window. On *Moskovskaya* a gang of youths loitered, chanting defiantly, empowered by destroying a president. Were they celebrating or considering something more sinister? For the first time I felt scared, threatened. It only needed one person to suggest that foreigners were a good target because they all had widescreen fifty-two inch plasma television in their apartments and we'd be attacked by looters. There were no policemen to save us, they'd all run away.

Was CNN right, was Kyrgyzstan falling into anarchy? Would we have to flee, expatriate refugees? If there were looters today, who could we expect tomorrow – the IMU, mafia gangs, drug lords, missionaries? I missed the Father of the Nation with his threatening eyebrows. I felt vulnerable going to bed in a country without a government. Maybe an authoritative Akayev wasn't so bad after all.

"Kyrgyz mob is calling in their country's doom while thinking they are salvaging it," an analyst predicted on the BBC.

What had the people done?

Chapter Twenty-Five – Living the Revolution

We went to bed at midnight when we couldn't bear to hear the phrase 'domino effect' any more. At three we were woken by gunshots, cracks echoing in the dark outside the window. We lay awake holding hands, waiting for Bill to call and tell us we were evacuating. We made plans. If we had to run for our lives, Matthew would grab Tom and I'd take our small emergency bag. Where we'd run to wasn't clear.

I felt scared. Tom was asleep on his side, legs curled towards his chest as he snuggled into the top corner of his cot. I'd hate to pull him from his dreams and run out into the cold night full of fear and danger.

The phone rang at seven. It wasn't Bill but Luigi in a panic.

"Did you see news? There is too much war. Yobs is looting randomly. They were in our building taking washing machines from shop. I so scared I want to cry. We must leaving now."

"But where can we go? We don't have visas to get into Kazakhstan. Will they let us in?"

"I know nothing! I call Bill but he no answer. My friend say no aeroplanes is leaving so we trapped, trapped! I can't stay here another night."

While Matthew calmed Luigi down, for the sake of his escalating blood pressure, I turned on the television for news of events outside. The morning after the people's revolution, Bishkek was smouldering. Euphoria had turned to vengeance and the mob had attacked the Akayev's shopping malls and Narodne supermarkets, smashing windows and stripping every item, locusts swarming over shelves and freezer cabinets.

"This shop belonged to the family, that is why it is ours," they shouted in justification.

But in the hysteria looting had become indiscriminate. The Chinese bazaar where I bought fresh ginger was a blackened shell, stunned stallholders crunching over glass looking for something to salvage. Turkish Beta Stores had been annihilated. Smoke drifted from broken windows leaving black scars up the walls. Television cameras peered through smashed windows and scanned across the empty caverns of its five floors of modernisation, now filled with upturned shelves, ripped boxes and shattered glass. The checkouts stood alone like tombstones. There'd been three deaths, CNN's anchorwoman told us breathlessly; a lady who'd fallen from the second floor of Dordoi Plaza, someone run over by a Lada with a sofa strapped to the roof and a looter shot by a Beta Stores Security guard.

"Because his receipt didn't tally with what was in his bag?" I asked sardonically.

Matthew went out, wanting to make his own judgement about the city's atmosphere. Bishkek was in shock, people stunned that their revolution had gone sour. Yesterday's jubilation had been destroyed with shop windows. On *Moskovskaya* a jewellery store had been smashed open and stripped by the crowd we'd seen from our flat. Narodne looked as though it had been gutted by a bomb, glass and packaging strewn by the blast. Staff stood outside crying and a man pulled up and shook everyone's hand in commiseration. At Beta Stores crowds were standing on the pavement, staring in disbelief.

"No photos!" shrieked a *babushka,* trying to shield the destruction from cameras. "I'm too ashamed. Kyrgyz people don't do this, they are quiet." But Kyrgyz people had done this and without any policemen to stop them, would they do it again that night?

Reports started filtering in from the BIWC network – when it came to a crisis the International Women were a far more effective source of information and help than British diplomats. Claudia From had spent the night with Ilke because a mob of three thousand had circled the Hyatt calling 'you're next, you're next'. Miraculously the hotel had survived but Gerhard was terrified and making battle plans for the night, busy buying every strand of barbed wire in the city.

Ben and Nicky were eating scrambled eggs for breakfast having slept calmly through the night, despite a perfume shop on the other side of their wall being destroyed. Lauren had been out to find milk and discovered shops empty or closed.

"What are we going to do for food with every supermarket destroyed," she asked? This was something I hadn't remembered to worry about yet. I went to the cupboard and counted cartons. I had ten litres of milk. When that ran out we'd have to buy a cow and put it in Ben and Nicky's garden.

Tanzilya arrived at 9am. I was trying to create an atmosphere of normality for Tom – and I had lots of writing to do. Ilke had already accused me of orchestrating the revolution just to sell my book. Tanzilya brought with her the opinions being circulated in Russian. According to a man on the trolleybus, the looting had been organised because people from Osh knew exactly where to go, despite it being their first visit to the capital.

"Who did he think arranged it?" I asked.

"Aidar Akayev."

"But his businesses were destroyed!"

"They say he had good insurance. His plan was to make it look as though only his father could keep control."

Others blamed the opposition, saying televisions and satellite dishes were rewards for marionette revolutionaries who'd brought them to power. Another theory was that the mafia were promoting disorder so that they could come in with guns and capitalise on the chaos.

"It's amazing for my generation," Tanzilya said, watching the CNN footage of Dordoi Plaza in ruins. "We were born Soviet but learnt to divide ourselves as Russian, Uzbek or Tatar when the Union fell apart. Today there's this revolution. What will we become now?"

It was a question many reporters were asking as they raced into the city, annoyed because the Kyrgyz had finished their revolution without them. For once everyone was talking about little Kyrgyzstan. We were reminded that its importance was its position; borders with countries associated with the War on Terror, Islamic radicals, drug trafficking and huge oil and gas resources. China was worried about its Uighur separatists; America wanted Kyrgyzstan as a buffer against Chinese expansionism and Russian colonialism and Russia wanted to maintain its historical influence, pushing America back a step in the New Great Game. All the big powers were playing, Kyrgyzstan the board at the crossroads of east and west. No-one wanted it to fall into an uncontrollable void of civil war and extremism.

As I scribbled in my journal I wondered whether American politicians were worrying that their policies to promote democracy and civil society had backfired. Anarchy and violence can't have been part of the plan. Or maybe they were; maybe America's strong man was already lined up to come in and take control. Condoleezza Rice was declaring, "...if we can encourage the various parties in Kyrgyzstan to move into a process that will then lead to the election of a government and move the process of democracy forward, it will have been a very good thing." Easy for her to say, she wasn't in Bishkek worrying about staying alive and finding milk for a thirsty seventeen-month-old.

The important question was – who was in control? Who would get the police back to work and save us that night from the rioters? According to CNN, Bakiev had been appointed acting president and prime minister by parliament; not bad – from defeated election candidate to president in twelve days. Kulov was Security Minister.

Unfortunately there were questions of legitimacy. Akayev had surfaced in Moscow and was accusing the opposition of staging a coup, insisting that only he was the country's lawful leader. According to Roza Otunbaeva, interim Foreign Minister, no-one had wanted a revolution and the opposition didn't stand for it. All they'd wanted was for Akayev to resign and instigate a constitutional and peaceful change of regime.

It was a volatile situation.

"All it needs is for Akayev to return with a hundred gunmen and we're in big trouble," Michael explained. "That's why I'm sending Kay and the boys to Almaty."

"They're leaving?"

"Just for a few days, while we see how things turn out. There's gonna be surprises in a country with two presidents. Why don't you go too?"

"Because we don't have visas. We're waiting for Bill to tell us whether we can get through without."

"Have you called your embassy?"

Our nearest embassy was in Almaty. It was closed for the Good Friday bank holiday. Rumour was the British Ambassador to Kazakhstan was in the Hyatt doing a deal to get us across the border. But this was just a rumour;

we'd heard nothing official from Bill. In fact, we'd heard nothing at all from Bill and if you believed every rumour circulating the city the water was poisoned, Islamic militants were preparing to storm parliament and only three policemen had turned up for work. All we could do was wait – and ration food and loo roll. I put on some washing. If we had to evacuate, at least we'd do so with clean underwear.

Throughout the afternoon we grew more anxious about what would happen that night. Apparently all Ambassadors were meeting to decide what to do with us. I wished they'd get on and decide: if we were fleeing to Almaty I'd rather do it in daylight. Ilke and Claudia From had already left, Ilke calling to tell me not to worry about being left behind – she could feel confident, she'd be watching us burn from the safety of her hotel room – and ask Techno Matt how to get the hard drive out of her computer.

Kulov was on KTR asking people to stay calm. He requested citizens to form teams, wear red armbands and help the police, to work together for the nation. Others questioned whether they were extra protection or vigilantes, security or a way to make personal vendettas official.

By 4.30pm – too late to reach Almaty before dark – I felt sick, rumours swirling people into panic.

"The UN is evacuating non-essential personnel."

"Americans are staying."

"Kumtor are moving people into safe houses."

"There's a convoy leaving for Almaty at five."

"No-one knows whether you can get across the border without a visa."

Should we stay or go? Should we move with Luigi to his nanny's house in the suburbs? Should we ask Dema to come over with his shotgun? Where was the official British advice? Wasn't this what embassies were for, helping their citizens in distress? You'd expect British embassies to be great in a crisis, to put the kettle on and dish out comfort and fruit cake. Unfortunately they appeared to be useless the world over. When I'd called the British embassy in Cairo on September 12th 2001, asking whether to stay in Egypt I was told, "of course, you must stay, ours is a beautiful country." With George Bush already planning The Retaliation I don't think they understood the significance of my question. Now, in Bishkek, I felt frightened and alone, trapped in a hostile city ready to erupt as the sun went down.

Neither Matthew nor I knew what to do for the best. Our heads were buzzing with rumours, gossip, opinions, ideas, recommendations and conjecture, too tired and overloaded to make a clear decision. A friend from the Swiss consulate, Heidi, phoned.

"I'm going on the UN convoy to Kazakhstan, are you coming?" Matthew and I looked at each other, then down at Baby Tom who was jigging to Twinkle Twinkle Little Star, the hip-hop version played on his toy telephone.

"No, we'll stay," I decided. I didn't want to take Tom out into the uncertainty of the night. Driving in the dark on dangerous roads in an old bus with a travel-sick baby seemed less appealing than being looted, especially as we might not be able to cross the border.

Had we made the right decision? When Tom fell asleep peacefully in his bed I thought yes, but when reports filtered though about rival gangs fighting on *Chui-Sovietskaya* my stomach went into a spin and I wished we were fleeing with the UN. Would we survive the night?

* * * * *

Someone was banging on our door. Matthew peered through the spy-hole.

"It's Grady." Grady lived on the first floor with Anna, his Russian wife. Anna told me she wanted to retire to Blackpool. It was good to have a neighbour with such aspirations. But Grady was useful in a revolution. He was big and muscled with a dog who barked a lot.

"I've found security guards," he said, "do you want to contribute?" Matthew went downstairs with our other neighbours and negotiated to pay a lot of money for two men with guns to sit inside and protect us. This was a good week to be in the business of security and glazing in Bishkek. I couldn't help wondering if we'd made a mistake: our new employees might be mates with the looters and let them in without a fight in return for a couple of DVD players.

I called Gina. Apart from Nicky, she was the only other member of Playgroup left in town. Maybe her husband would have some useful information to comfort us.

"Gina, how are you?"

"We're fine. We've got ten armed guards around the house, lots of peanut butter and candy and the boys are watching 'Finding Nemo'."

"Gina, it's a revolution not a sleep over!"

"You know, I heard it was a coup not a revolution because the opposition took power illegally."

This was the most intelligent thing Gina had ever said. I couldn't believe how calm she was. It was as though she had known what was going to happen. Maybe Gina was the CIA agent and had masterminded the whole thing on behalf of George Bush, just like Akayev said. I thought I'd test her.

"Gina, have you heard rumours about a forty-bedroom castle Akayev is building?" A picture of this palace in a US sponsored newspaper had been cited as inflammatory and the catalyst for riots in the south.

"Forty-bedrooms! Wow. Are they en-suite?" Nah, Gina wasn't CIA.

The official American advice, according to Gina, was to stay inside with lights out and curtains drawn. We obeyed and sat in silence on the sofa, waiting. My heart was beating so hard I felt sure it was banging like a war drum, telling the mob where we were hiding. With all the supermarkets stripped there were only private homes left to satisfy looters' greed.

My only consolation was that we were in an inconspicuous flat not a flashy house. Finally I was grateful to live in a vertical, brown shoebox with smelly bins outside the door. I thought of Gerhard at the Hyatt. We'd heard from Lauren that he was already besieged by thousands of jeering Kyrgyz, some circling on horseback, all desperate for one of the televisions, microwaves or luxurious bathrobes languishing in each room.

I could feel the suspense, the anticipation as we all waited for attack. I wanted to cry. Instead we made plans: looters were only interested in white goods so we'd stack the television, microwave and video by the door, ready to hand out. Hopefully this would distract them from our prize possessions – our *shyrdaks,* Shigaev oil-painting and Tom.

Gunshots cracked in the streets outside. They were coming. Adrenaline raced through my body. I had to do something so started packing more bags, ramming clothes and my journals into holdalls by torchlight, not realising that my panic caused its own momentum. Mentally I comforted myself: 'only ten more hours until the safety of dawn, then we're gone. I can't stand another night like this'. Taking photos out of frames I wondered whether we should put on our *ak-kalpaks*: according to an article written in the Bishkek Observer in happier times, you couldn't kill someone wearing an *ak-kalpak*.

"It's 8pm in Bishkek!" CNN reported sensationally. No-one had ever cared before. "Unemployed young men are gathering outside parliament, shouting slogans and making sure their revolution is complete. There's still anger on the streets, people impatient for change, determined their lives will improve." They showed footage of feisty crowds and Kulov the night before, standing on a car to appeal to the pack outside Tzum to leave the shop alone. He'd never made it to the casino.

The phone rang. It was Dirk.

"How are you?"

"Scared. Can't you hear the automatic gunfire rattling outside? Where are you?"

"The border."

"WHAT! You've gone too!"

"Calm down. I didn't want to leave, I was ordered to. My bank has to follow UN dictate, even if we think they're wrong."

"Are we the only people left? I feel so vulnerable."

"Go to the Hyatt."

"The Hyatt! That's the next target!"

"Gerhard will look after you."

"Gerhard doesn't need any more encumbrances. Lauren told us he's already protecting the whole Indian embassy, two bank managers with the contents of their vaults in huge holdalls, a few dozen journalists and even some ordinary guests."

"He's got extra security."

"Yeah, KelKel the student movement and the Kyrgyz national karate team armed with golf clubs."

"Golf clubs?"

"Exactly. They wanted weapons and it's all Gerhard had. They'll be lethal. The clubs are made by 'Head' and the karate team are convinced these are instructions on where to strike assailants. Gerhard's not sure whether to be more worried about the mob or law suits."

"I wish I was there," Dirk said wistfully. "It'll be like the fall of Sarajevo, everyone clustered together as the bombs were dropping." It was easier to romanticise the situation from the safety of the border. "You should be glad you're not here. It's chaos. No-one's being let through without a visa." Despite thinking we were going to die, I could at least be comforted we made the right decision.

"I gotta go, someone wants my passport. If the shit really hits the fan, call your Ambassador. He's at the Hyatt, he'll save you."

"Dirk, we've been waiting for advice from him all day. He's useless. He's not going to save us."

It was God who saved us. Suddenly, windows started rattling and branches scratched the glass. A huge storm howled down from the mountains, wind buffeting our block and swirling dust across the capital until we couldn't even see the shoebox opposite. Rain slashed in torrents, then hail; icy bullets from the Lord. We hadn't had a storm like this since our first summer. The timing was biblical, a plague to deliver us from evil. In God's tempest, all-night rampaging through the city didn't seem so appealing.

Tom and I had prayed at bedtime, asking God to bring us safely through the long night and protect Gerhard at the Hyatt. God had answered, blowing *ak-kalpaks* from heads and sending looters running from the Almighty's retribution.

"What sort of revolution is this when everyone goes home at the first drop of rain?" a disgusted journalist asked Gerhard, watching from the Hyatt steps as the crowd dissolved. Gerhard's reply was unprintable.

By 10.30pm it was quiet, eerily quiet. The shooting and sirens had stopped and I felt calm, as if the storm had washed away the city's anger. Exhausted we crawled into bed and slept until woken the next day at seven – by Tom singing rather than gunshot. Outside I could hear trolleybuses rattling past and the *malako* man intoning his products. At least we'd be able to buy milk, even if it wasn't pasteurised.

It was a normal Saturday, until the telephone relay started. The news was confusing. We were playing a huge international game of Chinese Whispers, people reporting what they'd heard then having it told back to them half an hour later as a completely different story. Before breakfast we'd learnt that the diplomatic compound had been burnt out; there was a British Airways flight leaving that night but it was already full; the UN was considering complete evacuation and the head of Kumtor had been kidnapped. Only the bit about the UN was true.

Lauren was more concerned about immediate survival issues. "How are we gonna cope without imported toilet paper? The thought of using that scratchy grey crepe makes my eyes water. And am I gonna have to use 'Barf' bleach and 'Bride' washing powder? I'm going on a shopping mission this afternoon, you need anything?"

The conclusion of many conversations was that we should get a Kazak visa from the re-opened embassy. The UN convoy had eventually reached Almaty at 4am, the Kazaks proving inflexible. Apparently the British Ambassador's comment was that he assumed people would rather be arrested in Kazakhstan than shot in Bishkek. So far, this was the extent of his official advice.

We walked the few blocks to the embassy. It was a reassuringly grey Bishkek day, people spitting on your feet and Ladas trying to run you over at traffic lights. If you'd been locked in a dark room for the last forty-eight hours you'd have no idea anything had changed.

Outside the embassy we met Ben and other ex-pat friends and cheerfully swapped news. The night having been quieter everyone was relieved and enjoying the kudos of having survived a revolution. Most were getting visas as precautions, although some admitted they were off to Almaty just to stock up on milk and soft toilet paper.

My greatest concern was finding bananas for Tom. Spotting some in a corner shop I stood in line, hoping to buy bread at the same time. I felt so Soviet; queuing for bread next to empty shelves, glass racks in cabinets broken in the haste to clear them. Most locals seemed to be concentrating on vital supplies, buying beer and pickles as if they were going to hibernate in front of films for the next few days. By the time I got to the counter there was one dry loaf and a spotted banana. I bought both gratefully.

Seeing me buoyed with success Matthew admitted that my occupation on the Kazak visa application had been entered as 'accompanying husband'. I wasn't about to get feminist, we were in a revolution after all. I'd retired at the age of twenty-six and although technically still a lawyer, had taken to putting 'housewife', 'mother' or 'writer' on forms, depending on who I aspired to be that day.

I wanted to make a pilgrimage to Beta Stores. We walked tentatively up *Manas*. It looked like a war zone. Smashed glass was strewn across pavements and shops had been emptied or boarded up. 'WE ARE WITH THE PEOPLE' had been daubed on walls in Russian and Kyrgyz. On corners people clustered around newspapers, trying to disseminate fact from gossip.

Outside Beta Stores people were still staring at the dead monument, upset that they'd missed out on the bargains. For years they'd wandered aisles looking at things they could never afford until Thursday night when everything had been available. We saw mums with new buggies, young lads in smart suits and even bin *babushkas* with Louis Vuitton handbags. Under a tree a man was blatantly selling looted bread on an upturned box, the new Kyrgyz black market.

Having made it to Beta without being mugged we continued tentatively to the White House. All there was to show for political upheaval were six broken windows. In Ala Too Square two soldiers were still guarding the flag. Men in leather coats and caps gathered around *Erkendik* to expound their politics, orating animatedly about whether Bakiev or Kulov would lead them fastest to prosperity.

The scrabble for power had already begun. Although the Supreme Court had annulled the elections, the new parliament, supported by Kulov, was claiming legitimacy, saying it was the people's representative. The old parliament, supported by Bakiev, was claiming only it had a lawful mandate. The status of the new parliament was controversial because its members had been elected in the fraudulent polls which were the catalyst for the revolution. With Kulov from the north and Bakiev from the south, civil war was brewing in a country which was, after all, only an artificial Soviet creation. The OSCE, led by Delphine's husband Philippe, was preparing to talk through a solution.

We ended up crossing town to see how Gerhard was. Finding him in the foyer I gave him a huge hug and he invited us for a 'revolutionary' cup of tea. Under the Hyatt's opulent red chandeliers we sat and ate 'revolutionary' scones and 'revolutionary' sandwiches, greeting ex-pats we hardly knew like old friends because surviving revolution was a bond.

Gerhard was desperate to narrate his tales of war.

"I don't know how many times I thought I was going to die." He guffawed and wiped strawberry jam from his moustache. "Last night my hotel was surrounded by lunatics. I was on the roof with my snipers – they don't have guns mind you, just catapults. Behind the mob I saw an old man carrying a huge satellite dish on his back like a snail. These people have no idea what to steal. Why didn't he take clothes or food or something useful? He was going to be very cross when he got home, plugged it in and still didn't have the porn channel."

His story was interrupted by two girls, desperate for his reassurance that their country wasn't ruined and not every rich foreigner was planning to leave. He gave them some verbal bolster, took a slurp of tea and continued.

"I waited for the end as night came down. When a convoy of jeeps turned up, men hanging out of the windows with machine guns, I expected to be shot. My security told me it was the opposition but the driver said they were the government. With two parliaments it's impossible to know who to believe anymore."

I only realised later why we were so hysterically happy, laughing and joking in the middle of the chaos: because we weren't dead. We'd lived through two nights of shooting and anarchy and felt invincible. We were obnoxious in our bravado, blasé about what else might come. With everything we'd survived, what danger was a battle between parliaments?

"I knew it was all over this morning," Gerhard concluded with a flourish, "because I saw a policeman stopping traffic and taking bribes. I was so happy I ran out, shook his hand and offered him breakfast. 'Corruption is back', I said to Chef, 'we are saved!'"

We were so relaxed we only just made it home in time to comply with the unofficial curfew. On television a sensationalist media were scrabbling for a story, desperate to smash our composure.

"Ten thousand Akayev supporters are marching from Kemin to take back the capital," CNN reported. We imagined another night of shooting and wondered if we should have gone to Almaty after all. Gina was hysterical.

"I've heard that a huge Akayev army's coming armed with Kalashnikovs."

"Gina, calm down. We've been to Kemin, there aren't ten thousand people there, just a few pensioners who are barely capable of crossing the road."

"They're coming on horses."

"It's a three-day hack from Kemin. No-one's coming to Bishkek in a hurry, and certainly not tonight." I wished the media considered the impact of their irresponsible and inaccurate reporting.

"Their leader's an ex-police chief so he'll know how to fight."

"Gina, what's happened, you were so calm yesterday?"

"That was before I ran out of cake mix. What am I gonna do now there's no Bey-da?"

Despite CNN's best efforts we passed a quiet night. There was no shooting, no civil war and no ten-thousand marchers, just a time change to daylight saving – quite an accomplishment as usually government approval was required. According to Dirk, who'd declared himself 'essential personnel' and returned to Bishkek, a pro-Akayev rabble *had* left Kemin in Ladas. They'd got as far as Tokmok where someone had opened a bottle of vodka and slaughtered a sheep, thus ending Akayev's come-back.

It was Easter Sunday. On the third day Jesus rose again but everyone in Bishkek was exhausted. We had Post-Revolution-Adrenaline Disorder. Revolution is hard work – nerves, fear, excitement, indecision, lack of sleep, change of plans and endless phone calls, never knowing if it's going to be daffodils or danger. We went to Hyatt brunch as planned. The missionaries from the Sacred Church of the Bleeding Heart were out with the hordes of kids God had given them.

"Isn't it wonderful, Jesus is risen!"

"Yep, he's done it again. Another good year to be Messiah."

"Did you hear about the revolution?" Missionaries love to gossip as much as us heathens. I explained I'd not been in a coma since Thursday and yes, I had heard about the revolution, I'd even heard the gunshots.

"Gunshots, wow! We didn't have guns out by us, praise God! But Paula and Jed had to flee for their lives 'cos smoke was pouring into their flat from burning shops below."

"Where do they live?"

"In *Dom Torgovli* on the corner of *Moskovskaya* and *Sovietskaya*." That was the horizontal grey shoebox we'd stayed in for our first week. I wondered if it had been destroyed. "Paula saw people dragging freezer cabinets upstairs, and she says to me, 'what are they going to do with those?'"

"Bath in them."

"Of course! Good job!"

While the International Community was eating brunch, a new regime was being organised down the corridor. I was looking out for Kulov. I wanted a kiss and an autograph. He never showed and by the time I'd chomped through four revolutionary courses, interspersed with conversations about where Paula and Jed were going to live, I wanted to crawl into bed in a cool, dark room of silence.

I didn't want to hear another word about Akayev, Bakiev, which parliament should be authorised and whether Narodne would open again. I was exhausted by 'ifs'; there were still so many questions and insecurities.

Outside, it was snowing.

"Even the weather's revolting," Dirk said. But it was having the desired effect. The Kyrgyz had run back to winter hibernation and Ala Too Square, scene of riots and uprisings, was deserted – except for two obedient, but freezing, soldiers guarding the flag.

I was tenser than I realised. As we drove up to our block I flinched at what sounded like the crack of gunfire. It was just the car driving over ice. Popular opinion was that the people of Kyrgyzstan just wanted to return to normal life. But with Akayev busy telling Moscow's media that he was the only elected and legitimate president of the Kyrgyz Republic and rumours of further riots if the new parliament was retained, we would just have to wait see what happened in the new Kyrgyzstan.

Chapter Twenty-Six – A New Kyrgyzstan?

The revolution in Kyrgyzstan was like a Bank Holiday weekend – all over by Tuesday. The schools were open, *babushkas* selling daffodils on street corners and international news networks had moved on to someone else's problems. After a weekend of storms and snow the sun was shining, spring bringing optimism to the shell-shocked city. Matthew returned to work with the computer hard drives. The only change was a faded brown stain on Mr Turd's office wall where a photo of Akayev had been removed.

A decision had been made about the parliaments, the old one agreeing to stand down and the new one accepting Bakiev as acting President. Now all they needed was Akayev's resignation. A few people gathered outside to complain but most were too busy sweeping up glass. We knew everything must be over when we had an email from Bill. He told us the situation was calm and advised caution and keeping well stocked with food: completely useless information five days late.

By Thursday it was difficult to believe that a week before gentle Kyrgyz had been throwing stones. They seemed ashamed; as if storming the White House was something crazy they'd done whilst drunk. But Akayev was being swiftly exorcised. The Bishkek Observer, always full of sycophantic headlines like *'Akayev has no Equal'*, had to quickly change editorials and put Kulov and Bakiev on the front page. 'Words of Akayev' had been replaced with an advert for a bank because no-one else was saying anything ridiculous enough.

Gina called with good news.

"Bishkek City Market's open! It wasn't looted, just a few windows broken, and there's an intact Narodne on *Ahunbayeva-Sovietskaya*, but don't get too excited 'cos there's no cake mix. Tzum's open too and I'm so relieved 'cos I was having withdrawal symptoms. I think I'll go there tomorrow and buy a handbag, just to celebrate."

Finding food post-revolution wasn't as difficult as feared – once we'd resigned ourselves that the days of Kellogg's cornflakes were over. I went shopping with Dema, trawling round corner shops which were well stocked with items looted from Beta Stores. I even found soft toilet paper, something I relayed quickly to Heidi and Ilke, still evacuated in Almaty and emailing for updates on the situation.

For a while we'd glimpsed modern life – three types of pasta, microwave popcorn, anchovies and a decent Japanese restaurant. Now we'd regressed to a Soviet era when everyone was grateful to queue for fresh cabbage: ironic considering the people's revolution was intended to improve a stagnated standard of living.

It wasn't just spoilt foreigners who were suffering. The euphoria of Akayev's demise had worn off and people were reflecting on what happened that day. There was confusion in the new Kyrgyzstan.

"What was this revolution for?" Valentina asked as we discussed politics and *demokrateecheski* at our Russian lesson. "We have two presidents, two parliaments, a leader from the north, a leader from the south, more mafia, more Afghan drugs, more unemployment and no Beta Stores. For what?"

"Bermet's gone." I reminded.

"Yes, that is good."

"And you no longer have a president who amends the constitution to give himself power to call referendums and veto legislation."

"Yes, that is good too. The Akayevs were corrupt and stole Kyrgyz money, but what have we got instead?" The complaint was, there was no-one new to trust, the 'opposition' were just recycled politicians from the old regime, men and women who once served under Akayev: Bakiev had been Akayev's prime minister until 2002.

"Revolution isn't revolution unless something changes apart from the leader," Valentina said.

The problem was that with a population of five million and only a small percentage educated and wealthy enough to be able to participate in politics, there weren't any new people to choose from. Was it better to have a president who'd already appropriated everything he wanted or a new lot hungry for perks? Apparently the Finance Minister was already appointing his family to important posts, actions condemned by donors as renewed corruption. Unfortunately, what the West labels 'nepotism', Central Asians call 'clan loyalty', tradition deeply rooted in culture and unlikely to be changed by a few seminars. 'Kyrgyz' means 'forty clans' and that's a lot of brothers competing for supremacy.

Kyrgyz emotions rose and fell in swells of euphoria and troughs of despair. By April spring optimism was definitely waning. Even the ardent revolutionaries of the south had stopped partying and started complaining. Protesting was the new national occupation. Now they'd discovered the art of demonstrating and the effects it could have, crowds gathered every day outside the White House or parliament, objecting about whatever had annoyed them the night before. Rumour was they were inspired more by wages than ideology, paid by whoever wanted their issue publicised.

On Monday they demanded Akayev's resignation, by Tuesday they wanted him impeached. On Wednesday they protested against the Issyk-Kul governor, on Thursday the subject was diesel prices. By Friday they insisted the Issyk-Kul governor – out of favour on Wednesday – be reinstated. When short on inspiration they simply complained that everyone wasn't rich two weeks after their revolution.

At work Matthew experienced two changes: a new age of co-operation from government departments and a new age of belligerence in villages. He didn't get too excited about the government. Allegedly they'd all been told to behave until after the presidential election, set for 10th July, when it was promised bribery and corruption would be re-instated.

In the villages Matthew decided they'd confused 'democracy' with 'anarchy'. They were changing governors every week; one group of *babushkas* appointing their man until another team stormed in and imposed their candidate. Everyone felt empowered in the People's Kyrgyzstan but didn't know what to do with that power so objected to everything – including all Matthew's project contracts which they demanded were renegotiated, not realising this would simply delay their supply of typhoid-free water. When there was nothing else to complain about they jumped on *mashrutkas* for Bishkek and joined the day's protest. With payments of 100 *som*, dinner and a bottle of vodka, there was good money to be made from insurrection.

Maybe this pseudo unrest was what was unnerving the UN. While the rest of us were strolling in the park and shopping at Bishkek City Market, the UN increased Bishkek's danger rating. Were they stupid or did they know something we didn't? Dirk's opinion was the former because this rating meant Jenna and the girls, now in Almaty after an aborted holiday in Istanbul, weren't allowed to return. Jenna was bored, Dirk was furious and the UN was still obsessing about the incident with the bananas outside Fatboys.

The Father of the Nation wasn't helping his country's recovery and stability – or UN nerves. Instead of giving up silently, as expected, he was taking credit for the lack of casualties, insisting he instructed police not to use violence and left quietly to prevent civil war. He misjudged his people. He was expecting them to say, 'Akayev, we love you. You didn't shoot and saved us when we strayed. Come back, we need you.' Instead, no-one turned up to his demonstration, sneering that he was a wimp. 'We want a hard-riding strong nomadic man of the mountains not a weedy scientist who runs away. Get lost, you're finished!'

He resigned in Moscow on 6th April with the provision he could retain his First President privileges, including immunity from prosecution and state mansions.

"I've only got a car and apartment," he claimed dejectedly.

"What happened to the gun and the horse?" Ben asked.

"A sad end for a president," Roza Otunbaeva said, "but he only built the Switzerland of Central Asia for his family."

This wasn't the end. It took parliament five days to vote to accept his resignation while outside people protested that he should face trial. Parliament did at least remove his privileges; it would have been sickening if he'd kept his presidential palace and huge *dacha* at Issyk-Kul, paid for with the country's money.

At Playgroup, hosted by Kay, there was relief that Akayev wouldn't be staging a violent comeback. Heidi, Ilke, Jenna and their children had finally returned from Almaty, the UN conceding that Bishkek didn't need to remain on the highest danger alert. This didn't indicate that they felt any less anxious about the situation; they just wanted Dirk to stop harassing them.

Gina was leading the conversation, ensuring she got maximum use from her one intelligent observation.

"What do you think, Ilke, was it a revolution or a coup? I heard it was a coup because the opposition took power illegally."

"My friend on a Swiss agricultural project says they're more worried about the grain crop because farmers were protesting when they should have been sowing," Nicky answered.

"What do you think Saf-fee-ya?" I was distracted trying to jump up and greet people without anyone noticing how filthy my feet were. There was no time for homemade pedicures in post-revolution Bishkek; I was too busy getting everything done that couldn't be left until tomorrow in case what I wanted wasn't there any more. I'd always regret not taking a photograph of Akayev's billboards on *Manas* before they were smashed.

Impatient for an answer Gina continued.

"Katya says this wasn't a Kyrgyz people's revolution, just a crowd of hooligans from Osh." So that was where Gina's astuteness was gleaned from: her new nanny. Natasha had been fired after feeding Bradley and John cat food rather than Bolognese sauce while Gina was at a felt symposium with the Blind Artisans of Kochkor.

"It's interesting you say that Gina." Michael, eavesdropping from his study, had decided to join us. "I've been interviewing students and they're frustrated by the betrayal of their democratic ideals. They wanted to camp in Ala Too Square and organise a slow-building momentum so that people could experience the emotions of civic education."

"But where would they go to the bathroom?" Gina could always be relied on to think of such issues.

"I'm sure something would have been arranged." Michael wasn't to be distracted. "We've been discussing this at work…"

"What, where to find a john?"

"No, no, whether Kyrgyzstan witnessed revolution or coup." Michael reached for a dictionary; Gina looked scared.

"The definition of 'revolution' is a 'forcible overthrow of a government or social order'."

"Well, we had that."

"And a 'coup' is a 'violent or illegal seizure of power'."

"Didn't we also have that?"

"So what was it, revolution or coup?"

"The American Embassy is calling it an 'event'," Jenna said.

"That's patronising."

"I heard 'uprising' was the non-controversial phrase of choice," Ilke remarked.

Michael picked up a Bishkek Observer. "At a press conference Bakiev said it was an accumulation of years of development in the democratic impulses of the Kyrgyz people; in here, Akayev says they were just an army of zombies from Nazaraliev's drug clinic."

Delphine arrived. As her husband was part of the OSCE delegation advising the new government we were hoping for some interesting insight. Gina rushed over to greet her.

"Hey Delphy! How was Paree? We're talkin' politics, what do you think, revolution or coup?"

"I think ze only difference is no Akayev and no Beta Store."

"And what does Philippe think?"

"He think I must go 'ome for summer to be safe so I am 'appy for zis revolution."

Walking home I thought about Delphine's comment. Was it the excuse of an unhappy woman or was Kyrgyzstan unsafe? Valentina said leaflets were being handed out suggesting people 'kill the Russians and take their property'. That explained the long queues outside the Russian embassy for permission to emigrate.

I'd always said to Matthew I'd not live in a country where I didn't feel comfortable walking around during the day: had that time come? I sensed more aggression on the streets. A man had jumped out at me doing karate kicks – but he was drunk rather than dangerous – and drivers were demonstrating even less patience at traffic lights. I'd given up swearing at them; they took no notice but Tom chanted, "'anker, 'anker, anker" the whole way home.

I smelt the guy in the park before I saw him, the male Kyrgyz odour of alcohol, cigarettes, body odour and sweet after shave. He was young and wearing jeans, leather jacket and black net vest. I slowed to let him pass and he slowed to level with me. Was I about to be mugged? All I had in my bag was a clean nappy and beaker of orange juice.

"Dyevooshka!" I prepared to confront him, trying to remember the best self-defence moves from classes in London.

"Dyevooshka!" What would Tom think when his mother started ramming her fingers into this man's eyes?

"Dyevooshka, skolka vremya?" I laughed with relief; he just wanted to know the time. Everyone in Bishkek always wanted to know the time. You'd think if it were that important they'd buy watches, especially as Rolexes only cost $2 at Dordoi bazaar.

"It's five-thirty," I told him gruffly. He shrugged.

"Thank you, and by the way, just because we've had a revolution doesn't mean everyone wants to hurt you." I felt guilty for my foreign paranoia.

The main Narodne re-opened at the end of April. This should have been a triumphant symbol of the city's recovery but apart from ex-pats rejoicing that they no longer had to traipse around every corner shop in Bishkek, there wasn't much joy in Kyrgyzstan. The aftermath of revolution was proving to be complicated. Thousands were squatting on land to the south of the capital, staking out plots and building crooked foundations. Bishkekers complained about this in Ala Too Square. Usen Kudaibergenov, who'd organised civilian patrols during the revolution and spoken out against land grabbers, was shot dead in his home. The Pinara Hotel was seized by its previous owners at gunpoint and Twelve Chimneys restaurant was commandeered by a crime lord from Issyk-Kul.

Kulov was warning of a counter revolution by criminals. The Supreme Court was occupied by people demanding the resignation of judges who'd rubber stamped the elections. Even a cosmonaut was appealing from outer space for a review of the results in his brother's constituency. Bermet returned to take her seat in parliament but was asked to leave when this caused more protests. The conclusion was she'd only risked a visit because they'd left the Swiss bank account pin codes taped to the bottom of Akayev's desk and someone had to retrieve them.

There were questions about the new leadership's legality: the constitution didn't specify who was in charge when the president was chased from office by paid rogues and drug zombies. Bakiev's answer was to set up lots of commissions, one to review Akayev business interests. Worryingly, the investigations were turning into Soviet-style purges. International companies and donors were appalled that they were being scrutinized. They were expected to hand over accounts and details of salaries to politicians, assuming the real purpose of this was for the new regime to work out who'd be best to bribe.

The justification, according to Interim Deputy Prime Minister Daniar Usenov, was that they'd already recovered millions for the state budget, calculated that the chandeliers in the presidential library cost US$15,000 and traced ownership of the mobile phone company, Bitel, to Aidar Akayev through a trail of offshore accounts in the Isle of Man, Seychelles and Liberia. He was requesting that Aidar return US$20 million.

"We'll find a way to spend the money," he reassured. "We could spend it on free breakfasts for school children, for example."

Most worryingly, according to Michael and other international commentators, was the power struggle developing between Bakiev and Kulov. After saving Bishkek from looters Kulov had resigned, allegedly in objection to Bakiev's personnel policies, distancing himself from the provisional government. He was running for president and was the northern favourite. Unfortunately, Bakiev was the southern favourite and it was feared that rather than unite the country, presidential elections would exacerbate the differences.

In Moscow Akayev was delighted, assuming that soon the people would want him back with his unifying eyebrows. Studying Bakiev and Kulov on the front of the Bishkek Observer I discovered a solution – as they both looked the same they could job share and no-one would notice. I explained my idea to Michael.

"Hm, it could work. You might not be far wrong actually; there are rumours that they're negotiating some sort of deal to run together for the good of the country. Apparently *Hizb-ut-Tahrir*, the Islamic movement, is hoping the political infighting will create disillusionment toward democracy and persuade people their Islamic caliphate is the answer. Sensing this, Bakiev and Kulov know a north-south divide is the last thing Kyrgyzstan can cope with."

"But who would be president?"

"That's the big question."

Matthew's office manager, Kumashai favoured Kulov. She even had a picture of him cut from a newspaper stuck to her fridge. Tom and I were at her flat for her baby's Forty Day Party. In the same way no-one truly believes someone is dead until forty days have passed, no-one celebrates the birth of a baby until it's forty days old, just in case – a primitive way of coping with high infant mortality.

Kumashai had given birth during the revolution – on the bathroom floor because the ambulance wasn't going anywhere that night. She'd named her child Felix after her hero. Following tradition, Kumashai and Felix had stayed at home, receiving few visitors to reduce their chances of being bewitched by the Evil Eye. Today was her opportunity to celebrate motherhood with cake, vodka and dodgy looking meat.

"Try some, it's delicious," Kumashai insisted. I chewed dutifully. It was dark red and sticking to my teeth.

"Umm, lovely, what is it?" I mumbled, unsuccessfully trying to wash it down with tea.

"It's horse." I coughed, dislodging the ball from the roof of my mouth and hiding the remaining piece under some beetroot salad. Kumashai pushed a bowl of caviar towards me, then sauerkraut and the inevitable garnish of raw onion. "Eat, eat, enjoy yourself!"

Fostered by the nomadic custom of welcoming every stranger because they were a means of communication, Kyrgyz hospitality is legendary – oppressive, Matthew would say. A host isn't happy unless you have food in your mouth the whole time you're visiting. The first food must be bread, the basis of life and therefore shown respect by never being thrown away. A sacred white drink should always be offered, often *koumys*. Kumashai was satisfying this tradition by providing milk for tea.

The meal was dominated by the pickled and smoky flavours of Russian cuisine, great for dinner but not quite so appetising at three in the afternoon.

"Try this," Kumashai insisted. "It's horse sausage made by turning the intestine inside-out so that the fat..."

"Can I have some cake?" Lauren interrupted, laughing. She escaped horse by claiming vegetarianism but I was sure I'd seen her ordering burgers by the Hyatt pool.

Kumashai had been Lauren's secretary before moving to Matthew's project and they'd remained friends, despite differences over eating horse. Also at the party were Kumashai's relations; a sister, cousin and Aunt from Kochkor, all with attached children. Miserable Cholpon from the office was unable to come as she'd broken her leg falling down a pothole in stilettos.

"I've never been in a room with so many five-year olds," Lauren remarked as Jalbek, Kumashai's nephew, drove a lorry over her foot. I didn't like to tell her most of them were nearer two, single women are very sensitive about such things I'd learnt from watching Sex and the City.

Kumashai lifted Felix from his cot, which I was relieved to see had been 'Made in China' and didn't include a catheter or hole for poo. He was tightly swaddled in blue blankets, the archetypal Kyrgyz baby with fat cheeks squeezed into caricature by a tight bonnet. His huge brown eyes were hooded by lids folded low and pulled tight to the flat bridge of his nose. Bristles of black hair bordered the face where his head had been shaved according to tradition. He hiccupped.

"Must be cold," said Aunty from Kochkor and rushed off to find another blanket.

"I hope he is strong man like his namesake," Kumashai said, gazing at her child.

"D'you think he'll be president?" Lauren asked.

"Maybe in thirty years."

"No, Kulov."

"Oh yes, he is our hero."

"According to Valentina my Russian teacher, lots of people are scared of him. Because he's come up through the security services they think he'll turn Kyrgyzstan into a police state."

"Didn't he used to be head of Kyrgyzstan's KGB?" Lauren asked.

"He looks cute in uniform." Kumashai was obsessed.

"He's very short," I'd seen Kulov at an International Business Council drinks reception at the Hyatt. It had been the highlight of my evening.

"Kulov can't speak Kyrgyz," said Aunt from Kochkor. It was true; rumour was he'd fail his language exam. "Can you speak Kyrgyz?" she asked me.

"No, I can't." It was shameful, after two years in the country and the Bishkek Observer's best efforts. "But Tom can speak Russian. He says 'malako' and 'vada'. And he rolled over yesterday." I wished I hadn't said this. My mum had reminded me that most babies do this at six months.

"How old is he?" Aunt queried.

"Sixteen months."

"And he doesn't walk!" As Gina so eloquently put it, he was still 'getting round on his fanny'. I wasn't worried about Tom, just bored of defending him against accusations of being retarded. Kochkor Aunty had jumped up from her seat and was peering at Tom anxiously.

"You've done it now," Lauren whispered.

"He must do exercises," Aunt said, "and..." There'd be an onion and vodka remedy next; there was always an onion and vodka remedy.

While Kochkor Aunty lectured me on Kyrgyz physiotherapy I watched Kumashai with Felix and thought back to our first telephone call when I'd been worried about finding a doctor. So much had changed: Akayev had gone, Beta Stores was a wreck and I'd become a mother, referring to myself in the third person. Motherhood had altered the focus of my life and with it my interpretation of the world. Events were now condensed into how they affected mothers; suicide bombs, abductions, soldiers killed in Iraq, all pain for women who'd lost children they'd given years of their lives to.

My expectations had changed. I'd mellowed, relaxed into my role of international mother, prepared to accept that in my situation I couldn't always do everything The Books advised and that didn't make me wrong. I was less judgemental, of myself and others, wanting to apologise to Iona for being incredulous that she turned up to Playgroup late and without make-up. I accepted that being a mother was a kaleidoscope of emotions with days when you did cope and days when you didn't because I wasn't perfect and my child wasn't perfect. The only certainty was that life was more complicated...

"...and every evening tap feet with pine branches, rub with vodka and bind each leg with hot towels and onions," Kochkor Aunt concluded, passing me the horse-intestine sausage.

...especially in Kyrgyzstan.

Chapter Twenty-Seven – Massacre in Andijan

On 13th May Central Asia hit international headlines again, reporters dusting off the phrase 'domino effect' and predicting anarchy. In Andijan, a town in Uzbekistan's Ferghana Valley just across the border from Osh, demonstrators were demanding Karimov's resignation. An administration building had been occupied, cinemas set on fire and a prison stormed, freeing hundreds of inmates. It was similar to our revolution – until Karimov's police started shooting; killing hundreds of people if you believed international media, or a few nasty terrorists if you believed Karimov.

The catalyst for the riots was the imprisonment of 23 businessmen who Karimov had branded 'Islamic extremists'. Human rights organisations were concerned by Karimov's use of the word 'terrorist', claiming US support encouraged the Uzbek government policy of torture by calling it 'anti-terrorist measures'.

A few friends emailed, concerned for our safety. We explained gently that they had the wrong 'Stan'; our violent uprising had been two months before. Hundreds of refugees fled to Kyrgyzstan. The international community demanded a full investigation but were denied access.

Karimov was unrepentant, but most of his allies didn't seem to care. The EU announced it would 'suspend further deepening' of EU-Uzbek cooperation, for a short time. America called mildly for restraint on both sides, anxious to protect the use of its airbase in Uzbekistan. Russia expressed support against terrorists and China signed a lucrative oil deal.

This was the answer to why revolution had happened in Kyrgyzstan, the most liberal of Central Asian states. According to his counterparts Akayev was too lenient, doing crazy things like allowing opposition parties – Turkmenbashi had suppressed all opposition since 1985. Karimov blamed IMU chaos in Kyrgyzstan on Akayev doing nothing but 'grinning stupidly'.

'Dissidents,' Karimov once said in the Uzbek parliament, 'must be shot in the forehead! If necessary I'll shoot them myself.' Apparently he also boiled opponents, a true descendent of Emir Nasrullah of Bukhara who in 1842 beheaded two English diplomats, players of the Great Game.

Susi's husband Pete flew in from Geneva and spent a week listening to stories of murdered husbands and lost children, trying to determine whether each person should be given refugee status. The fate of the 500 Uzbek refugees was monitored by the world, the Kyrgyz provisional government forced to publicly showcase its first piece of international diplomacy. Uzbekistan, Kazakhstan, Russia, China and America all watched to see who Kyrgyzstan would favour. Should it pacify its bullying neighbour and sole supplier of natural gas by repatriating the refugees or satisfy the UN and America, its biggest donor, by adhering to international conventions?

It occurred to me that world politics were like Sudoku puzzles. Military alliances, pipeline routes, counter-terrorism activities and trade agreements were all numbers which countries juggled between their rows, columns and boxes, taking care not to place a wrong number in the wrong square because that would cause ripples of retaliation, ending the game. Kyrgyzstan might look like a mere comma dividing the huge phrases of Kazakhstan and China but it had somehow become vital in the dynamics of the region.

Amidst regional uncertainty our immediate future became more settled. Funding had been reshuffled – again – and we really were leaving at the end of October. It was comforting to have a date, one which allowed escape before winter snow but plenty of time for a last pilgrimage to Issyk-Kul.

Where we would go next was less settled. Since deciding to be a lawyer at the age of thirteen, my life had been planned. I'd set off on a path of A-levels, university, law school, training and qualification which I never thought to question until Matthew suggested moving to Egypt. Now my life wasn't plotted I had exciting choices: should we move to Ouagadougou in Burkina Faso where they suffered from desertification and recurring droughts; Arkhangelsk in northern Russia, described optimistically by Matthew's boss as 'on the coast and free from tourists', or England where everything was very expensive and it always rained?

I'd had amazing adventures in obscure places but I wasn't sure I could take the pain of arriving and leaving a new country again. I was tired of having to panic buy a year's supply of clothes in one morning.

"I thought we'd agreed to settle, at least for a while," I queried Matthew when he came home talking of rural Vietnam. I accepted that after the quirks of Central Asia I might soon be bored with being able to buy Heinz baked beans whenever I wanted but hoped to stay long enough to at least unpack our wedding presents.

"They're great projects." There were always going to be great projects in extraordinary places. I'd known that when I married him but still wasn't sure I could commit to a lifetime of displacement. I sensed it was time for a career decision.

Apart from dreading goodbyes there was another reason why I didn't want to move to a paddy field: I was pregnant. I'd found out just after the revolution, Matthew paling when I showed him a test stick with a blue line.

"You were trying too!"

"I know, but the reality seems much scarier." Baby Number 2 was due on 1st January, an inconvenient date if you like wild New Year parties. I was much calmer about this pregnancy, the strange functions of my body less mysterious. I'd not even picked up a pregnancy book. I felt guilty for neglecting Number 2; with Tom I'd known what was going on inside me every week. This time, distracted by more obvious demands, I sometimes forgot anyone was in there.

With your first child every day is an experiment, your learning curve vertical as you struggle to work out what to feed them and whether they're too young for play dough. With the second child, Jenna told me, you just get on with it because you don't have time to worry what's right any more.

I'd foolishly assumed that I'd enjoy my second pregnancy with the support of the NHS. I didn't relish becoming Dr Gideon's training model again. Feeling braver and less in need of medical reassurance I wondered whether it was irresponsible to go without check-ups.

I was looking forward to seeing mad Dr Bucket, although I felt ashamed that in two years my Russian had barely improved. I could say that I didn't want to know if it was a girl or boy – avoiding another 'penis scrotum' incident – but I still couldn't discuss whether baby's bladder measurements were correct.

Tom was indifferent to the news of a sibling, too busy cooking aubergines in the kitchen we'd made from cardboard boxes. Trying to engender interest I asked him whether he'd like a brother or sister.

"A biscuit," he replied.

With a month to go before presidential elections, Kyrgyzstan exploded in the heat. A parliamentary deputy was gunned down on a busy Bishkek street – but no-one was surprised because he was a dodgy businessman with mafia connections. A hotel was attacked by crowds in Osh – but no-one was surprised because it was owned by a dodgy businessman with mafia connections. The White House was stormed, again – by supporters of a dodgy businessman with mafia connections who'd been disqualified from running for president because he had Kazak citizenship.

The Kyrgyz had adapted quickly to their new regime: if they didn't like something they took over a government building. It was déjà-vu: offices closed, Tzum was evacuated and supermarkets were emptied and boarded up. Cars drove around the city droning out public service announcements: 'Dear Citizens, Kyrgyzstan is our home, we must look after it.' Bakiev accused Akayev of organising the riots in an attempt to discredit the elections.

The only difference was that the police didn't run away and instead formed orderly lines and dispersed crowds with tear gas and water canons. The OSCE were delighted to see the results of their €600,000 funding. Matthew heard shooting from his office and feared this was our Andijan.

Into this mayhem rode Alastair, a twenty-eight year old teacher from England who'd spent the past four years cycling 64,000 kilometres around the world, to be stopped in his forty-ninth country by Kyrgyz police in ski-jump caps.[28] Alastair was searching for us because I'd 'met' him through a travel-writing website, not that I'm in the habit of meeting men over the Internet. He found us at Ben and Nicky's. As was tradition during White House stormings we'd adjourned to their garden where Tom and Siana were

---

[28] Alastair Humphreys has written two books about his trip; see www.alastairhumphreys.com

throwing sand at each other. They had a volatile relationship, kissing one minute then fighting the next. It was exhausting never knowing whether it was going to be love or violence.

We were eating homemade ice-lollies when Alastair arrived.

"You're very calm," he said, ducking to avoid a cherry Tom was aiming at Siana. "Hardened ex-pats now?"

"When you've lived through one revolution the second's much easier," I explained pompously, "it's like pregnancy, you know what's coming."

"I thought the last revolution created a new Kyrgyzstan?"

"It's sad but nothing's really changed."

"There's an arrest warrant for Bermet's husband," Ben pointed out.

"And the White House is now guarded by soldiers," Nicky added helpfully.

"Who spend most of their time chatting up girls through the fence."

"But policemen are still taking bribes on every corner."

"I know. I just had to pay 20 *som* to cycle down *Manas*."

"While government salaries are so low you're never going to change this," Matthew said authoritatively. "Donors should stop holding conferences on corruption and spend the money on salaries. It's been shown elsewhere in the world; increase salaries, corruption stops and government revenue rises."

"That sounds too sensible," said Nicky.

"And would put a lot of international consultants out of work," Ben added.

"I was talking to Gerhard about this the other day," I said. "He's got a good idea about the administration of Kyrgyzstan as he spends most of his time with government ministers. He says that rather than forcing inappropriate economic models on the country, donors should provide international experts for each ministry. The Kyrgyz lack expertise so how can they be expected to successfully run a country?"

"America runs it for them," Ben yelled over his shoulder as he disappeared round the corner to find Siana.

"With contradictory policies that don't work."

"Gerhard also says that until America stops making compromises for oil and global terrorism, foreign policy will always be hypocritical."

"Exactly," Matthew agreed. "How much has America compromised to get airbases in Kyrgyzstan and Uzbekistan? Look at the reaction to Andijan, the US is willing to overlook anything in exchange for a landing strip."

"Did America start the revolution?" Alastair asked.

"Our journalist friend Michael believes that without the civil society projects stirring up feelings of discontent, people would have remained passive," I explained. "He thinks the momentum *was* started by outside interference. Bakiev maintains it was a people's revolution because the impetus came from them and no-one was prepared for it."

"So what has the revolution actually achieved?" Alastair asked.

We thought about this while Siana tried to grab Tom's lolly and he whacked her on the head with it.

"A new public holiday."

"Re-fitted Narodnes."

"Different bickering and ineffectual politicians."

"Unrealistic expectations."

"So, not a lot then."

"Kumashai says Kulov will save the country."

"Trouble is the Kyrgyz believe he'll make them rich overnight, they don't realise that development is a lengthy process."

"She said Kulov was now supported by Akayev."

"Akayev sees Kulov as his best chance to retain influence and businesses."

"Michael said he saw Aidar in town."

"I saw Bermet at the Hyatt."

"Did they forget more pin codes?"

"I just hope they don't raid Narodne again," I said. "We're almost out of milk."

"Don't worry, we've got plenty in stock," Nicky reassured. "More tea Alastair?"

Fortunately the cycle of revolution was broken and there was no looting that night – the protesters said they'd come back when it was cooler. It was hot, so hot local girls forgot to wear bras under their skimpy chiffon tops and stiletto heels sank into melting tarmac. The city was a furnace blasting out the forty-degree hairdryer heat we thought we'd left behind in Egypt. All anyone could do was lie by the pool and pant – apart from Bin *Babushka* who seemed to be impervious to the heat and still wore her thick winter coat, woolly tights and boots. Everyone who could went to Issyk-Kul so life calmed down in Bishkek. Weeks went by without murders or demonstrations.

The new topic for discussion at Playgroup was 'are you going home for the election?' Gina, Ilke, Delphine and Jenna were leaving, Jenna saying she'd rather fly to America when she chose than be forced back to Almaty by the UN. Kay, Penny, Nicky and I were staying, not expecting another revolution now the element of surprise had gone.

In the heat haze the build up to the election started. Billboards of Bakiev appeared across town. He had his arms crossed defiantly, was superimposed over a picture of a factory and was wearing a blue tank top – well, he was an engineer. Most were resigned that Bakiev would win because being from the south with a Russian wife and Uzbek uncle he had good ethnic coverage. His chances of success were greatly increased when his only rival, Kulov, stood down. Critics said it was because Kulov was scared of failing his Kyrgyz language exam. Bakiev and Kulov claimed they'd come to an agreement to save the country from splitting: if Bakiev won Kulov would be Prime Minister.

The greatest concern was voter apathy. Authorities were worried that people wouldn't bother voting because they'd all be in Issyk-Kul. There were promotional adverts on KTR – Nargiza, Tom's hairdresser, starring in one.

Matthew's colleagues were called to a meeting and told to vote, but not *who* to vote for. This was an improvement.

I hoped the situation would remain stable – and Narodne remain open – because my sister Demelza and boyfriend Charlie were coming to visit. A revolution wouldn't help my sightseeing schedule. When people fly 7000 kilometres to visit you feel responsible that they have a good time, especially when they bring a box of cornflakes and gravy granules as gifts.

Demelza and Charlie were active types, unlikely to be content discussing potty training at Playgroup. Aware of this, and bolstered by having two more people to help mop up vomit, I decided to brave a road trip – one with as few bends as possible. I researched destinations, reinstating the guidebooks and consulting Nicky, knowing that there was so much more to Kyrgyzstan than I was capable of showing my guests. Our compromise was to circumnavigate Issyk-Kul. This would enable Demelza and Charlie to experience the Riviera of Central Asia as well as satisfying my ultimate Kyrgyz dream – a night in a mouldy *yurt*.

Chapter Twenty-Eight – Meeting Anna Petrovna

Alastair stayed for three weeks, waiting for an Iranian visa which never came. He gave a presentation on his trip in Ben and Nicky's garden making us all feel ashamed for complaining about toilet roll post-revolution – what's a scratch on your bum compared to mending punctures in a minus-forty degree Siberian winter?

Three days after he left, Kurmanbek Bakiev was voted president with a majority of 89% and no riots: it was still forty degrees so no-one could be bothered to protest. Everybody was happy. The OSCE said there was tangible progress on democracy – these were the freest and fairest elections to ever take place in Central Asia; Akayev said he was going to head up a science institute in Moscow and I felt more comfortable receiving Demelza and Charlie now that the risk of messy revolution had passed.

In two-and-a half years we'd only had three visitors – my parents and Lorna, Tom's godmother – so it was a novelty to welcome Demelza and Charlie. Egypt had been very different. Aswan was a tourist attraction and I'd taken so many visitors on a camel trip through the desert that the locals called me 'Tour Leader'.

Friends, like most Brits, weren't as informed about Kyrgyzstan's attractions. Kyrgyzstan is one of the few places on the planet still undiscovered. It's so remote Rough Guide hasn't found it yet. Although the Kyrgyz government talk about exploiting their natural tourist resources they've no idea how to do it so Kyrgyzstan remains a gem of obscurity, free from packs of people and obtrusive tour buses. Travellers can destroy the remoteness they seek so I felt fortunate to have known Kyrgyzstan while still unspoilt.

Although we left the city in forty-degrees, Dema's jeep was stacked with coats, socks and jumpers as well as a cot, potty, baby bath, sun-cream and water because I knew the heat could be deceptive. Along the edges of the main road east, watermelon sellers were still waking up, uncurling from the iron beds which were home for the season. Some had put up tents or shelters next to their mountains of fruit but most just hid under blankets, scant privacy from the ceaseless traffic roaring by.

We turned right at the power station and took the highway towards the lake. This was apparently an international standard road but the surface was rutted and flocks of sheep herded up the middle of its lanes. Red combine harvesters lumbered between fields, hunched over their wheels of teeth where bedding rolls and watermelons were stowed. Kazaks in Japanese jeeps roared past, swerving to avoid sheep.

The road followed the Chui River which creates the boundary between Kyrgyzstan and Kazakhstan. The river curved and crashed over boulders, grey and narrow in places, wide and shallow in others. It was difficult to believe that this innocuous stretch of water had carved out the vast Chui valley over millions of years. On its banks people emerged from bushes where they'd stopped to pee and herders watched cattle graze along the shore. Long, low white buildings were set back behind concrete walls, abandoned *kolkhoz* of the Soviet Union. In the independent Kyrgyz Republic, farmers lived in straw shacks with awnings for their Ladas and buckets of tomatoes for sale on their doorsteps.

It seemed exciting that the mountains to the left were in Kazakhstan. They were parched brown and stony, just another bump in a vast land without borders until Stalin had decided to make them a frontier. To the right, across the valley floor, the Kyrgyz mountains rose in layers. First the foothills, grass faded by the sun. Then swathes of deeper green, undulating pastures where the *yurts* were hidden. Above them was the snow line, white peaks tucked into clouds. Clefts and ridges formed gullies of shadow.

We skirted Tokmok and joined the lower road as it entered the apple village. I asked Dema to stop and buy some but he shook his head dismissively.

"They're not good yet. I'll bring some for you in September when I go hunting, they'll be sweet then." I'd learnt that it was easier not to argue. Tom was yelling 'TRAKTOR!' every two minutes. Kyrgyz villages are a little boy's dream, the streets busy with dented and rusting tractors, each with a red star on their radiator.

"How come Dema knows everyone?" Demelza asked.

"Why d'you say that?"

"Because they're all flashing at him."

They were telling him about police speed traps. Desperate to make extra money to supplement meagre salaries, officers pointed what looked like old grey hairdryers at cars. Despite the warning we were pulled over three times. As was custom Dema politely shook each policeman's hand before arguing vehemently about being stopped. We had to pay one fine, Dema muttering about corruption as he got back into the car.

"Forty *som* with a receipt or twenty without. It's a disgrace! I bet officers in England aren't so dishonest." I comforted him by explaining that fines in England were over $100 and you didn't even need policemen, black boxes could catch you and send a bill in the post. This seemed to calm him down and we continued to Issyk-Kul without incident.

We were staying at Raduga, a new resort built with a loan from Dirk's bank. Checking in was easy for me because as Anna Petrovna and Ivan Ivanovich were always resting in sanatoria I knew all the words. It felt good to be finally using phrases which had sounded so ridiculous repeated rote in the sitting room. Our rooms were in the *corpus*, a long, dull building with speakers blasting Russian pop music outside the windows. Lunch was salad of peas and diced carrots smeared with mayonnaise, followed by greasy soup with mutton, cabbage and potatoes floating in it then fatty chunks of chicken with rice, all washed down with apricots dissolving in water, which I now knew was called *kompot*. It was served quickly and in silence by a girl in a green uniform.

"I feel like we're in a concentration camp," Demelza whispered.

We spent the afternoon on the beach so that Demelza and Charlie could experience Central Asian holiday making. To our right a group of young people were sharing a crate of beer and a watermelon. To our left a man was sunbathing in Speedos and an *ak-kalpak*. At the water's edge a *babushka* snorted strands of green mucus into the lake. Goats grazed at the next-door beach. Behind us two women dug holes with a small child in between shots of vodka.

At lunchtime other diners had drunk vodka like wine, honouring the phrase that a good Kyrgyz never leaves the room before the bottle is empty. The alcohol consumption statistics had come out the week before and 42 million litres of vodka and 39 million litres of beer had reportedly been sold in Kyrgyzstan the previous year – and that didn't include the moonshine. Matthew found it difficult to remain patient with villagers who resented paying a few *som* for clean water when they spent much more on vodka.

Behind us thunder was rumbling in the mountains. From the water we looked back to a purple sky. Tom didn't want to swim, despite Dema's persistent efforts, so we took a walk on the pier. An odd couple approached us. The girl was young and looked like Anna Petrovna with long, straight blond hair. The only difference was length of skirt – Anna Petrovna always wore hers demurely at knee length, this girl's was nudging her upper thighs. She was with an older, swarthy man whose black chest hair burst from a Hawaiian shirt – what would Ivan Ivanovich say?

"Could you take our photo please," she asked in polite English, holding out a camera. They posed together with the unfettered blue of Issyk-Kul behind them. "We are first time together. We met on Internet and Mario has come from Mexico to see me. We hope to marry and live in America. This country is not good after revolution."

"You don't like Bakiev?"

"He is just the same as Akayev." She had a point; he'd started to smile like Akayev on the front page of the Bishkek Observer and travelled in an ostentatious convoy which caused similar traffic disruption. Commentators had given Bakiev until Christmas to deal with poverty and unemployment to avoid a Russian scenario: two revolutions in one year. The people were no longer afraid of complaining and were very aware of the effect they could have on government.

However, the first thing Bakiev had done was renovate the front of the White House – new president, new fountain. The second thing, prompted by China and Russia at an SCO summit, was question the necessity of the American base, controversial because Karimov had just served notice-to-quit for the base in Uzbekistan.

Rumsfeld, and later Condi, dashed over offering extra friendship, and money, panicking because they were losing all their convenient flight paths to Afghanistan. China and Russia, desperate to counterbalance America's influence, called for 'multi-polar world order'. America accused them of bullying their neighbours then declared that Bakiev was 'in no position to ask us to leave'. Bakiev bravely retorted that Kyrgyzstan would not serve as a site for someone else's political games. Anna Petrovna was only concerned what this bickering meant for her future.

"I hope Bakiev not make American angry so they not give us visa."

"You could live here."

"Oh no! Mario say I have nice legs but he not want my home."

Next morning after breakfast – mince and bulgur wheat pies – we repacked the jeep with potties and baths and headed for Karakol. It had rained hard all night, clearing the air so that the sun was hot in a sky fragmented with puffs of white cloud. I read names as we passed through villages – Grigorievka, Jarkynbaev, Chong-Oruktu. Matthew had bought me a map of the region with places printed in Cyrillic. The paper was thick and smelt of adventures. I'd folded it into a concertina. Around the blue lake were ever-deepening circles of orange indicating mountains climbing higher above the plateau. Jagged patches of white showed the eternal snow line.

We swung round the far end of Issyk-Kul where the road veered away from the lake towards the Kazak border. Beyond Karakol, Kazakhstan collided with China and the eastern tip of Kyrgyzstan, uncharted territory deep in the Tien Shan. The water was a shimmering mirage behind lines of poplars and fields of humped hayricks. Rows of yellow sunflowers looked east and the air smelled of hot sun-dried pastures and herbs which crunched into fragrances of rosemary and mint when you stepped on them.

Karakol was the largest red blob on my map. It had once been a thriving frontier town and garrison, perched on the outer edge of the Soviet Union with only remote mountains between it and China. Its significance lost, it now had a parochial feel, frequented only by mountaineers heading for unexplored peaks and farmers bringing livestock to Sunday market. Locals claimed to still be recovering from the shock of the break up of the Soviet Union, annoyed that they now had to work for a living rather than be cared for by the state. Most spent days tending orchards; Karakol was still famous for its apples.

We were met by Smeagol, a small Kyrgyz lady with a dark plait reaching to her bum and a studded denim outfit left over from the Eighties. Her name was actually Mirgul – *gul* means flower in Kyrgyz hence Aigul, Moonflower and Mirgul, Peace-flower – but the first time Matthew said it I heard Smeagol and it stuck. I couldn't help thinking of Tolkien in Kyrgyzstan. With names like Nazgul and bleak, craggy mountains, I wondered whether he'd snuck behind the Iron Curtain for inspiration.

Smeagol took us to the market; a row of stalls covered with tarpaulin balanced on sticks. She was then supposed to show us a picnic spot Matthew recommended. Unfortunately Smeagol didn't know this and my Russian was failing me. I was trying to say, "we drive towards Kerege-Tash and turn right at the first water pump" but couldn't remember my vocabulary and couldn't find my dictionary. I stuttered at Smeagol and waved my hands uselessly.

"I'm sorry, I've forgotten the Russian word.

"Try and show me."

I felt pretty foolish playing charades in the middle of Karakol but had little choice. I bent down and indicated something near the ground.

"It's small." Smeagol was good. "Flaps its wings?"

"*Nyet!*" I was trying to mime someone pumping water.

"You have puncture?"

"*Nyet.*" I took a bottle of water from the jeep and tipped it up when I pumped.

"*Kalonka?*"

"*Da!*"

We got there eventually, loaded with chicken, tomatoes, cucumber and a watermelon the size of a small child. The picnic spot was up a hill on the edge of the tree line where cows were grazing thick grass studded with pink, blue and yellow flowers. Matthew had eaten *besh barmak* here but still managed to describe it as picturesque with a river, slopes of pines and huge views of the mountains across the valley in Kazakhstan. I remembered this trip because his colleagues had picked pine branches, telling Matthew to put them in the wardrobe to deter moths. This I'd dutifully done, until they'd moulted. I was still picking needles out of our jumpers.

We were staying at Elita *gastinitsa* in the suburbs of Karakol. It was run by Olga, a fearsome woman who had thighs capable of squashing Tom in the event of disobedience. She wore the national costume of Russian matrons; socks with flip flops and a shapeless floral dress.

"Can we have *casha* for breakfast?" I asked timidly. Matthew had warned me it would be spam, grim at the best of times, let alone before 8am.

"*Nyet!*" Olga snapped. "I choose the breakfast."

Breakfast, I've realised, defines nationality. Matthew's Danish colleagues eat salami, cheese and gherkins, ridiculing our fried eggs. Russians like fried spam, pasta, peas and mince and bulgur wheat pasties. If you were lucky they'd make *casha*, semolina, something we'd been converted to eating for breakfast since trying it on a trip to Issyk-Kul. I wished hosts would serve local products, *lepioshka*, jam and *kaimak*; delicious and much less hassle than making pasties – although Matthew pointed out eating *kaimak* would increase the risk of contracting Brucellosis, a nasty disease found in dairy products, but not spam.

Tom and I wandered the streets around the guesthouse. Despite being five minutes from the centre of town there was a rural feel. Homes were white

Slavic cottages with low eaves and ornately carved wooden window frames painted green or pale blue. Surrounding them were gardens thick with flowers and neat rows of vegetables. Orchards spilled over fences, branches heavy with apples, plums, apricots and pears. Mountain-fresh water gushed through ditches and cows and goats grazed the lush grass.

A man in a David Beckham t-shirt was making *lepioshka*. He slapped a lump of white dough onto a rounded board, turning it quickly in his hands to stretch the edges before placing it inside his domed clay oven. We bought a loaf, so fresh it was too hot to touch. I felt a deep sense of contentment. It was like being home in the village, people looking up from watering tomatoes to smile and wave.

Tom was now a little man with definite opinions. After eating his *lepioshka* he didn't want to stay in his buggy but walk in concentric circles around a *kalonka* with me holding his hand. If Dema had been there he would have obliged. Dema would do anything for Tom, including walking in concentric circles around a *kalonka*. This wasn't helpful because Tom was learning how to get his own way and cried for Dema whenever distressed or wanting something.

Eventually I gave up trying to explore and stomped back to Elita muttering about my tempestuous child. Matthew accused me of oscillating between calling Tom gorgeous and horrible; it's a mother's prerogative. Nearing the guesthouse I heard two women chatting to each other as they picked fruit. They were hidden deep in a green thicket of bushes. If I'd been with Matthew he would have made me walk on, too shy to want to attract attention. The good thing about visitors, especially ones who ask so many questions, is a renewal of your sense of curiosity. It's easy to become stagnated by routine so that you forget to look at things with fresh eyes. I slowed my angry pace to watch and was rewarded by a hand shoved through the fence loaded with raspberries.

"*Malina!*" shouted Tom who'd decided to cheer up.

The woman's name was Tolkun and she and her sister, Barool, who was concealed by a pear tree, were born in Karakol and had never been to Bishkek. Like so many Kyrgyz women they lived within the parameters of their plot, wandering occasionally to the side of the road in slippers to watch traffic pass and swap gardening notes with neighbours. I wondered if they were bored or more contented in their simple life than those of us who exhausted ourselves chasing around the modern world with gadgets, technology and expectations.

Tolkun smiled as she passed up more raspberries. She had gold teeth, a blue headscarf and silver discs hanging from her ears, traditional jewellery passed on through generations. She wouldn't let me leave until the pocket of Tom's buggy was full of fruit. I arrived at Elita calmed by their simple domesticity. It was a golden summer evening smelling of roses and the musty apple trees whose branches brushed our window.

"This is what the journey's for, a chance to explore and get to know the Kyrgyz better," I told Matthew later on the phone.

"Their kindness humbles me," he admitted, "even if their maintenance skills are exasperating. Remember I told you about that family of four living in the guard house of a chlorination unit in Talas? The father was the guard and the tiny room was his wage. They insisted I come in for tea and *lepioshka*. These people are so generous, even when they have nothing." I went to sleep content, lulled by my encounter with Tolkun and Barool.

Chapter Twenty-Nine – The Jailoo

I enjoyed my spam for breakfast. I ate it with cold eggy-bread, which was also delicious smeared with *smarodeena*. Strange pregnancy eating habits can be useful when breakfasting in Kyrgyzstan. We waved good-bye to Olga, who'd been charmed by Dema's gruff kindness and ability to fix her carburettor, and returned to the market for fresh *lepioshka*. After wandering around the wooden Russian orthodox cathedral, set in a garden of marigolds and potatoes, we set off, at last, for my night in a *jailoo*.

Outside Karakol more potatoes were growing, acres of green rows topped with white flowers, some being hoed by men in *ak-kalpaks*. Horses pulled carts carrying huge mounds of hay, shaggy green edges dragging along the road. They were driven by young boys perched behind the wooden yokes which curved across the horses' necks, dwarfed by the load. Goats stood on hind legs to reach fresh leaves in trees. Toddlers in woollen bonnets and tights traced patterns in the dust with sticks. *Babushkas* draped clumps of brown wool over fences to dry. Between each village were avenues of poplars, behind which the mountains rose majestically, piebald with snow.

The road was corrugated with potholes and patches of tarmac. Tom said "oi" every time we bounced over a rut and I hoped baby Number Two was swimming in enough liquid. Gradually the lake came back into focus, a haze of blue at the bottom of potato fields. On the north shore the sky was ominously grey and by the time we reached Jeti Oguz, a valley famous for huge red rocks and *yurts*, it had started to rain.

An hour later my English optimism that 'it was brighter over there' had started to wane. The lake was parallel with the road but I couldn't see the other side. It was dark with thick grey clouds, rain turning picturesque villages into muddy roads of desolate squalor. I felt sorry for the holiday makers who'd saved all year for their week at the beach. Some huddled bravely under trees wrapped in towels but most were walking dejectedly back to cold chalets. It wasn't going to be much fun camping in a tent which smelt of damp sheep. I considered asking Dema to drive us back to Bishkek but I knew that if I didn't persevere I'd never visit a *jailoo*. At least I could say I'd spent a night in a *yurt*, even if it was miserable.

We turned left after *Bokonbayeva* and followed a track through *Toora-Suu*.

"This is one of Matthew's villages," I told Demelza and Charlie. I was proud of Matthew's work. Unlike a lot of well-meaning development projects his wasn't installing unsuitable technology or telling villagers how to deal with conditions they'd survived for hundreds of years. Matthew's project was simply providing a basic need.

"He was here last month for the opening ceremony." Grateful *babushkas* had pumped water for the KTR cameras. Luigi had cut a ribbon and become an honorary member of the village, which meant he had to pay annual water tax. Mr Turd had refused to inaugurate the VIP[29] latrine at the chlorination plant, not getting the joke. The completion of *Toora-Suu's* water system had been a very positive achievement. It was a shame that there was no money for chlorine and a girl was still filling a kettle from a puddle.

Outside *Toora-Suu* the hills closed in, forcing the track to curve right. We were in the base of a huge valley. To east and west grassy slopes swept grandly into the distance. In front of us the ground rose steeply, rushing up to mountains we knew were there but couldn't see. In the distance, perched high on the second tier of mountains, were two white yurts, so small they could have been button mushrooms in the green.

"Is that where we're staying?" Charlie asked incredulously.

"Yup," I replied.

Dema drove doggedly on, putting the jeep into four wheel drive so we could churn though thick mud and cross deep streams. Even with the extra grip we skidded and lurched upwards in frightening angles and my head banged relentlessly on the window. Distances were deceptive. The *yurts* appeared to grow no larger as we pitched and rolled through gullies gouged into the hillside.

Tom was yelling, positive that he did not want to spend a night in this place. As we crested the steepest rise he had a little vomit in defiant protest over six hours spent in the car. Physically and emotionally exhausted, I no longer cared that he'd aimed straight down my cleavage. I was more relaxed about puke now, having acclimatised to his gagging. Rather than initiate full outfit change at the roadside I'd just say "oh dear" and have a bit of a dab with a wet wipe.

By the time we arrived the family had gathered to greet us. I must have been a bedraggled site with puke crusting in my cleavage.

"Welcome to our *jailoo*, I am Aida." Aida had the high, flat cheekbones typical of her race. Her face was testament to a life in the mountains; her skin weathered by the elements, eyes narrowed against the sun. She introduced her husband Ooluk, a tall, dark man who nodded curtly and Gulzada and Tonya, two women who looked so similar to Aida they had to be sisters.

Aida explained that her brother, Alibek, lived with his family in the *yurts* we could see across the *jailoo*. He was hosting six distinguished men who were on their *adehayet*, rest holiday. Rather than stay in an Issyk-Kul sanatoria to take the healing waters they were enjoying a Kyrgyz detox; ten days in the mountains drinking mare's milk every two hours, breathing clean air and abstaining from vodka.

"One of the men is our boss," Aida explained. "He is renting this *jailoo* and owns all the animals. I am looking after the horses and yaks and my brother the sheep and cows. Our boss is a very rich and important man."

---

[29] Ventilated Improved Pit

Aida invited us for tea and we stooped to enter the first *yurt*, leaving damp shoes on the mat. The door was blue with carved panels of red and yellow, patches of brightness in the gloom. Inside was cosy, warmed by a stove on which the kettle boiled. Next to it was a barrel of *koumys*, a large ladle tipped against its side. A worn, green and orange *shyrdak* covered the floor and a red and gold embroidered *tush kiz* covered the back wall. Bags, coats and satchels of papers hung on the curved red wooden frame and eiderdowns were piled on the metal *sunduk*, a large chest used to carry a nomadic bride's trousseau. A thin curtain hung from roof slats to the right, partitioning off the cooking area where the stove was propped up with stones. Most food was prepared outside over an open fire, when it wasn't raining.

We sat cross-legged at the low, round table while Aida served tea from a silver samovar. There was no need to ask for more. She watched carefully and if you had not sipped recently, reached out for your bowl which she half filled, polite tradition so that the tea did not cool before you drank it. Gulzada pressed *koumys* and food on us; round, unleavened loaves of *lepioshka*, bowls of rancid butter, apricot or *smarodeena* jam, thick cream and plates of cold mutton, the cut of which was difficult to determine.

Tonya's sons Ermish and Orus watched shyly from the doorway. To keep warm they wore layers of random clothing, multiple jumpers and jackets. Their cheeks were ruddy patches in elliptical brown faces and they smelt of outdoor life, happily a comforting haze of wood smoke rather than cow dung.

"*Amereekanka toristka?*" Gulzada asked. I explained that I was English but lived in Bishkek because my husband was a water engineer. "Is he blond and young and disliking *besh barmak?*" She gabbled excitedly in Russian and I translated for Demelza and Charlie.

"She knows Matthew, met him at a village meeting when he ranted because they'd not painted the tap stands."

"Please tell him our union painted the stands but it's now peeling off so can we have more money to do it again," Gulzada asked. I promised to pass on the message.

There was a shout from outside and Aida looked at her watch. "They will be here soon. Please excuse me to milk the mares." Leaving Tom with Charlie and Demelza I followed her outside into the rain. Two jeeps were moving slowing across the valley from the *yurts* on the other side. I was surprised that exercise was not part of the *adehayet*.

In a pen behind the *yurt* Aida knelt subserviently at the rounded belly of a horse while Ooluk held the head. Jets of white liquid drummed into her pail and by the time it was full the six men were sitting expectantly on a long, low bench, holding out their mugs for the warm milk. They welcomed me, amused to find a western woman encroaching on their retreat.

The boss was called Chingiz and implied that he owned a piece of everything in Kyrgyzstan. He'd been popular with the Akayevs but had survived the revolution and purges that followed. The friends were his chiefs of staff. One offered me his cup. The milk was surprisingly thin, sweet like juice from a coconut. They advised me to sip gently – the milk's purpose was to cleanse the digestive system, its effects immediate.

In the *yurt* Demelza and Charlie were wondering how to entertain a child in a wet *jailoo*. Aida found a ceramic flute tucked into the red frame and showed Tom how to make a noise by placing fingers over the holes and blowing. The low notes resonated around the tent and Tom was so excited with this discovery he puffed and grinned, looking up proudly after each hoot for congratulations. This filled ten minutes. Ermish and Orus were playing a game called *torwus korgul*, moving stones around an oval, wooden board in which sixteen holes were carved. Tom interrupted and was happily occupied shuffling stones until he decided it was more fun throwing them – ten more minutes gone. Plucking the *komuz* occupied another ten minutes and taking Dema's cap on and off, a further five. Eventually I let Tom go outside in the mud where he was so desperate to be and he and Gulzada threw bread to the gobbling turkeys and their fluffy chicks.

With Tom distracted I wandered off to the toilet – a long-drop in a shed with a panoramic view of the valley. Although Aida's was a working *yurt* she was also set up to accommodate visitors. She was part of the Community Based Tourism (CBT) group, a network of enterprising Kyrgyz supported by Swiss Aid who opened their homes to tourists. This enabled foreigners to experience the uniqueness of nomadic life while supporting struggling families with extra dollars.

Aida's family, like most Kyrgyz shepherds, were semi nomadic. They spent the winter in a village on the valley floor and rode up into the *jailoo* in late May or June. Traditionally they took their homes with them but sadly for my romantic notions of nomadic life it appeared that *yurts* were losing popularity to stone hovels and shacks of corrugated asbestos. Aida told me excitedly that her boss had promised to build them a hut. Nomadic life was changing, modernising in a slow, Kyrgyz way. Pastures were being rented rather than occupied according to family custom and lessees were told they could build structures as long as they removed them at the lease end. As a result hillsides were marred by skeletons of bricks and rusting railway carriages rather than dotted with unobtrusive *yurts* and the richest men had access to the best pastures.

Eventually, at six, the rain stopped. Everything was quiet while we listened to drops dripping off the grass. The clouds drifted apart allowing pale yellow rays of sun to squeeze through from a glimpse of blue sky. The valley was a natural amphitheatre, enclosed by green mountains, meadows of wild flowers stretching in both directions. Smoke was rising from Alibek's chimney and I could hear distant echoes of cows mooing as they were herded home across the valley floor.

According to the orange band on my map we were between 2000 and 3000 metres high. Behind us grey glaciers were cascading between peaks in infinite slowness. Around us was an intricate network of valleys, interlocking like arteries and veins.

At last I had penetrated the mysteries of the mountains, their façades no longer one-dimensional. I could finally appreciate the true character of Kyrgyzstan and how it affected those who lived there. Unfortunately, I still wasn't satisfied. The more I saw the more I wanted to infiltrate the mountains, to travel on into them to places rarely seen, places only reachable on horseback. I started to make fantastical plans to return for a trek, not really believing it would ever happen.[30]

Dinner was delicious; a deep basin of *plov* which tasted faintly of wood smoke from the fire it had been cooked on. Even Tom sat still long enough to eat, shovelling chunks of mutton in with an orange fork held in a clenched fist, shouting "*yurt*" when he thought he wasn't getting enough attention. Tommybek, as Dirk called him, was a true Kyrgyz boy. He'd perfected the Central Asian Squat, loved *yurts,* Shoro, Soviet tractors, gnawing meat off bones, flirting with skinny girls and *lepioshka*. He called this 'more-vodka'. It was going to be embarrassing when he started yelling "I need more-vodka!" in Tesco.

"How old is he?" Aida asked.

"Twenty-one months."

"And he doesn't walk?" I waited for the advice, wondering what her onion and vodka remedy would be.

"But he's very good at talking," Dema interrupted, "so don't criticise my *Droog* Tomas. He speaks Russian and English. He says "dog"..."

"*Sabaka*," said Tom obligingly.

"...trolleybus, Tzum, apple and strawberry and can even work the radio in my jeep." Aida was forced to admit he was the most talented, but immobile, child she'd ever met.

The men came for their last dose of mare's milk at dusk. The solid greyness had gone and the sky was pink with the promise of better weather for tomorrow. The only sounds were natural: gushing water in a river; whinnying horses; dogs barking across the valley. With her duties completed Aida rolled out long cushions called *tushuks* for our beds and placed a flickering candle next to the stove.

To save awkwardness Charlie, Dema and Ooluk moved to the second *yurt* leaving Demelza, Tom and I to share with the rest of the family. While I settled Tom into his cot Tonya sat outside softly strumming the *komuz* and singing. Her plaintive nasal chants undulated around us, merging with the rushing water as she told tales of ancient nomads. I lay snugly in my sleeping bag enjoying the warmth of the stove. Above me seventy-four red roof struts radiated from the round *tunduk* like sun rays and all the colours of the

---

[30] Eighteen months after leaving Kyrgyzstan I did return and rode through Chong Kemin valley with Nicky, Kay and another friend.

274

embroidered lining emanated into a warm feeling of cosiness. Like my baby I felt I was enveloped in a womb.

The rain returned, with gale force winds, around midnight. Water drummed loudly on the already sodden felt, leaking into Tom's strategically placed potty. Gusts buffeted us so hard I was convinced we'd leave the ground. The walls didn't quite meet the earth allowing icy drafts to squeeze through. The stove had gone out and it was so cold I could see clouds of my breath in the torchlight. Nicky later told me that on their last visit the door had burst off and a *yurt* had blown away. It was a good job she'd forgotten to share this information before we went or I'd have never slept and spent the whole night clinging to a roof strut.

As it was my rest was broken by poking Tom to check he was still alive; I had terrible images of waking to find him cold and hard. I felt guilty that I wanted a night in a *yurt* so much I was willing to risk my child developing hypothermia. I'd wrapped him in blankets and towels, put on his sun hat and said a few prayers but I still touched his neck periodically for reassuring warmth. In between I slept surprisingly well, the *koumys* barrel pressing against my feet, seduced by the romance of it all.

For Aida there was little romance. I heard her rise at 5.30am and watched as she tied her headscarf, stoked the fire and left to milk the mares. Through the door my first tantalising glimpse of snow capped mountains tempted me out into the dawn. An orange glow delineated jagged ridges at the top of the valley and across the roaring river sheep bleated as they spread over the hillside, watched by a solitary herdsman. Finally, I was in my elusive calendar picture

I walked to a stream and looked back at the *yurt* where Aida and Ooluk eked out an existence from the land. It was surrounded by mud and muck, the horses penned behind. There were no vegetables, no fruits and no deviation from the diet of bread, rice and meat; no variety of scenery, work or company and no escape from the proximity of the violent elements. Up here with them, I could appreciate how the vast soaring dimensions of uninterrupted grass, so beautiful to me because of its remoteness, could become oppressively lonely. It was easy for me to enjoy washing in icy melt water because soon I would be going down to hot showers and the cacophony of distractions which make us so stressed and exhausted.

After *casha* for breakfast Gulzada harnessed horses to ride higher into the mountains to check the yaks who preferred the cooler air. Ermish and Orus were to go with her, taken from childhood early by the responsibility of helping support the family. Folklore tells of children born into the saddle and Kyrgyz can often ride before they can walk. Perhaps mindful of this Gulzada grabbed Tom and hoisted him onto the horse. Holding her whip and dangling the reigns he looked completely at ease and happily let Gulzada lead him round and round the *yurts*.

"Do you think this life will continue?" I asked Tonya. "Will your sons follow the path of you and your family?"

"While there are herds they will need to be taken to the summer pasture," she replied, "and while there are no other jobs the young people have no choice but to take that work."

I prised Tom from his horse and we left on foot, to spare him the indignity of puking. We strode down the hill through wet knee-length grass which hid pink, yellow and blue flowers. Each time we turned to wave goodbye the *yurts* shrunk a little until they were tiny dots in the crease of the valley, dwarfed by the magnitude of the mountains they clung to. I wondered, as we turned a corner and they were lost to view; if I return next year, will they be there?

At the foot of the valley we rejoined Dema and took a muddy farm track, popping out in a yard where a family were stamping merrily on a melding roll of felt.

"*Salaam!* How are you?" Although their dog barked they welcomed us without surprise, as if four foreigners often drove into their garden while they were making carpets. With legendary Kyrgyz hospitality *babushka* insisted we eat *kaimak* and drink *chai*, clutching at my hand through the jeep window. Eventually I explained we had a long drive ahead.

"Where are you going?" one of the children asked.

"Bishkek," I replied.

"Ooh, that is far," she said, "I went to Balykchy once."

It was a different southern shore to the day before. The lake was a Mediterranean blue and cheering holiday makers ran in and out of the water. In the distance we could see the mountains Matthew had told me were there, fresh snow gleaming in the sun. We drove through barren canyons of crumbly yellow and orange rocks, inhabited only by scrubby bushes with prolific purple flowers. Along the roadside bare-chested men scythed meadows of hay in casual rows while others skinned cows or picnicked in the shade of their combine harvesters. We rushed through the villages on my map, making swift progress along the red line to Bishkek until something clunked and whined in the engine and Dema pulled over muttering nasty words in Russian.

"Oh dee-yah," said Tom.

Fortunately we'd stopped in a village with an interesting Soviet war memorial so while Dema lifted the bonnet and sorted his tools – he kept them in a white patent handbag under his seat – we persuaded Tom he didn't need to help and walked across for a closer look. It was a huge metal structure, images moulded in iron filigree to create a giant skeletal poster for Soviet propaganda. On the right a woman raised a sword while on the left a man held the hammer in the middle of a sickle. Names of the dead were listed in between. We walked around it, Tom leading Charlie and telling him, in his eclectic mix of Russian and English, about the dog he'd spotted. He even got the case right.

"You're very relaxed," Demelza commented, looking at Dema whose head was still under the bonnet.

"This happens all the time. Last week the starter motor fell off in Ala Too Square."

"What did you do?"

"Push."

When Dema called us back I presumed the engine was fixed enough to get us home. The jeep started at least and we bounced on steadily to Balykchy where we were stopped at the level crossing to let the racing-green train curve past. With a backward glance at the lake we turned into the pass, the last hurdle of our journey to the *Chui* valley. It was Friday-night rush hour, cars hurtling past buses on blind corners. Their haste made the pass a death trap, watched over by mournful faces etched onto granite gravestones at each precipitous bend. I felt grateful I'd lit a candle for journey mercies in Karakol's cathedral.

"Look at the goats," I said as a distraction tactic when Dema, unable to contain himself any longer, overtook a pea-green Lada with visibility of five metres. The goats were grazing individually on ledges stepping up the steep mountain side as if spectators in a grandstand. One slip and they'd fall into the icy-green water frothing below. A scrap-metal lorry lumbered towards us, its high sides wedges of bed heads and steel plates holding hundreds of smaller pieces in. Dema swerved back into our lane in front of the Lada.

"Where's that going?" Demelza asked. I explained about manhole covers and the Chinese steel industry and how these precarious trucks made the pass even more lethal as drivers became desperate to overtake them. I wasn't surprised to see an accident. A lorry had overturned after colliding with a black Mercedes. It lay on the side of the road, a slain beast with innards of girders and manhole covers spilling from its belly.

"Stupid Kyrgyz drivers," Dema muttered.

"The car number plate's Kazakh."

"They're terrible too."

"Or maybe Uzbek."

"None of them can drive properly, only Russians." It was good to see that revolution hadn't altered Dema's colonial arrogance.

I was glad to leave the angles of the pass behind and speed once again through Slavic villages. It was dusk. The apple sellers had given up for the day and men on horseback were herding sheep and cattle home across the road. Children were collecting water, dragging heavy churns on handcarts and gardeners set piles of raked leaves on fire creating a haze of smoke which merged with the sunset. Birds swooped into trees to roost and *babushkas* rocked babies on laps.

As we entered Bishkek the watermelon sellers were preparing for bed. It didn't look as though they'd made many sales. The warm city air smelt of *shashlik*, lights glowed from shop doors and music drifted from outdoor restaurants. Pointing out some of my favourite Soviet buildings to Demelza and Charlie it felt truly like coming home, ironic when it would soon be time to start extraction procedures – organising shippers, packing and saying goodbye to Tom's favourite cashier in Narodne. I was aware of time passing, reminded by my body notching up weeks with its own unstoppable clock.

"Will you be sad to leave?" Charlie asked. I tried to explain the dichotomy of feelings: that I'd become attached to Kyrgyzstan but there were inconveniences I couldn't wait to escape; that I was looking forward to England but sad the adventure was ending; that I'd try to ignore the finality of leaving so I wouldn't get nostalgic about my last trip to Narodne. I remembered a Russian word which would best answer the question; *danyet*, yes-no, a convenient contradiction covering all options.

Although I'd never have believed it that first night when our world was grey and bleak, I'd been happy in Kyrgyzstan. Once it had stopped raining I'd discovered it was a beautiful country, one of extraordinary experiences and generous people. I'd learnt to overcome my frustrations about what I couldn't buy and appreciate the unique things I could – *lepioshka*, *kaimak*, buckets of fruit and *ak-kalpaks*. With western commercialisation encroaching on the capital, I felt fortunate to have lived in Bishkek before the McDonald's franchise arrived.

Although I was aware there was so much I hadn't explored, I felt satisfied I had made the most of my time, especially as I'd spent most of it pregnant or breastfeeding. I'd slept in a *yurt*, ridden a horse, knew how to make felt, learnt to love Soviet concrete and could finally say 'hello' in Russian. And I'd survived a revolution and the first twenty-one months of motherhood. Where could we possibly go next to find greater challenges?

Epilogue

Shortly after our return from the *jailoo* Tanzilya's university course ended and she went 'home' to Russia. I cried. Not because I'd have to be a full-time mum again but because she'd become part of our family. Too young to understand the significance of this goodbye Tom touched a finger to our tears saying, "eyes, wet."

Gina left permanently in August, her year's extension up. She went back to HQ in Washington DC, emailing about how Bradley loved baseball and asking whether Tom was still getting around on his fanny. Sister Kathy was called back to America, asked to help in a shelter for those affected by the New Orleans floods. She gave up her work in Kyrgyzstan with reluctance.

Lauren left for New York to run the marathon and enjoy a more balanced sexual dynamic. Delphine never returned from her voluntary evacuation, the stress of cooking soufflé with Central Asian power surges finally proving too much for her. Penny returned to Saskatchewan, (pronounced Sas-kat-toon), in Canada to join the Kumtor Bishkek Alumni Wives. Clorise's husband was posted to Islamabad, she and Tula bravely moving with him. I was now convinced he was CIA.

Many friends remained in Bishkek. Michael resigned from his job so that he could write the first biography of Akayev. Nicky and Ben bought a tandem and were planning to cycle around Issyk-Kul. Dirk and Jenna, tired of their new housekeeper who washed bathroom floors with toilet paper, had decided they missed fly swats arranged in flower vases and were trying to find Zarema who'd moved to Karakol. Ilke upset Soren and shocked the international community by giving up smoking and suggesting that cigarettes no longer be raffle prizes. Claudia From, looking for new challenges after her term of presidency was up, took an advisory role on the Kyrgyz Olympic Committee.

High fences went up around Beta Stores as workmen started to clear out the debris and resurrect the shop. Revolution Tour t-shirts went on sale in Tzum: 'Tbilisi 2003; Kiev 2004; Bishkek 2005; Andijan/Tashkent Cancelled.' The country remained unsettled. Another parliamentary deputy was shot, another dodgy businessman with mafia connections. Bakiev was accused of failing to deliver any of his revolution promises and redistributing bad money. Post-revolution virtue had worn off and corruption had returned.

Bermet and Aidar were disqualified as parliamentary deputies. Aidar lost his immunity from prosecution and was being investigated for money laundering and illegal privatisation of property. Tanayev, Akayev's unpopular Prime Minister, was charged with abuse of office and embezzling state resources. He tried to run away to China but border guards spotted his huge quiff and sent him back to prison in Bishkek. He decided to run for parliament, a seat conveniently vacated by another murdered deputy. Although it was unclear who would vote for him, this gave him six weeks of immunity from prosecution, time to plan a better escape route.

Most days there were at least three protests to choose from in Bishkek: anti-Kulov, pro-Kulov or Lets Keep Trying for a bit of Free Land. The protest which caused the most disruption was a march by Russian pensioners who grid-locked the city every time they crossed a road.

The anti-Kulov protest set up outside parliament by Ryspek dispersed the day we left. It ended the same way as all the others: in anti-climax with promises from the government everyone knew would be ignored. The careers of Ryspek and Kulov did not go as planned. Kulov distanced himself from Bakiev, resigned from government and organised opposition protests in Ala Too Square. Failing to incite the revolution needed to bring him to power he disappeared into obscurity. Ryspek, crime lord and suspected murderer, was voted into parliament. A month later he was gunned down outside a mosque on the outskirts of Bishkek.

Matthew left Kyrgyzstan with the self-proclaimed record for most *besh barmaks* eaten in one day and job satisfaction: he'd piped clean water to 300,000 people and survived an investigation by the Prosecutor General. Franco Maccaroni wasn't so lucky; he was arrested, accused of tax evasion, embezzlement and using false documents.

An impact assessment of the project was done in Issyk-Kul. Despite a few broken pumps villagers reported positive results: they were ill less often and attendance was up 20% at school because children didn't spend so much time walking to fetch water. Even Mr Turd was happy, thanking Matthew and presenting him with a certificate for conscientious work on National Civil Engineers Day. "When you first arrived I thought, 'who is this child, he won't know anything'. Now I know better and you have proved yourself a friend of Kyrgyzstan." Kumashai cried.

Tom left Kyrgyzstan on two feet. He suddenly got off his fanny and walked alone on Saturday 20th August at 6.35pm, encouraged by my pleas that I couldn't hold off the accusations of his being retarded much longer. Matthew and I were emotional at the sight of our independent little boy running round the flat giggling at his new freedom. Next day in the park he saw a man jogging. "Funny man running," he said and chased after him.

I left Kyrgyzstan seven months pregnant. I thought this was apt. I'd arrived in Bishkek four months pregnant and left gaining three months, grey hairs and a mostly cheerful little boy. Baby Number Two was also a boy. We went for a scan to find out – Matthew didn't want his child known as slang for a turd for nine months. Sadly Bucket was no longer at the Rotdorm, whether this was because he'd moved on or the building had finally collapsed I wasn't told. We went to a 'new' clinic funded by Japanese Aid. It was clean, well-ordered and boring.

I said goodbye to my favourite parts of Bishkek as leaves yellowed in the weakening sun and snow crept further down the mountains. Matthew cried as he left his office and Tom went into quiet decline, unable to say a proper goodbye to *Droog* Dema. Sadly he'd forget his precious Kyrgyz days when *yurts* and more-vodka were his favourite things. But some memories are left, small sensations in the back of his mind. Looking at the photo of riding Gulzada's horse Tom frowns and says, "that's me at the mountains, isn't it?"

He'll always be my Revolution Baby.

In explanation and acknowledgement...

My writing career started as therapy. I'd moved from a City lawyer job to being alone all day in Aswan, southern Egypt. Not wanting to fall into bored lethargy I started writing a journal, recording all the extraordinary occurrences of every day. I sent extracts by email to friends who replied that I should write a book. Having nothing better to do I acquiesced, discovering a love of turning events into words so that now writing is an obsession. Trying to sell that first book, Puddles in the Desert, I learnt about the difficulties of publishing. Years later I was still being rejected by publishers and agents for not being a 'well-known face'.

I would have given up were it not for the support of six people: Matthew, my husband, who listened patiently to years of deliberation and self-doubt and *still* encouraged me to persevere, providing invaluable technical support; Lucy Irvine and Brigid Keenan who gave me the confidence to keep writing; Jackie Floyd who read my manuscript, believed in it enough to rekindle my enthusiasm and gave her time to help me improve it; Nick Kemp who created a cover so stunning I had to finish a book worthy to put inside and Alastair Humphreys who taught me that self-publishing is not failing.

Thank you all.

Names and identities have been changed to protect privacy but everything recorded here was said to me by someone at some time.

www.saffiafarr.com

Glossary

adehayet – rest holiday
ak-kalpak – white, conical felt hats worn by Kyrgyz men
aksakal – 'white beard' – term given to old, respected men
ala kiz – felt carpet made with melded colours
Amereekanka – American woman
Angleechanka – English woman
arik – drainage ditch
babushka – grandmother
banya – public baths
bazaarchik – small market
besh barmak – dish made with every part of a sheep, served with noodles for celebrations and festivals
bishkek – wooden spoon for stirring fermented mare's milk
biznizman – businessman
blinis – pancakes
borsok – small diamonds of fried dough, a traditional Ramadan food
casha – semolina
chai – tea
chiy – mats made from woven reeds, used to line the walls of *yurts*
da – yes
dacha – holiday home
demokrateecheski – democracy
danyet – yes/no
dereva – tree
derevna – village
dobra ootra – good morning
dom – home
droog – friend
dyedushka – grandfather
dyevooshka – young woman
elechek – traditional Kyrgyz hat worn by women
gastinitsa – guest house
jenshcheena – older woman
kaimak – thick, almost clotted, cream
kalonka – water standpipe
keffir – a sour, yoghurt drink
kochkor muyuz – an ornamental ram's horn design
kolkhoz – Soviet collective farms
kompot – a drink made from fruit
komuz – a small wooden guitar-like instrument with three strings
koumys – fermented mare's milk
kurak – patchwork
kurt – hard balls of white curd cheese

kyyak – stringed instrument played with a bow
lagman – a Kyrgyz dish of noodles and mutton
lepioshka – round, unleavened bread
malako – milk
malina – raspberries
malinki – little
manaschi – the bards and narrators of the Manas epic
mashrutka – mini buses used for public transport
nyet – no
Nooruz – a festival of Muslim New Year and spring equinox
oblast – province, there are seven provinces in Kyrgyzstan
pajalsta – please
pensionnat – small hotel
ploha – bad
plov – a Kyrgyz dish of rice, carrot and mutton
precass – an order, used in this context as medical instructions
rayon – district, there are 42 *rayons* in Kyrgyzstan
salaam – Kyrgyz greeting
samsi – meat or cheese pies
shaman – a spiritual messenger following the beliefs of shamanism
shampanski – champagne
shashlik – kebabs
shyrdak – overstitched felt carpet made with pieces of symmetrical colours
smarodeena – blackcurrant jam
som – Kyrgyz currency
spaceeba – thank you
shto – what?
sunduk – trunk, part of a nomad bride's trousseau
tunduk – the circular vent with cross pattern found at the top of a *yurt*
tush kiz – large embroidered panel traditionally hung above a marriage bed
tushuk – long cushions used as mattresses
Ulak tartysh – game played with a dead goat and two teams on horse back
vada – water
yurt – round felt tent, traditional home of nomadic shepherds
zdrastvooytyeh – hello

ADB – Asian Development Bank
BIWC – Bishkek International Women's Club
DFID – Department for International Development
IMF – International Monetary Fund
IMU – Islamic Movement of Uzbekistan
NGO – Non Governmental Organisation
OSCE – Organisation for Security and Co-operation in Europe
SCO – Shanghai Co-operation Organisation
UNHCR – The United Nations High Commissioner for Refugees
USAID – United States Agency for International Development

Information Sources

Quotes and information have been taken from the following sources:

The Bishkek Observer; The Times of Central Asia; The Bishkek Herald; Caspian Business News; Institute for War and Peace Reporting; United Nations Millennium Declaration – September 2000; The New York Times; The Financial Times; The Guardian; The Economist; Associated Press
www.eurasianet.org
www.news.bbc.co.uk
www.reuters.com
www.akipress.com
www.opendemocracy.net

Bibliography

Aitmatov, Chingiz, *The Day Lasts More Than a Hundred Years* (Boston & Moscow, Moscow, 2000)

Anderson, John, *Kyrgyzstan: Central Asia's Island of Democracy?* (Harwood Academic Publishers, Amsterdam, 1999)

Art of Silk Road 2002

Child, Greg, *Over the Edge: The True Story of Four American Climbers' Kidnap and Escape in the Mountains of Central Asia* (Villard Books, 2002)

Hickman, Katie, *Daughters of Britannia: The Lives and Times of Diplomatic Wives* (Flamingo, London, 2000)

Hopkirk, Peter, *The Great Game: On Secret Service in High Asia* (Oxford University Press, 2001)

Imanaliev, K, *Kyrgyzstan: The Word about Homeland* (Uchkun, Bishkek, 2004)

Kadyrov, V, *The Art of Nomads* (Rarity, Bishkek, 2003)

Kaplan, Robert D, *The Coming Anarchy: Shattering the Dreams of the Post Cold War* (Vintage, New York, 2000)

Keenan, Brigid, *Diplomatic Baggage: The Adventures of a Trailing Spouse* (John Murray, London, 2005)

Kleveman, Lutz, *The New Great Game: Blood and Oil in Central Asia* (Atlantic Books, London 2003)

Mayhew, Bradley, Plunkett, Richard and Richmond, Simon, *Central Asia* (Lonely Planet, Hawthorn, 2000)

Maillart, Ella, *Turkestan Solo* (TPP, London, 2005)

Murray, Craig, *Murder in Samarkand: A British Ambassador's Controversial Defiance of Tyranny in the War on Terror* (Mainstream Publishing, Edinburgh, 2006)

Nazaroff, Paul, *Hunted Through Central Asia: On the Run from Lenin's Secret Police* (Oxford Paperbacks, 2002)

Prior, Daniel, *Bishkek Handbook: Inside and Out* (AKCENT Information Agency, Bishkek, 1994)

ed. *Manas: The Epic Vision of Theodor Herzen* (Far Flung Press, Bishkek, 1995)

Rashid, Ahmed, *The Resurgence of Central Asia: Islam or Nationalism?* (Zed Books, 1994)

Jihad: The Rise of Militant Islam in Central Asia (Penguin, London, 2003)

Sogge, David, *Give and Take: What's the Matter with Foreign Aid?* (Zed Books, London, 2002)

Stewart, Rowan and Weldon, Susie, *Kyrgyzstan: Heartland of Central Asia* (Odyssey Publications, Hong Kong, 2003)

Stewart, Stanley, *In the Empire of Genghis Khan: A Journey Among Nomads* (Flamingo, London, 2001)

Thorpe, Meredith, *Glimpses of Village Life in Kyrgyzstan* (Sonun Jer, Bishkek, 2004)

Thubron, Colin, *The Lost Heart of Asia* (Penguin Books, London, 2004)

Tisch, Sarah J and Wallace, Michael B, *Dilemmas of Development Assistance: The What, Why and Who of Foreign Aid* (Westview Press, London, 1994)

Tolstoy, Alexandra, *The Last Secrets of the Silk Road: Four girls follow Marco Polo across 5,000 miles* (Profile Books, London, 2003)

Whitlock, Monica, *Beyond the Oxus: The Central Asians* (John Murray, London, 2002)

Whittell, Giles, *Extreme Continental: Blowing Hot and Cold Through Central Asia* (Indigo, London 1996)

For more about Kyrgyzstan and its artisans

Altyn Kol: a group of women who make traditional crafts and organise felt making days: altyn_kol@mail.ru

Art of the Silk Road: information about artists: www.artofsilkroad.com

Ashu Guesthouse in Chong Kemin valley: www.ashu.ctc.kg

CBT: offers *yurt* stays and provides unique insights into Kyrgyz life: www.cbtkyrgyzstan.kg

Dilbar Fashion House: www.dilbarfashion.com

Kyrgyz Heritage: a range of *kurak* (patchwork) and embroidered products: kyrheritage@saimanet.kg

Kyrgyz Style: handmade felt products: www.kyrgyzstyle.kg

NoviNomad: specialise in eco-tourism, trekking and horse riding – www.novinomad.com

Shepherd's Life: *yurt* stays: www.tourism.elcat.kg

Printed in the United Kingdom
by Lightning Source UK Ltd.
124189UK00002B/52-498/A